WALT DISNEY's

SILLY SYMPHONIES

Publisher: **GARY GROTH**
Editor of This Edition: **DAVID GERSTEIN**
Cover and Interior Design: **KAYLA E.** (this edition)
DEAN MULLANEY (material from earlier edition)
Production: **PAUL BARESH**
Color Restoration: **DIGIKORE STUDIOS with PAUL BARESH**
Associate Publisher: **ERIC REYNOLDS**

Walt Disney's Silly Symphonies 1935-1939 Starring Donald Duck and the Big Bad Wolf is copyright © 2023 Disney Enterprises, Inc. All contents copyright © 2023 Disney Enterprises, Inc. unless otherwise noted. Text of "Introduction," and introductory texts for individual stories, by J. B. Kaufman are © 2023 J. B. Kaufman. All rights reserved.

Permission to quote or reproduce material for reviews must be obtained from the publisher.

Fantagraphics Books, Inc. | 7563 Lake City Way NE | Seattle WA 98115 | (800) 657-1100
Visit us at *fantagraphics.com* | Follow us on Twitter at *@fantagraphics* and on Facebook at *facebook.com/fantagraphics*

First printing: December 2023
ISBN 978-1-68396-890-0
Printed in China
Library of Congress Control Number: 2022943408

EDITOR'S NOTE: The first edition of this anthology, released in 2017 by IDW Publishing under The Library of American Comics imprint, was compiled and edited by Dean Mullaney. David Gerstein, consulting editor on that release, wishes to thank Mr. Mullaney for supporting this revised edition.

Special thanks from the earlier and current editorial teams to Curt Baker, Danielle Digrado, Julie Dorris, Iliana Lopez, and Ken Shue at Disney Publishing Worldwide; Becky Cline, Kevin Kern, and Joanna Pratt at the Walt Disney Archives; and Holly Brobst and Michael Buckhoff at the Walt Disney Photo Library. Additional thanks to Justin Eisinger, Sarah Gaydos, Didier Ghez, Thomas Jensen, Larry Lowery, Alonzo Simon, Germund Von Wowern, Hake's Americana, and Heritage Auctions.

Front cover art by Jukka Murtosaari, originally published in Finnish *Walt Disney Hassunkuriset Sinfoniat*, 1996 (XFC M 1996).

ALSO AVAILABLE

The Complete Carl Barks Disney Library
Walt Disney's Donald Duck: "Maharajah Donald" (Vol. 4)
Walt Disney's Uncle Scrooge: "Cave of Ali Baba" (Vol. 23)

Disney Afternoon Adventures
TaleSpin: Flight of the Sky-Raker (Bobbi JG Weiss, Michael T. Gilbert, Romano Scarpa, and others; Vol. 2)
Chip 'n Dale Rescue Rangers: The Count Roquefort Case (Bobbi JG Weiss, Doug Gray, Lee Nordling, and others; Vol. 3)

Disney Masters
Mickey Mouse: The Monster of Sawtooth Mountain (Paul Murry; Vol. 21)
Uncle Scrooge: Operation Galleon Grab (Giorgio Cavazzano; Vol. 22)
Mickey Mouse: The Riddle of Brigaboom (Romano Scarpa; Vol. 23)

Silly Symphonies
Walt Disney's Silly Symphonies 1932-1935 Starring Bucky Bug and Donald Duck (Al Taliaferro with Earl Duvall, Merrill De Maris, and Ted Osborne)
Walt Disney's Silly Symphonies 1935-1939 Starring Donald Duck and the Big Bad Wolf (Al Taliaferro with Carl Barks, Merrill De Maris, and Ted Osborne)

One-Shots and Specials
Disney Comics: Around the World in One Hundred Years (20+ international creators, including Carl Barks, Floyd Gottfredson, Daan Jippes, Freddy Milton, Don Rosa, and Romano Scarpa; Target Stores exclusive)
Disney One Saturday Morning Adventures (40+ international creators, including Daan Jippes, Laura McCreary, and Scott Gimple)
Donald Duck: Donald's Happiest Adventures (Lewis Trondheim and Nicolas Keramidas)
Scrooge McDuck: The Dragon of Glasgow (Joris Chamblain and Fabrizio Petrossi)
Uncle Scrooge and Donald Duck: Bear Mountain Tales (20 international creators, including Carl Barks, Don Rosa, Daniel Branca, and Giorgio Cavazzano)
Uncle Scrooge and Donald Duck in Les Misérables and War and Peace (Giovan Battista Carpi)
Walt Disney's Uncle Scrooge: The Diamond Jubilee Collection (Carl Barks with William Van Horn and Daan Jippes)

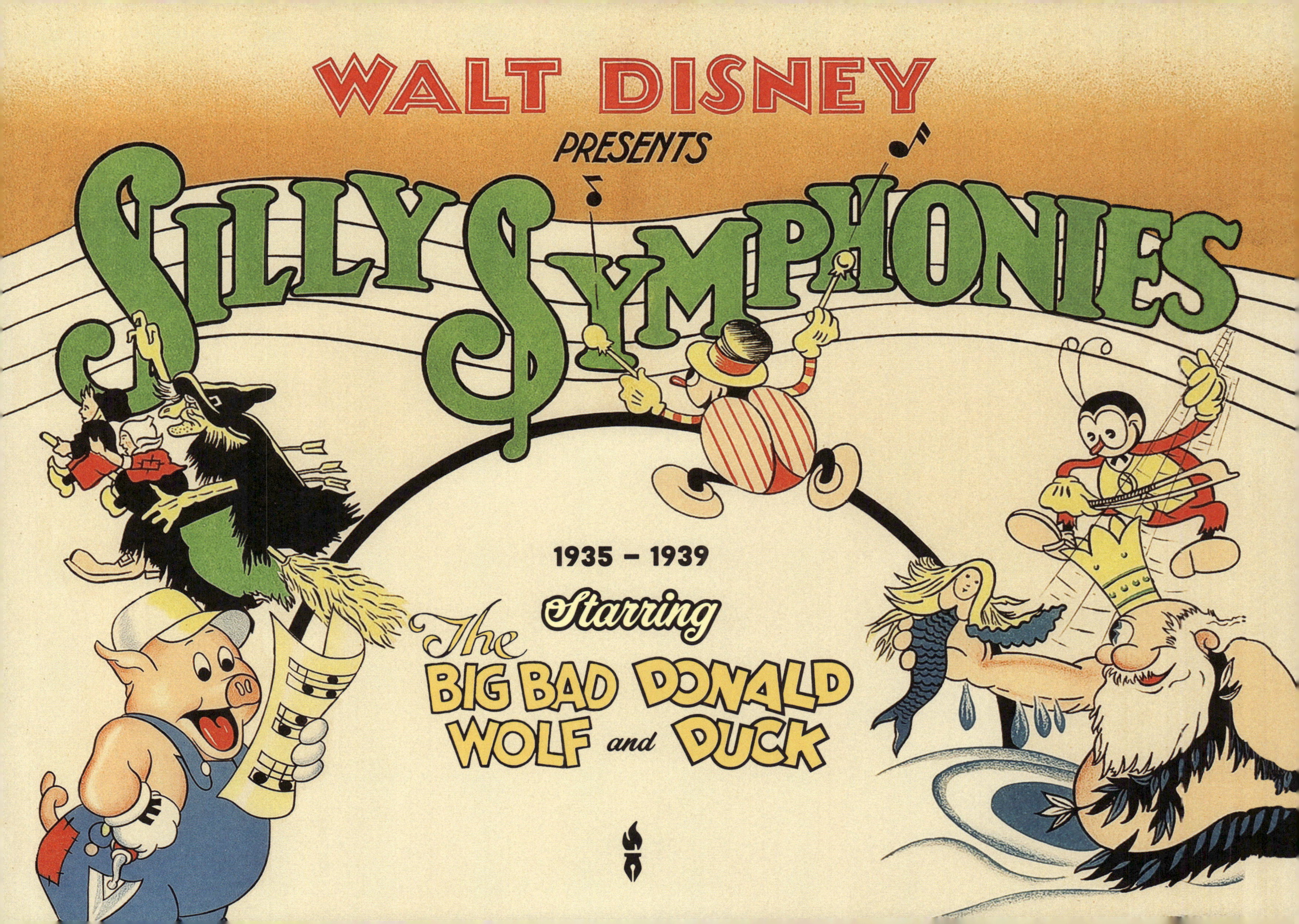
WALT DISNEY
PRESENTS
SILLY SYMPHONIES
1935 – 1939
Starring
The BIG BAD WOLF and DONALD DUCK

CONTENTS

THREE LITTLE KITTENS 12
July 28 - October 20, 1935
Written by Ted Osborne, drawn by Al Taliaferro

THE LIFE AND ADVENTURES OF ELMER ELEPHANT 26
October 27, 1935 - January 12, 1936
Written by Ted Osborne, drawn by Al Taliaferro

THE FURTHER ADVENTURES OF THE THREE LITTLE PIGS . . 40
January 19 - August 23, 1936
Written by Ted Osborne, drawn by Al Taliaferro

DONALD DUCK 74
August 30, 1936 - December 5, 1937
Written by Ted Osborne, penciled by Floyd Gottfredson (October 3 and 10, 1937)
and Al Taliaferro (all others), inked by Al Taliaferro

SNOW WHITE AND THE SEVEN DWARFS 142
December 12, 1937 - April 24, 1938
Written by Merrill de Maris, drawn by Hank Porter, assisted by Bob Grant

THE PRACTICAL PIG 164
May 1 - August 7, 1938
Written by Merrill de Maris, drawn by Al Taliaferro

MOTHER PLUTO 180
April 23 - June 4, 1933
Written by Ted Osborne, drawn by Al Taliaferro

THE FARMYARD SYMPHONY 192
October 23 - November 27, 1938
Written by Merrill de Maris, drawn by Al Taliaferro

TIMID ELMER 200
December 4, 1938 - February 12, 1939
Plotted by Bianca Majolie, Ferdinand Horvath, Carl Barks, and Walt Kelly, scripted
by Merrill de Maris, drawn by Al Taliaferro

A NOTE ON COLORING: Sharp-eyed readers may notice some minor color inconsistency in
these pages. We have chosen to present an authentic reproduction of the comics' original colors in order to
preserve their historic appeal.

This content has been reprinted in its entirety as first created in 1935-1939.

Many stories were created during an earlier time and may include cartoon violence, historically dated material,
or gags that depict smoking and gunplay. We present them here with a caution to the reader that they reflect
the era in which they were produced.

This title includes negative depictions and mistreatment of people or cultures. These stereotypes were
wrong then and are wrong now. Rather than remove this content, we want to acknowledge its harmful
impact, learn from it and spark conversation to create a more inclusive future together. Disney is
committed to creating stories with inspirational and aspirational themes that reflect the rich diversity
of the human experience around the globe. To learn more about how stories have impacted society,
please visit **www.disney.com/StoriesMatter**

INTRODUCTION

by J.B. Kaufman

IT'S NOT DIFFICULT TO UNDERSTAND why the 1930s and early '40s are widely regarded as the "Golden Age" of the Walt Disney studio. The Disney films of those years were marked by a distinctive, original quality that proved irresistible to audiences of the time, and is no less appealing today. The same quality distinguished the studio's ancillary activities, including its comic strips. Readers of Fantagraphics' previous Volume 1 can vouch for the early years of the *Silly Symphony* Sunday comics. This newspaper feature, based on an innovative series of animated cartoons with a musical orientation, debuted in 1932 Although its story material was based only loosely on that of the films, the strip mirrored the freshness and charm of the Silly Symphonies themselves.

In this second volume, covering a period from the summer of 1935 through early 1939, the *Symphony* comics continue to reflect their cinematic namesakes, the favorites that readers were seeing every week at the movies. At the Disney studio of the 1930s, however, nothing stood still for very long. As the studio continued to pioneer new ideas and techniques and to refine its artistic standards, its films evolved and became radically unlike those of the early years. Inevitably, those changes were reflected in the comics. The progress of the *Silly Symphony* strip in these pages charts the maturation of the Disney studio into new and unfamiliar territory.

The strips reproduced here can be broken down into four distinct phases. They begin where they left off at the end of Volume 1, with discrete continuities based, more or less faithfully, on individual films. Writer Ted Osborne and artist Al Taliaferro had, after working as a team for more than a year, established a pattern: taking a Silly Symphony's plot as a starting point, they would hatch a parallel story of their own. The relationship between the film version and the comics version could be complex and varied, providing no end of intrigue for the latter-day Disney enthusiast who compares the two. The convention of rhyming dialogue, established at the outset of the strip in 1932 (and by this time adopted in many of the films), continued for the moment. Taliaferro maintained his impressive artistic facility, keeping pace with the Disney animators and rendering a variety of characters *exactly* as they appeared in the films—sometimes with poses that seemed to come directly from the screen.

As before, the stories chosen for the strip were selected from key films in the series. *Three Orphan Kittens*, released in 1935, was notable for the elegant sophistication of its visual effects, and would go on to win the Academy Award as the best cartoon of the year. Its corresponding comic continuity, "Three Little Kittens," retained the bare bones of the film's concept and changed almost everything else. *Elmer Elephant* (1936), about the troubles of a little jungle misfit, likewise inspired a comic continuity that retained the film's setting and characters, but took their story in a new direction. The appearance of a new continuity based on *Three Little Pigs* probably seemed counterintuitive in 1936; the film had been released three years earlier. But, in fact, the new story was a multilayered device. *Three Little Pigs* had

MICKEY MOUSE
PRESENTS
A WALT DISNEY
SILLY SYMPHONY
The
THREE LITTLE PIGS
UNITED ARTISTS PICTURE
In TECHNICOLOR!

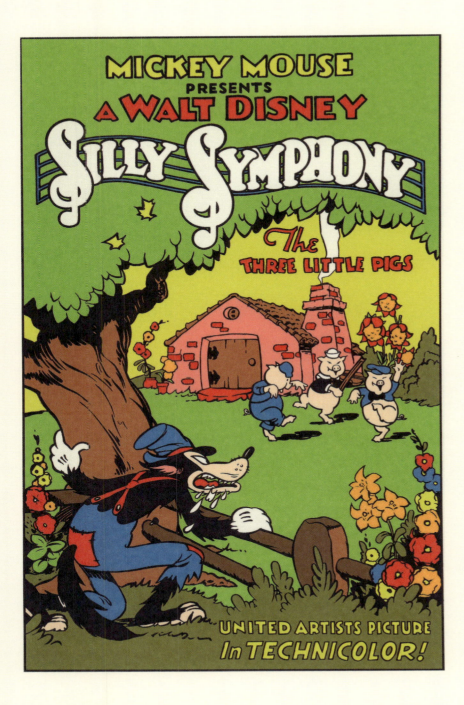

been one of the hit movies of 1933—it remains today, arguably, the most successful one-reel cartoon ever produced—and by 1936 it had already inspired two Pig sequels: *The Big Bad Wolf* (1934) and *Three Little Wolves* (1936). Now Osborne and Taliaferro crafted a continuity that incorporated elements of the original film and the first sequel, but leaned heavily on the *second* sequel, due for imminent release to movie houses—then topped that with a series of original gags and plot details that were common to *none* of the films.

The *Silly Symphony* comic strip marked its first major turning point in the late summer of 1936, launching a new long-running continuity, not built around an individual story, but designed simply as a starring vehicle for Donald Duck. There was a precedent for this departure. Donald's first-ever appearance in the comics had occurred two years earlier in the *Symphony* strip, in a continuity based on the film *The Wise Little Hen* (and now preserved in *Silly Symphonies* Volume 1). His role had been intended as a single isolated appearance —but Donald made a strong first impression, and neither the movies nor the comics were about to let him go so easily. Soon he could be seen again, onscreen and on the comic page, as a regular member of Mickey Mouse's supporting cast. The squawking, belligerent Duck quickly developed a fan following, and began to evolve into a major Disney character with star potential of his own.

In the meantime, Al Taliaferro, the artist who had first introduced Donald to the comic page, was developing his own special fondness for the character. Taliaferro had ambitions for a separate comic strip starring the Duck, and pressured Walt Disney for a chance to try out his idea. Walt's answer was to give artist and duck a trial run, turning over the *Silly Symphony* Sunday strip to Donald for what amounted to an extended audition. Osborne and Taliaferro, for so long charged with creating episodic pictorial narratives based on the Silly Symphonies, now shifted gears to begin producing weekly slapstick comedies for the studio's short-tempered new cartoon star. Ultimately the trial lasted for well over a year, a continuity collected and preserved in this volume.

This was a significant development in more ways than one. Though observers outside the studio might not have guessed it, the days of the cinematic Silly Symphonies were numbered. Once the Disney studio's most prestigious product, they were gradually being replaced in Walt's priorities by a still more ambitious venture: a *feature-length* cartoon. *Snow White and the Seven Dwarfs*, a seemingly impossible undertaking, had been in story development for two years by the autumn of 1936 and was moving inexorably into production. As it did so, it absorbed some of the top animation talent in the studio—talent that had once been reserved for the Silly Symphonies.

For the time being, of course, this shift was imperceptible outside the studio walls. Silly Symphonies, including some of the best, would continue to appear on movie screens and in the comics for several years to come. But in the meantime the launch of the *Donald Duck* continuity, in what was still nominally the *Silly Symphony* space, had a marked effect on the tenor of the Disney Sunday comic page. The *Symphonies*, with their constantly changing landscape of stories and characters, had held pride of place at the top of the page, with reliable *Mickey Mouse* holding court in the lower portion. Now the page changed course and became, in effect, a showcase for the two most popular *continuing* Disney stars. The convention of rhyming dialogue, a staple of the *Symphony* comics from 1932 on, disappeared in the *Donald* strips—and, in fact, dialogue of any kind was drastically curtailed. Although created by the same writer and artist who had produced the earlier *Symphony* stories, the strip now became largely a compendium of sight gags.

The months of the *Donald Duck* continuity, August 1936 to early December 1937, coincided with the Duck's rise to a new prominence in the movies. Now he was no longer simply a member of Mickey Mouse's supporting cast, but the star of his own series of cartoons. In time his popularity would come to rival that of Mickey himself. The comic continuity built on this new celebrity status and also contributed to it in some ways. One notable event occurred in October 1937, when Osborne and Taliaferro added a group of new characters to the Disney pantheon: Donald's nephews Huey, Dewey, and Louie. Typically, new Disney characters were introduced on the screen, then worked their way into comics, storybooks, and other showcases. This time the influence flowed in the opposite direction: Donald's nephews made such a hit with newspaper readers that they were soon featured in the animated cartoons as well. They went on to take their places among the best-known Disney characters.

In the end, Donald did pass his audition with flying colors. From Taliaferro's viewpoint, the extended newspaper series accomplished its objective, demonstrating that the Duck was more than capable of carrying his own comic strip. Tellingly, during the last months of the run, the original title panel, "Silly Symphony featuring Donald Duck," was replaced by a new panel reading simply "Donald Duck." And, indeed, by this time a new *Donald Duck* daily strip was in the works, to debut in newspapers early in 1938. In the movies, and now in the comics, Donald had arrived.

Simultaneously, many other activities were taking place at the Disney studio—most spectacularly, continuing work on *Snow White and the Seven Dwarfs*. As the challenges of this monumental undertaking mounted, Walt pressed on undaunted, fired by an enthusiasm that spread to the rest of his staff and carried them along with him. Their efforts culminated in a film that would make history, transform the fortunes of the Disney studio, and exercise a powerful influence on the film industry at large. As *Snow White* approached completion during the summer of 1937, the studio and its distributor laid plans to unveil their feature as a special Christmas attraction across the nation. The Disney marketing experts marshaled their forces, mounting a spectacular promotional campaign. A key element in that campaign was the comics: the *Silly Symphony* comic page, having demonstrated its useful versatility, provided a ready-made showcase for the latest Disney triumph.

Hampered by production delays, *Snow White* ultimately failed to meet its nationwide December opening date. A single theater, Hollywood's Carthay Circle, opened the film before the end of December 1937; the rest of America and the world had to wait until 1938. Nonetheless the carefully coordinated promotional campaign rolled into action on schedule, unleashing a flood of *Snow White*-related press and merchandise. And the *Silly Symphony* comic strip entered the third major phase of its history, giving over its prized position at the top of the comics page to a twenty-week retelling of Snow White's story.

For the first time since 1932, Al Taliaferro relinquished the artistic reins—the *Snow White* continuity was written by Merrill de Maris and drawn by Hank Porter, assisted by Bob Grant. Together they invested the tale with a quaint storybook quality. By the time the film began to open at theaters across America in the early months of 1938, the Sunday comic page had been whetting audiences' appetites for several weeks—as it had routinely done for the Silly Symphonies. Just as with the Symphonies, the comics adaptation maintained a loose fidelity to the film, at times closely mirroring the screen continuity, at other times veering into unfamiliar story material (including some gags and plot ideas that had originally been developed for the film, but were dropped during pre-production). The full run

Walt Disney's
ELMER ELEPHANT
ELMER
LINEN-LIKE AND SEWED

SILLY SYMPHONY FEATURING
DONALD DUCK
and his
MIS ADVENTURES
by WALT DISNEY
THE BIG LITTLE BOOK

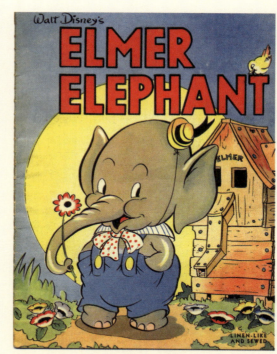

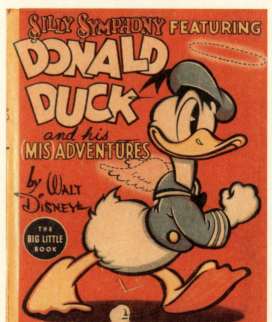

OPPOSITE: A latter-day serigraph reproduction of the 1933 Silly Symphony poster for *Three Little Pigs*. Image courtesy Heritage Auctions.

ABOVE: A 1938 Elmer Elephant picture book, published by Whitman, in which Mickey and Pluto make guest appearances. Image courtesy Heritage Auctions.

LEFT: A 1937 *Big Little Book* from Whitman featuring Al Taliaferro's art from the "Donald Duck" series in *Silly Symphonies*. Image courtesy Heritage Auctions.

WALT DISNEY'S
The
PRACTICAL PIG
SILLY SYMPHONY
© W.D.P.
R.K.O. RADIO PICTURE IN TECHNICOLOR

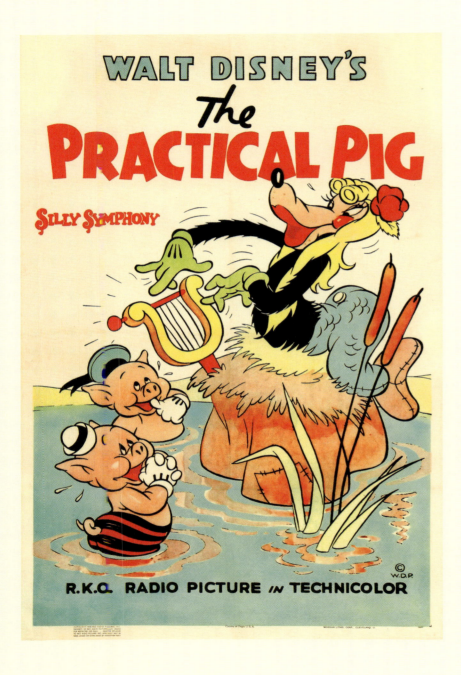

of the story is reproduced in this volume, where *Snow White* enthusiasts can savor and compare the screen and print versions.

Snow White's adventure came to its happy ending late in April 1938. The Sunday comic feature then shifted gears once again, and, for the first time in nearly two years, returned to its original mission: retelling stories from the Silly Symphonies. Merrill de Maris, the writer of the *Snow White* continuity, remained in place as the strip's writer; but Al Taliaferro, now established as the artist behind the new *Donald Duck* comic strip, compounded his workload by returning to the *Silly Symphony* page as well.

So the *Symphonies* were back in their original spot, but with some key differences. By this time it was official: the Silly Symphony film series was coming to an end, phased out as Disney's top animation talent was shifted to a multitude of new feature projects. The last of the *Symphonies*, *The Ugly Duckling*, was completed and in the can by the autumn of 1938. But that and other titles were carefully held back, released to theaters on an intermittent schedule that extended well into 1939. The Sunday comic feature continued as well, adapting storylines from the series—with new title panels that announced each individual story, minus the unifying rubric of "Silly Symphonies." The early convention of rhyming dialogue, dropped for Donald Duck's launch in 1936, likewise did not return. In every way, readers were encouraged to see the new continuities as individual self-contained works, rather than entries in an ongoing series.

As before, these mini-narratives were based on key Disney films. The studio's production of *The Practical Pig*, yet another sequel to *Three Little Pigs*, was complete by May 1938 when its comic continuity appeared, but most movie audiences had not yet seen it; its theatrical release would be delayed for nearly a year. By contrast, *Mother Pluto* and *Farmyard Symphony* had already been released to theaters and were familiar to viewers (*Mother Pluto*, in particular, had been released nearly two years before its comic continuity appeared in newspapers). In all these stories de Maris and Taliaferro followed standard procedure and based their continuities loosely on the films, hewing closely to some elements of the original stories but combining those elements with other ideas that were wholly original to the comics. *Farmyard Symphony*, in its screen form, has practically no plot; the comic version builds on a minor running gag from the film and spins it into a tale with a moralizing twist.

This volume ends with an intriguing anomaly: a story that was *planned* as a movie short, but never completed. On pages 27-38 the reader can see the earlier continuity based on the 1936 short *Elmer Elephant*. By the end of 1936 that film had aroused enough interest that the Disney story department set to work on a sequel to be titled "Timid Elmer." Their story was never realized as a film, but late in 1938 de Maris and Taliaferro adapted "Timid Elmer" to the comics. Its reprinting here provides a rare luxury: a glimpse of an unfinished Disney film story. The comic version varies from the film scenario—given the creative liberties that Taliaferro and the strip's writers routinely took with film stories—but that only adds to the interest of this unique sidelight.

By February 1939 the *Silly Symphony* Sunday strip had appeared in newspapers for a full seven years—years in which it had explored, adapted, and generally reflected the wide-ranging activities of the Disney studio itself. The Silly Symphony film series would come to an end in 1939, but the comic strip had built up its own momentum and was not about to quit. Far from it; by 1939, the strip had become a versatile platform, capable of sustaining its own vein of comic art for years to come. ♫

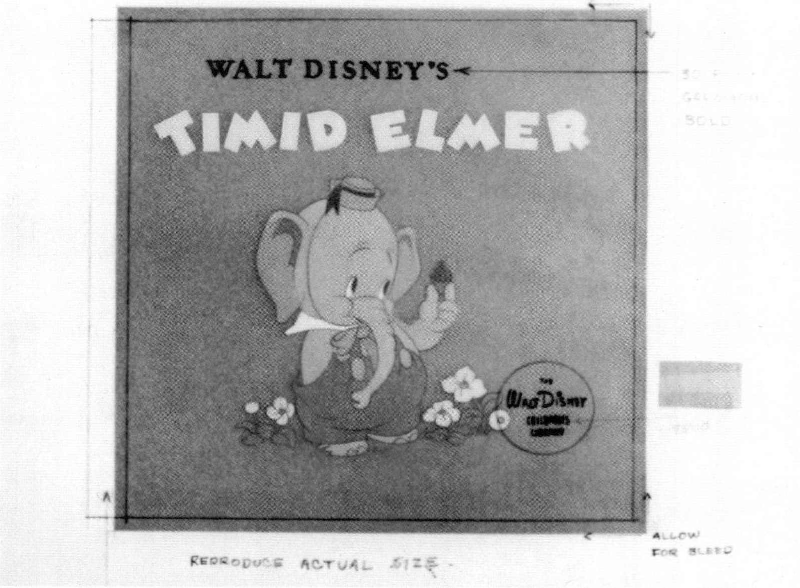
WALT DISNEY'S
TIMID ELMER
REPRODUCE ACTUAL SIZE.
ALLOW FOR BLEED

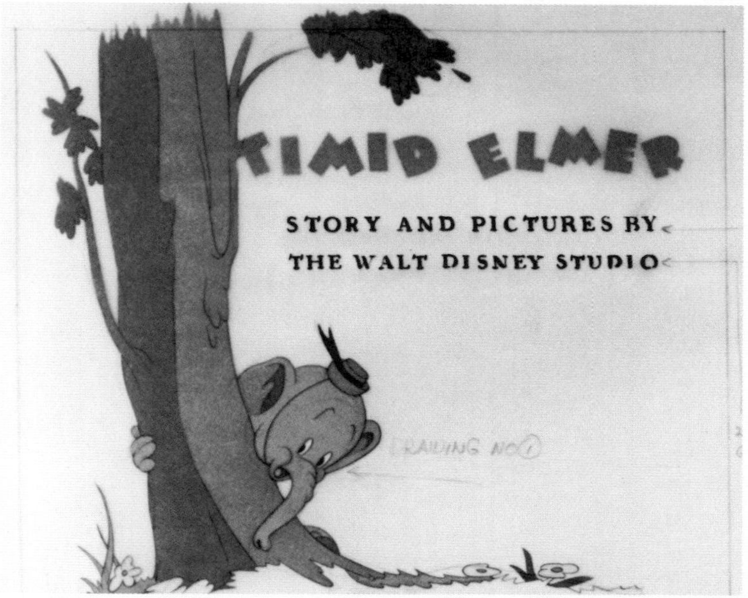
TIMID ELMER
STORY AND PICTURES BY
THE WALT DISNEY STUDIO

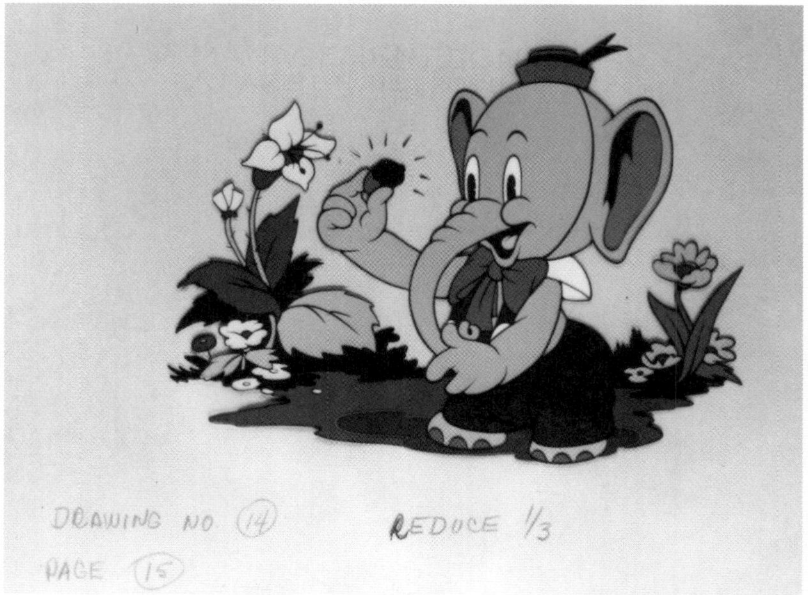
DRAWING NO (14)
REDUCE 1/3
PAGE (15)

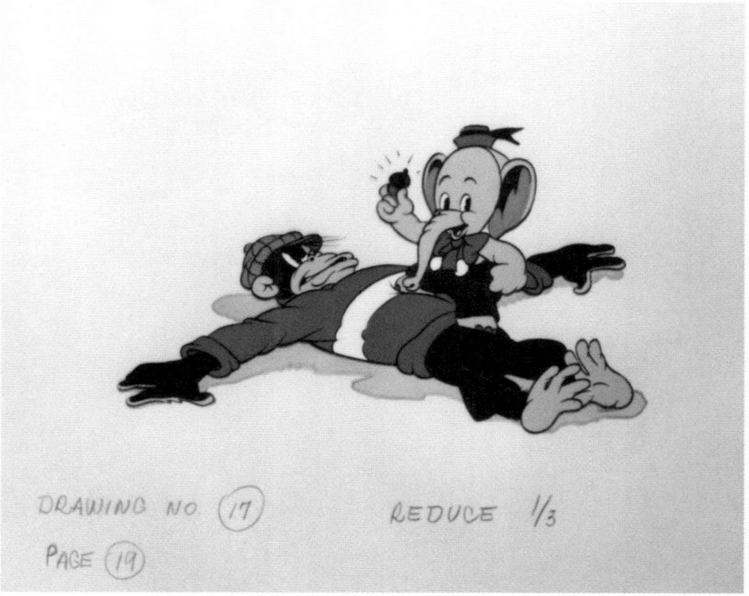
DRAWING NO (17)
REDUCE 1/3
PAGE (19)

OPPOSITE: A 1939 one-sheet poster for Disney's *The Practical Pig* theatrical cartoon. Image courtesy Heritage Auctions.

LEFT: While "Timid Elmer" was still in development as a cartoon, Disney and publisher Whitman planned a large-size storybook, for which Al Taliaferro drew original illustrations reinked and enhanced from his Sunday strips. When the cartoon plans were shelved, Whitman issued "Timid Elmer" only as a smaller book illustrated with original strip art. Eight of Taliaferro's specialty drawings appeared with a short retelling in the 1940 anthology book *The Walt Disney Parade*, but the rest went unused at the time. Images courtesy Walt Disney Photo Library.

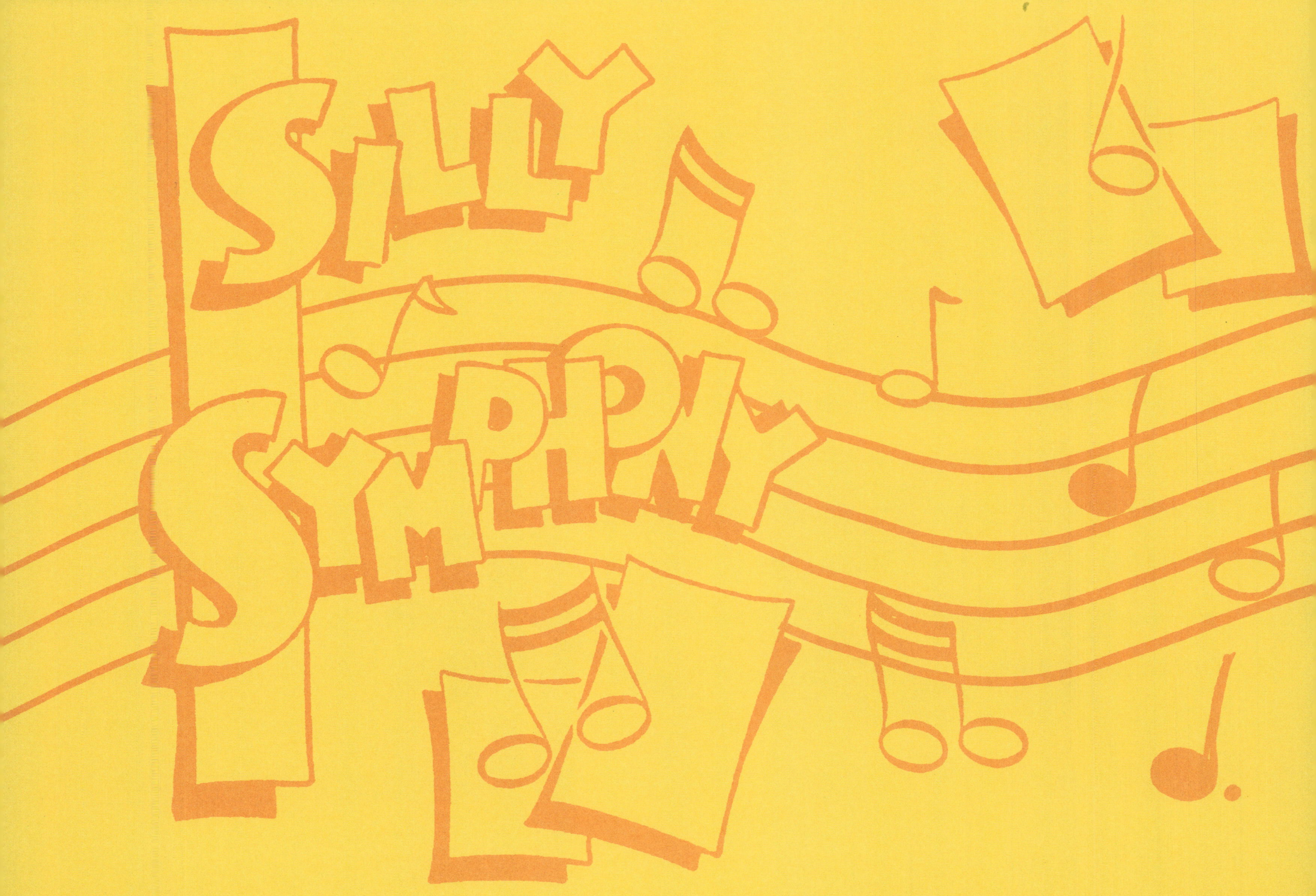
Silly
Symphony

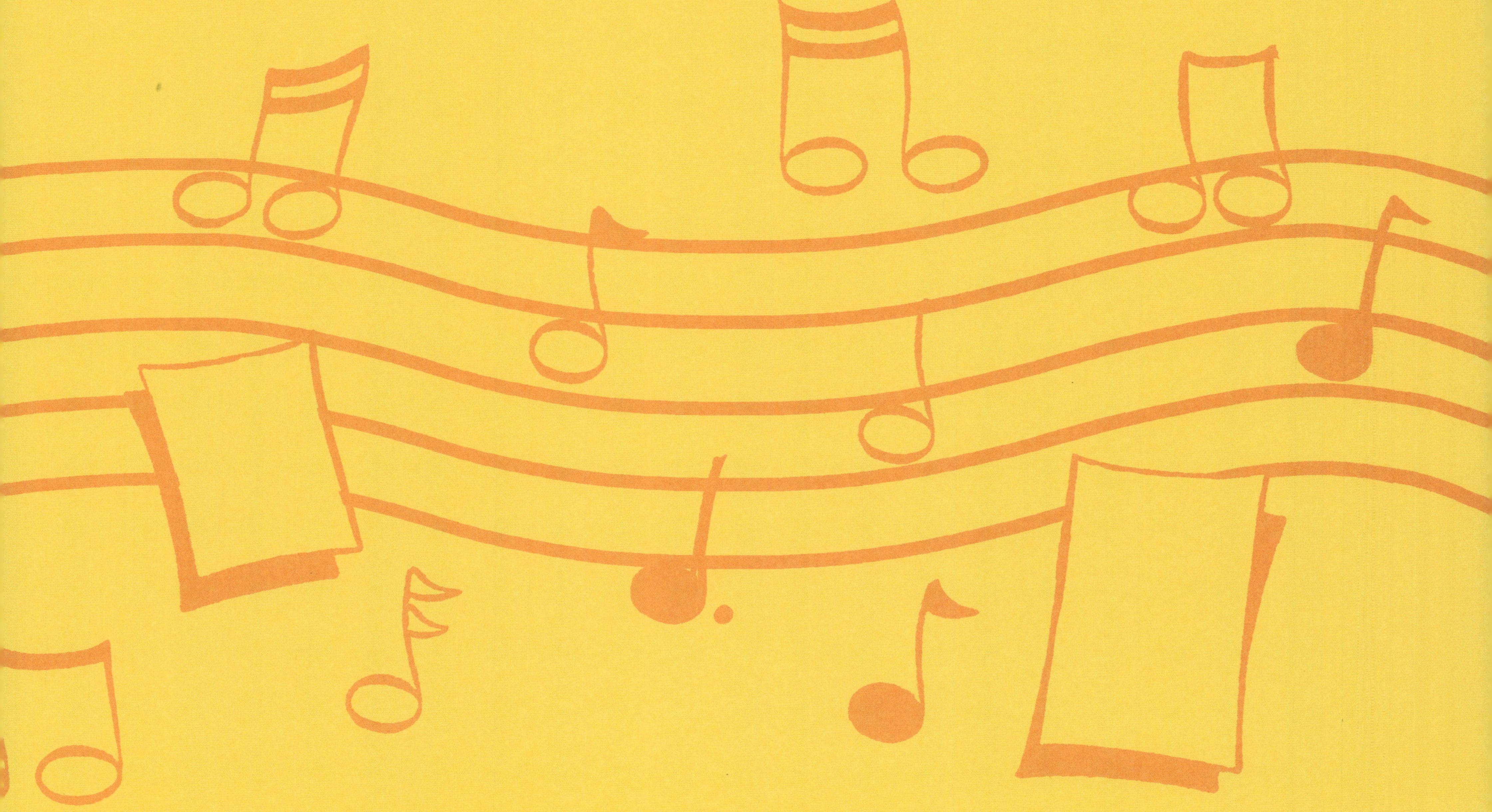

THREE LITTLE KITTENS

July 28 - October 20, 1935
Written by Ted Osborne, drawn by Al Taliaferro

IN THE ACADEMY AWARD-WINNING short *Three Orphan Kittens*, the kittens of the title take refuge in a family home, cause mischief, and are eventually discovered and adopted by the little girl of the household. The comic continuity, "Three Little Kittens," retains that basic concept, but changes almost all the details. The kittens in the film enter the house after being abandoned in a snowstorm in the dead of night; the comic story takes place on a warm, sunny afternoon, and the kittens are merely fleeing neighborhood boys and a watchdog. The movie kittens' mischief in the house includes a creative musical sequence on the keys of a piano; their comics counterparts settle for tangled yarn, broken vases, and other customary destruction. Perhaps most noticeably, the maid featured in the film is nowhere to be seen in the comic continuity, and the adult who wants to throw the kittens out is the little girl's father.

The film's story is told from the viewpoint of the kittens. The humans function as incidental players, glimpsed only by way of their feet and hands; their faces are never shown. (This approach was repeated in other animal-centric Disney films, turning up a full twenty years later in *Lady and the Tramp*.) The comic continuity retains this device, and takes it a step further: the humans' dialogue is never heard. Even when one of the kittens floods a box of cigars with water, the father's violent reaction is only *suggested*, and we are left to imagine his colorful language for ourselves.

—J.B. KAUFMAN

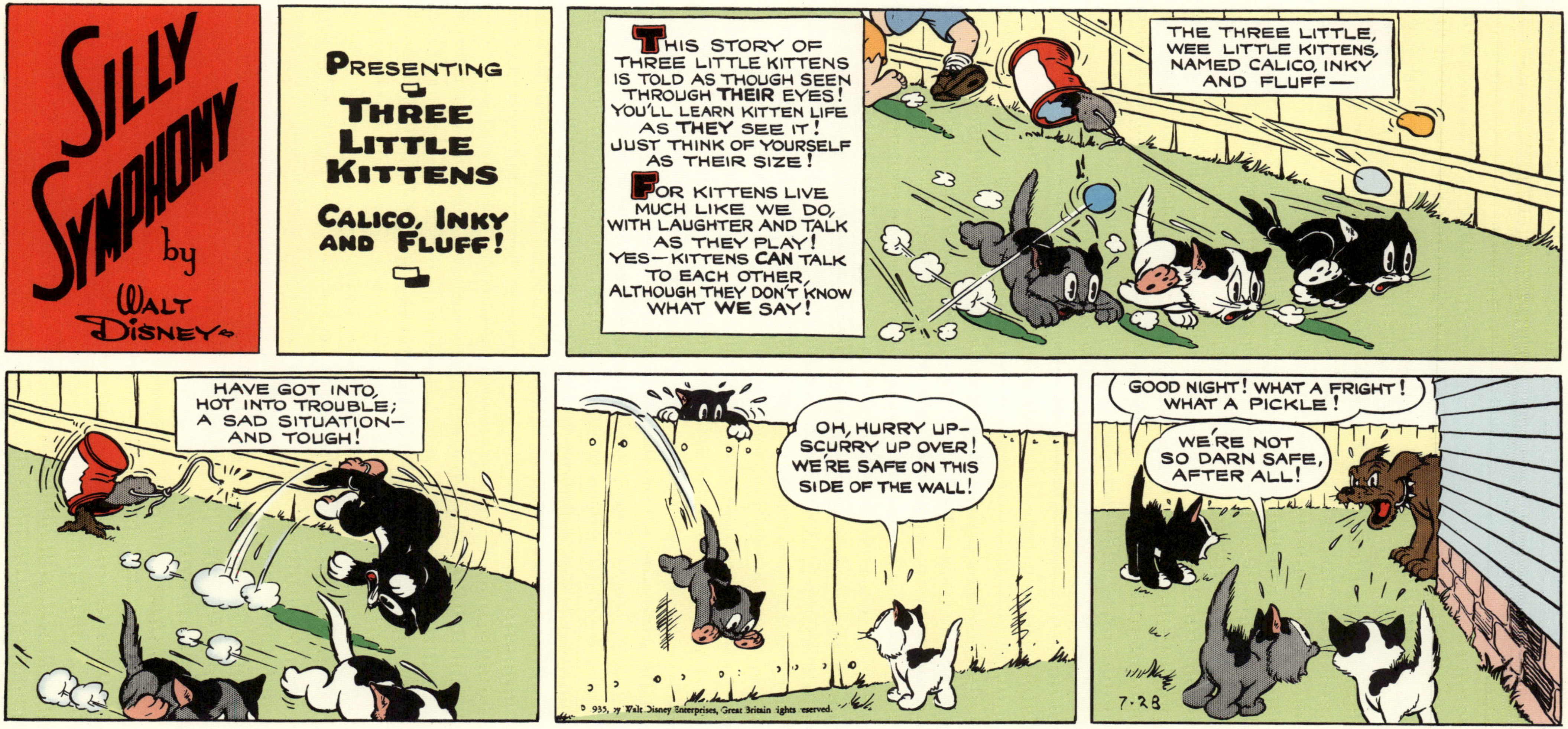

SILLY SYMPHONY by WALT DISNEY
PRESENTING
THREE LITTLE KITTENS
CALICO, INKY AND FLUFF!
THIS STORY OF THREE LITTLE KITTENS IS TOLD AS THOUGH SEEN THROUGH THEIR EYES! YOU'LL LEARN KITTEN LIFE AS THEY SEE IT! JUST THINK OF YOURSELF AS THEIR SIZE!
FOR KITTENS LIVE MUCH LIKE WE DO, WITH LAUGHTER AND TALK AS THEY PLAY! YES—KITTENS CAN TALK TO EACH OTHER, ALTHOUGH THEY DON'T KNOW WHAT WE SAY!
THE THREE LITTLE, WEE LITTLE KITTENS, NAMED CALICO, INKY AND FLUFF—
HAVE GOT INTO, HOT INTO TROUBLE; A SAD SITUATION— AND TOUGH!
OH, HURRY UP— SCURRY UP OVER! WE'RE SAFE ON THIS SIDE OF THE WALL!
GOOD NIGHT! WHAT A FRIGHT! WHAT A PICKLE!
WE'RE NOT SO DARN SAFE, AFTER ALL!
7-28

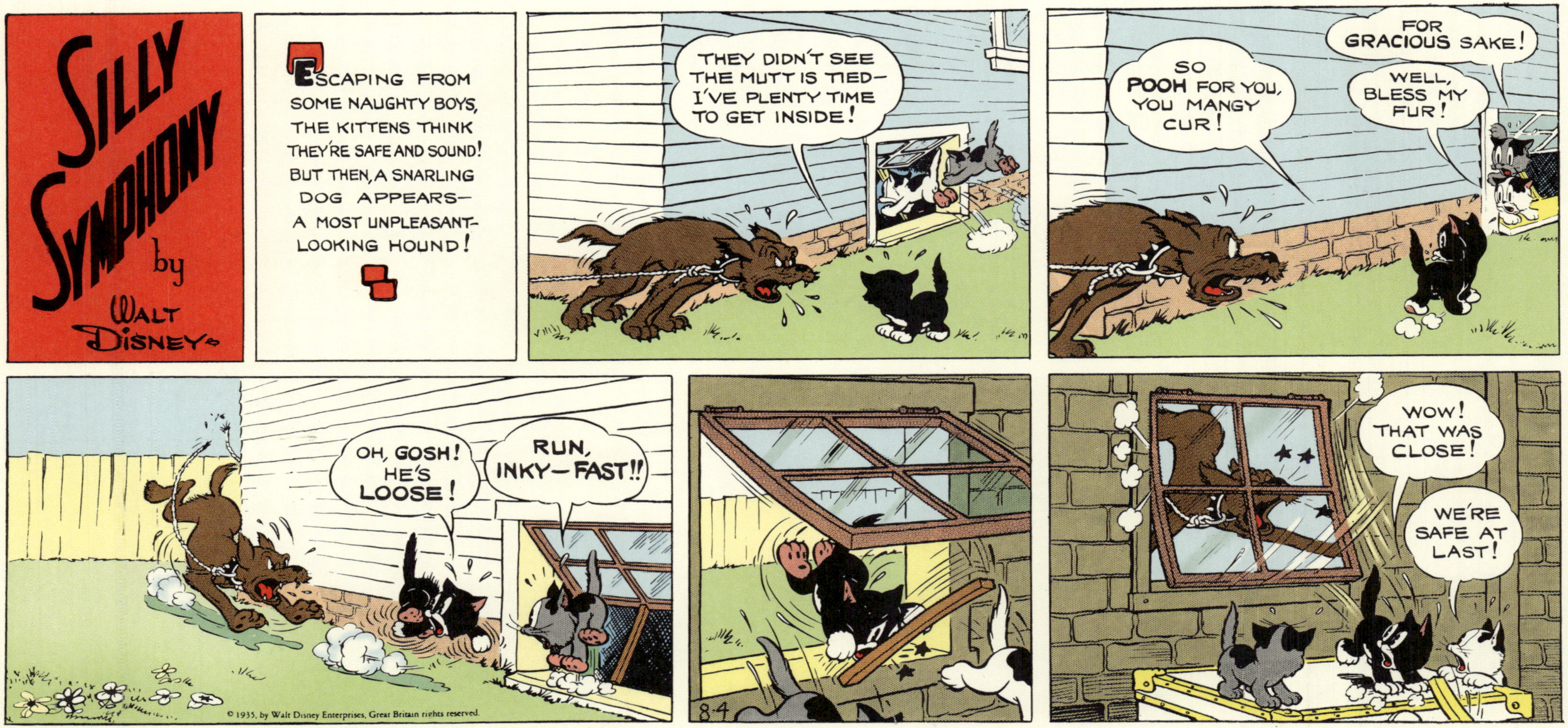
SILLY SYMPHONY
by
WALT DISNEY
ESCAPING FROM SOME NAUGHTY BOYS, THE KITTENS THINK THEY'RE SAFE AND SOUND! BUT THEN, A SNARLING DOG APPEARS— A MOST UNPLEASANT-LOOKING HOUND!
THEY DIDN'T SEE THE MUTT IS TIED— I'VE PLENTY TIME TO GET INSIDE!
SO POOH FOR YOU, YOU MANGY CUR!
FOR GRACIOUS SAKE!
WELL, BLESS MY FUR!
OH, GOSH! HE'S LOOSE!
RUN, INKY—FAST!!
© 1935, by Walt Disney Enterprises, Great Britain rights reserved.
WOW! THAT WAS CLOSE!
WE'RE SAFE AT LAST!

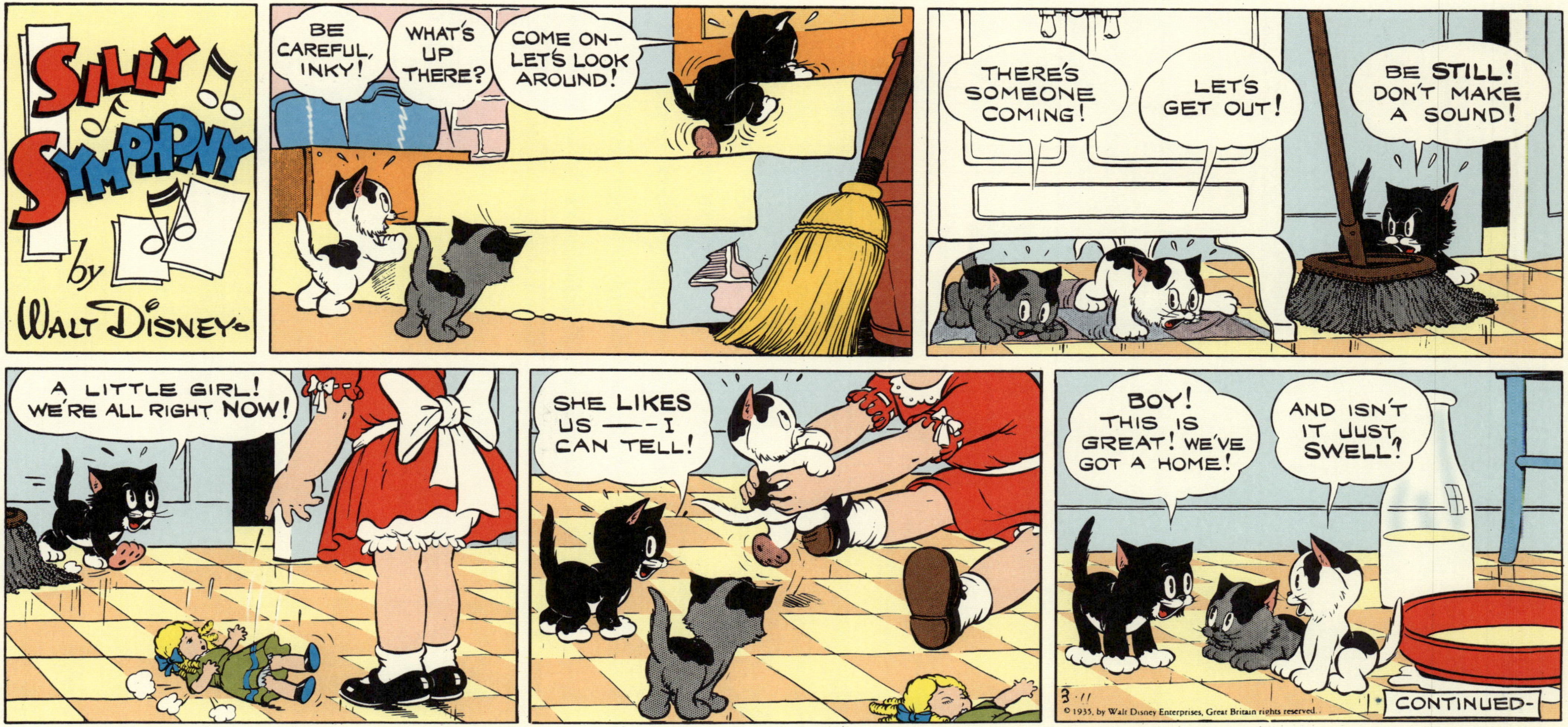

SILLY SYMPHONY
by
WALT DISNEY
BE CAREFUL, INKY!
WHAT'S UP THERE?
COME ON— LET'S LOOK AROUND!
THERE'S SOMEONE COMING!
LET'S GET OUT!
BE STILL! DON'T MAKE A SOUND!
A LITTLE GIRL! WE'RE ALL RIGHT NOW!
SHE LIKES US —— I CAN TELL!
BOY! THIS IS GREAT! WE'VE GOT A HOME!
AND ISN'T IT JUST SWELL?
© 1935, by Walt Disney Enterprises, Great Britain rights reserved.
CONTINUED-

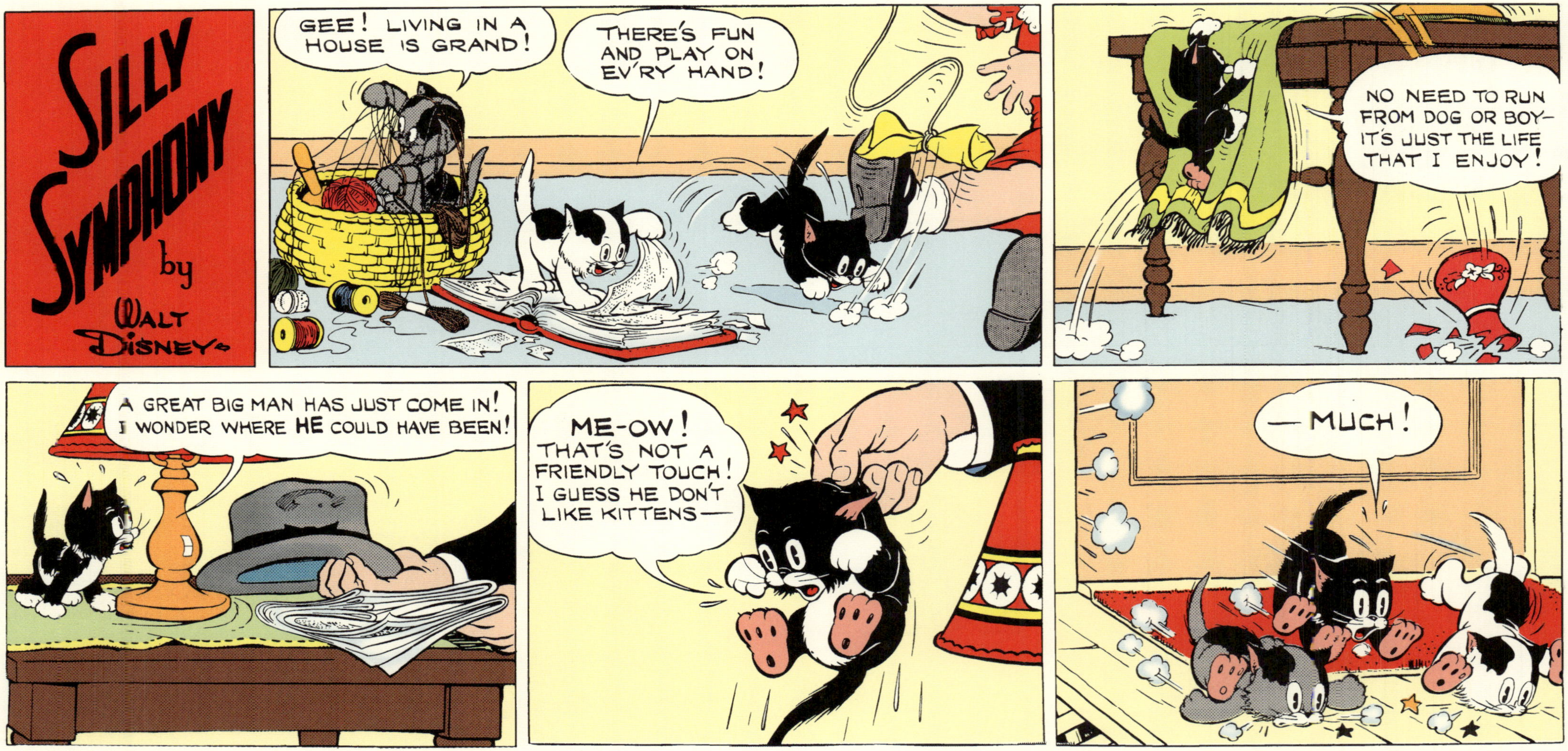
SILLY SYMPHONY
by
WALT DISNEY
GEE! LIVING IN A HOUSE IS GRAND!
THERE'S FUN AND PLAY ON EV'RY HAND!
NO NEED TO RUN FROM DOG OR BOY— IT'S JUST THE LIFE THAT I ENJOY!
A GREAT BIG MAN HAS JUST COME IN! I WONDER WHERE HE COULD HAVE BEEN!
ME-OW! THAT'S NOT A FRIENDLY TOUCH! I GUESS HE DON'T LIKE KITTENS—
—MUCH!

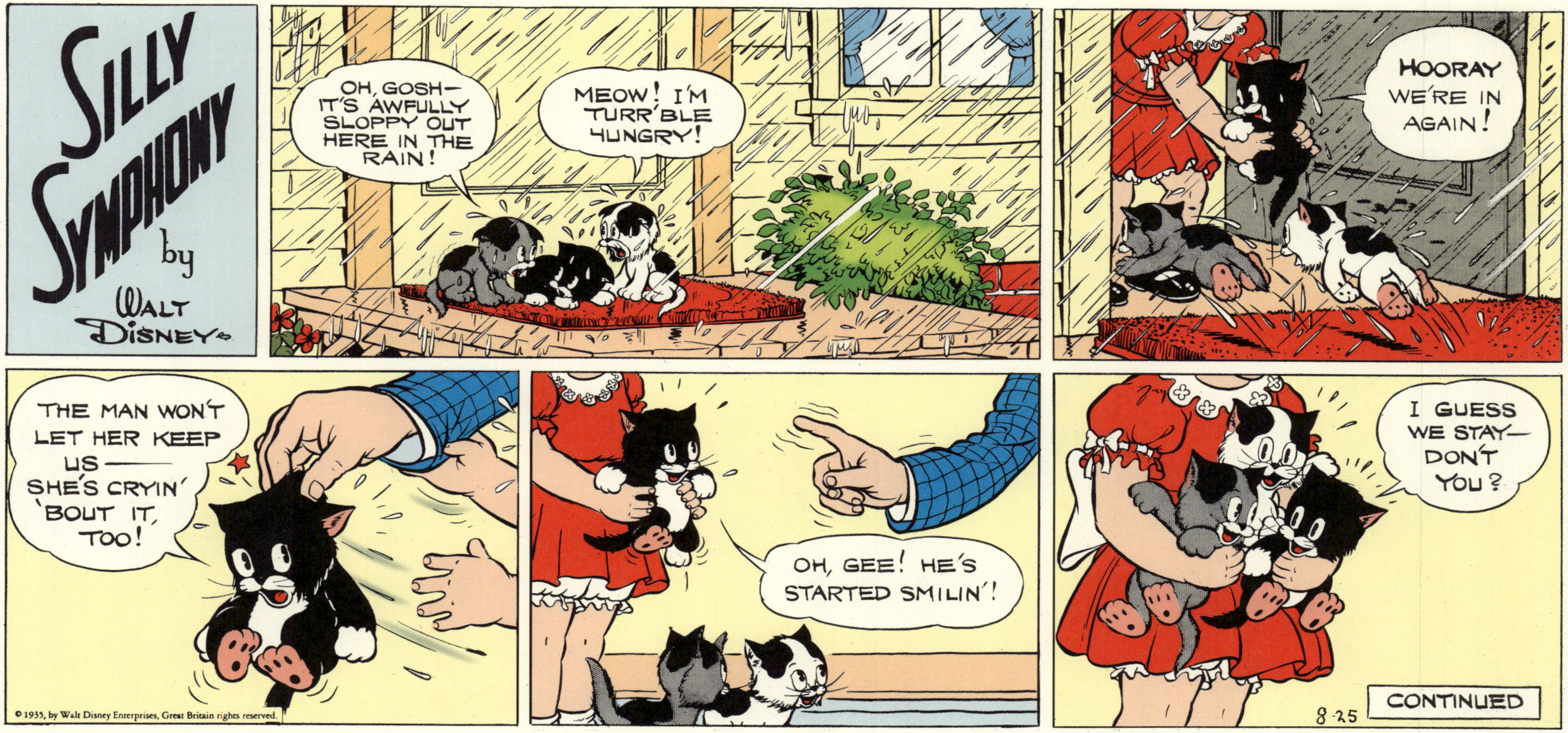
SILLY SYMPHONY
by
WALT DISNEY
OH, GOSH— IT'S AWFULLY SLOPPY OUT HERE IN THE RAIN!
MEOW! I'M TURR'BLE HUNGRY!
HOORAY WE'RE IN AGAIN!
THE MAN WON'T LET HER KEEP US—— SHE'S CRYIN' 'BOUT IT, TOO!
© 1935, by Walt Disney Enterprises, Great Britain rights reserved.
OH, GEE! HE'S STARTED SMILIN'!
I GUESS WE STAY— DON'T YOU?
8-25
CONTINUED

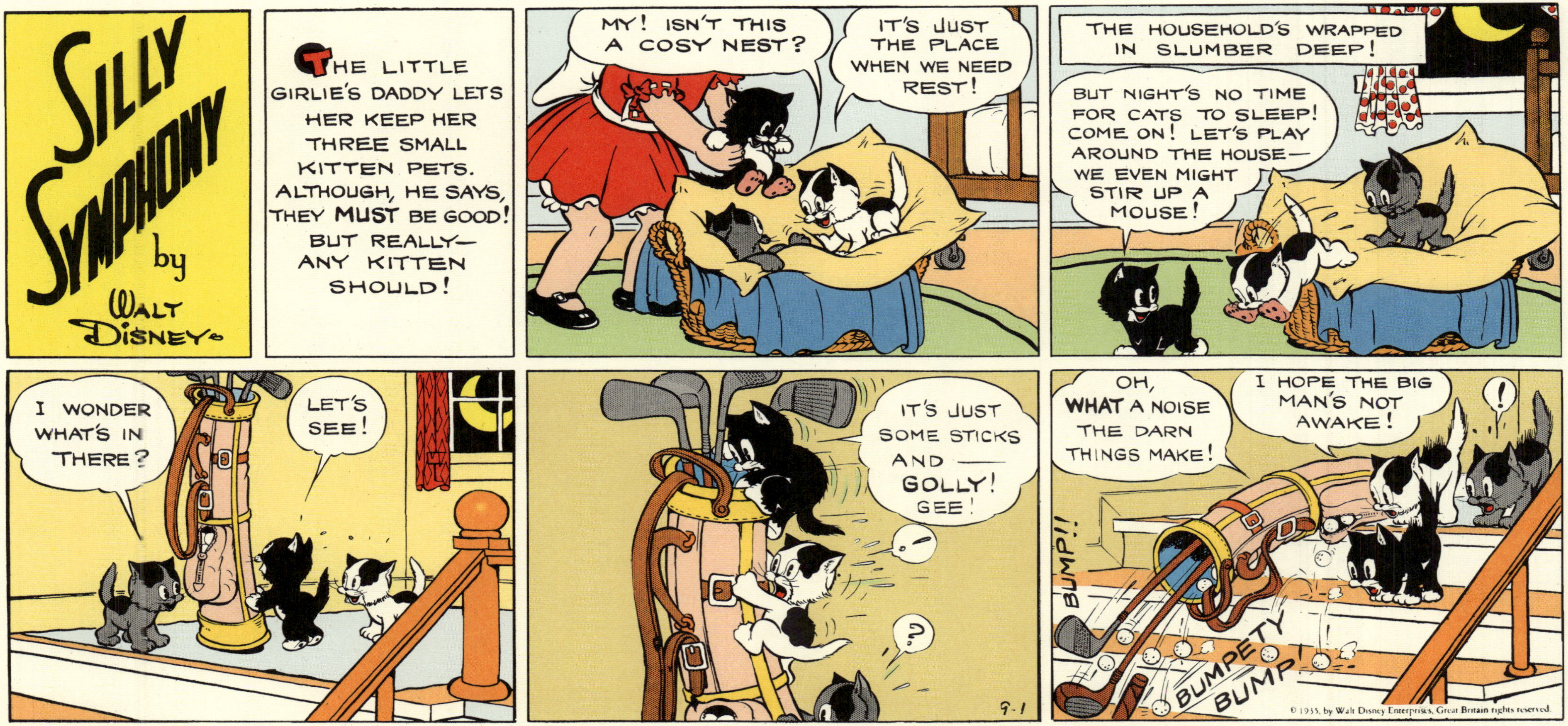
SILLY SYMPHONY
by
WALT DISNEY
THE LITTLE GIRLIE'S DADDY LETS HER KEEP HER THREE SMALL KITTEN PETS. ALTHOUGH, HE SAYS, THEY MUST BE GOOD! BUT REALLY— ANY KITTEN SHOULD!
MY! ISN'T THIS A COSY NEST?
IT'S JUST THE PLACE WHEN WE NEED REST!
THE HOUSEHOLD'S WRAPPED IN SLUMBER DEEP!
BUT NIGHT'S NO TIME FOR CATS TO SLEEP! COME ON! LET'S PLAY AROUND THE HOUSE— WE EVEN MIGHT STIR UP A MOUSE!
I WONDER WHAT'S IN THERE?
LET'S SEE!
IT'S JUST SOME STICKS AND —— GOLLY! GEE!
?
9-1
OH, WHAT A NOISE THE DARN THINGS MAKE!
I HOPE THE BIG MAN'S NOT AWAKE!
!
BUMP!!
BUMPETY BUMP!
© 1935, by Walt Disney Enterprises, Great Britain rights reserved.

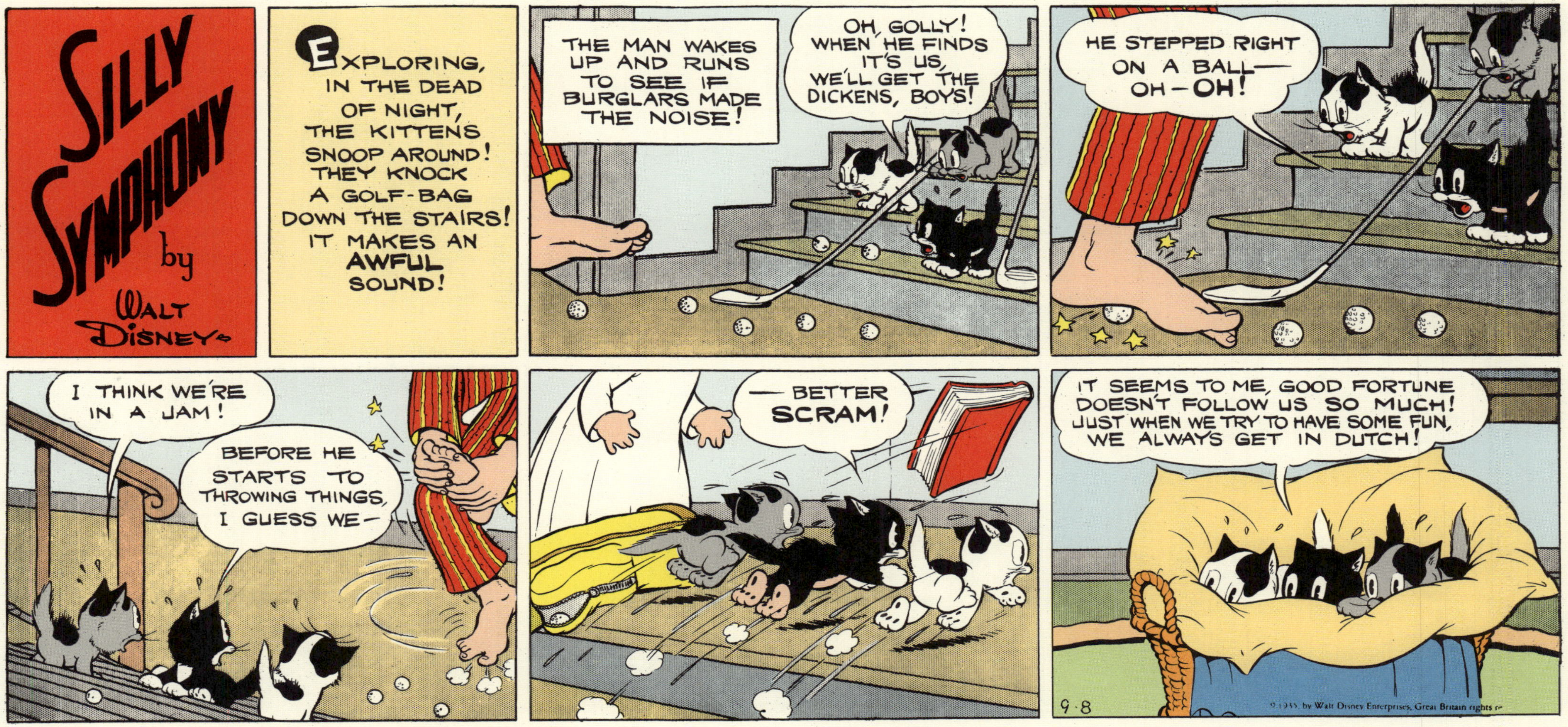
SILLY SYMPHONY
by
WALT DISNEY
EXPLORING, IN THE DEAD OF NIGHT, THE KITTENS SNOOP AROUND! THEY KNOCK A GOLF-BAG DOWN THE STAIRS! IT MAKES AN AWFUL SOUND!
THE MAN WAKES UP AND RUNS TO SEE IF BURGLARS MADE THE NOISE!
OH, GOLLY! WHEN HE FINDS IT'S US, WE'LL GET THE DICKENS, BOYS!
HE STEPPED RIGHT ON A BALL— OH—OH!
I THINK WE'RE IN A JAM!
BEFORE HE STARTS TO THROWING THINGS, I GUESS WE—
—BETTER SCRAM!
IT SEEMS TO ME, GOOD FORTUNE DOESN'T FOLLOW US SO MUCH! JUST WHEN WE TRY TO HAVE SOME FUN, WE ALWAYS GET IN DUTCH!
9·8

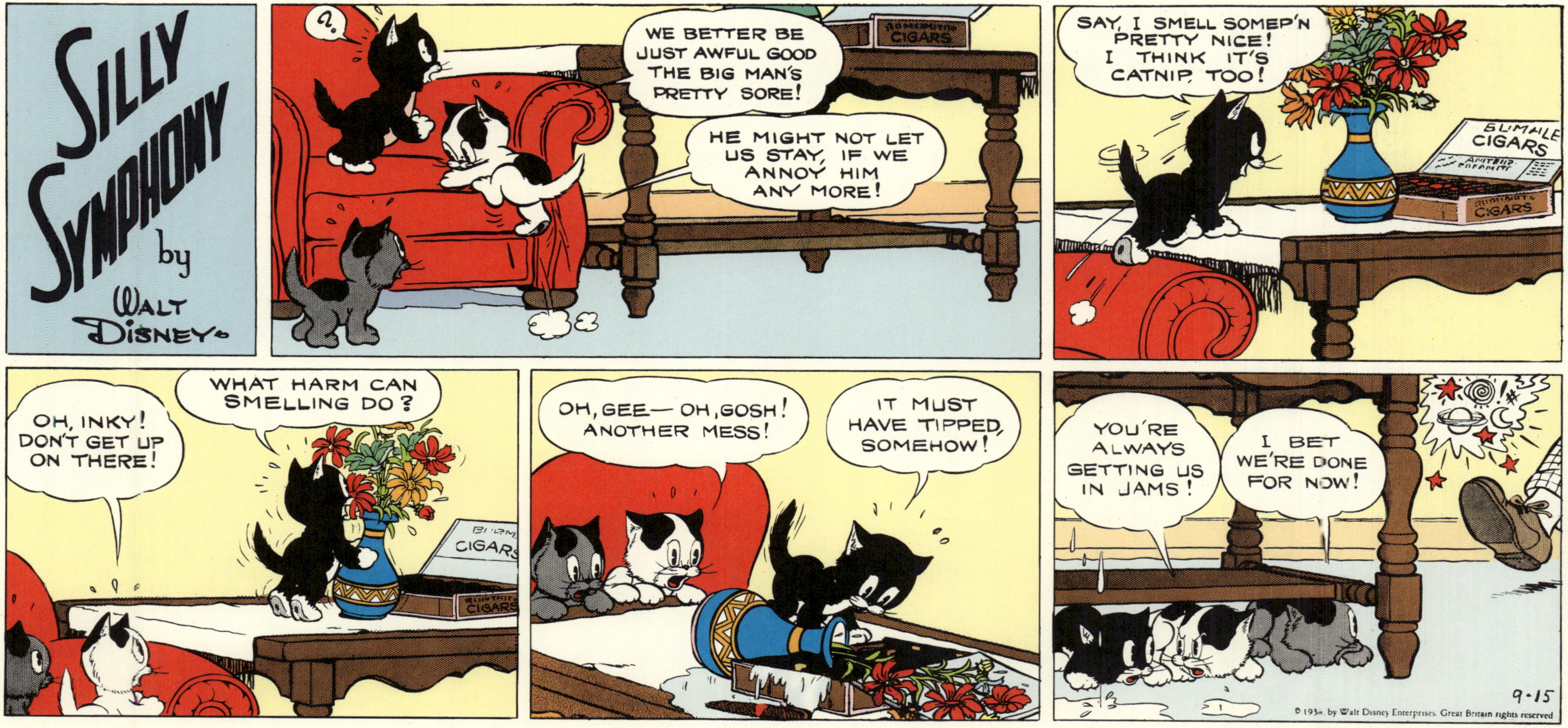
SILLY SYMPHONY
by
WALT DISNEY
?
WE BETTER BE JUST AWFUL GOOD THE BIG MAN'S PRETTY SORE!
HE MIGHT NOT LET US STAY, IF WE ANNOY HIM ANY MORE!
CIGARS
SAY, I SMELL SOMEP'N PRETTY NICE! I THINK IT'S CATNIP, TOO!
CIGARS
OH, INKY! DON'T GET UP ON THERE!
WHAT HARM CAN SMELLING DO?
CIGARS
OH, GEE— OH, GOSH! ANOTHER MESS!
IT MUST HAVE TIPPED, SOMEHOW!
YOU'RE ALWAYS GETTING US IN JAMS!
I BET WE'RE DONE FOR NOW!
9-15
© 193 by Walt Disney Enterprises. Great Britain rights reserved

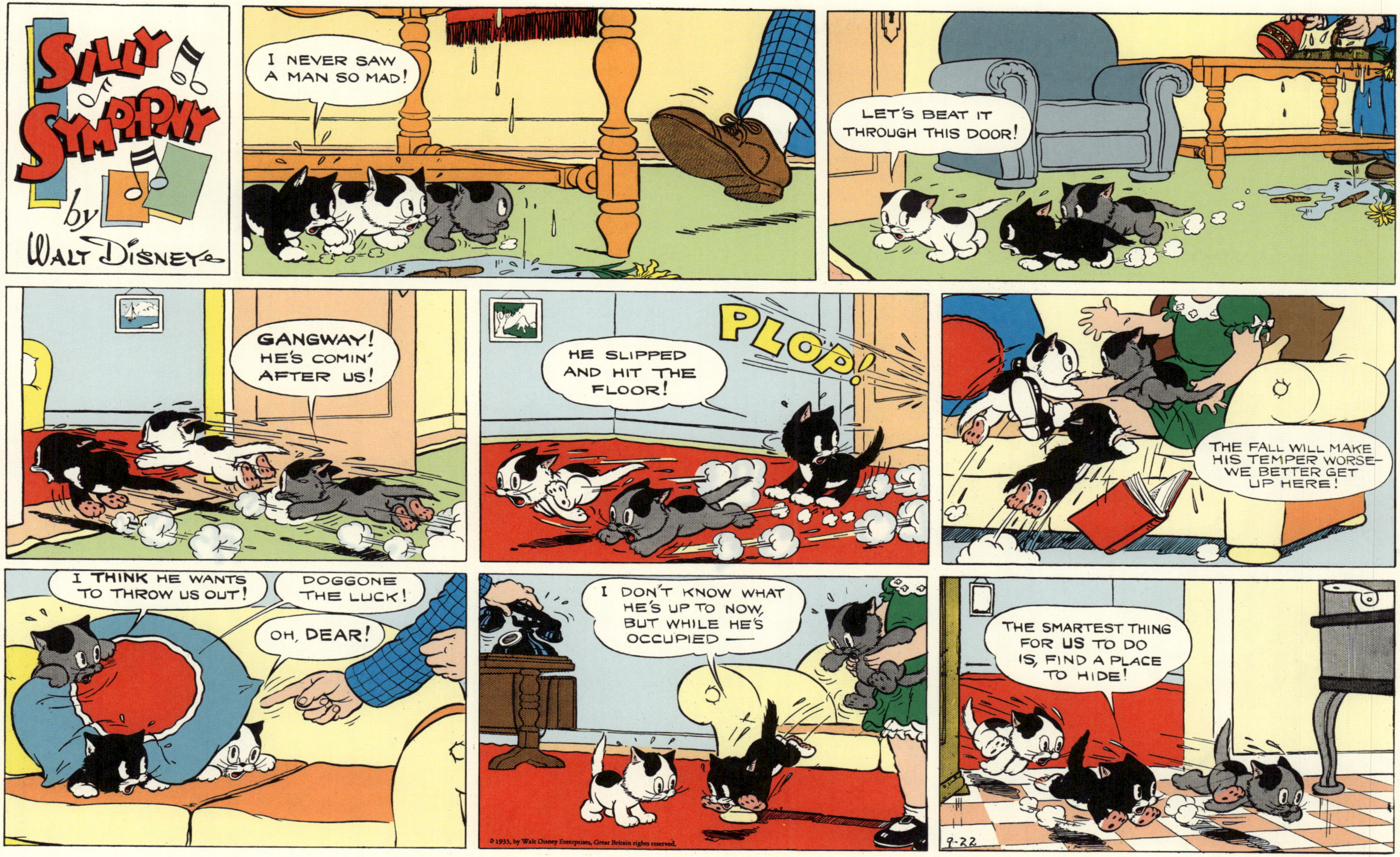
SILLY SYMPHONY
by WALT DISNEY
I NEVER SAW A MAN SO MAD!
LET'S BEAT IT THROUGH THIS DOOR!
GANGWAY! HE'S COMIN' AFTER US!
HE SLIPPED AND HIT THE FLOOR!
PLOP!
THE FALL WILL MAKE HIS TEMPER WORSE— WE BETTER GET UP HERE!
I THINK HE WANTS TO THROW US OUT!
DOGGONE THE LUCK!
OH, DEAR!
I DON'T KNOW WHAT HE'S UP TO NOW, BUT WHILE HE'S OCCUPIED —
© 1935, by Walt Disney Enterprises, Great Britain rights reserved.
THE SMARTEST THING FOR US TO DO IS, FIND A PLACE TO HIDE!
9-22

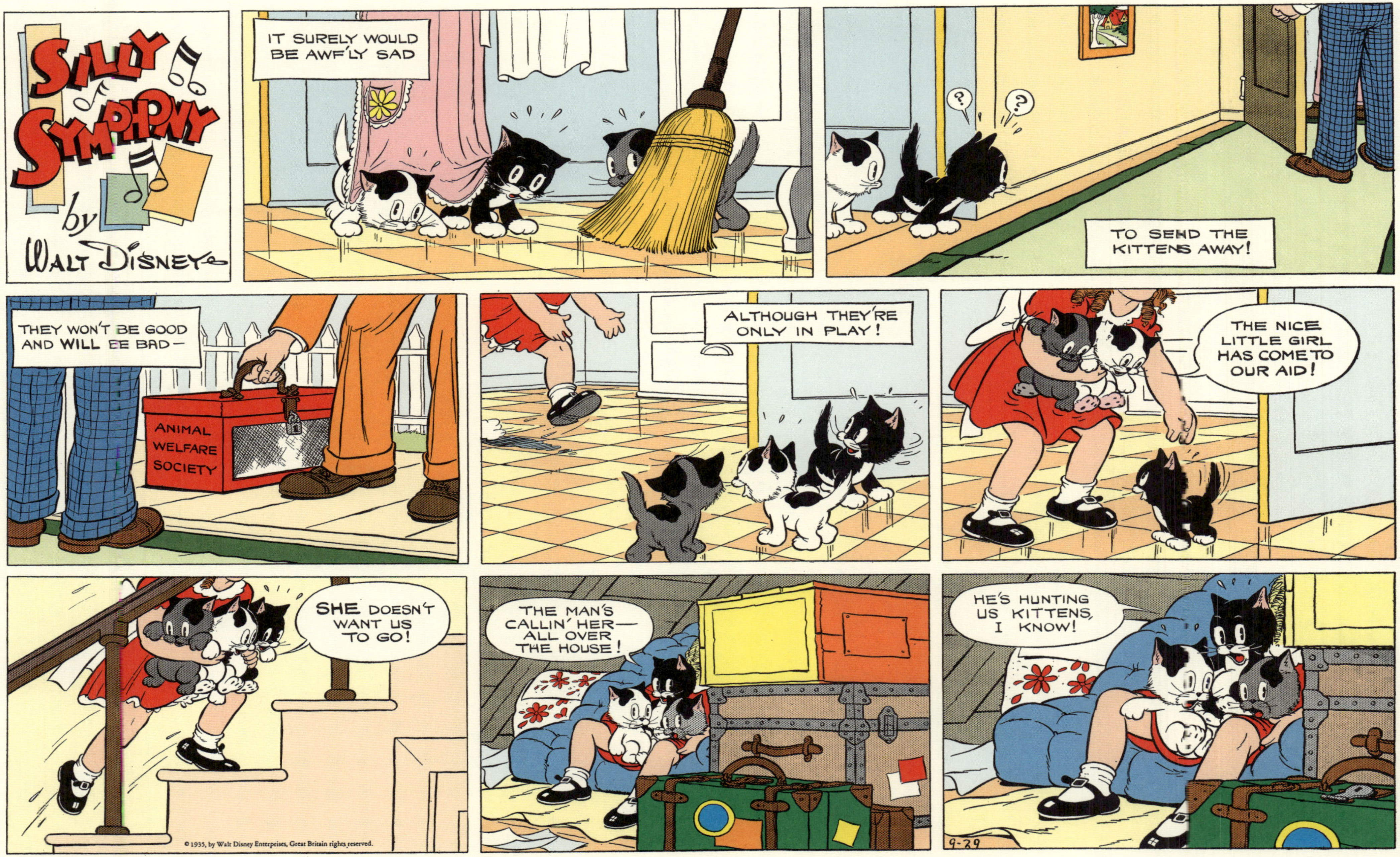
SILLY SYMPHONY
by
WALT DISNEY
IT SURELY WOULD BE AWF'LY SAD
?
?
TO SEND THE KITTENS AWAY!
THEY WON'T BE GOOD AND WILL BE BAD—
ANIMAL WELFARE SOCIETY
ALTHOUGH THEY'RE ONLY IN PLAY!
THE NICE LITTLE GIRL HAS COME TO OUR AID!
SHE DOESN'T WANT US TO GO!
© 1935, by Walt Disney Enterprises, Great Britain rights reserved.
THE MAN'S CALLIN' HER— ALL OVER THE HOUSE!
HE'S HUNTING US KITTENS, I KNOW!
9-29

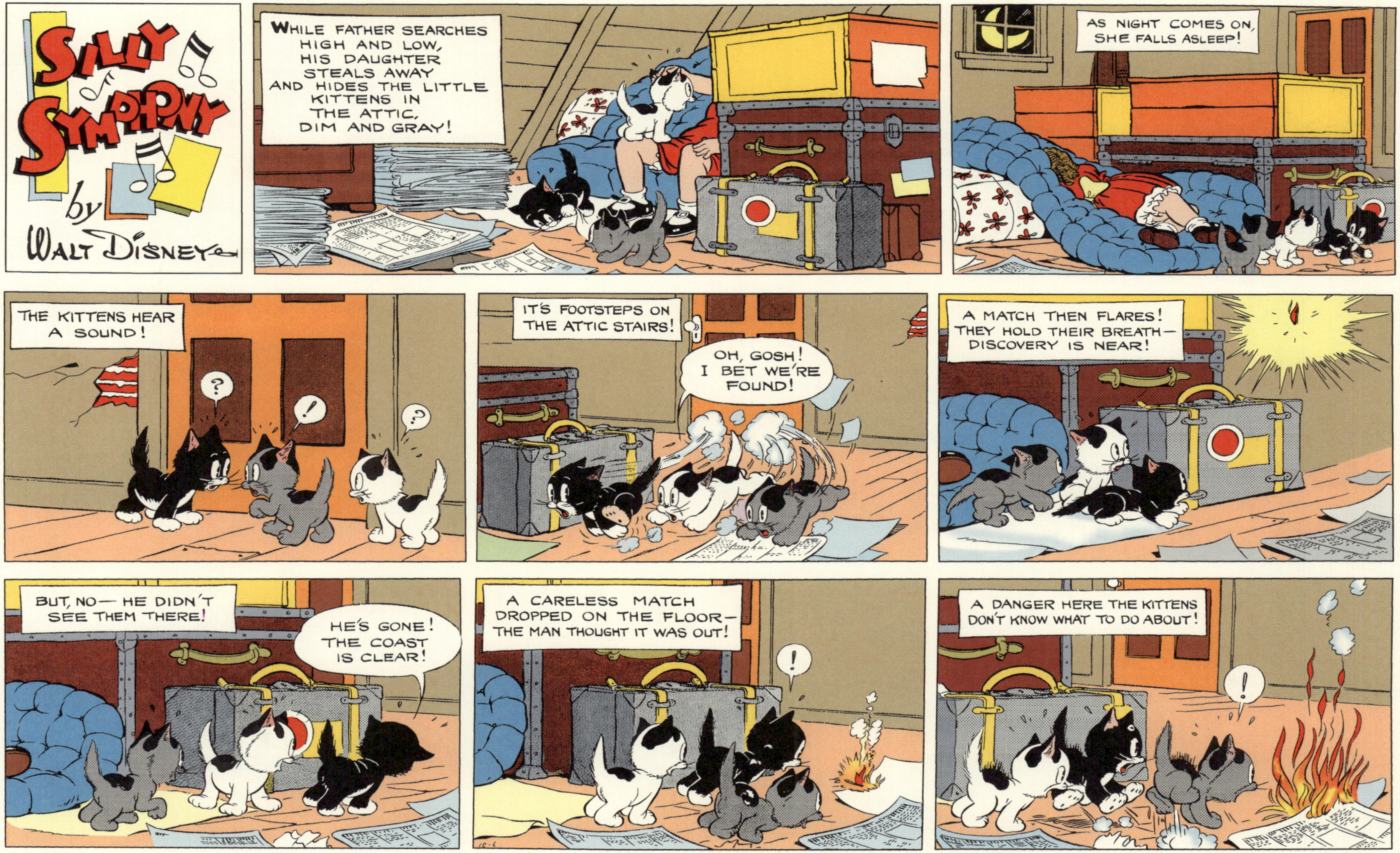
SILLY SYMPHONY
by WALT DISNEY
WHILE FATHER SEARCHES HIGH AND LOW, HIS DAUGHTER STEALS AWAY AND HIDES THE LITTLE KITTENS IN THE ATTIC, DIM AND GRAY!
AS NIGHT COMES ON, SHE FALLS ASLEEP!
THE KITTENS HEAR A SOUND!
?
!
?
IT'S FOOTSTEPS ON THE ATTIC STAIRS!
OH, GOSH! I BET WE'RE FOUND!
A MATCH THEN FLARES! THEY HOLD THEIR BREATH— DISCOVERY IS NEAR!
BUT, NO— HE DIDN'T SEE THEM THERE!
HE'S GONE! THE COAST IS CLEAR!
A CARELESS MATCH DROPPED ON THE FLOOR— THE MAN THOUGHT IT WAS OUT!
!
A DANGER HERE THE KITTENS DON'T KNOW WHAT TO DO ABOUT!
!

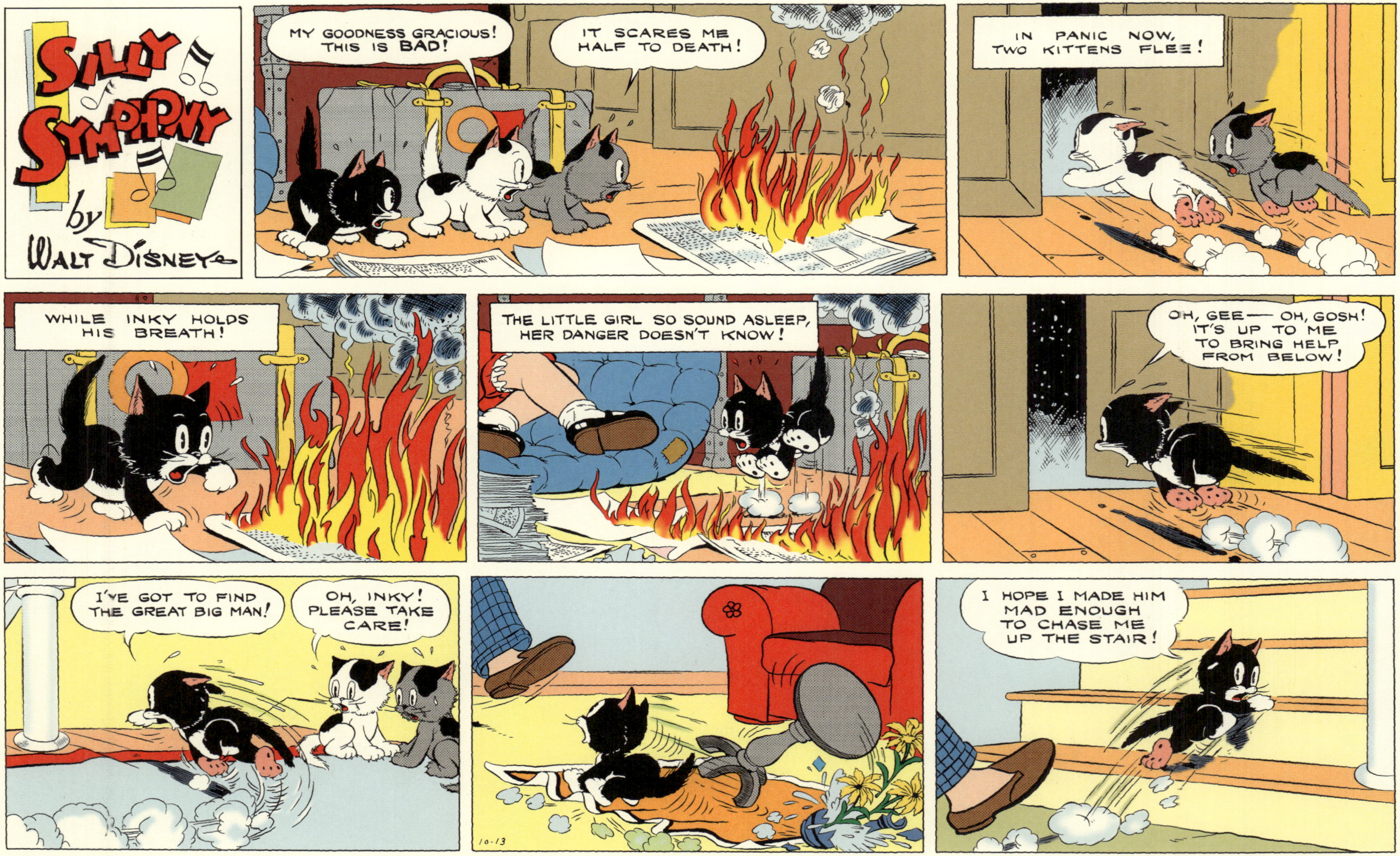
SILLY SYMPHONY
by WALT DISNEY
MY GOODNESS GRACIOUS! THIS IS BAD!
IT SCARES ME HALF TO DEATH!
IN PANIC NOW, TWO KITTENS FLEE!
WHILE INKY HOLDS HIS BREATH!
THE LITTLE GIRL SO SOUND ASLEEP, HER DANGER DOESN'T KNOW!
OH, GEE— OH, GOSH! IT'S UP TO ME TO BRING HELP FROM BELOW!
I'VE GOT TO FIND THE GREAT BIG MAN!
OH, INKY! PLEASE TAKE CARE!
10-13
I HOPE I MADE HIM MAD ENOUGH TO CHASE ME UP THE STAIR!

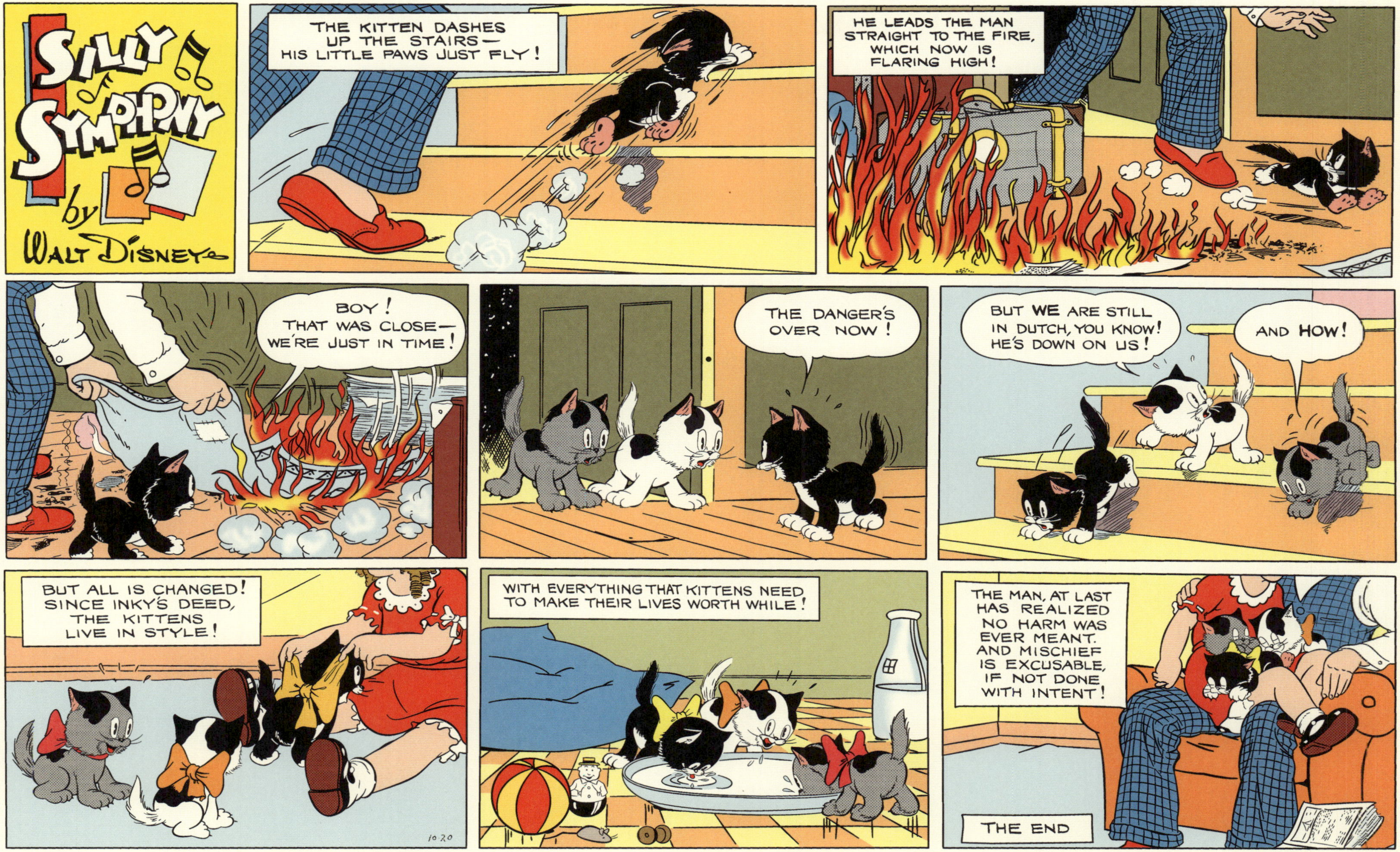
SILLY SYMPHONY
by
WALT DISNEY
THE KITTEN DASHES UP THE STAIRS— HIS LITTLE PAWS JUST FLY!
HE LEADS THE MAN STRAIGHT TO THE FIRE, WHICH NOW IS FLARING HIGH!
BOY! THAT WAS CLOSE— WE'RE JUST IN TIME!
THE DANGER'S OVER NOW!
BUT WE ARE STILL IN DUTCH, YOU KNOW! HE'S DOWN ON US!
AND HOW!
BUT ALL IS CHANGED! SINCE INKY'S DEED, THE KITTENS LIVE IN STYLE!
10 20
WITH EVERYTHING THAT KITTENS NEED TO MAKE THEIR LIVES WORTH WHILE!
THE MAN, AT LAST HAS REALIZED NO HARM WAS EVER MEANT. AND MISCHIEF IS EXCUSABLE, IF NOT DONE WITH INTENT!
THE END

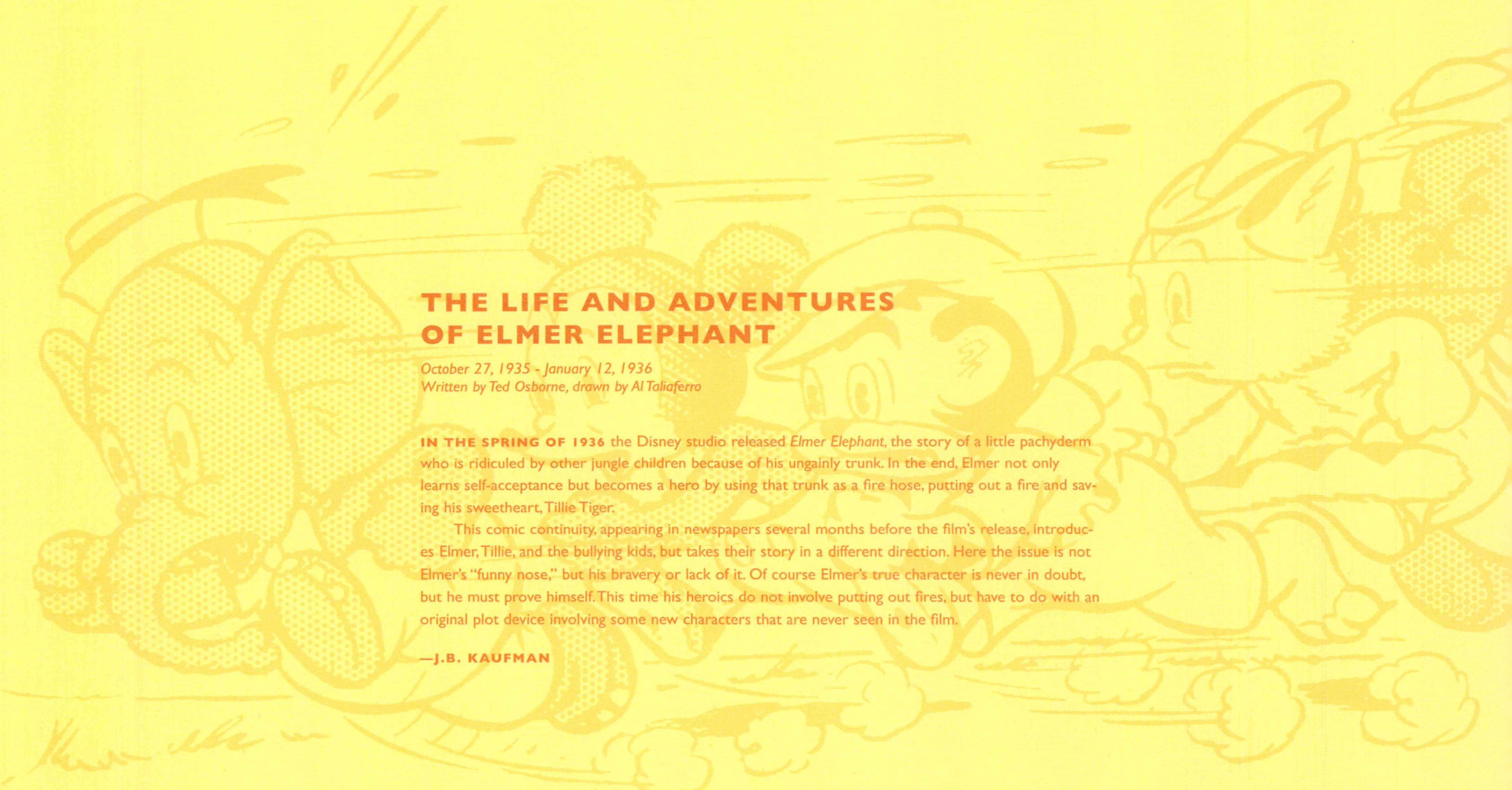

THE LIFE AND ADVENTURES OF ELMER ELEPHANT

October 27, 1935 - January 12, 1936
Written by Ted Osborne, drawn by Al Taliaferro

IN THE SPRING OF 1936 the Disney studio released *Elmer Elephant*, the story of a little pachyderm who is ridiculed by other jungle children because of his ungainly trunk. In the end, Elmer not only learns self-acceptance but becomes a hero by using that trunk as a fire hose, putting out a fire and saving his sweetheart, Tillie Tiger.

This comic continuity, appearing in newspapers several months before the film's release, introduces Elmer, Tillie, and the bullying kids, but takes their story in a different direction. Here the issue is not Elmer's "funny nose," but his bravery or lack of it. Of course Elmer's true character is never in doubt, but he must prove himself. This time his heroics do not involve putting out fires, but have to do with an original plot device involving some new characters that are never seen in the film.

—**J.B. KAUFMAN**

SILLY SYMPHONY
by
WALT DISNEY
Registered U.S. Patent Office
THE LIFE AND ADVENTURES OF ELMER ELEPHANT
HEY, FELLERS! LOOK! WELL, BLOW ME DOWN! SEE WHAT'S JUST ARRIVED IN TOWN!
WHAT'S YER NAME?
WHERE ARE YA FROM?
COME ON! ANSWER! ARE YA DUMB?
HE DOESN'T LOOK SO VERY BRIGHT!
I'M ELMER!
YEAH? YA WANNA FIGHT?
ME? FIGHT? O'COURSE NOT! GOSH! WHAT FOR? I ONLY FIGHT WHEN I GET SORE!
YAAAH! HE DON'T WANNA FIGHT! HE'S YELLER!
BABY! MAMMA'S 'ITTLE FELLER!
WHERE'S YOUR MAMMA? DO YOU MISS HER?
COWARD! YELLOW! SISSY—KISSER!
WELL, I DON'T LIKE TO FIGHT, BUT GEE! IF THAT'S WHAT YOU GUYS THINK OF ME, AND FIGHT IS WHAT YOU WANT, ALL RIGHT!
COME ON! PUT UP YOUR HANDS! LET'S FIGHT!
STOP THAT, YOU GREAT BIG BULLY, YOU! I SAW WHAT YOU WERE TRYING TO DO!
10-27
SUCH COWARDS AND RUFFIANS I DESPISE! PICK ON SOMEBODY YOUR OWN SIZE!

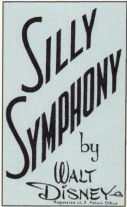

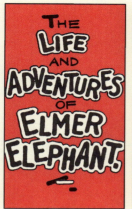

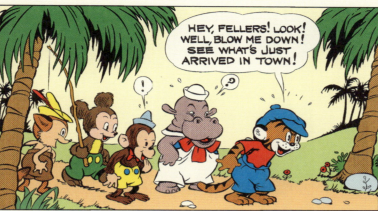

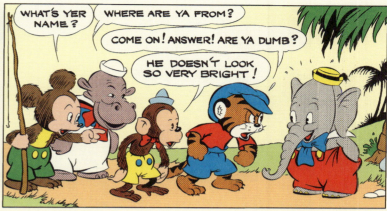

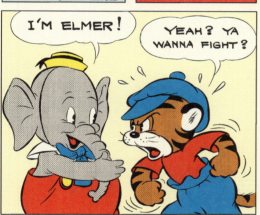

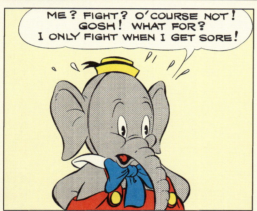

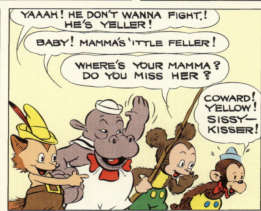

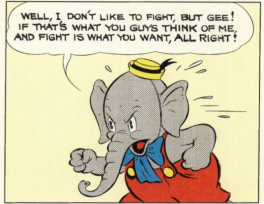

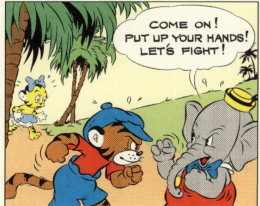

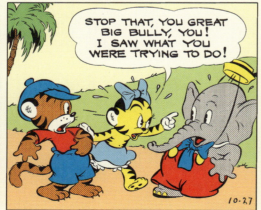

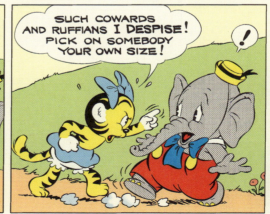

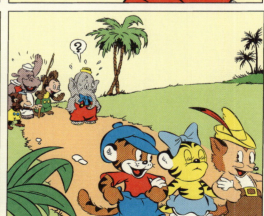

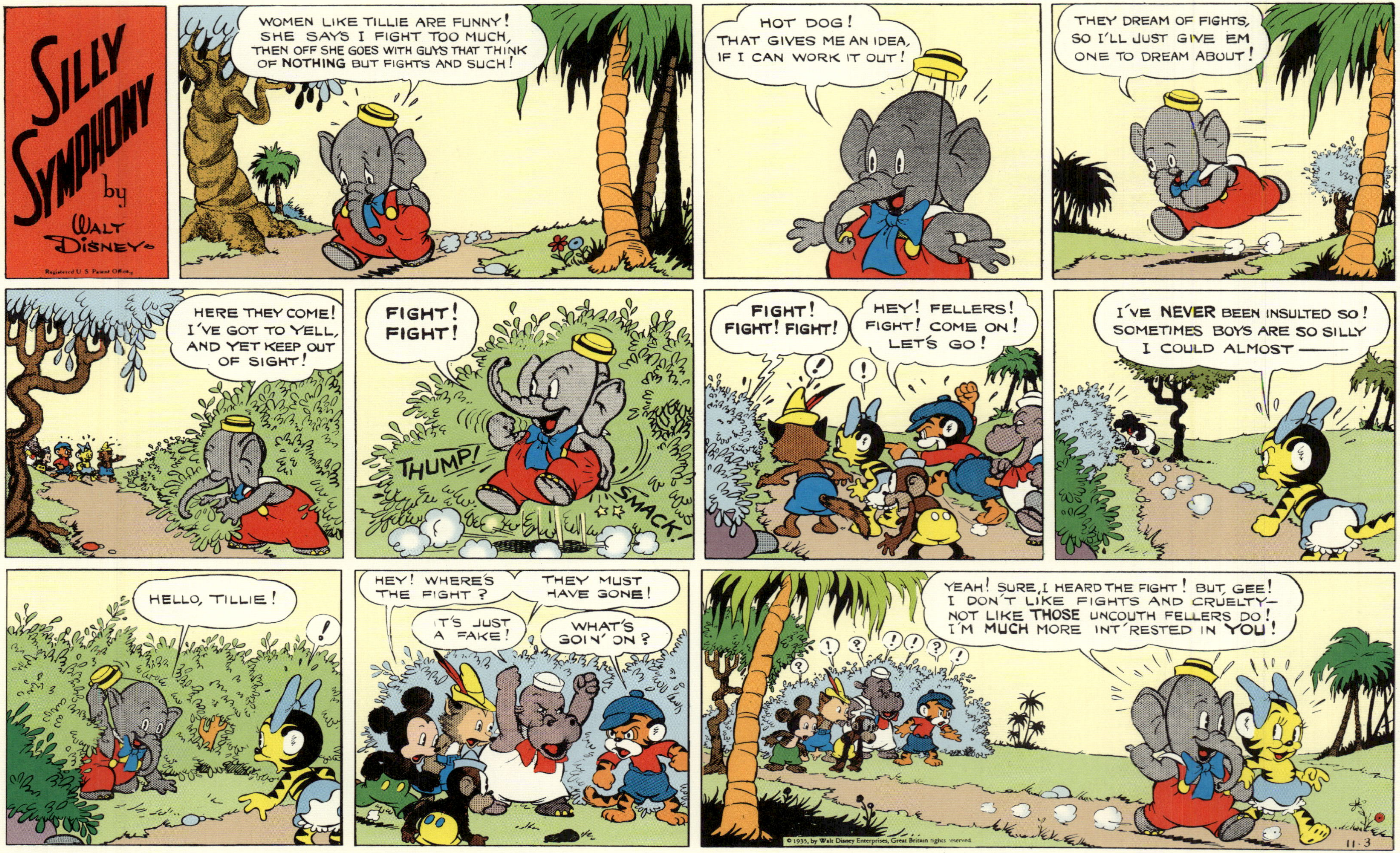
SILLY SYMPHONY
by WALT DISNEY
WOMEN LIKE TILLIE ARE FUNNY! SHE SAYS I FIGHT TOO MUCH, THEN OFF SHE GOES WITH GUYS THAT THINK OF NOTHING BUT FIGHTS AND SUCH!
HOT DOG! THAT GIVES ME AN IDEA, IF I CAN WORK IT OUT!
THEY DREAM OF FIGHTS, SO I'LL JUST GIVE 'EM ONE TO DREAM ABOUT!
HERE THEY COME! I'VE GOT TO YELL, AND YET KEEP OUT OF SIGHT!
FIGHT! FIGHT!
THUMP!
SMACK!
FIGHT! FIGHT! FIGHT!
HEY! FELLERS! FIGHT! COME ON! LET'S GO!
I'VE NEVER BEEN INSULTED SO! SOMETIMES BOYS ARE SO SILLY I COULD ALMOST ——
HELLO, TILLIE!
HEY! WHERE'S THE FIGHT?
THEY MUST HAVE GONE!
IT'S JUST A FAKE!
WHAT'S GOIN' ON?
YEAH! SURE, I HEARD THE FIGHT! BUT, GEE! I DON'T LIKE FIGHTS AND CRUELTY— NOT LIKE THOSE UNCOUTH FELLERS DO! I'M MUCH MORE INT'RESTED IN YOU!
© 1935, by Walt Disney Enterprises, Great Britain rights reserved
11-3

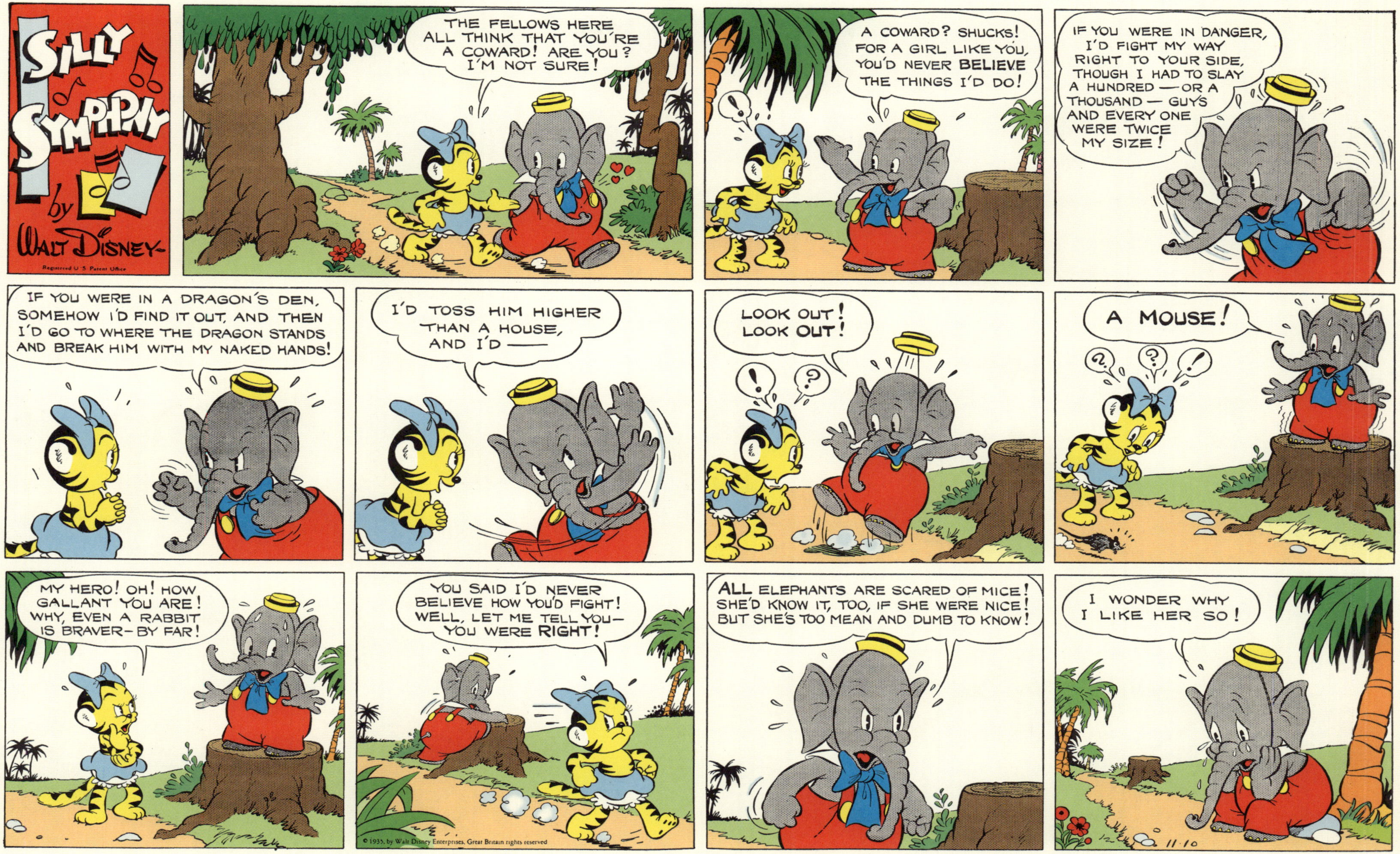
SILLY SYMPHONY
by WALT DISNEY
Registered U.S. Patent Office
THE FELLOWS HERE ALL THINK THAT YOU'RE A COWARD! ARE YOU? I'M NOT SURE!
A COWARD? SHUCKS! FOR A GIRL LIKE YOU, YOU'D NEVER BELIEVE THE THINGS I'D DO!
IF YOU WERE IN DANGER, I'D FIGHT MY WAY RIGHT TO YOUR SIDE, THOUGH I HAD TO SLAY A HUNDRED — OR A THOUSAND — GUYS AND EVERY ONE WERE TWICE MY SIZE!
IF YOU WERE IN A DRAGON'S DEN, SOMEHOW I'D FIND IT OUT, AND THEN I'D GO TO WHERE THE DRAGON STANDS AND BREAK HIM WITH MY NAKED HANDS!
I'D TOSS HIM HIGHER THAN A HOUSE, AND I'D ——
LOOK OUT! LOOK OUT!
A MOUSE!
MY HERO! OH! HOW GALLANT YOU ARE! WHY, EVEN A RABBIT IS BRAVER– BY FAR!
YOU SAID I'D NEVER BELIEVE HOW YOU'D FIGHT! WELL, LET ME TELL YOU– YOU WERE RIGHT!
© 1935, by Walt Disney Enterprises. Great Britain rights reserved
ALL ELEPHANTS ARE SCARED OF MICE! SHE'D KNOW IT, TOO, IF SHE WERE NICE! BUT SHE'S TOO MEAN AND DUMB TO KNOW!
I WONDER WHY I LIKE HER SO!
11·10

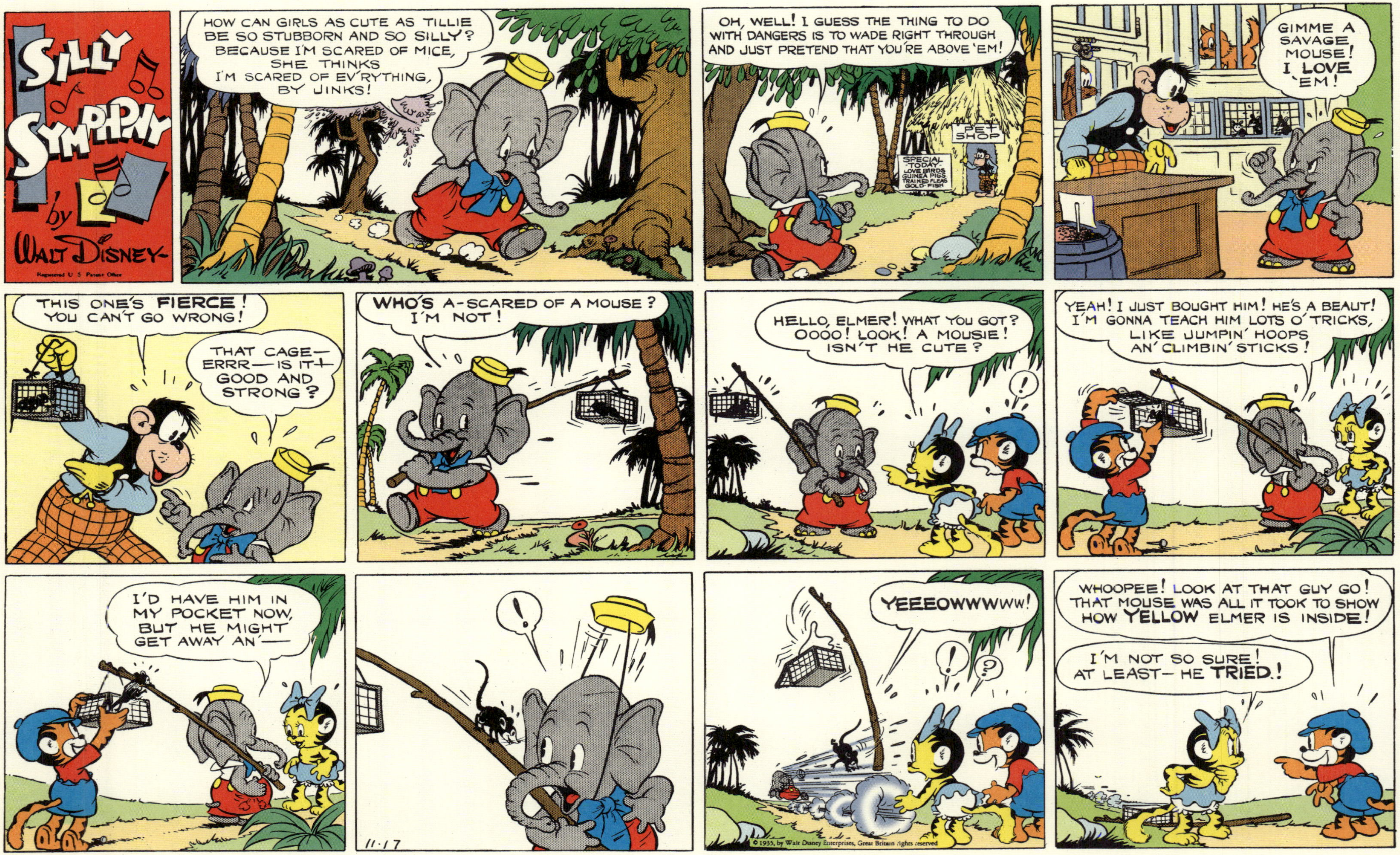
SILLY SYMPHONY
by
WALT DISNEY
Registered U.S. Patent Office
HOW CAN GIRLS AS CUTE AS TILLIE BE SO STUBBORN AND SO SILLY? BECAUSE I'M SCARED OF MICE, SHE THINKS I'M SCARED OF EV'RYTHING, BY JINKS!
OH, WELL! I GUESS THE THING TO DO WITH DANGERS IS TO WADE RIGHT THROUGH AND JUST PRETEND THAT YOU'RE ABOVE 'EM!
PET SHOP
SPECIAL TODAY LOVE BIRDS GUINEA PIGS TRAINED FLEAS GOLD-FISH
GIMME A SAVAGE MOUSE! I LOVE 'EM!
THIS ONE'S FIERCE! YOU CAN'T GO WRONG!
THAT CAGE— ERRR—IS IT— GOOD AND STRONG?
WHO'S A-SCARED OF A MOUSE? I'M NOT!
HELLO, ELMER! WHAT YOU GOT? OOOO! LOOK! A MOUSIE! ISN'T HE CUTE?
!
YEAH! I JUST BOUGHT HIM! HE'S A BEAUT! I'M GONNA TEACH HIM LOTS O' TRICKS, LIKE JUMPIN' HOOPS AN' CLIMBIN' STICKS!
I'D HAVE HIM IN MY POCKET NOW, BUT HE MIGHT GET AWAY AN'—
!
11-17
YEEEOWWWWWW!
!
?
© 1935, by Walt Disney Enterprises, Great Britain rights reserved
WHOOPEE! LOOK AT THAT GUY GO! THAT MOUSE WAS ALL IT TOOK TO SHOW HOW YELLOW ELMER IS INSIDE!
I'M NOT SO SURE! AT LEAST— HE TRIED.!

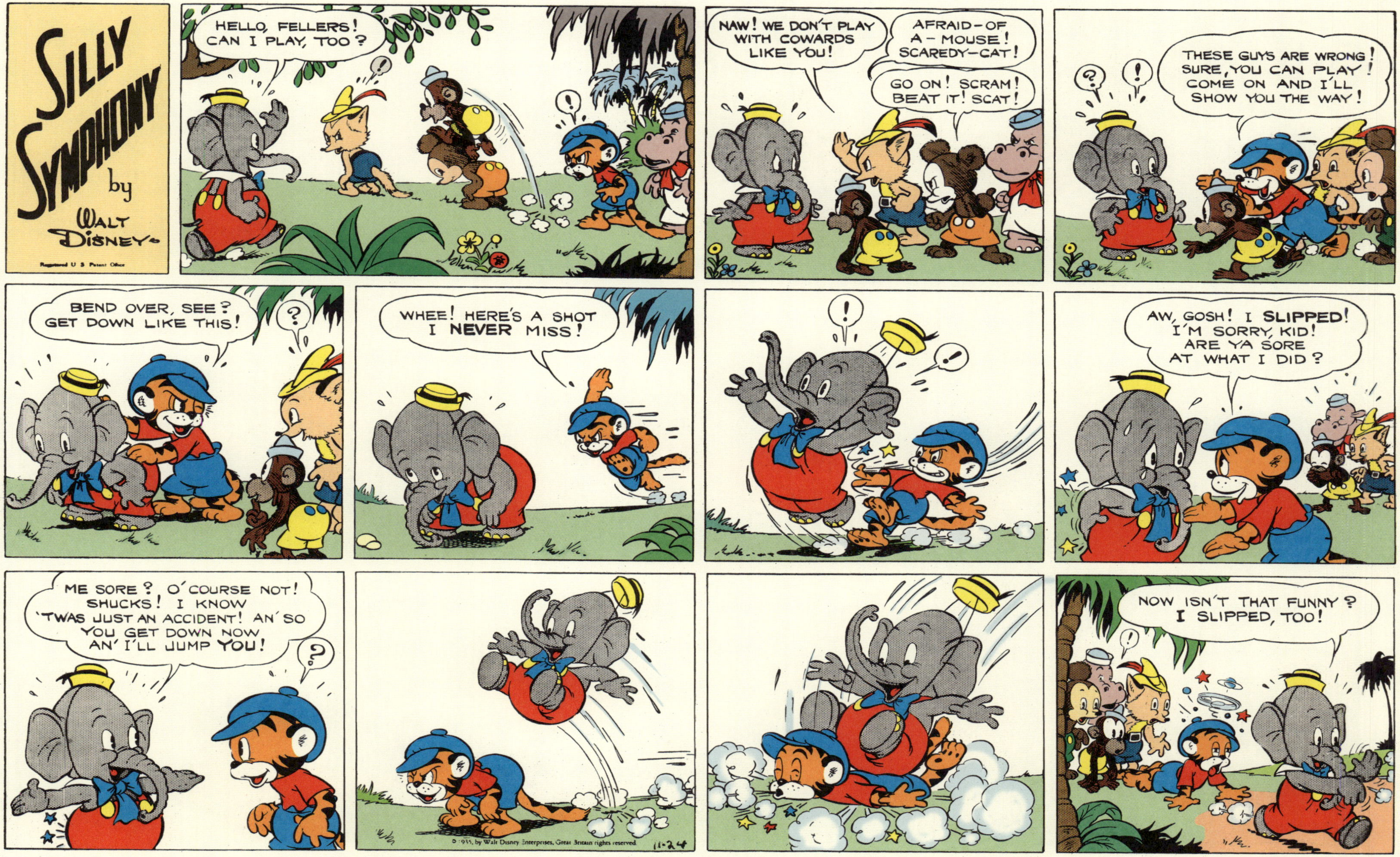
SILLY SYMPHONY
by
WALT DISNEY
Registered U S Patent Office
HELLO, FELLERS! CAN I PLAY, TOO?
NAW! WE DON'T PLAY WITH COWARDS LIKE YOU!
AFRAID-OF A-MOUSE! SCAREDY-CAT!
GO ON! SCRAM! BEAT IT! SCAT!
THESE GUYS ARE WRONG! SURE, YOU CAN PLAY! COME ON AND I'LL SHOW YOU THE WAY!
BEND OVER, SEE? GET DOWN LIKE THIS!
WHEE! HERE'S A SHOT I NEVER MISS!
AW, GOSH! I SLIPPED! I'M SORRY, KID! ARE YA SORE AT WHAT I DID?
ME SORE? O'COURSE NOT! SHUCKS! I KNOW 'TWAS JUST AN ACCIDENT! AN' SO YOU GET DOWN NOW AN' I'LL JUMP YOU!
© 1935, by Walt Disney Enterprises, Great Britain rights reserved
11-24
NOW ISN'T THAT FUNNY? I SLIPPED, TOO!

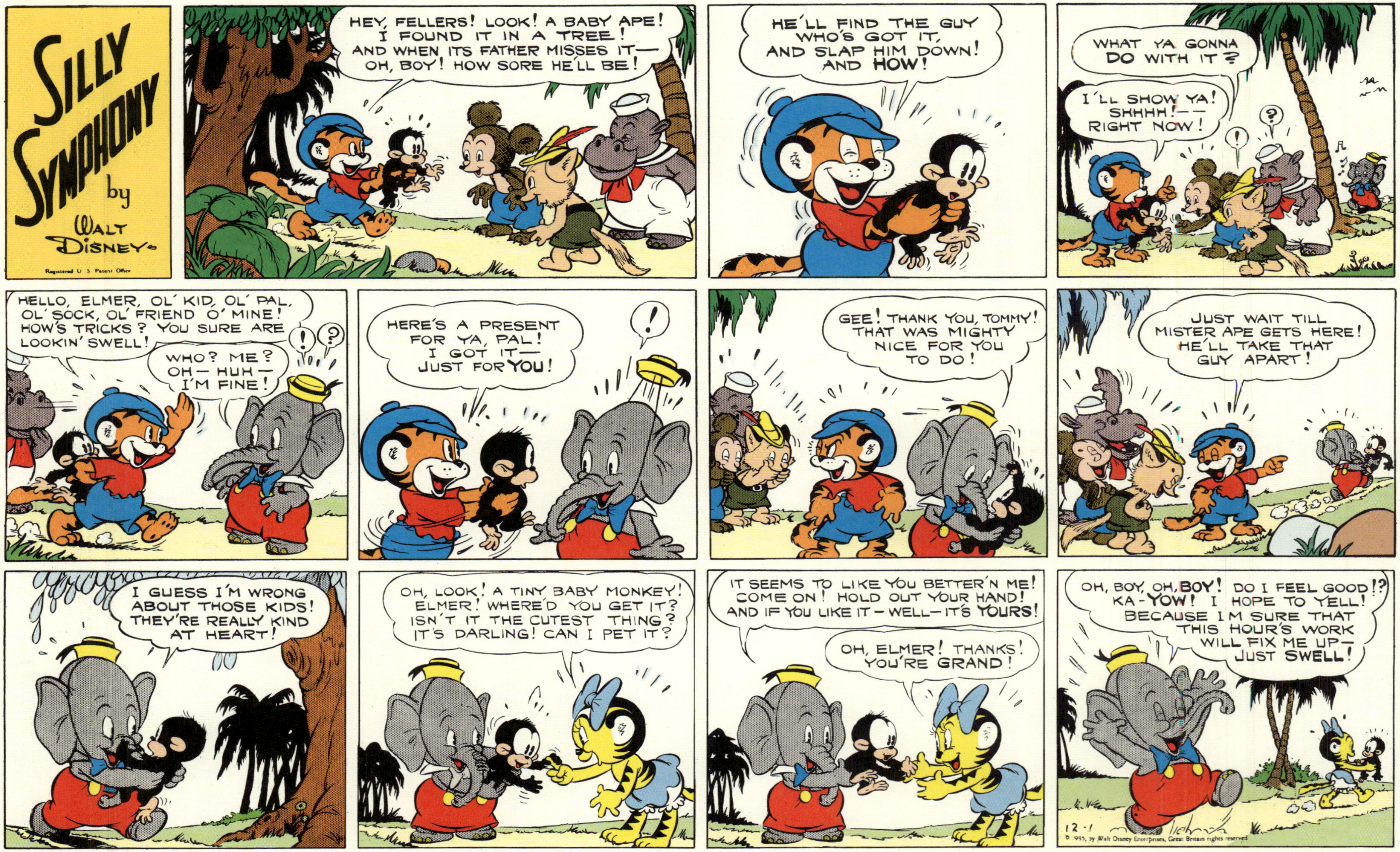
SILLY SYMPHONY by WALT DISNEY
Registered U.S. Patent Office
HEY, FELLERS! LOOK! A BABY APE! I FOUND IT IN A TREE! AND WHEN ITS FATHER MISSES IT— OH, BOY! HOW SORE HE'LL BE!
HE'LL FIND THE GUY WHO'S GOT IT, AND SLAP HIM DOWN! AND HOW!
WHAT YA GONNA DO WITH IT?
I'LL SHOW YA! SHHHH!— — RIGHT NOW!
HELLO, ELMER, OL' KID, OL' PAL, OL' SOCK, OL' FRIEND O' MINE! HOW'S TRICKS? YOU SURE ARE LOOKIN' SWELL!
WHO? ME? OH — HUH — I'M FINE!
HERE'S A PRESENT FOR YA, PAL! I GOT IT— JUST FOR YOU!
GEE! THANK YOU, TOMMY! THAT WAS MIGHTY NICE FOR YOU TO DO!
JUST WAIT TILL MISTER APE GETS HERE! HE'LL TAKE THAT GUY APART!
I GUESS I'M WRONG ABOUT THOSE KIDS! THEY'RE REALLY KIND AT HEART!
OH, LOOK! A TINY BABY MONKEY! ELMER! WHERE'D YOU GET IT? ISN'T IT THE CUTEST THING? IT'S DARLING! CAN I PET IT?
IT SEEMS TO LIKE YOU BETTER'N ME! COME ON! HOLD OUT YOUR HAND! AND IF YOU LIKE IT — WELL — IT'S YOURS!
OH, ELMER! THANKS! YOU'RE GRAND!
OH, BOY, OH, BOY! DO I FEEL GOOD!? KA-YOW! I HOPE TO YELL! BECAUSE I'M SURE THAT THIS HOUR'S WORK WILL FIX ME UP— JUST SWELL!
12-1
© 1935, by Walt Disney Enterprises, Great Britain rights reserved

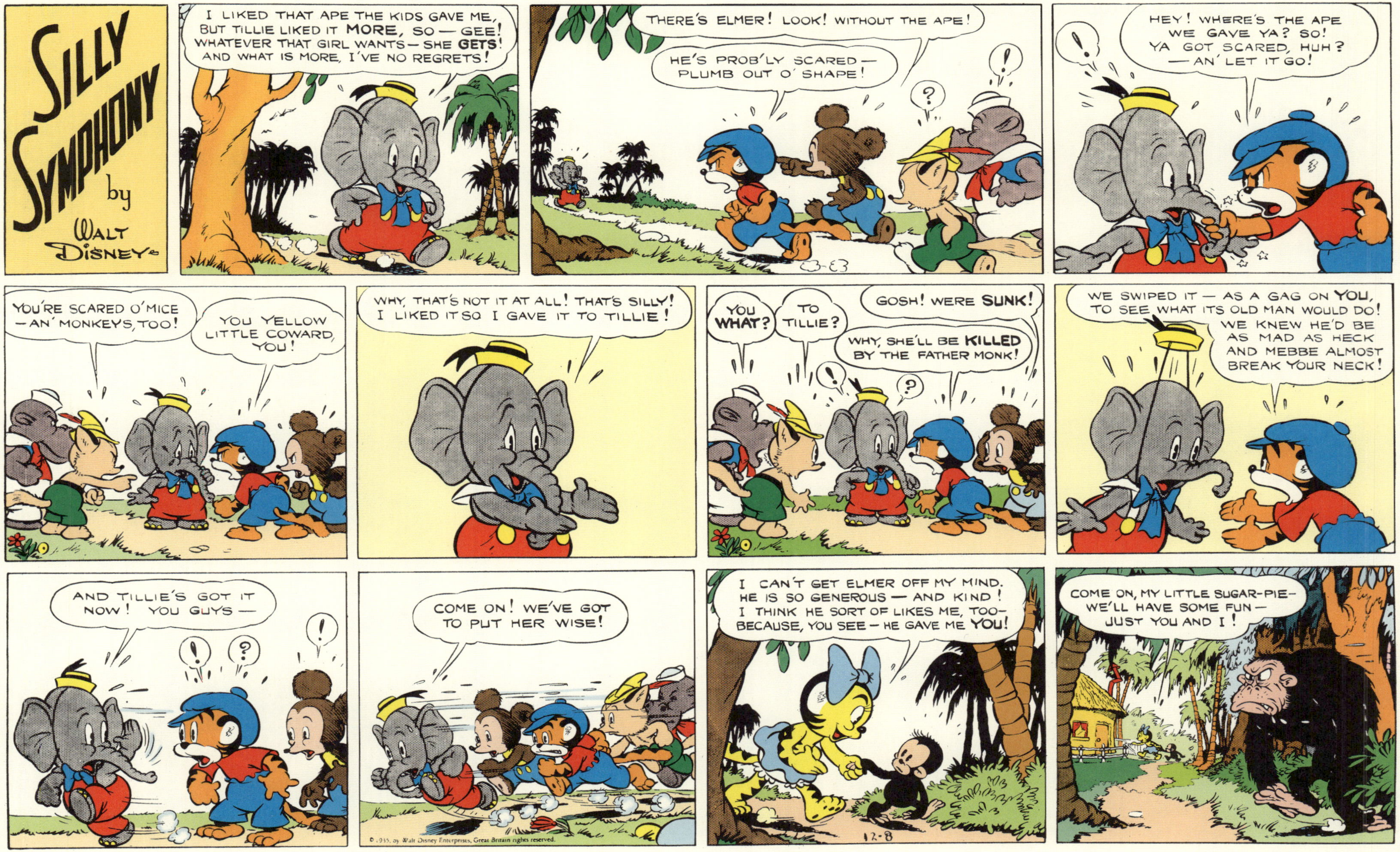
SILLY SYMPHONY by WALT DISNEY
I LIKED THAT APE THE KIDS GAVE ME, BUT TILLIE LIKED IT MORE, SO — GEE! WHATEVER THAT GIRL WANTS — SHE GETS! AND WHAT IS MORE, I'VE NO REGRETS!
THERE'S ELMER! LOOK! WITHOUT THE APE!
HE'S PROB'LY SCARED — PLUMB OUT O' SHAPE!
HEY! WHERE'S THE APE WE GAVE YA? SO! YA GOT SCARED, HUH? — AN' LET IT GO!
YOU'RE SCARED O' MICE — AN' MONKEYS, TOO!
YOU YELLOW LITTLE COWARD, YOU!
WHY, THAT'S NOT IT AT ALL! THAT'S SILLY! I LIKED IT SO I GAVE IT TO TILLIE!
YOU WHAT?
TO TILLIE?
GOSH! WE'RE SUNK!
WHY, SHE'LL BE KILLED BY THE FATHER MONK!
WE SWIPED IT — AS A GAG ON YOU, TO SEE WHAT ITS OLD MAN WOULD DO!
WE KNEW HE'D BE AS MAD AS HECK AND MEBBE ALMOST BREAK YOUR NECK!
AND TILLIE'S GOT IT NOW! YOU GUYS —
COME ON! WE'VE GOT TO PUT HER WISE!
© 1935, by Walt Disney Enterprises, Great Britain rights reserved.
I CAN'T GET ELMER OFF MY MIND. HE IS SO GENEROUS — AND KIND! I THINK HE SORT OF LIKES ME, TOO — BECAUSE, YOU SEE — HE GAVE ME YOU!
12-8
COME ON, MY LITTLE SUGAR-PIE — WE'LL HAVE SOME FUN — JUST YOU AND I!

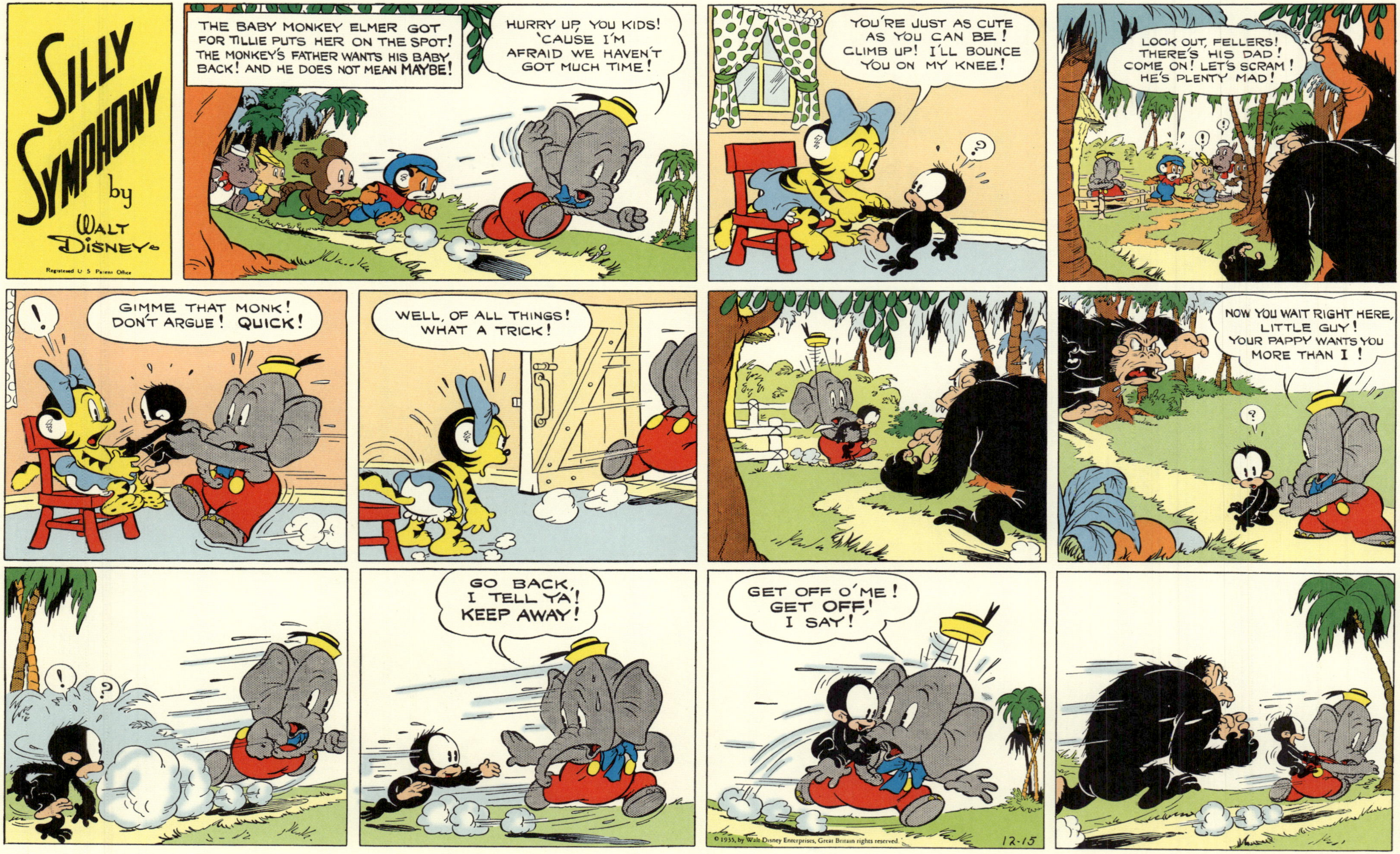

SILLY SYMPHONY
by
WALT DISNEY
Registered U S Patent Office
THE BABY MONKEY ELMER GOT FOR TILLIE PUTS HER ON THE SPOT! THE MONKEY'S FATHER WANTS HIS BABY BACK! AND HE DOES NOT MEAN MAYBE!
HURRY UP, YOU KIDS! 'CAUSE I'M AFRAID WE HAVEN'T GOT MUCH TIME!
YOU'RE JUST AS CUTE AS YOU CAN BE! CLIMB UP! I'LL BOUNCE YOU ON MY KNEE!
?
LOOK OUT, FELLERS! THERE'S HIS DAD! COME ON! LET'S SCRAM! HE'S PLENTY MAD!
!
GIMME THAT MONK! DON'T ARGUE! QUICK!
WELL, OF ALL THINGS! WHAT A TRICK!
NOW YOU WAIT RIGHT HERE, LITTLE GUY! YOUR PAPPY WANTS YOU MORE THAN I!
?
! ?
GO BACK, I TELL YA! KEEP AWAY!
GET OFF O'ME! GET OFF! I SAY!
© 1935, by Walt Disney Enterprises, Great Britain rights reserved
12-15

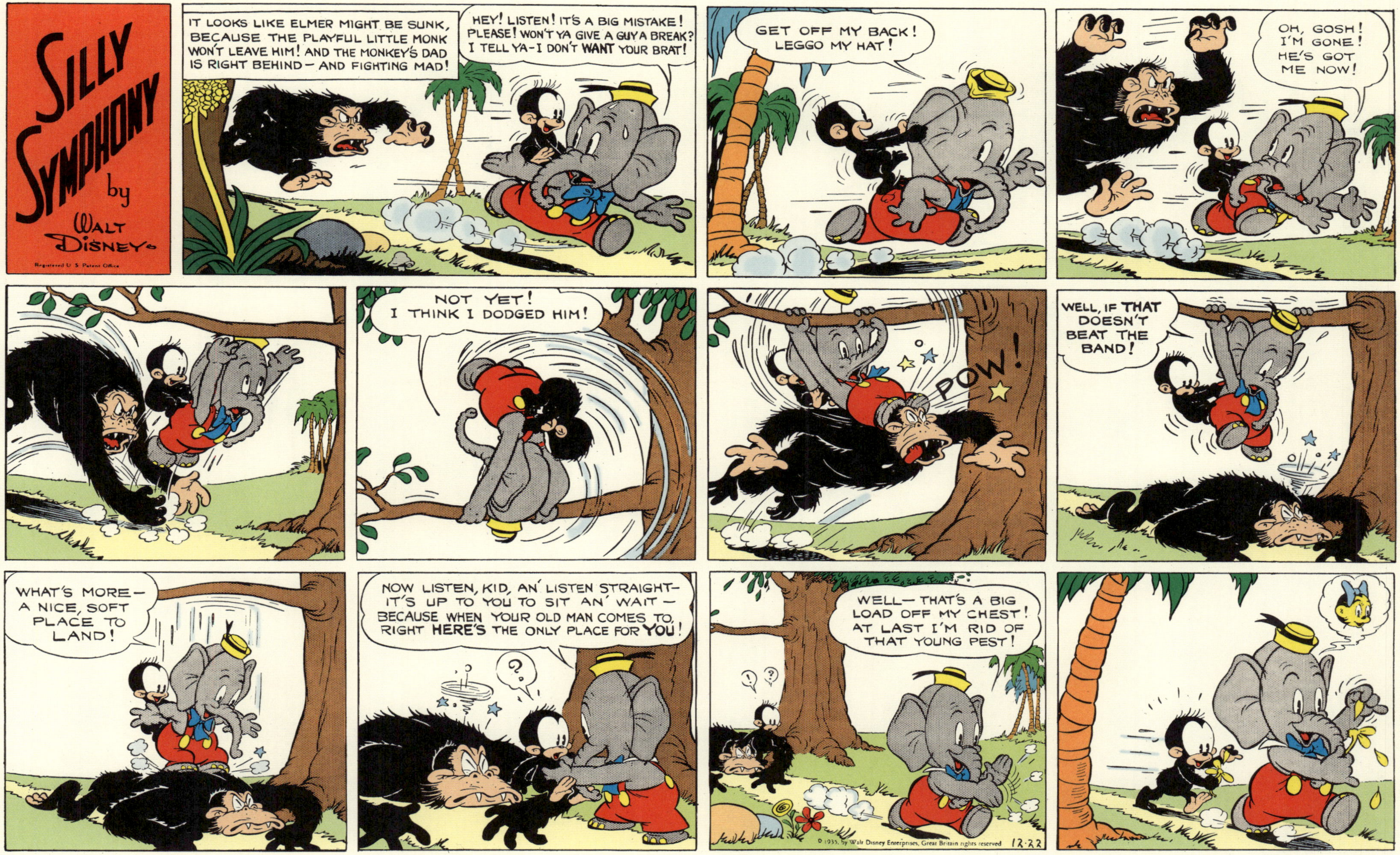
SILLY SYMPHONY
by
WALT DISNEY
Registered U. S. Patent Office
IT LOOKS LIKE ELMER MIGHT BE SUNK, BECAUSE THE PLAYFUL LITTLE MONK WON'T LEAVE HIM! AND THE MONKEY'S DAD IS RIGHT BEHIND — AND FIGHTING MAD!
HEY! LISTEN! IT'S A BIG MISTAKE! PLEASE! WON'T YA GIVE A GUY A BREAK? I TELL YA - I DON'T WANT YOUR BRAT!
GET OFF MY BACK! LEGGO MY HAT!
OH, GOSH! I'M GONE! HE'S GOT ME NOW!
NOT YET! I THINK I DODGED HIM!
POW!
WELL, IF THAT DOESN'T BEAT THE BAND!
WHAT'S MORE — A NICE, SOFT PLACE TO LAND!
NOW LISTEN, KID, AN' LISTEN STRAIGHT — IT'S UP TO YOU TO SIT AN' WAIT — BECAUSE WHEN YOUR OLD MAN COMES TO, RIGHT HERE'S THE ONLY PLACE FOR YOU!
?
!?
WELL — THAT'S A BIG LOAD OFF MY CHEST! AT LAST I'M RID OF THAT YOUNG PEST!
© 1935, by Walt Disney Enterprises, Great Britain rights reserved
12-22

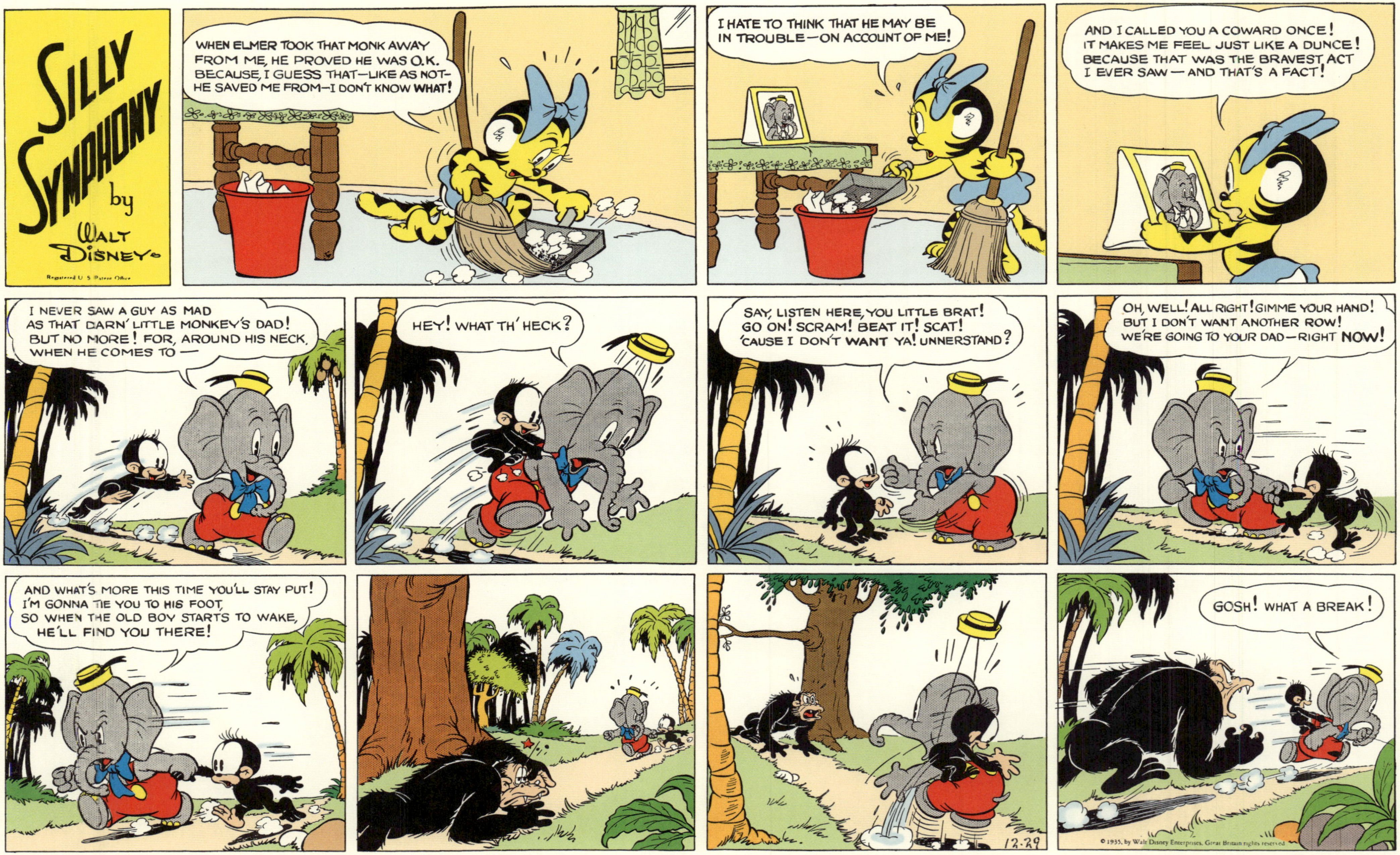
SILLY SYMPHONY by WALT DISNEY
Registered U.S. Patent Office
WHEN ELMER TOOK THAT MONK AWAY FROM ME, HE PROVED HE WAS O.K. BECAUSE, I GUESS THAT—LIKE AS NOT—HE SAVED ME FROM—I DON'T KNOW WHAT!
I HATE TO THINK THAT HE MAY BE IN TROUBLE—ON ACCOUNT OF ME!
AND I CALLED YOU A COWARD ONCE! IT MAKES ME FEEL JUST LIKE A DUNCE! BECAUSE THAT WAS THE BRAVEST ACT I EVER SAW — AND THAT'S A FACT!
I NEVER SAW A GUY AS MAD AS THAT DARN' LITTLE MONKEY'S DAD! BUT NO MORE! FOR, AROUND HIS NECK, WHEN HE COMES TO —
HEY! WHAT TH' HECK?
SAY, LISTEN HERE, YOU LITTLE BRAT! GO ON! SCRAM! BEAT IT! SCAT! 'CAUSE I DON'T WANT YA! UNNERSTAND?
OH, WELL! ALL RIGHT! GIMME YOUR HAND! BUT I DON'T WANT ANOTHER ROW! WE'RE GOING TO YOUR DAD—RIGHT NOW!
AND WHAT'S MORE THIS TIME YOU'LL STAY PUT! I'M GONNA TIE YOU TO HIS FOOT, SO WHEN THE OLD BOY STARTS TO WAKE, HE'LL FIND YOU THERE!
12-29
GOSH! WHAT A BREAK!
© 1935, by Walt Disney Enterprises. Great Britain rights reserved

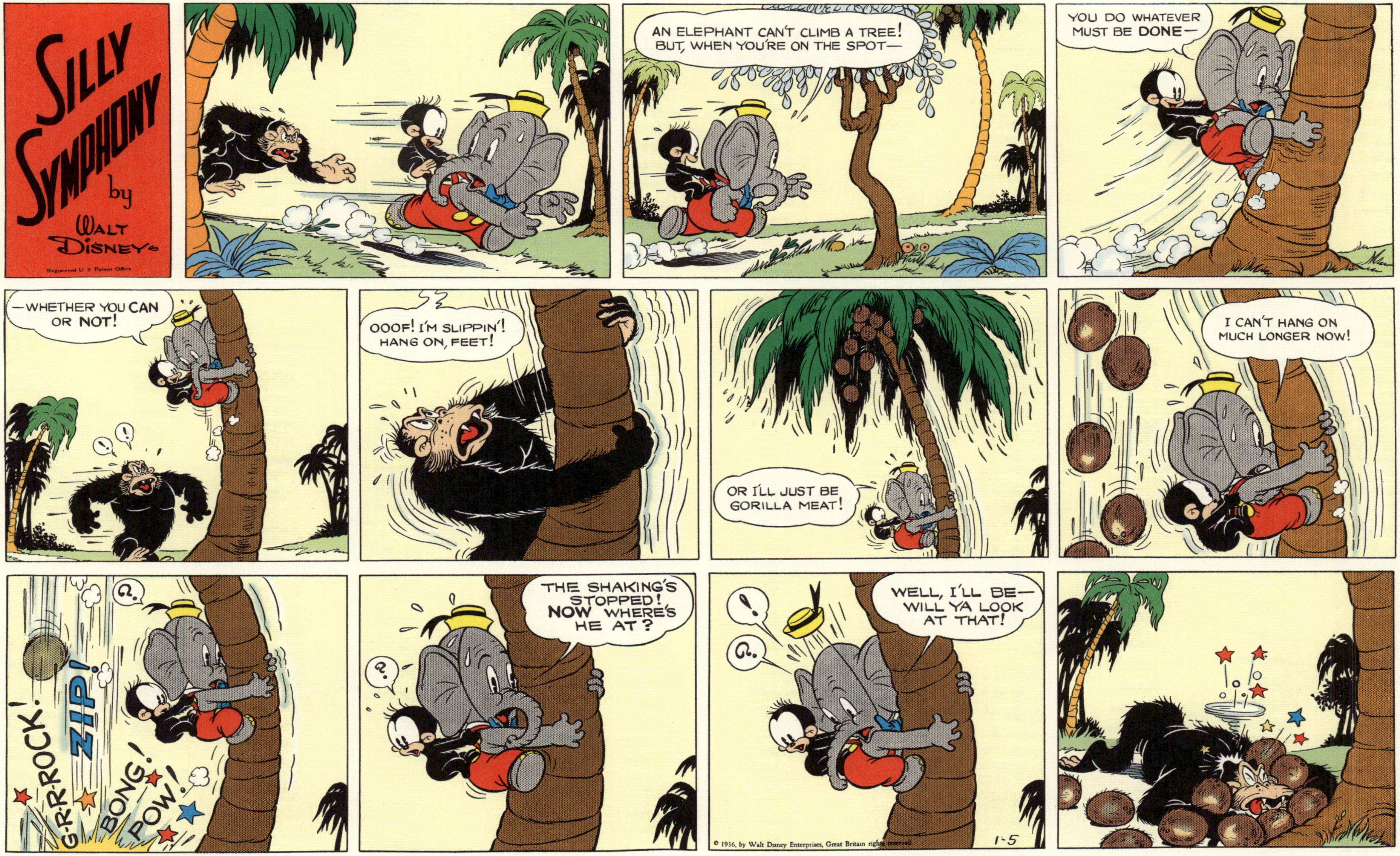
SILLY SYMPHONY
by
WALT DISNEY
Registered U. S. Patent Office
AN ELEPHANT CAN'T CLIMB A TREE! BUT, WHEN YOU'RE ON THE SPOT—
YOU DO WHATEVER MUST BE DONE—
—WHETHER YOU CAN OR NOT!
OOOF! I'M SLIPPIN'! HANG ON, FEET!
OR I'LL JUST BE GORILLA MEAT!
I CAN'T HANG ON MUCH LONGER NOW!
G-R-R-ROCK! ZIP! BONG! POW!
THE SHAKING'S STOPPED! NOW WHERE'S HE AT?
WELL, I'LL BE— WILL YA LOOK AT THAT!
© 1936, by Walt Disney Enterprises, Great Britain rights reserved.
1-5

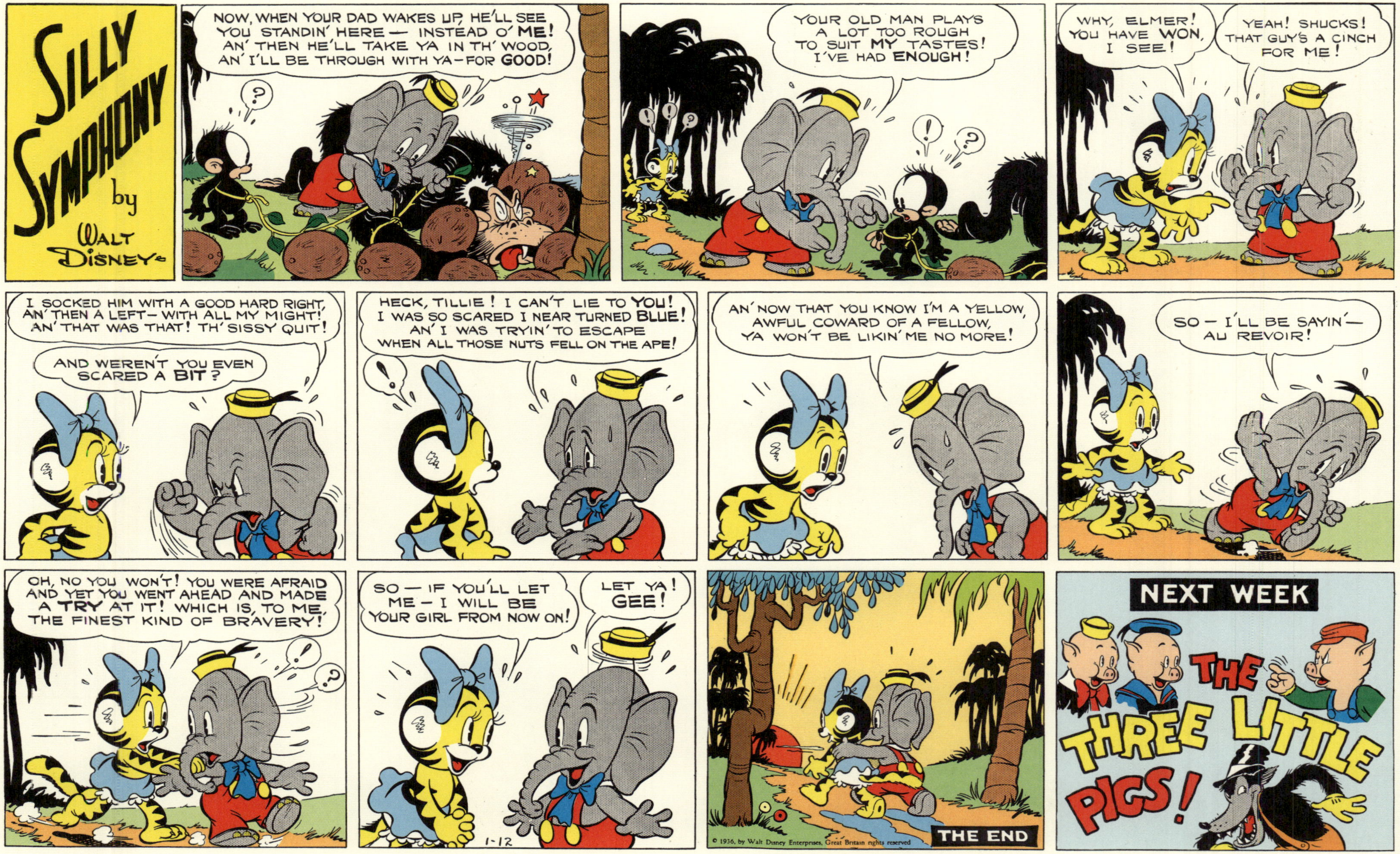
SILLY SYMPHONY by WALT DISNEY
NOW, WHEN YOUR DAD WAKES UP, HE'LL SEE YOU STANDIN' HERE — INSTEAD O' ME! AN' THEN HE'LL TAKE YA IN TH' WOOD, AN' I'LL BE THROUGH WITH YA—FOR GOOD!
YOUR OLD MAN PLAYS A LOT TOO ROUGH TO SUIT MY TASTES! I'VE HAD ENOUGH!
WHY, ELMER! YOU HAVE WON, I SEE!
YEAH! SHUCKS! THAT GUY'S A CINCH FOR ME!
I SOCKED HIM WITH A GOOD HARD RIGHT, AN' THEN A LEFT—WITH ALL MY MIGHT! AN' THAT WAS THAT! TH' SISSY QUIT!
AND WEREN'T YOU EVEN SCARED A BIT?
HECK, TILLIE! I CAN'T LIE TO YOU! I WAS SO SCARED I NEAR TURNED BLUE! AN' I WAS TRYIN' TO ESCAPE WHEN ALL THOSE NUTS FELL ON THE APE!
AN' NOW THAT YOU KNOW I'M A YELLOW, AWFUL COWARD OF A FELLOW, YA WON'T BE LIKIN' ME NO MORE!
SO — I'LL BE SAYIN' — AU REVOIR!
OH, NO YOU WON'T! YOU WERE AFRAID AND YET YOU WENT AHEAD AND MADE A TRY AT IT! WHICH IS, TO ME, THE FINEST KIND OF BRAVERY!
SO — IF YOU'LL LET ME — I WILL BE YOUR GIRL FROM NOW ON!
LET YA! GEE!
1-12
© 1936, by Walt Disney Enterprises, Great Britain rights reserved
THE END
NEXT WEEK
THE THREE LITTLE PIGS!

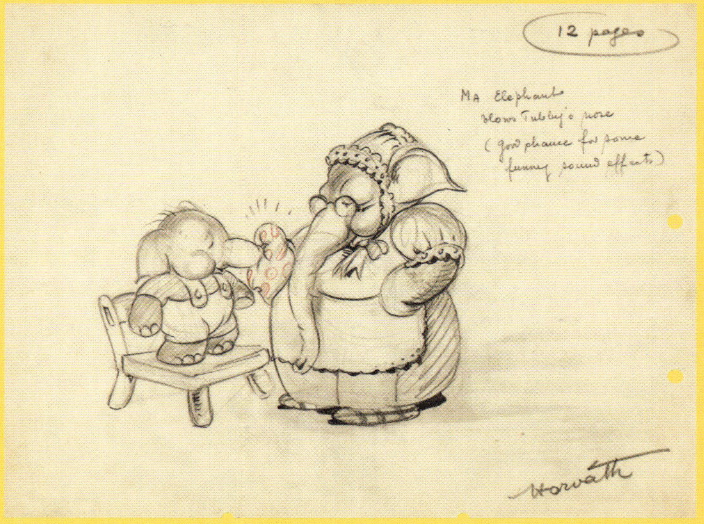
12 pages
Ma Elephant blows Tubby's nose (Good chance for some funny sound effects)
Horvath

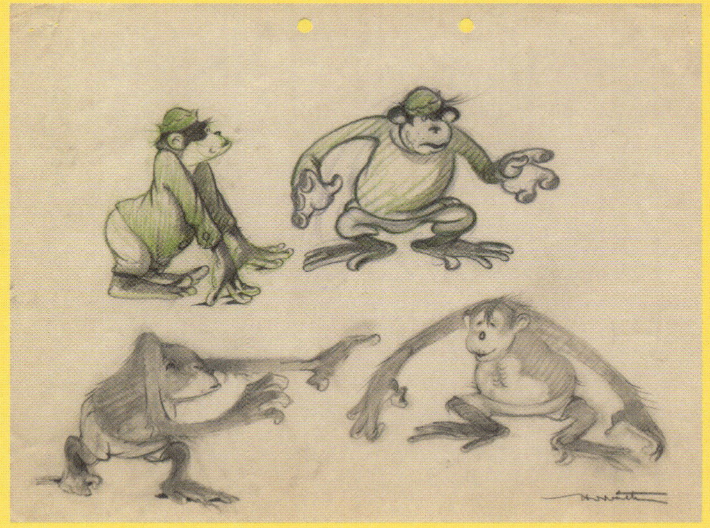

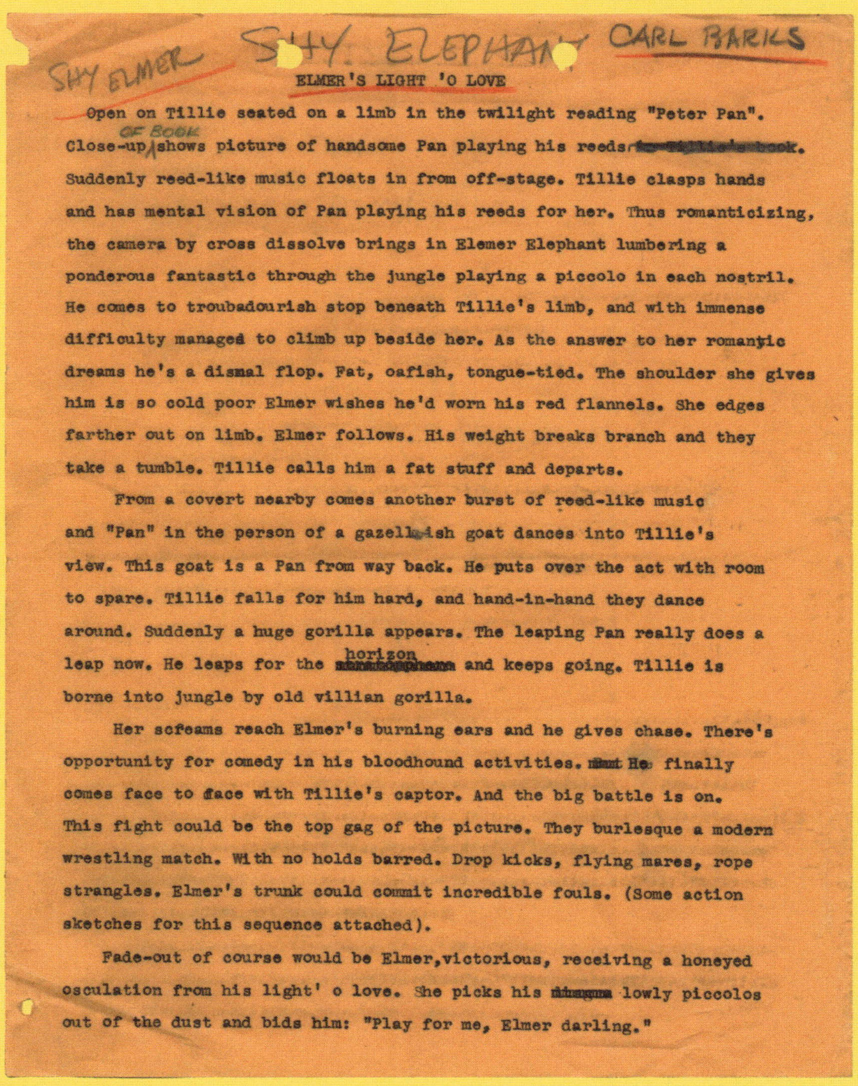
SHY ELMER SHY ELEPHANT CARL BARKS

ELMER'S LIGHT 'O LOVE

Open on Tillie seated on a limb in the twilight reading "Peter Pan". Close-up OF BOOK shows picture of handsome Pan playing his reeds ~~by Tillie's book~~. Suddenly reed-like music floats in from off-stage. Tillie clasps hands and has mental vision of Pan playing his reeds for her. Thus romanticizing, the camera by cross dissolve brings in Elemer Elephant lumbering a ponderous fantastic through the jungle playing a piccolo in each nostril. He comes to troubadourish stop beneath Tillie's limb, and with immense difficulty managed to climb up beside her. As the answer to her romantic dreams he's a dismal flop. Fat, oafish, tongue-tied. The shoulder she gives him is so cold poor Elmer wishes he'd worn his red flannels. She edges farther out on limb. Elmer follows. His weight breaks branch and they take a tumble. Tillie calls him a fat stuff and departs.

From a covert nearby comes another burst of reed-like music and "Pan" in the person of a gazellish goat dances into Tillie's view. This goat is a Pan from way back. He puts over the act with room to spare. Tillie falls for him hard, and hand-in-hand they dance around. Suddenly a huge gorilla appears. The leaping Pan really does a leap now. He leaps for the horizon ~~[illegible]~~ and keeps going. Tillie is borne into jungle by old villian gorilla.

Her screams reach Elmer's burning ears and he gives chase. There's opportunity for comedy in his bloodhound activities. ~~But~~ He finally comes face to face with Tillie's captor. And the big battle is on. This fight could be the top gag of the picture. They burlesque a modern wrestling match. With no holds barred. Drop kicks, flying mares, rope strangles. Elmer's trunk could commit incredible fouls. (Some action sketches for this sequence attached).

Fade-out of course would be Elmer, victorious, receiving a honeyed osculation from his light' o love. She picks his ~~[illegible]~~ lowly piccolos out of the dust and bids him: "Play for me, Elmer darling."

LEFT: Early character studies by Ferdinand Horvath: Elmer, still in an early stage as "Tubby," from the short that would become *Elmer Elephant* (1936); Gooch Gorilla, from the planned sequel "Timid Elmer" (c. 1937). See the "Timid Elmer" comics adaptation later in this book for more about the project. Images courtesy Heritage Auctions (top) and Disney Publishing Worldwide (bottom).

RIGHT: Early story outline by Carl Barks for "Timid Elmer," under the variant title "Elmer's Light o' Love." Image courtesy Disney Publishing Worldwide.

THE FURTHER ADVENTURES
OF THE THREE LITTLE PIGS

January 19 - August 23, 1936
Written by Ted Osborne, drawn by Al Taliaferro

THE UNEXPECTED WORLDWIDE SUCCESS of *Three Little Pigs* in 1933 elevated the Pigs and the Big Bad Wolf to a level of popularity that rivaled that of Mickey Mouse and his gang. Inevitably, the Disney studio brought them back to the screen in sequels to the original film. The first sequel, *The Big Bad Wolf*, was released in April 1934. Two years later, the *Silly Symphony* comic strip heralded the second sequel, *Three Little Wolves*, which introduced three nasty little lupine offspring and was released to theaters roughly halfway through this continuity's run in newspapers.

The resulting comic tale is a delightful concoction that blends gags and visuals from *Three Little Wolves*, and sidelong glances at the first two films, with new story material that appears in none of the films. Disney aficionados can enjoy combing these strips for images drawn from the films—perhaps most obviously the exterior of the Wolf's house at the base of a tree, pictured as it appears in *Three Little Wolves*.

Equally delightful is the original material. *Three Little Wolves* is perhaps the wittiest of the Pig films, featuring the Wolf's disguise as Little Bo Peep (!) and climaxing with the Wolf Pacifier, an elaborate machine invented by Practical Pig. These devices are nowhere to be seen in the comic version, but in their place we get other wildly improbable schemes by the Wolf, including more outlandish disguises. Writer Ted Osborne endows Practical Pig with some subtly droll touches of character development: compelled to drop everything to once again go rescue his brothers from the Wolf, he's not frightened or concerned, merely annoyed at the inconvenience. Even when he himself is trapped and tied up, Practical Pig maintains his cool, criticizing the Wolf for his shoddy workmanship.

In other details, too, Osborne shows his hand. Note the passage in which the Wolf impersonates a Boy Scout leader. The Boy Scouts of America were at the height of their popularity in the 1930s and the organization's influence was reflected in the movies and elsewhere in pop culture. Here the Wolf's recruiting station features the Scout motto, "Be Prepared;" he correctly demonstrates knot-tying and other woodcraft, and even includes a reference to Ernest Thompson Seton (one of the founders of the Scouts). Similarly, when the Wolf turns sculptor and crafts a couple of Pig decoys, he invokes the names of Rodin and Phidias. The combination of this subtle wit with a healthy dose of slapstick makes this continuity a worthy counterpart to *Three Little Wolves*, as well as a gem of comic art in its own right.

—J.B. KAUFMAN

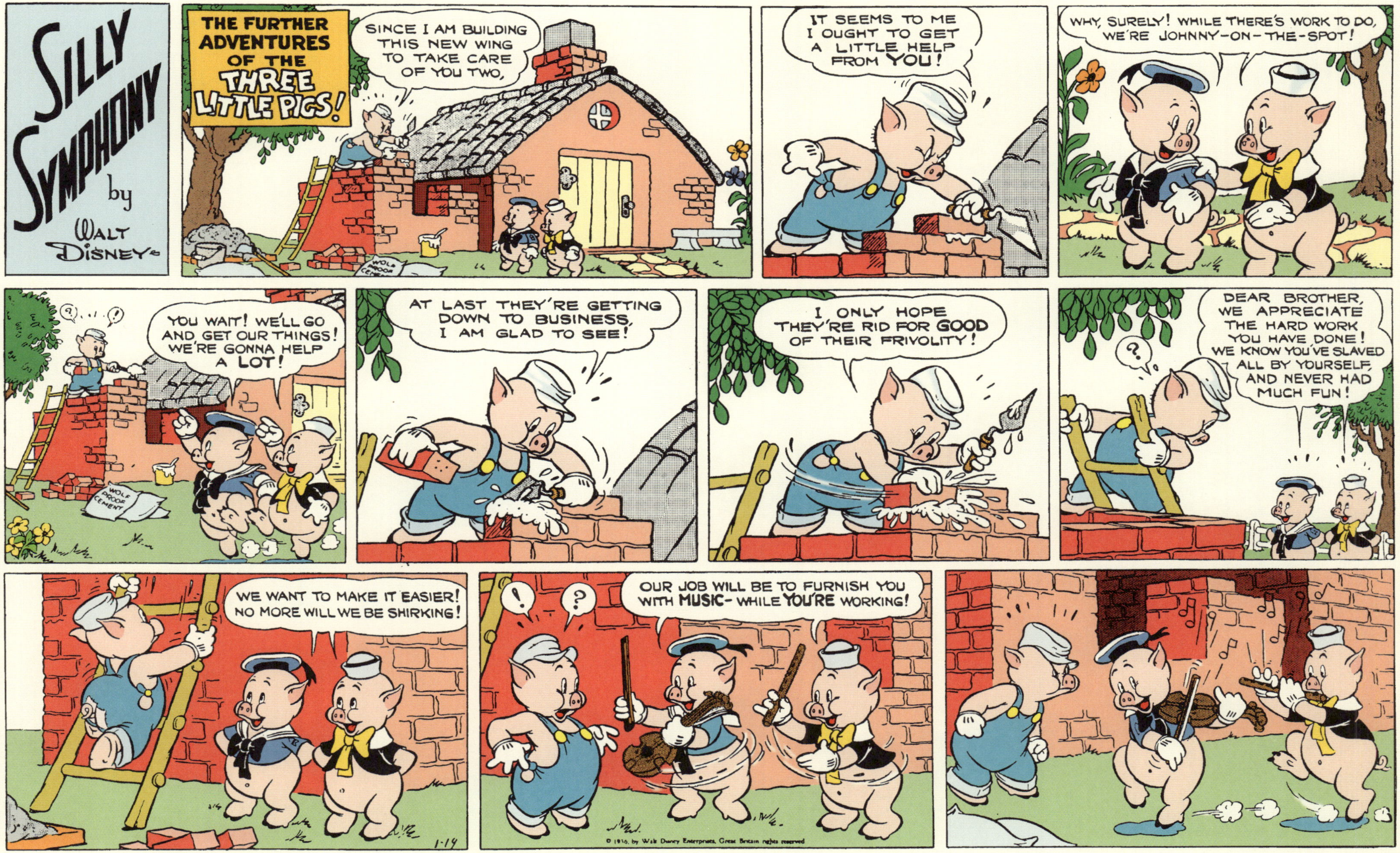
SILLY SYMPHONY
by
WALT DISNEY
THE FURTHER ADVENTURES OF THE THREE LITTLE PIGS!
SINCE I AM BUILDING THIS NEW WING TO TAKE CARE OF YOU TWO,
WOLF PROOF CEMENT
IT SEEMS TO ME I OUGHT TO GET A LITTLE HELP FROM YOU!
WHY, SURELY! WHILE THERE'S WORK TO DO, WE'RE JOHNNY-ON-THE-SPOT!
YOU WAIT! WE'LL GO AND GET OUR THINGS! WE'RE GONNA HELP A LOT!
WOLF PROOF CEMENT
AT LAST THEY'RE GETTING DOWN TO BUSINESS, I AM GLAD TO SEE!
I ONLY HOPE THEY'RE RID FOR GOOD OF THEIR FRIVOLITY!
DEAR BROTHER, WE APPRECIATE THE HARD WORK YOU HAVE DONE! WE KNOW YOU'VE SLAVED ALL BY YOURSELF, AND NEVER HAD MUCH FUN!
WE WANT TO MAKE IT EASIER! NO MORE WILL WE BE SHIRKING!
1-19
OUR JOB WILL BE TO FURNISH YOU WITH MUSIC- WHILE YOU'RE WORKING!
© 1936, by Walt Disney Enterprises, Great Britain rights reserved

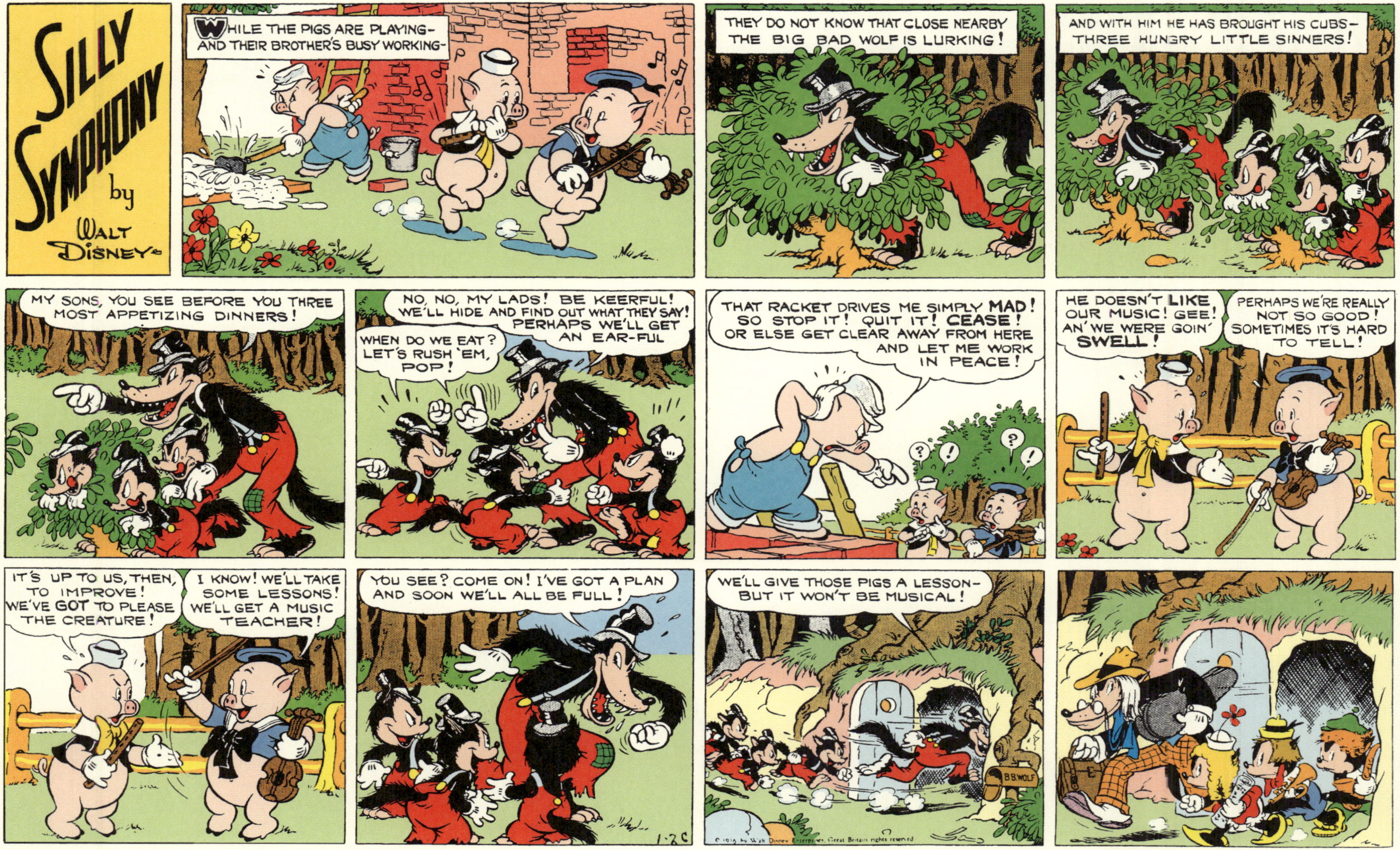
SILLY SYMPHONY by WALT DISNEY
WHILE THE PIGS ARE PLAYING- AND THEIR BROTHER'S BUSY WORKING-
THEY DO NOT KNOW THAT CLOSE NEARBY THE BIG BAD WOLF IS LURKING!
AND WITH HIM HE HAS BROUGHT HIS CUBS- THREE HUNGRY LITTLE SINNERS!
MY SONS, YOU SEE BEFORE YOU THREE MOST APPETIZING DINNERS!
NO, NO, MY LADS! BE KEERFUL! WE'LL HIDE AND FIND OUT WHAT THEY SAY! PERHAPS WE'LL GET AN EAR-FUL
WHEN DO WE EAT? LET'S RUSH 'EM, POP!
THAT RACKET DRIVES ME SIMPLY MAD! SO STOP IT! QUIT IT! CEASE! OR ELSE GET CLEAR AWAY FROM HERE AND LET ME WORK IN PEACE!
HE DOESN'T LIKE OUR MUSIC! GEE! AN' WE WERE GOIN' SWELL!
PERHAPS WE'RE REALLY NOT SO GOOD! SOMETIMES IT'S HARD TO TELL!
IT'S UP TO US, THEN, TO IMPROVE! WE'VE GOT TO PLEASE THE CREATURE!
I KNOW! WE'LL TAKE SOME LESSONS! WE'LL GET A MUSIC TEACHER!
YOU SEE? COME ON! I'VE GOT A PLAN AND SOON WE'LL ALL BE FULL!
WE'LL GIVE THOSE PIGS A LESSON- BUT IT WON'T BE MUSICAL!
B.B.WOLF

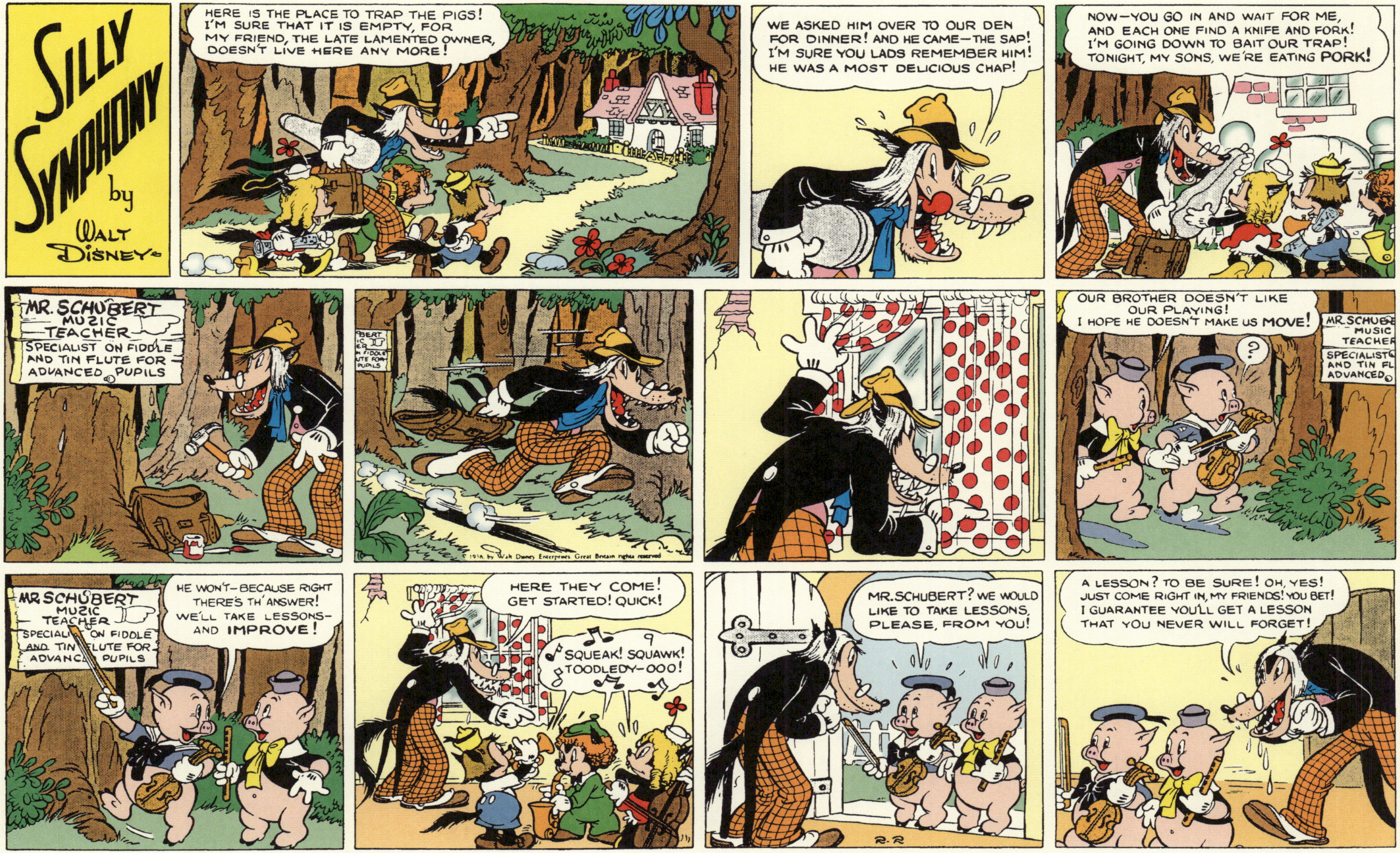
SILLY SYMPHONY
by WALT DISNEY
HERE IS THE PLACE TO TRAP THE PIGS! I'M SURE THAT IT IS EMPTY, FOR MY FRIEND, THE LATE LAMENTED OWNER, DOESN'T LIVE HERE ANY MORE!
WE ASKED HIM OVER TO OUR DEN FOR DINNER! AND HE CAME—THE SAP! I'M SURE YOU LADS REMEMBER HIM! HE WAS A MOST DELICIOUS CHAP!
NOW—YOU GO IN AND WAIT FOR ME, AND EACH ONE FIND A KNIFE AND FORK! I'M GOING DOWN TO BAIT OUR TRAP! TONIGHT, MY SONS, WE'RE EATING PORK!
MR. SCHUBERT MUZIC TEACHER SPECIALIST ON FIDDLE AND TIN FLUTE FOR ADVANCED PUPILS
© 1936 by Walt Disney Enterprises Great Britain rights reserved
OUR BROTHER DOESN'T LIKE OUR PLAYING! I HOPE HE DOESN'T MAKE US MOVE!
?
HE WON'T—BECAUSE RIGHT THERE'S TH' ANSWER! WE'LL TAKE LESSONS—AND IMPROVE!
HERE THEY COME! GET STARTED! QUICK!
SQUEAK! SQUAWK! TOODLEDY—OOO!
MR. SCHUBERT? WE WOULD LIKE TO TAKE LESSONS, PLEASE, FROM YOU!
R.R
A LESSON? TO BE SURE! OH, YES! JUST COME RIGHT IN, MY FRIENDS! YOU BET! I GUARANTEE YOU'LL GET A LESSON THAT YOU NEVER WILL FORGET!

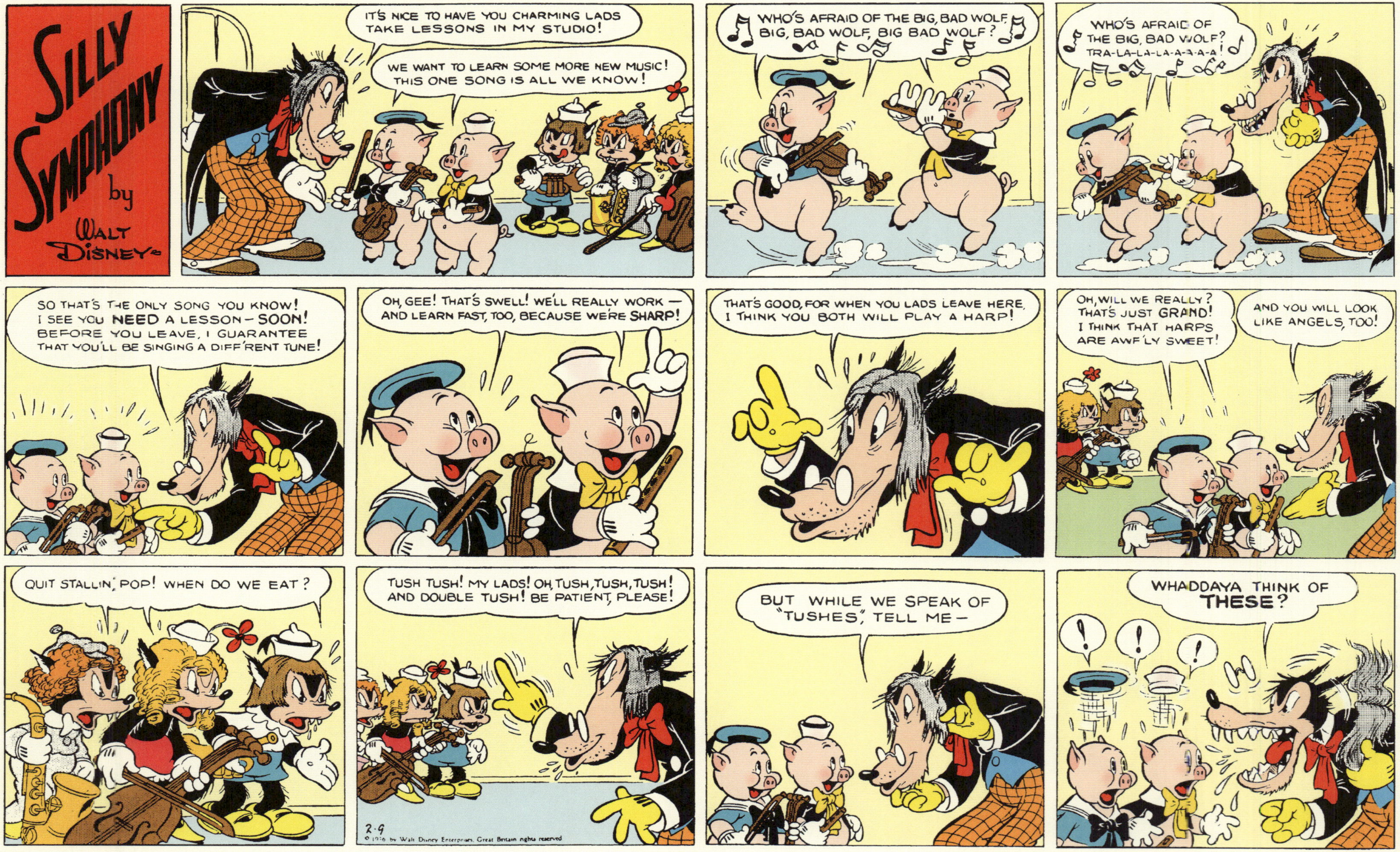
SILLY SYMPHONY by WALT DISNEY
IT'S NICE TO HAVE YOU CHARMING LADS TAKE LESSONS IN MY STUDIO!
WE WANT TO LEARN SOME MORE NEW MUSIC! THIS ONE SONG IS ALL WE KNOW!
WHO'S AFRAID OF THE BIG, BAD WOLF, BIG, BAD WOLF, BIG BAD WOLF?
WHO'S AFRAID OF THE BIG, BAD WOLF? TRA-LA-LA-LA-A-A-A!
SO THAT'S THE ONLY SONG YOU KNOW! I SEE YOU NEED A LESSON – SOON! BEFORE YOU LEAVE, I GUARANTEE THAT YOU'LL BE SINGING A DIFF'RENT TUNE!
OH, GEE! THAT'S SWELL! WE'LL REALLY WORK — AND LEARN FAST, TOO, BECAUSE WE'RE SHARP!
THAT'S GOOD, FOR WHEN YOU LADS LEAVE HERE, I THINK YOU BOTH WILL PLAY A HARP!
OH, WILL WE REALLY? THAT'S JUST GRAND! I THINK THAT HARPS ARE AWF'LY SWEET!
AND YOU WILL LOOK LIKE ANGELS, TOO!
QUIT STALLIN', POP! WHEN DO WE EAT?
TUSH TUSH! MY LADS! OH, TUSH, TUSH, TUSH! AND DOUBLE TUSH! BE PATIENT, PLEASE!
2-9
© 1936 by Walt Disney Enterprises. Great Britain rights reserved
BUT WHILE WE SPEAK OF "TUSHES," TELL ME –
WHADDAYA THINK OF THESE?
!
!
!

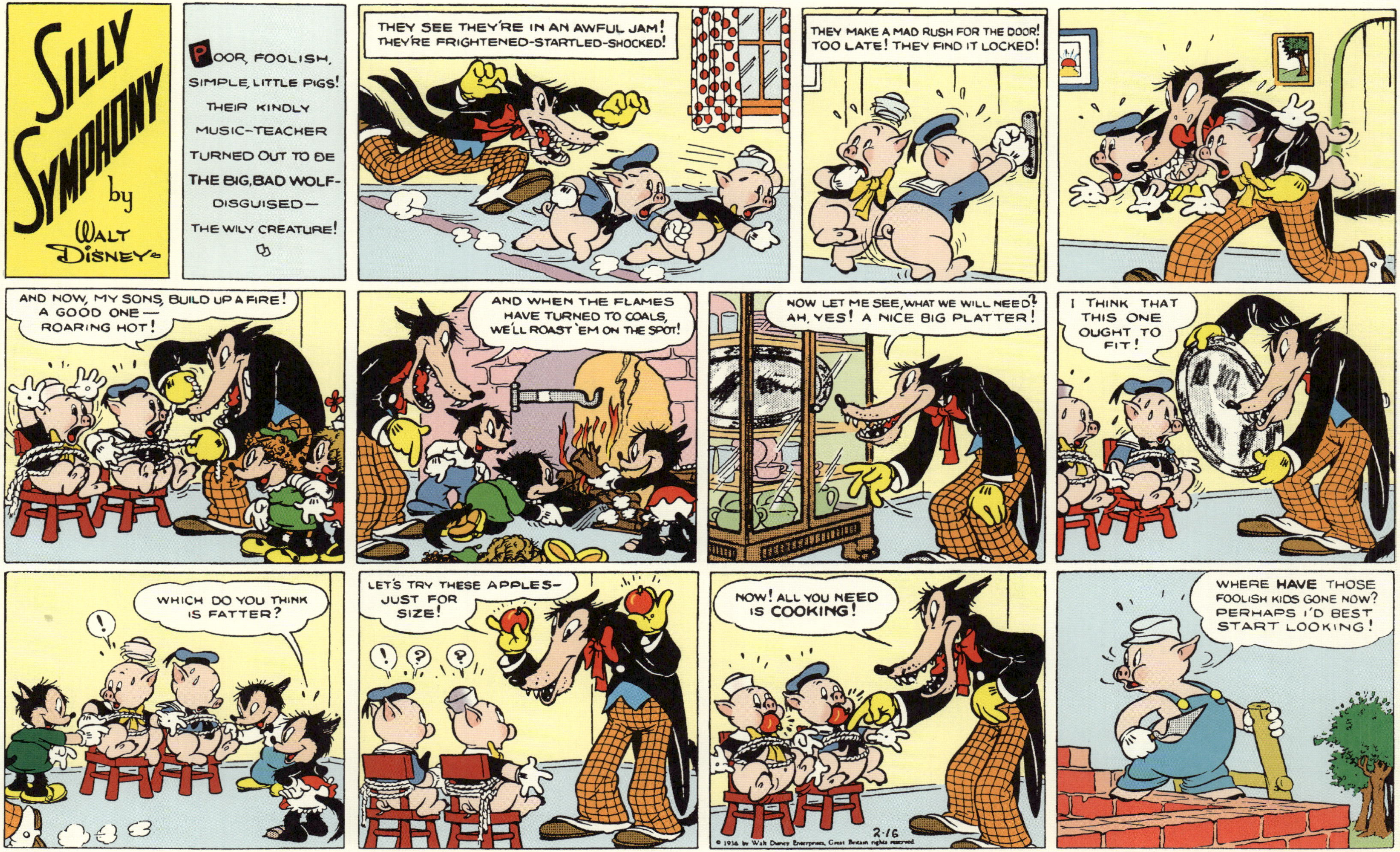
SILLY SYMPHONY
by WALT DISNEY
POOR, FOOLISH, SIMPLE, LITTLE PIGS! THEIR KINDLY MUSIC-TEACHER TURNED OUT TO BE THE BIG, BAD WOLF- DISGUISED- THE WILY CREATURE!
THEY SEE THEY'RE IN AN AWFUL JAM! THEY'RE FRIGHTENED-STARTLED-SHOCKED!
THEY MAKE A MAD RUSH FOR THE DOOR! TOO LATE! THEY FIND IT LOCKED!
AND NOW, MY SONS, BUILD UP A FIRE! A GOOD ONE— ROARING HOT!
AND WHEN THE FLAMES HAVE TURNED TO COALS, WE'LL ROAST 'EM ON THE SPOT!
NOW LET ME SEE, WHAT WE WILL NEED? AH, YES! A NICE BIG PLATTER!
I THINK THAT THIS ONE OUGHT TO FIT!
!
WHICH DO YOU THINK IS FATTER?
LET'S TRY THESE APPLES- JUST FOR SIZE!
! ? ?
NOW! ALL YOU NEED IS COOKING!
2·16
© 1936 by Walt Disney Enterprises, Great Britain rights reserved
WHERE HAVE THOSE FOOLISH KIDS GONE NOW? PERHAPS I'D BEST START LOOKING!

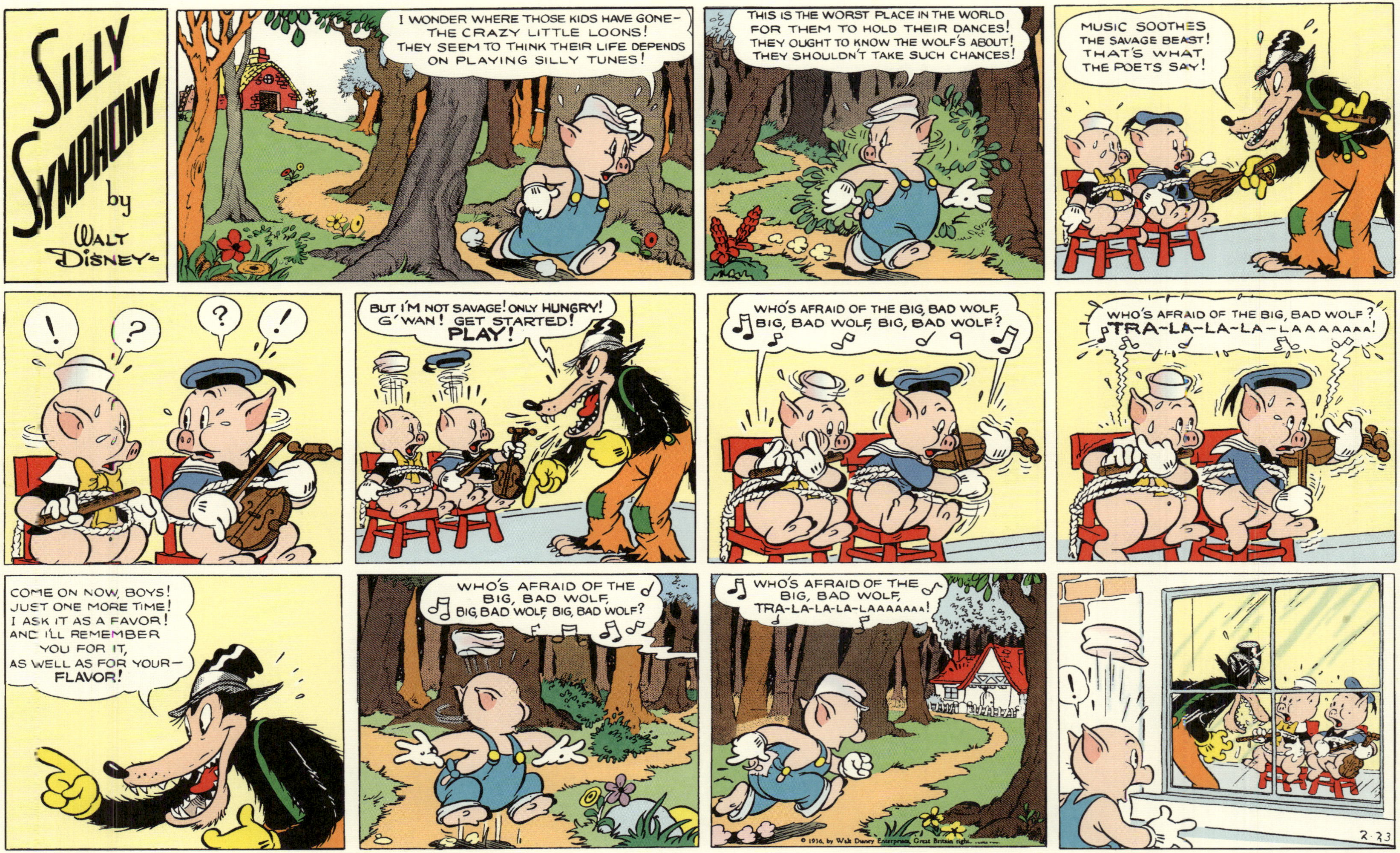
SILLY SYMPHONY by WALT DISNEY
I WONDER WHERE THOSE KIDS HAVE GONE— THE CRAZY LITTLE LOONS! THEY SEEM TO THINK THEIR LIFE DEPENDS ON PLAYING SILLY TUNES!
THIS IS THE WORST PLACE IN THE WORLD FOR THEM TO HOLD THEIR DANCES! THEY OUGHT TO KNOW THE WOLF'S ABOUT! THEY SHOULDN'T TAKE SUCH CHANCES!
MUSIC SOOTHES THE SAVAGE BEAST! THAT'S WHAT THE POETS SAY!
! ? ? !
BUT I'M NOT SAVAGE! ONLY HUNGRY! G'WAN! GET STARTED! PLAY!
WHO'S AFRAID OF THE BIG, BAD WOLF, BIG, BAD WOLF, BIG, BAD WOLF?
WHO'S AFRAID OF THE BIG, BAD WOLF? TRA-LA-LA-LA-LAAAAAAA!
COME ON NOW, BOYS! JUST ONE MORE TIME! I ASK IT AS A FAVOR! AND I'LL REMEMBER YOU FOR IT, AS WELL AS FOR YOUR— FLAVOR!
WHO'S AFRAID OF THE BIG, BAD WOLF, BIG, BAD WOLF, BIG, BAD WOLF?
WHO'S AFRAID OF THE BIG, BAD WOLF, TRA-LA-LA-LA-LAAAAAAA!
© 1936, by Walt Disney Enterprises, Great Britain rights
!
2-23

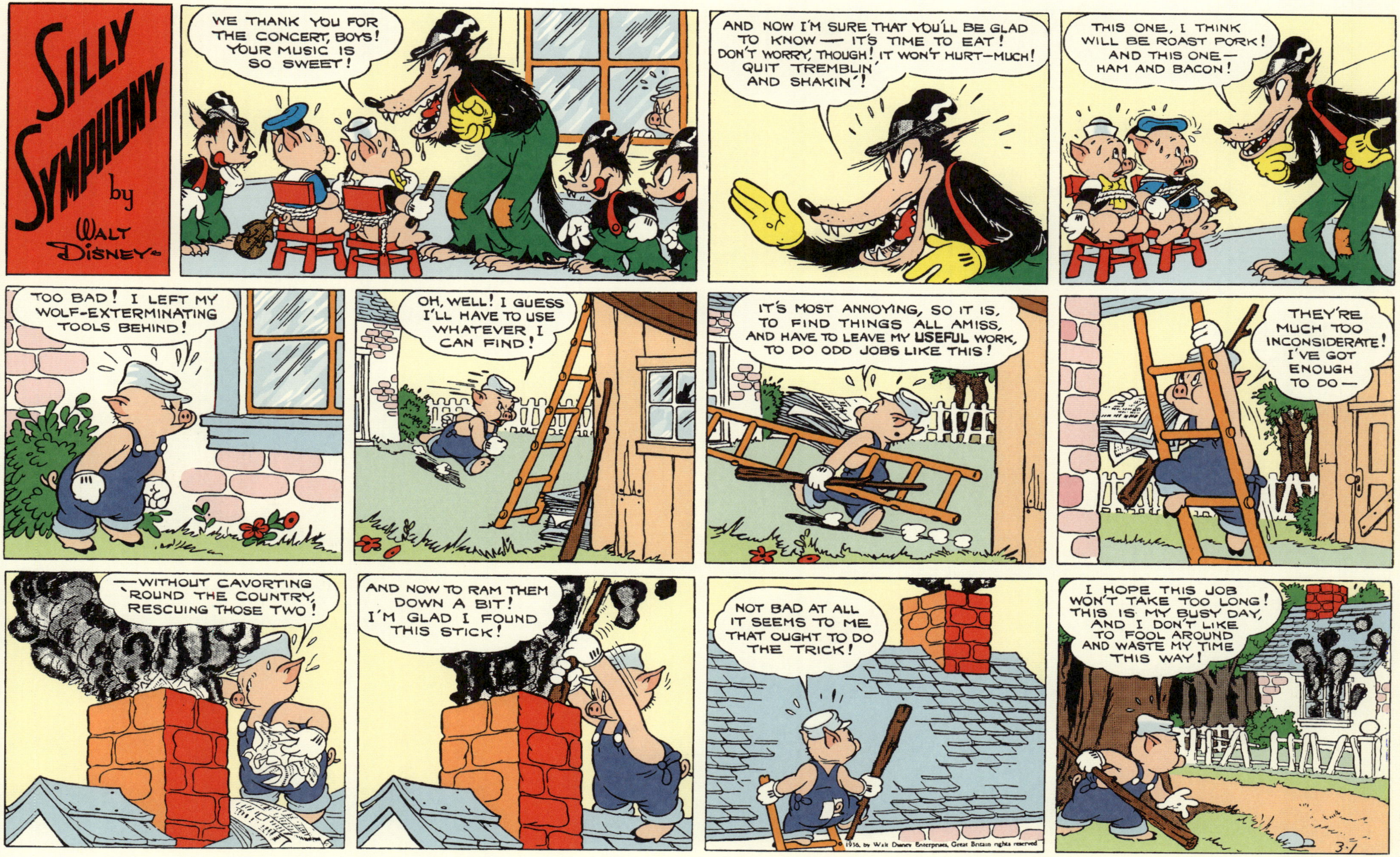
SILLY SYMPHONY
by
WALT DISNEY
WE THANK YOU FOR THE CONCERT, BOYS! YOUR MUSIC IS SO SWEET!
AND NOW I'M SURE THAT YOU'LL BE GLAD TO KNOW — IT'S TIME TO EAT! DON'T WORRY, THOUGH! IT WON'T HURT—MUCH! QUIT TREMBLIN' AND SHAKIN'!
THIS ONE, I THINK WILL BE ROAST PORK! AND THIS ONE— HAM AND BACON!
TOO BAD! I LEFT MY WOLF-EXTERMINATING TOOLS BEHIND!
OH, WELL! I GUESS I'LL HAVE TO USE WHATEVER I CAN FIND!
IT'S MOST ANNOYING, SO IT IS, TO FIND THINGS ALL AMISS, AND HAVE TO LEAVE MY USEFUL WORK, TO DO ODD JOBS LIKE THIS!
THEY'RE MUCH TOO INCONSIDERATE! I'VE GOT ENOUGH TO DO—
—WITHOUT CAVORTING 'ROUND THE COUNTRY, RESCUING THOSE TWO!
AND NOW TO RAM THEM DOWN A BIT! I'M GLAD I FOUND THIS STICK!
NOT BAD AT ALL IT SEEMS TO ME THAT OUGHT TO DO THE TRICK!
© 1936, by Walt Disney Enterprises, Great Britain rights reserved
I HOPE THIS JOB WON'T TAKE TOO LONG! THIS IS MY BUSY DAY, AND I DON'T LIKE TO FOOL AROUND AND WASTE MY TIME THIS WAY!
3-1

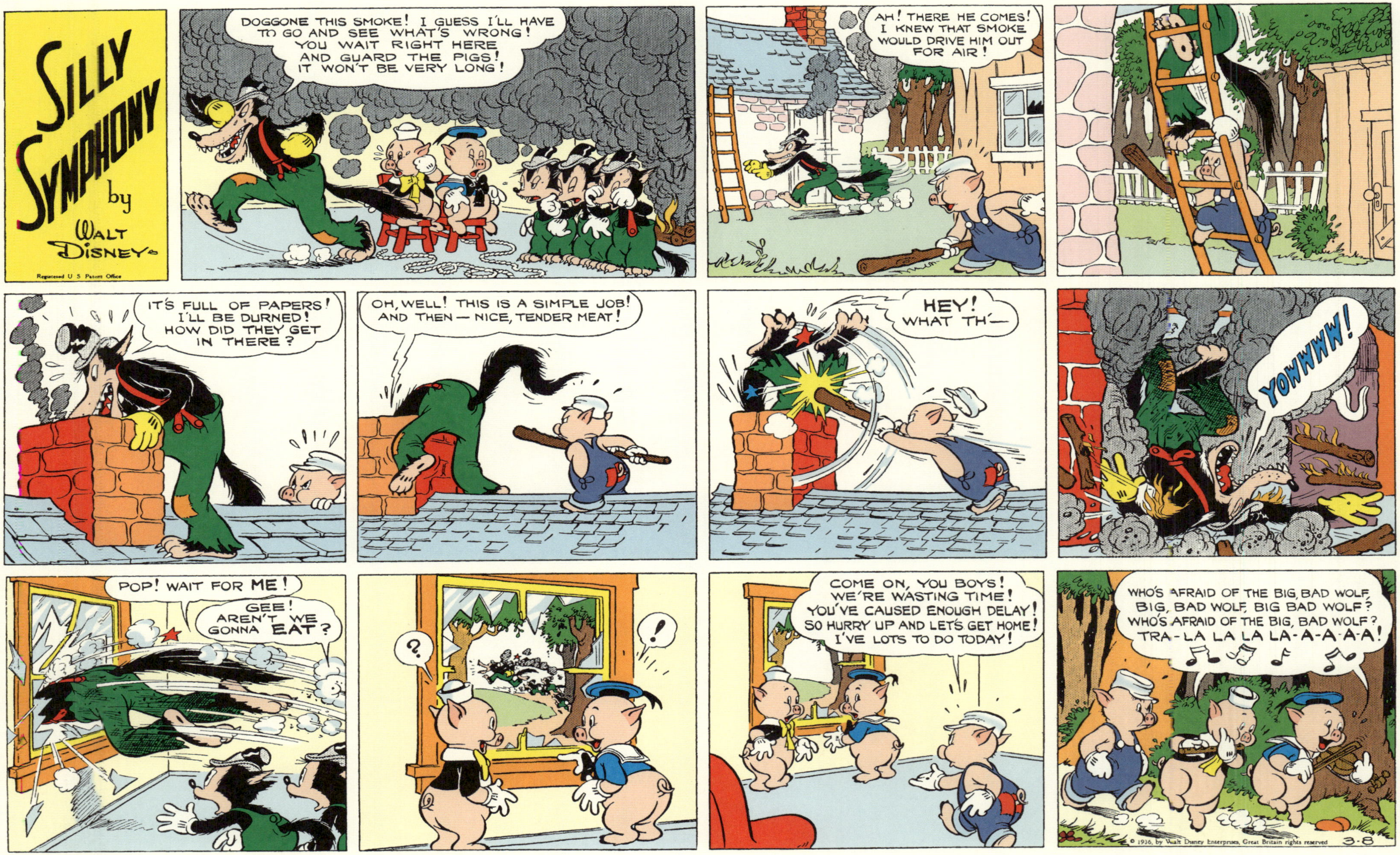
SILLY SYMPHONY
by
WALT DISNEY
Registered U S Patent Office
DOGGONE THIS SMOKE! I GUESS I'LL HAVE TO GO AND SEE WHAT'S WRONG! YOU WAIT RIGHT HERE AND GUARD THE PIGS! IT WON'T BE VERY LONG!
AH! THERE HE COMES! I KNEW THAT SMOKE WOULD DRIVE HIM OUT FOR AIR!
IT'S FULL OF PAPERS! I'LL BE DURNED! HOW DID THEY GET IN THERE?
OH, WELL! THIS IS A SIMPLE JOB! AND THEN — NICE, TENDER MEAT!
HEY! WHAT TH'—
YOWWWW!
POP! WAIT FOR ME!
GEE! AREN'T WE GONNA EAT?
?
!
COME ON, YOU BOYS! WE'RE WASTING TIME! YOU'VE CAUSED ENOUGH DELAY! SO HURRY UP AND LET'S GET HOME! I'VE LOTS TO DO TODAY!
WHO'S AFRAID OF THE BIG, BAD WOLF, BIG, BAD WOLF, BIG BAD WOLF? WHO'S AFRAID OF THE BIG, BAD WOLF? TRA-LA LA LA LA-A-A-A-A!
© 1936, by Walt Disney Enterprises, Great Britain rights reserved
3-8

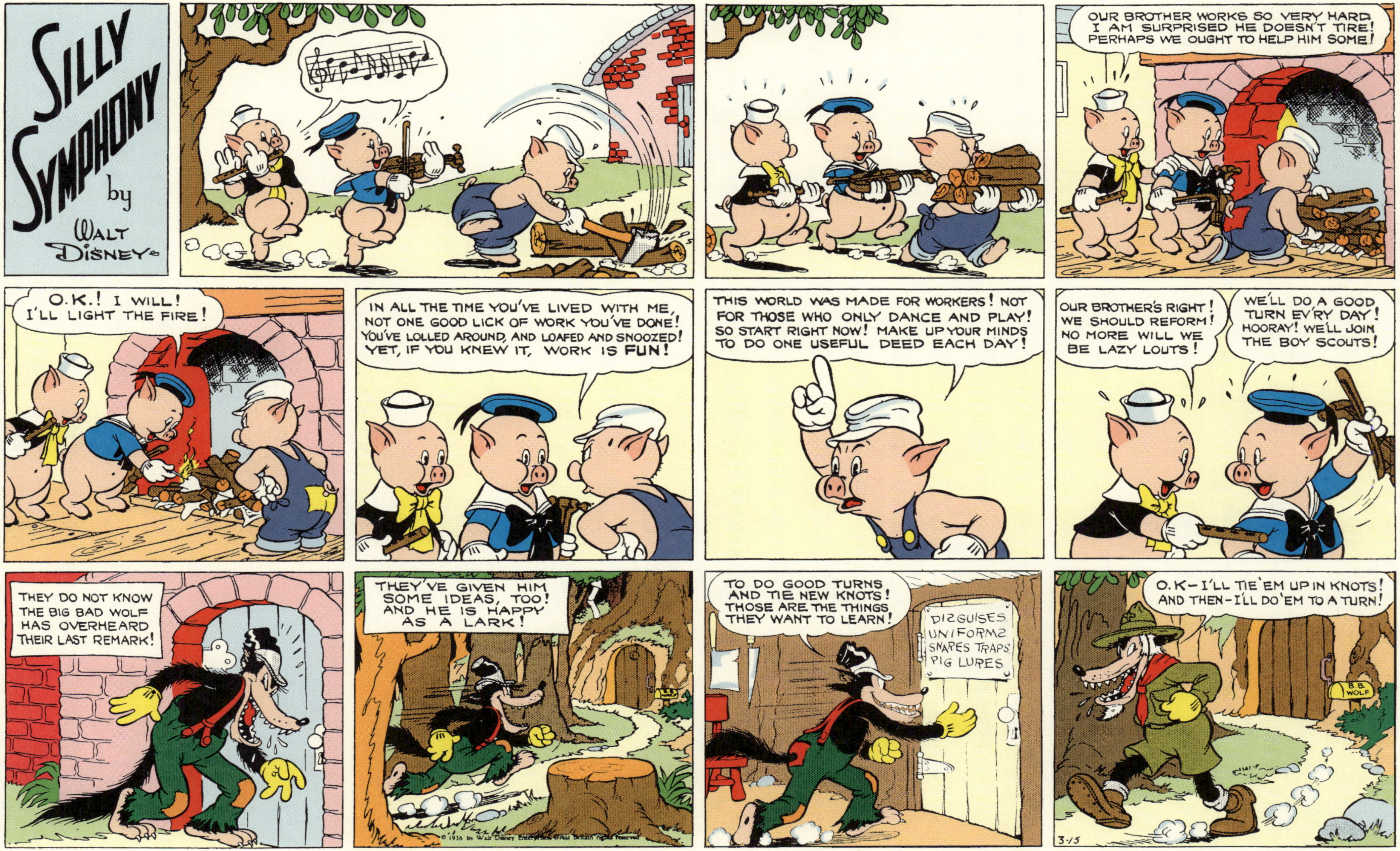
SILLY SYMPHONY
by
WALT DISNEY
OUR BROTHER WORKS SO VERY HARD I AM SURPRISED HE DOESN'T TIRE! PERHAPS WE OUGHT TO HELP HIM SOME!
O.K.! I WILL! I'LL LIGHT THE FIRE!
IN ALL THE TIME YOU'VE LIVED WITH ME, NOT ONE GOOD LICK OF WORK YOU'VE DONE! YOU'VE LOLLED AROUND, AND LOAFED AND SNOOZED! YET, IF YOU KNEW IT, WORK IS FUN!
THIS WORLD WAS MADE FOR WORKERS! NOT FOR THOSE WHO ONLY DANCE AND PLAY! SO START RIGHT NOW! MAKE UP YOUR MINDS TO DO ONE USEFUL DEED EACH DAY!
OUR BROTHER'S RIGHT! WE SHOULD REFORM! NO MORE WILL WE BE LAZY LOUTS!
WE'LL DO A GOOD TURN EV'RY DAY! HOORAY! WE'LL JOIN THE BOY SCOUTS!
THEY DO NOT KNOW THE BIG BAD WOLF HAS OVERHEARD THEIR LAST REMARK!
THEY'VE GIVEN HIM SOME IDEAS, TOO! AND HE IS HAPPY AS A LARK!
TO DO GOOD TURNS AND TIE NEW KNOTS! THOSE ARE THE THINGS THEY WANT TO LEARN!
DISGUISES
UNIFORMS
SNARES TRAPS
PIG LURES
O.K.—I'LL TIE 'EM UP IN KNOTS! AND THEN—I'LL DO 'EM TO A TURN!
B.B. WOLF
3-15

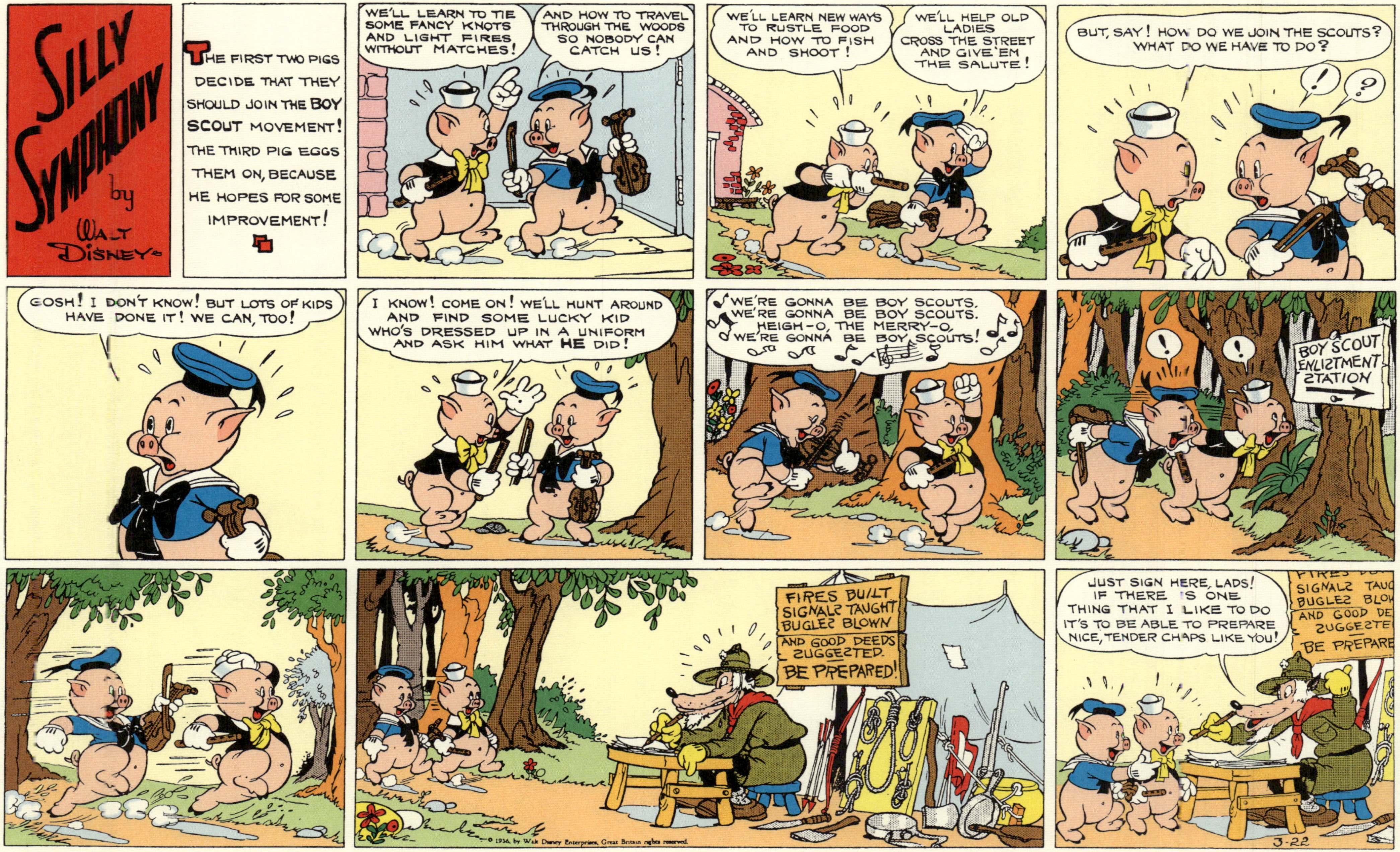
SILLY SYMPHONY by WALT DISNEY
THE FIRST TWO PIGS DECIDE THAT THEY SHOULD JOIN THE BOY SCOUT MOVEMENT! THE THIRD PIG EGGS THEM ON, BECAUSE HE HOPES FOR SOME IMPROVEMENT!
WE'LL LEARN TO TIE SOME FANCY KNOTS AND LIGHT FIRES WITHOUT MATCHES!
AND HOW TO TRAVEL THROUGH THE WOODS SO NOBODY CAN CATCH US!
WE'LL LEARN NEW WAYS TO RUSTLE FOOD AND HOW TO FISH AND SHOOT!
WE'LL HELP OLD LADIES CROSS THE STREET AND GIVE 'EM THE SALUTE!
BUT, SAY! HOW DO WE JOIN THE SCOUTS? WHAT DO WE HAVE TO DO?
!
?
GOSH! I DON'T KNOW! BUT LOTS OF KIDS HAVE DONE IT! WE CAN, TOO!
I KNOW! COME ON! WE'LL HUNT AROUND AND FIND SOME LUCKY KID WHO'S DRESSED UP IN A UNIFORM AND ASK HIM WHAT HE DID!
WE'RE GONNA BE BOY SCOUTS, WE'RE GONNA BE BOY SCOUTS. HEIGH-O, THE MERRY-O, WE'RE GONNA BE BOY SCOUTS!
!
!
BOY SCOUT ENLISTMENT STATION
FIRES BUILT SIGNALS TAUGHT BUGLES BLOWN
AND GOOD DEEDS SUGGESTED
BE PREPARED!
© 1936, by Walt Disney Enterprises, Great Britain rights reserved.
JUST SIGN HERE, LADS! IF THERE IS ONE THING THAT I LIKE TO DO IT'S TO BE ABLE TO PREPARE NICE, TENDER CHAPS LIKE YOU!
3-22

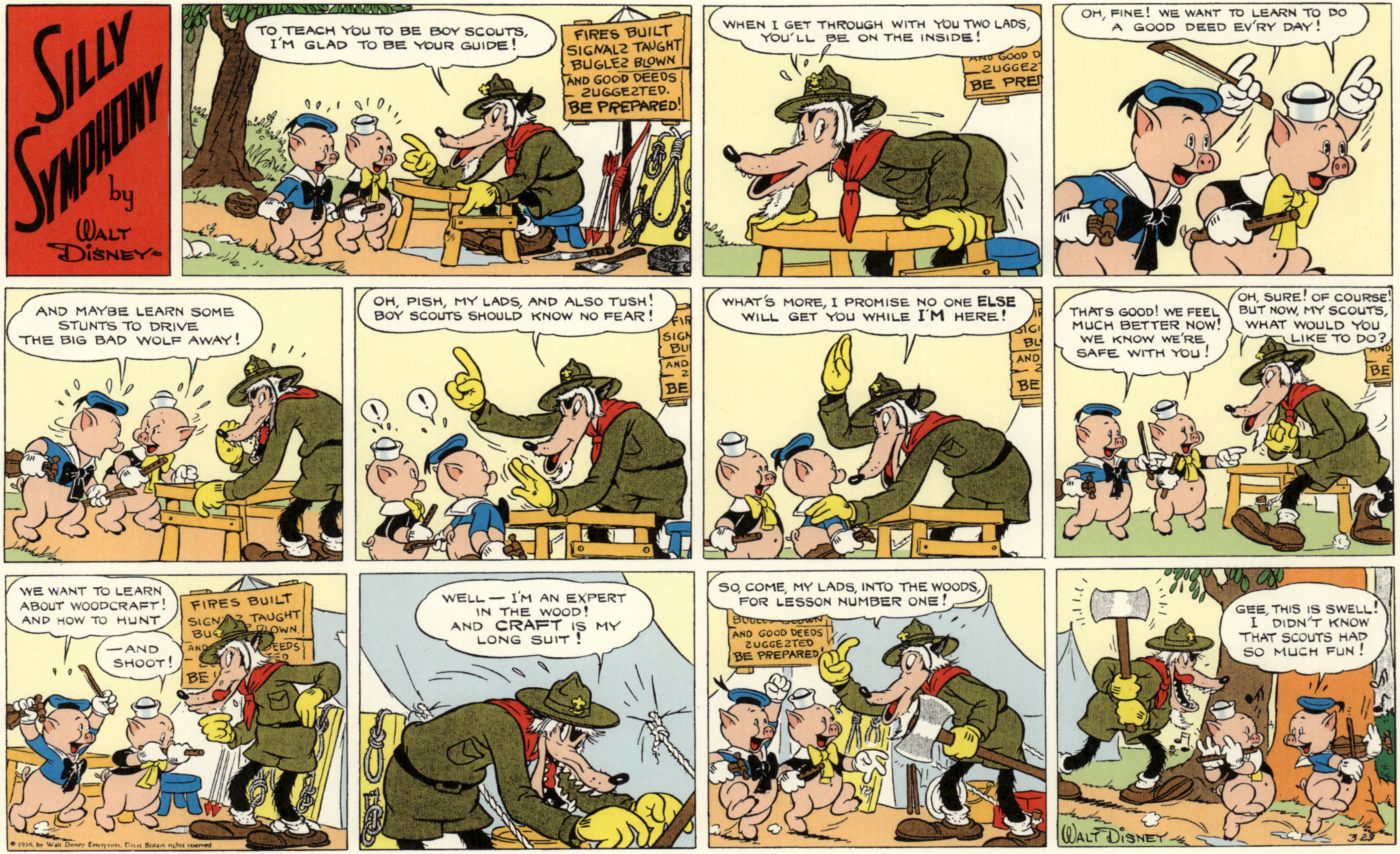
SILLY SYMPHONY by WALT DISNEY
TO TEACH YOU TO BE BOY SCOUTS, I'M GLAD TO BE YOUR GUIDE!
FIRES BUILT SIGNALZ TAUGHT BUGLEZ BLOWN AND GOOD DEEDS ZUGGEZTED. BE PREPARED!
WHEN I GET THROUGH WITH YOU TWO LADS, YOU'LL BE ON THE INSIDE!
OH, FINE! WE WANT TO LEARN TO DO A GOOD DEED EV'RY DAY!
AND MAYBE LEARN SOME STUNTS TO DRIVE THE BIG BAD WOLF AWAY!
OH, PISH, MY LADS, AND ALSO TUSH! BOY SCOUTS SHOULD KNOW NO FEAR!
WHAT'S MORE, I PROMISE NO ONE ELSE WILL GET YOU WHILE I'M HERE!
THAT'S GOOD! WE FEEL MUCH BETTER NOW! WE KNOW WE'RE SAFE WITH YOU!
OH, SURE! OF COURSE! BUT NOW, MY SCOUTS, WHAT WOULD YOU LIKE TO DO?
WE WANT TO LEARN ABOUT WOODCRAFT! AND HOW TO HUNT
—AND SHOOT!
WELL — I'M AN EXPERT IN THE WOOD! AND CRAFT IS MY LONG SUIT!
SO, COME, MY LADS, INTO THE WOODS, FOR LESSON NUMBER ONE!
AND GOOD DEEDS ZUGGEZTED BE PREPARED!
GEE, THIS IS SWELL! I DIDN'T KNOW THAT SCOUTS HAD SO MUCH FUN!
WALT DISNEY 3-29
© 1936, by Walt Disney Enterprises, Great Britain rights reserved

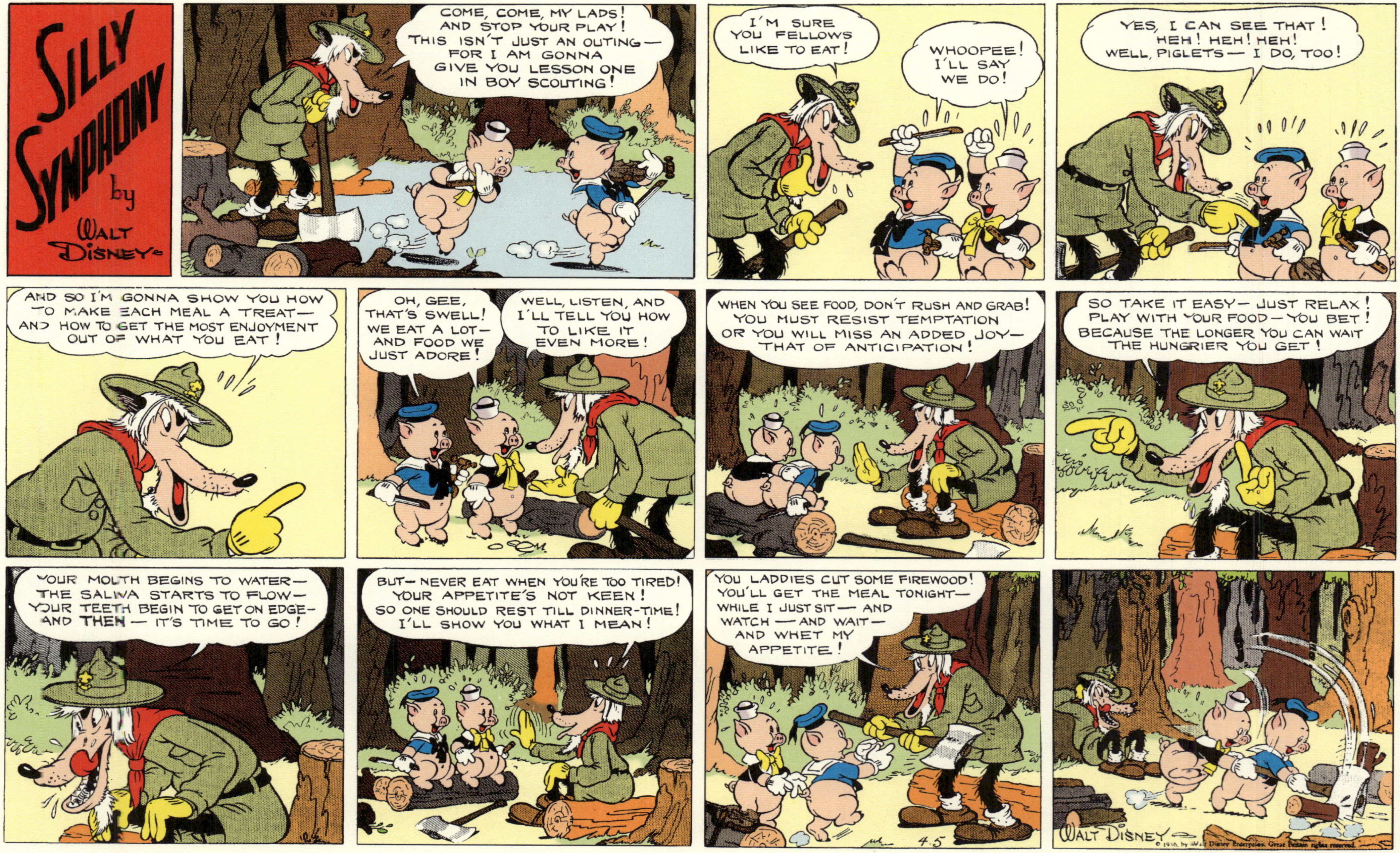
SILLY SYMPHONY by WALT DISNEY
COME, COME, MY LADS! AND STOP YOUR PLAY! THIS ISN'T JUST AN OUTING— FOR I AM GONNA GIVE YOU LESSON ONE IN BOY SCOUTING!
I'M SURE YOU FELLOWS LIKE TO EAT!
WHOOPEE! I'LL SAY WE DO!
YES, I CAN SEE THAT! HEH! HEH! HEH! WELL, PIGLETS — I DO, TOO!
AND SO I'M GONNA SHOW YOU HOW TO MAKE EACH MEAL A TREAT— AND HOW TO GET THE MOST ENJOYMENT OUT OF WHAT YOU EAT!
OH, GEE, THAT'S SWELL! WE EAT A LOT— AND FOOD WE JUST ADORE!
WELL, LISTEN, AND I'LL TELL YOU HOW TO LIKE IT EVEN MORE!
WHEN YOU SEE FOOD, DON'T RUSH AND GRAB! YOU MUST RESIST TEMPTATION OR YOU WILL MISS AN ADDED JOY— THAT OF ANTICIPATION!
SO TAKE IT EASY— JUST RELAX! PLAY WITH YOUR FOOD— YOU BET! BECAUSE THE LONGER YOU CAN WAIT THE HUNGRIER YOU GET!
YOUR MOUTH BEGINS TO WATER— THE SALIVA STARTS TO FLOW— YOUR TEETH BEGIN TO GET ON EDGE— AND THEN — IT'S TIME TO GO!
BUT— NEVER EAT WHEN YOU'RE TOO TIRED! YOUR APPETITE'S NOT KEEN! SO ONE SHOULD REST TILL DINNER-TIME! I'LL SHOW YOU WHAT I MEAN!
YOU LADDIES CUT SOME FIREWOOD! YOU'LL GET THE MEAL TONIGHT— WHILE I JUST SIT— AND WATCH —AND WAIT— AND WHET MY APPETITE!
4-5
WALT DISNEY

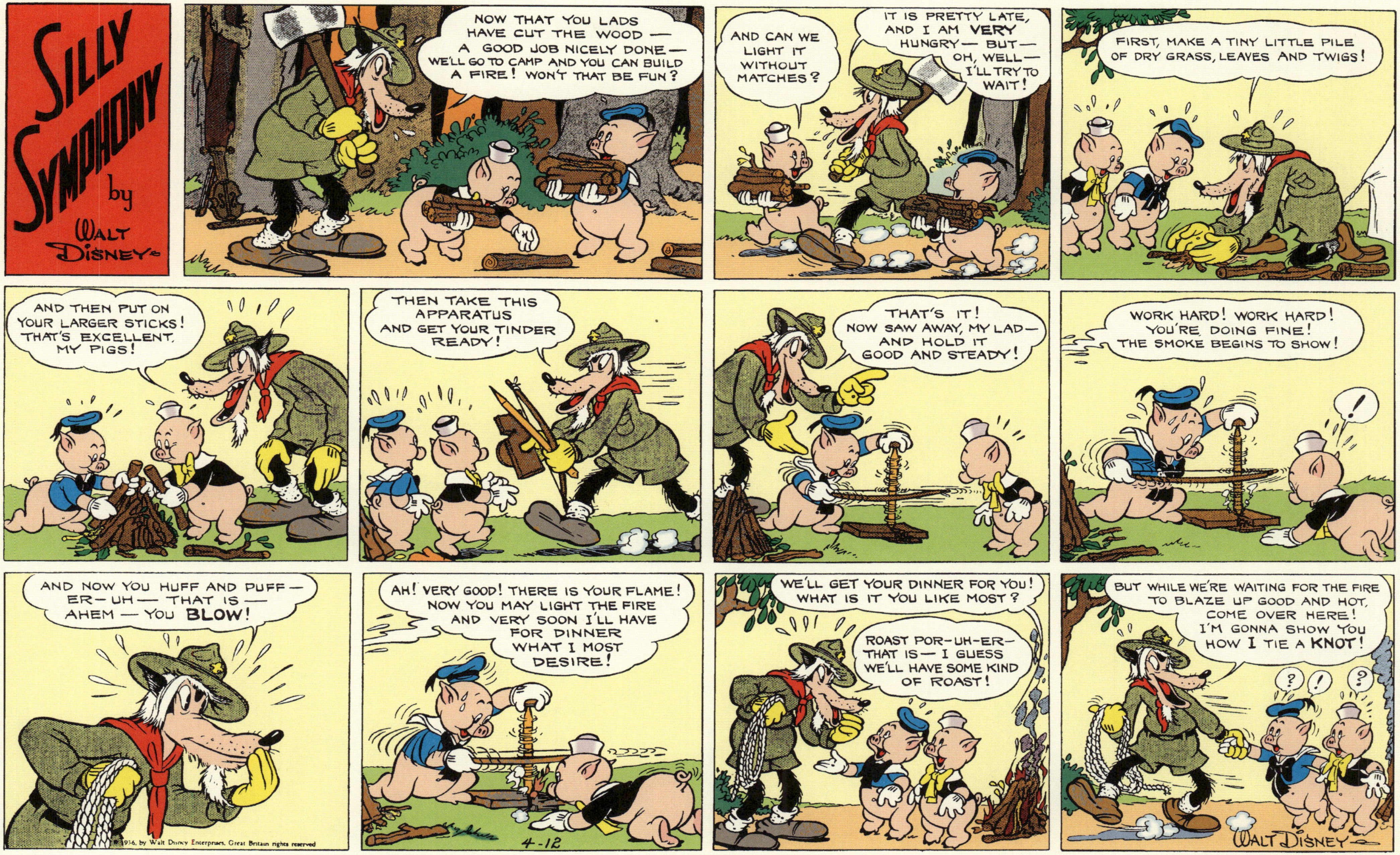

SILLY SYMPHONY
by
WALT DISNEY
NOW THAT YOU LADS HAVE CUT THE WOOD — A GOOD JOB NICELY DONE — WE'LL GO TO CAMP AND YOU CAN BUILD A FIRE! WON'T THAT BE FUN?
AND CAN WE LIGHT IT WITHOUT MATCHES?
IT IS PRETTY LATE, AND I AM VERY HUNGRY — BUT — OH, WELL — I'LL TRY TO WAIT!
FIRST, MAKE A TINY LITTLE PILE OF DRY GRASS, LEAVES AND TWIGS!
AND THEN PUT ON YOUR LARGER STICKS! THAT'S EXCELLENT, MY PIGS!
THEN TAKE THIS APPARATUS AND GET YOUR TINDER READY!
THAT'S IT! NOW SAW AWAY, MY LAD — AND HOLD IT GOOD AND STEADY!
WORK HARD! WORK HARD! YOU'RE DOING FINE! THE SMOKE BEGINS TO SHOW!
!
AND NOW YOU HUFF AND PUFF — ER — UH — THAT IS — AHEM — YOU BLOW!
© 1936, by Walt Disney Enterprises. Great Britain rights reserved
AH! VERY GOOD! THERE IS YOUR FLAME! NOW YOU MAY LIGHT THE FIRE AND VERY SOON I'LL HAVE FOR DINNER WHAT I MOST DESIRE!
4-12
WE'LL GET YOUR DINNER FOR YOU! WHAT IS IT YOU LIKE MOST?
ROAST POR—UH—ER— THAT IS — I GUESS WE'LL HAVE SOME KIND OF ROAST!
BUT WHILE WE'RE WAITING FOR THE FIRE TO BLAZE UP GOOD AND HOT, COME OVER HERE! I'M GONNA SHOW YOU HOW I TIE A KNOT!
? ! ?
WALT DISNEY

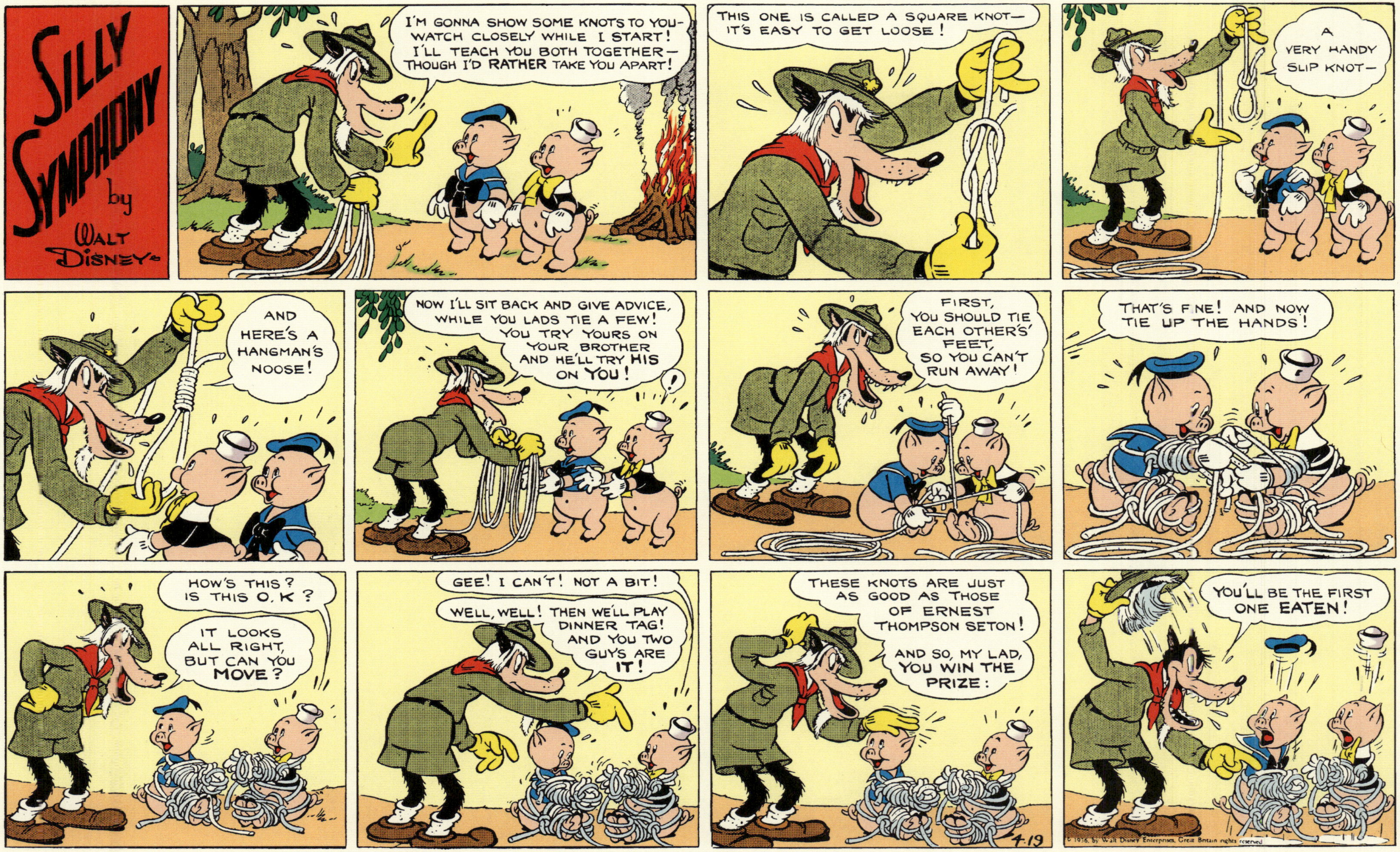
SILLY SYMPHONY
by
WALT DISNEY
I'M GONNA SHOW SOME KNOTS TO YOU— WATCH CLOSELY WHILE I START! I'LL TEACH YOU BOTH TOGETHER— THOUGH I'D RATHER TAKE YOU APART!
THIS ONE IS CALLED A SQUARE KNOT— IT'S EASY TO GET LOOSE!
A VERY HANDY SLIP KNOT—
AND HERE'S A HANGMAN'S NOOSE!
NOW I'LL SIT BACK AND GIVE ADVICE, WHILE YOU LADS TIE A FEW! YOU TRY YOURS ON YOUR BROTHER AND HE'LL TRY HIS ON YOU!
!
FIRST, YOU SHOULD TIE EACH OTHER'S FEET, SO YOU CAN'T RUN AWAY!
THAT'S FINE! AND NOW TIE UP THE HANDS!
HOW'S THIS? IS THIS O.K?
IT LOOKS ALL RIGHT, BUT CAN YOU MOVE?
GEE! I CAN'T! NOT A BIT!
WELL, WELL! THEN WE'LL PLAY DINNER TAG! AND YOU TWO GUYS ARE IT!
THESE KNOTS ARE JUST AS GOOD AS THOSE OF ERNEST THOMPSON SETON!
AND SO, MY LAD, YOU WIN THE PRIZE:
4-19
YOU'LL BE THE FIRST ONE EATEN!
© 1936, by Walt Disney Enterprises, Great Britain rights reserved

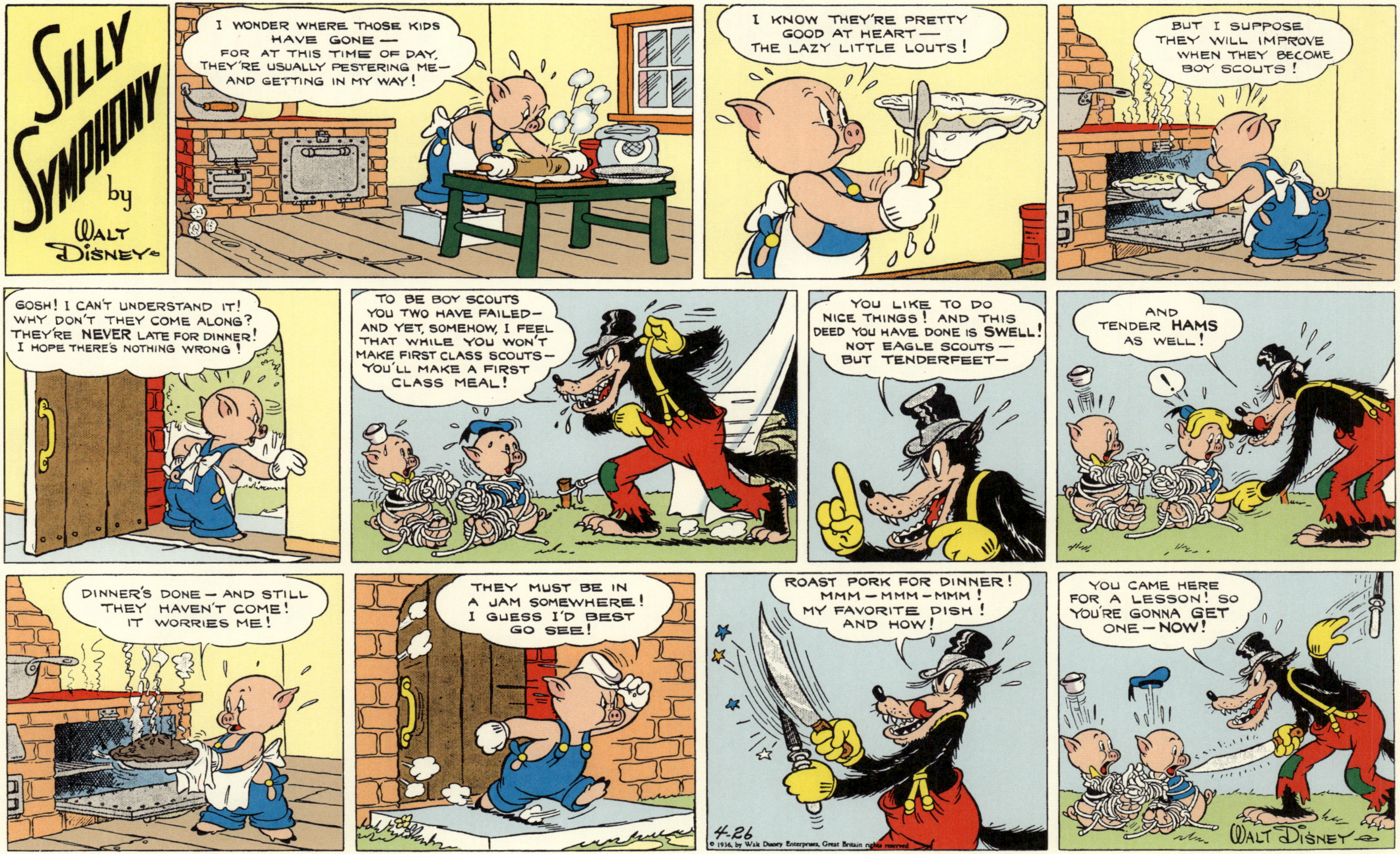
SILLY SYMPHONY by WALT DISNEY
I WONDER WHERE THOSE KIDS HAVE GONE — FOR AT THIS TIME OF DAY, THEY'RE USUALLY PESTERING ME— AND GETTING IN MY WAY!
I KNOW THEY'RE PRETTY GOOD AT HEART— THE LAZY LITTLE LOUTS!
BUT I SUPPOSE THEY WILL IMPROVE WHEN THEY BECOME BOY SCOUTS!
GOSH! I CAN'T UNDERSTAND IT! WHY DON'T THEY COME ALONG? THEY'RE NEVER LATE FOR DINNER! I HOPE THERE'S NOTHING WRONG!
TO BE BOY SCOUTS YOU TWO HAVE FAILED— AND YET, SOMEHOW, I FEEL THAT WHILE YOU WON'T MAKE FIRST CLASS SCOUTS— YOU'LL MAKE A FIRST CLASS MEAL!
YOU LIKE TO DO NICE THINGS! AND THIS DEED YOU HAVE DONE IS SWELL! NOT EAGLE SCOUTS— BUT TENDERFEET—
AND TENDER HAMS AS WELL!
!
DINNER'S DONE — AND STILL THEY HAVEN'T COME! IT WORRIES ME!
THEY MUST BE IN A JAM SOMEWHERE! I GUESS I'D BEST GO SEE!
ROAST PORK FOR DINNER! MMM — MMM — MMM! MY FAVORITE DISH! AND HOW!
4-26
© 1936, by Walt Disney Enterprises, Great Britain rights reserved
YOU CAME HERE FOR A LESSON! SO YOU'RE GONNA GET ONE — NOW!
WALT DISNEY

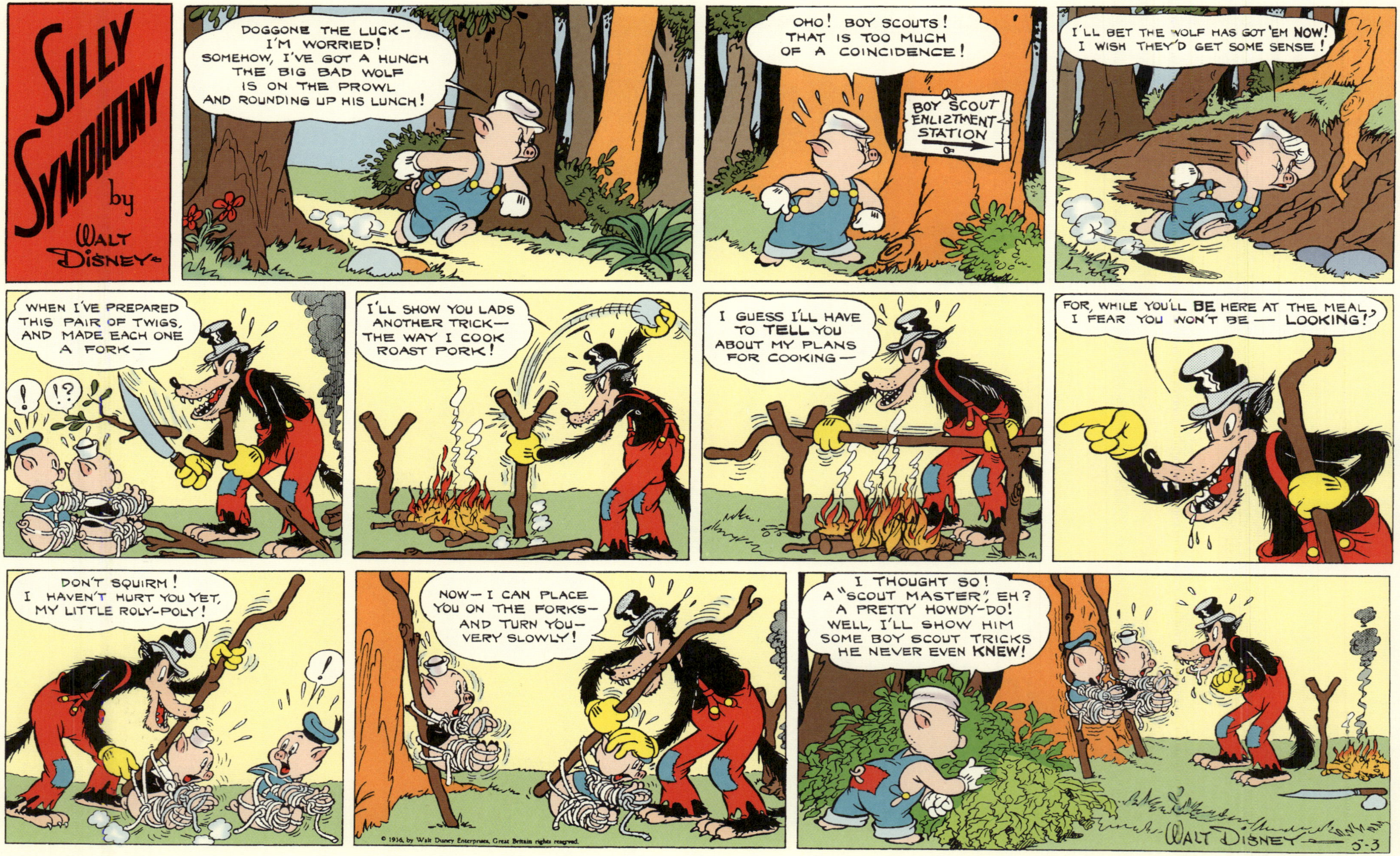
SILLY SYMPHONY by WALT DISNEY
DOGGONE THE LUCK— I'M WORRIED! SOMEHOW, I'VE GOT A HUNCH THE BIG BAD WOLF IS ON THE PROWL AND ROUNDING UP HIS LUNCH!
OHO! BOY SCOUTS! THAT IS TOO MUCH OF A COINCIDENCE!
BOY SCOUT ENLIZTMENT STATION
I'LL BET THE WOLF HAS GOT 'EM NOW! I WISH THEY'D GET SOME SENSE!
WHEN I'VE PREPARED THIS PAIR OF TWIGS, AND MADE EACH ONE A FORK—
!
!?
I'LL SHOW YOU LADS ANOTHER TRICK— THE WAY I COOK ROAST PORK!
I GUESS I'LL HAVE TO TELL YOU ABOUT MY PLANS FOR COOKING—
FOR, WHILE YOU'LL BE HERE AT THE MEAL, I FEAR YOU WON'T BE — LOOKING!
DON'T SQUIRM! I HAVEN'T HURT YOU YET, MY LITTLE ROLY-POLY!
!
NOW— I CAN PLACE YOU ON THE FORKS— AND TURN YOU— VERY SLOWLY!
© 1936, by Walt Disney Enterprises. Great Britain rights reserved.
I THOUGHT SO! A "SCOUT MASTER," EH? A PRETTY HOWDY-DO! WELL, I'LL SHOW HIM SOME BOY SCOUT TRICKS HE NEVER EVEN KNEW!
WALT DISNEY
5-3

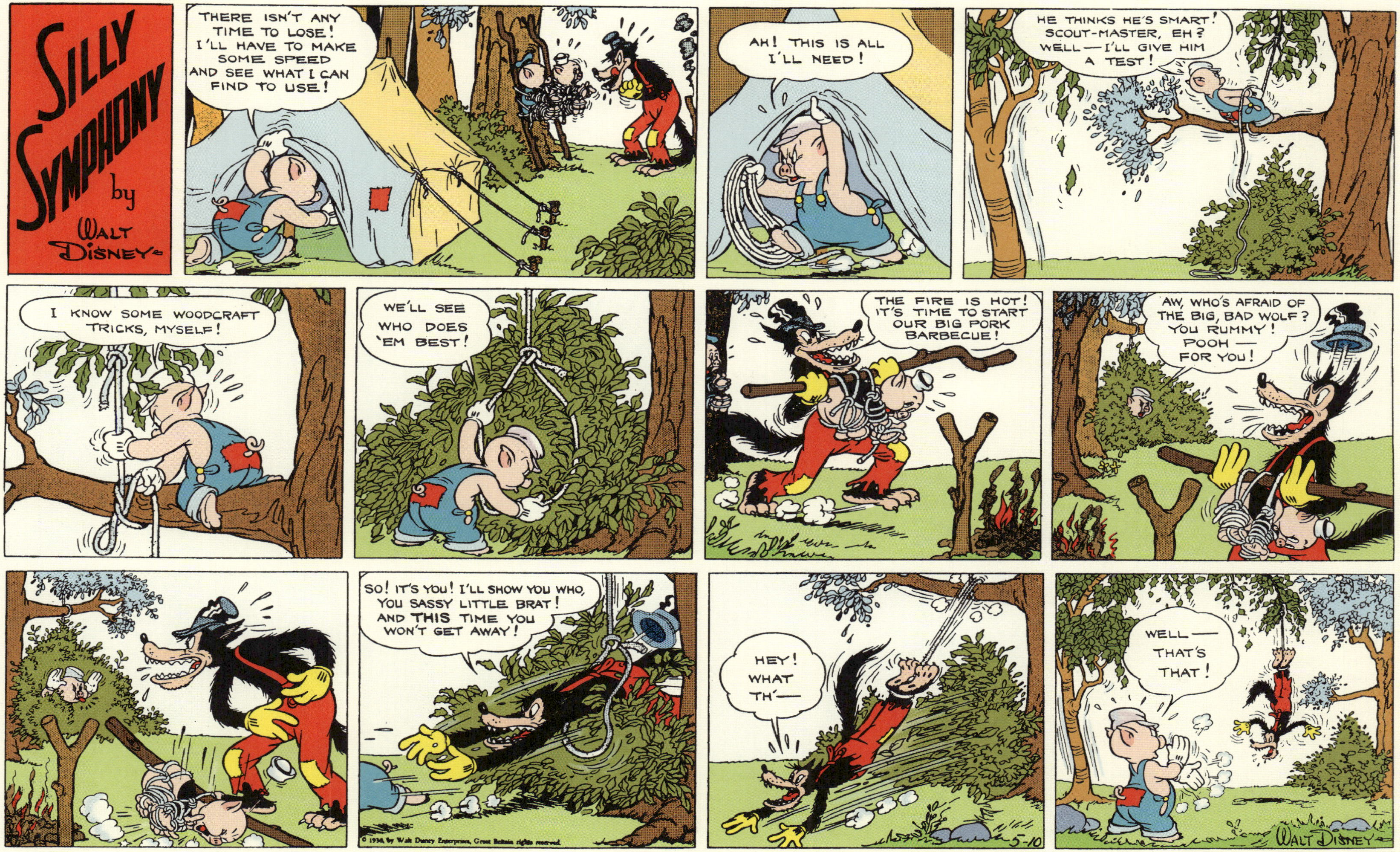
SILLY SYMPHONY
by
WALT DISNEY
THERE ISN'T ANY TIME TO LOSE! I'LL HAVE TO MAKE SOME SPEED AND SEE WHAT I CAN FIND TO USE!
AH! THIS IS ALL I'LL NEED!
HE THINKS HE'S SMART! SCOUT-MASTER, EH? WELL — I'LL GIVE HIM A TEST!
I KNOW SOME WOODCRAFT TRICKS, MYSELF!
WE'LL SEE WHO DOES 'EM BEST!
THE FIRE IS HOT! IT'S TIME TO START OUR BIG PORK BARBECUE!
AW, WHO'S AFRAID OF THE BIG, BAD WOLF? YOU RUMMY! POOH — FOR YOU!
SO! IT'S YOU! I'LL SHOW YOU WHO, YOU SASSY LITTLE BRAT! AND THIS TIME YOU WON'T GET AWAY!
© 1936, by Walt Disney Enterprises, Great Britain rights reserved.
HEY! WHAT TH'—
5-10
WELL — THAT'S THAT!
WALT DISNEY

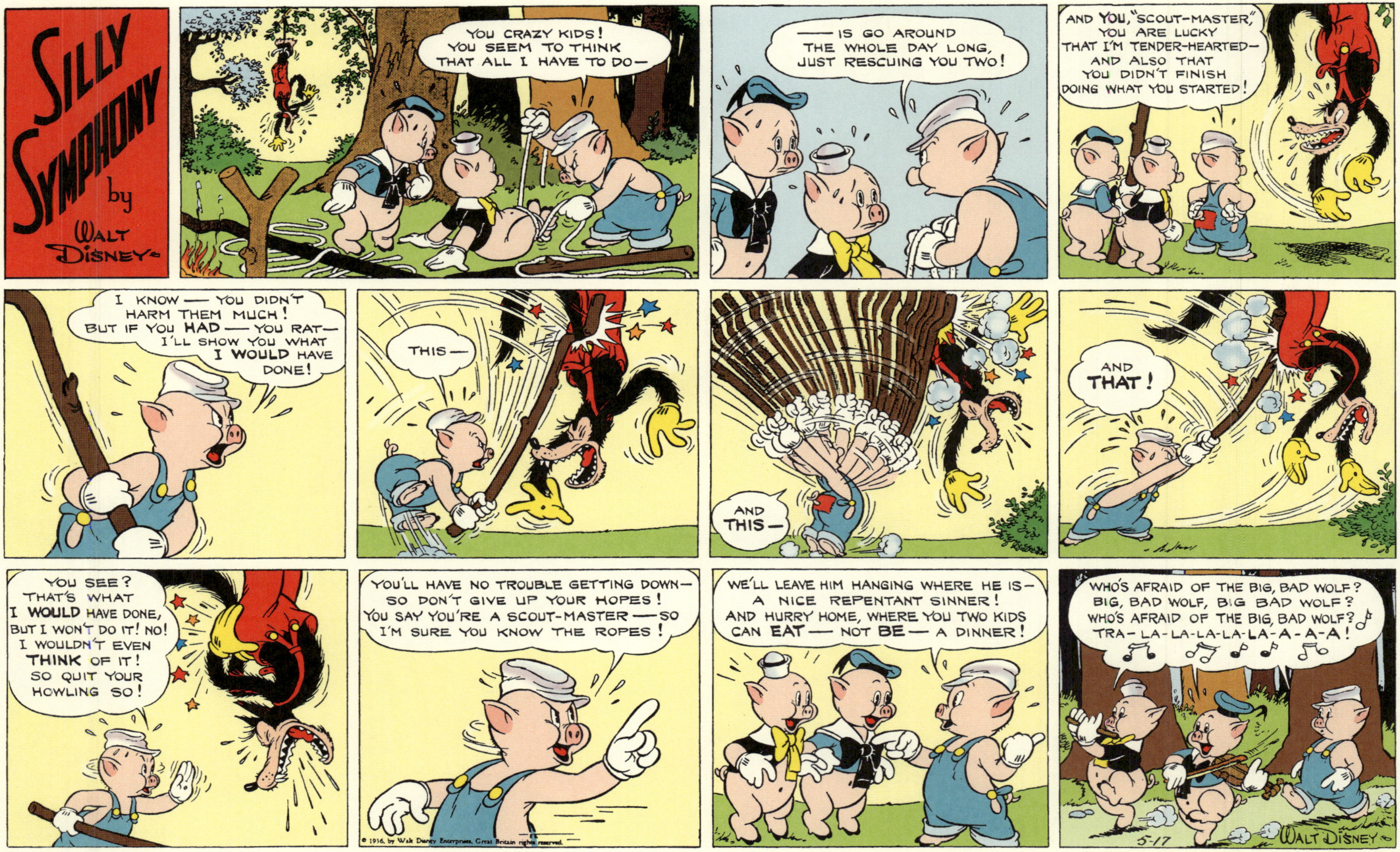
SILLY SYMPHONY
by WALT DISNEY
YOU CRAZY KIDS! YOU SEEM TO THINK THAT ALL I HAVE TO DO—
—IS GO AROUND THE WHOLE DAY LONG, JUST RESCUING YOU TWO!
AND YOU, "SCOUT-MASTER," YOU ARE LUCKY THAT I'M TENDER-HEARTED—AND ALSO THAT YOU DIDN'T FINISH DOING WHAT YOU STARTED!
I KNOW — YOU DIDN'T HARM THEM MUCH! BUT IF YOU HAD — YOU RAT— I'LL SHOW YOU WHAT I WOULD HAVE DONE!
THIS—
AND THIS—
AND THAT!
YOU SEE? THAT'S WHAT I WOULD HAVE DONE, BUT I WON'T DO IT! NO! I WOULDN'T EVEN THINK OF IT! SO QUIT YOUR HOWLING SO!
YOU'LL HAVE NO TROUBLE GETTING DOWN—SO DON'T GIVE UP YOUR HOPES! YOU SAY YOU'RE A SCOUT-MASTER —SO I'M SURE YOU KNOW THE ROPES!
© 1936, by Walt Disney Enterprises. Great Britain rights reserved.
WE'LL LEAVE HIM HANGING WHERE HE IS—A NICE REPENTANT SINNER! AND HURRY HOME, WHERE YOU TWO KIDS CAN EAT — NOT BE — A DINNER!
WHO'S AFRAID OF THE BIG, BAD WOLF? BIG, BAD WOLF, BIG BAD WOLF? WHO'S AFRAID OF THE BIG, BAD WOLF? TRA-LA-LA-LA-LA-LA-A-A-A!
5-17
WALT DISNEY

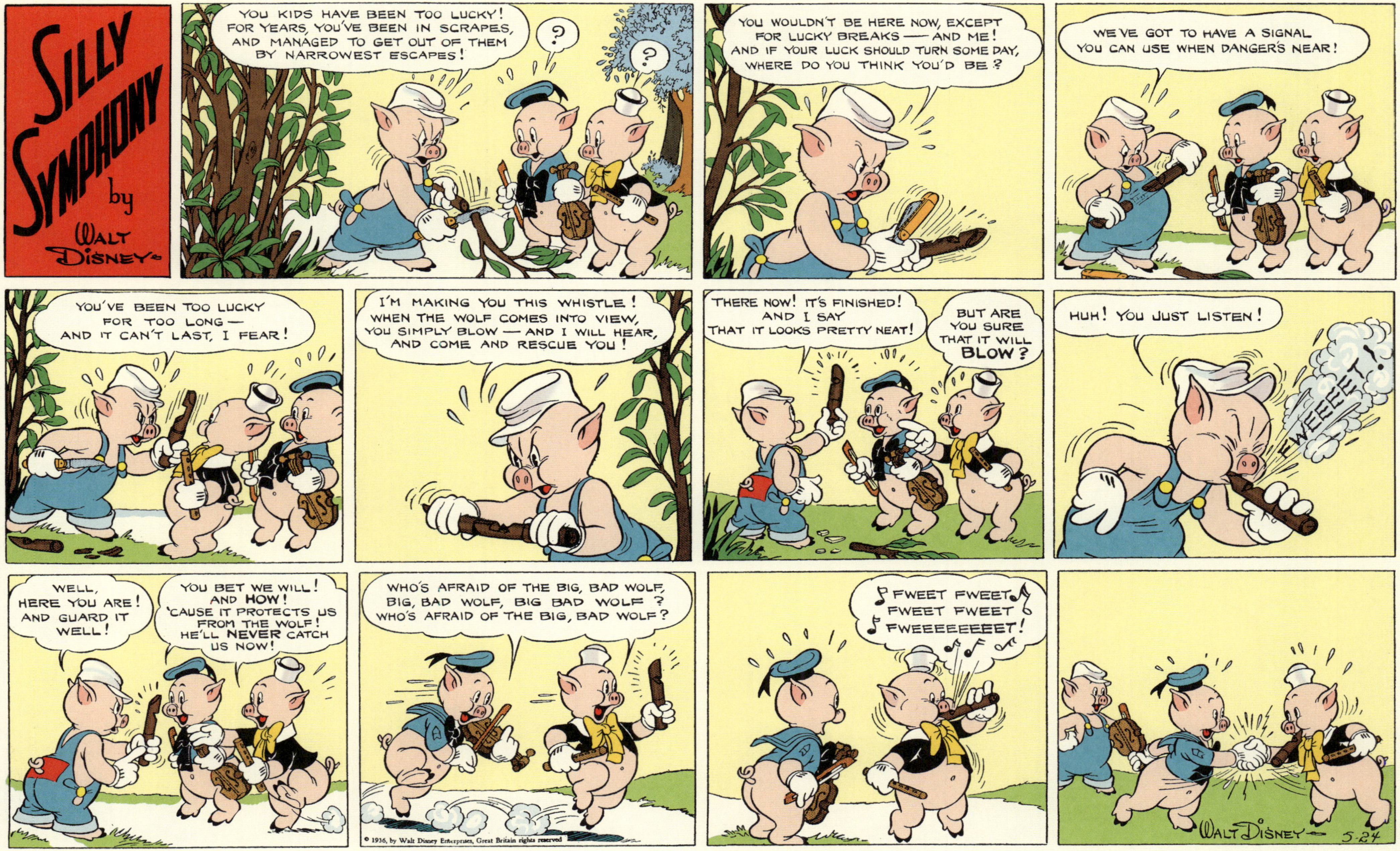
SILLY SYMPHONY
by
WALT DISNEY
YOU KIDS HAVE BEEN TOO LUCKY! FOR YEARS, YOU'VE BEEN IN SCRAPES, AND MANAGED TO GET OUT OF THEM BY NARROWEST ESCAPES!
?
?
YOU WOULDN'T BE HERE NOW, EXCEPT FOR LUCKY BREAKS — AND ME! AND IF YOUR LUCK SHOULD TURN SOME DAY, WHERE DO YOU THINK YOU'D BE?
WE'VE GOT TO HAVE A SIGNAL YOU CAN USE WHEN DANGER'S NEAR!
YOU'VE BEEN TOO LUCKY FOR TOO LONG — AND IT CAN'T LAST, I FEAR!
I'M MAKING YOU THIS WHISTLE! WHEN THE WOLF COMES INTO VIEW, YOU SIMPLY BLOW — AND I WILL HEAR, AND COME AND RESCUE YOU!
THERE NOW! IT'S FINISHED! AND I SAY THAT IT LOOKS PRETTY NEAT!
BUT ARE YOU SURE THAT IT WILL BLOW?
HUH! YOU JUST LISTEN!
FWEEEET!
WELL, HERE YOU ARE! AND GUARD IT WELL!
YOU BET WE WILL! AND HOW! 'CAUSE IT PROTECTS US FROM THE WOLF! HE'LL NEVER CATCH US NOW!
WHO'S AFRAID OF THE BIG, BAD WOLF, BIG, BAD WOLF, BIG BAD WOLF? WHO'S AFRAID OF THE BIG, BAD WOLF?
© 1936, by Walt Disney Enterprises, Great Britain rights reserved
FWEET FWEET FWEET FWEET FWEEEEEEEET!
WALT DISNEY 5-24

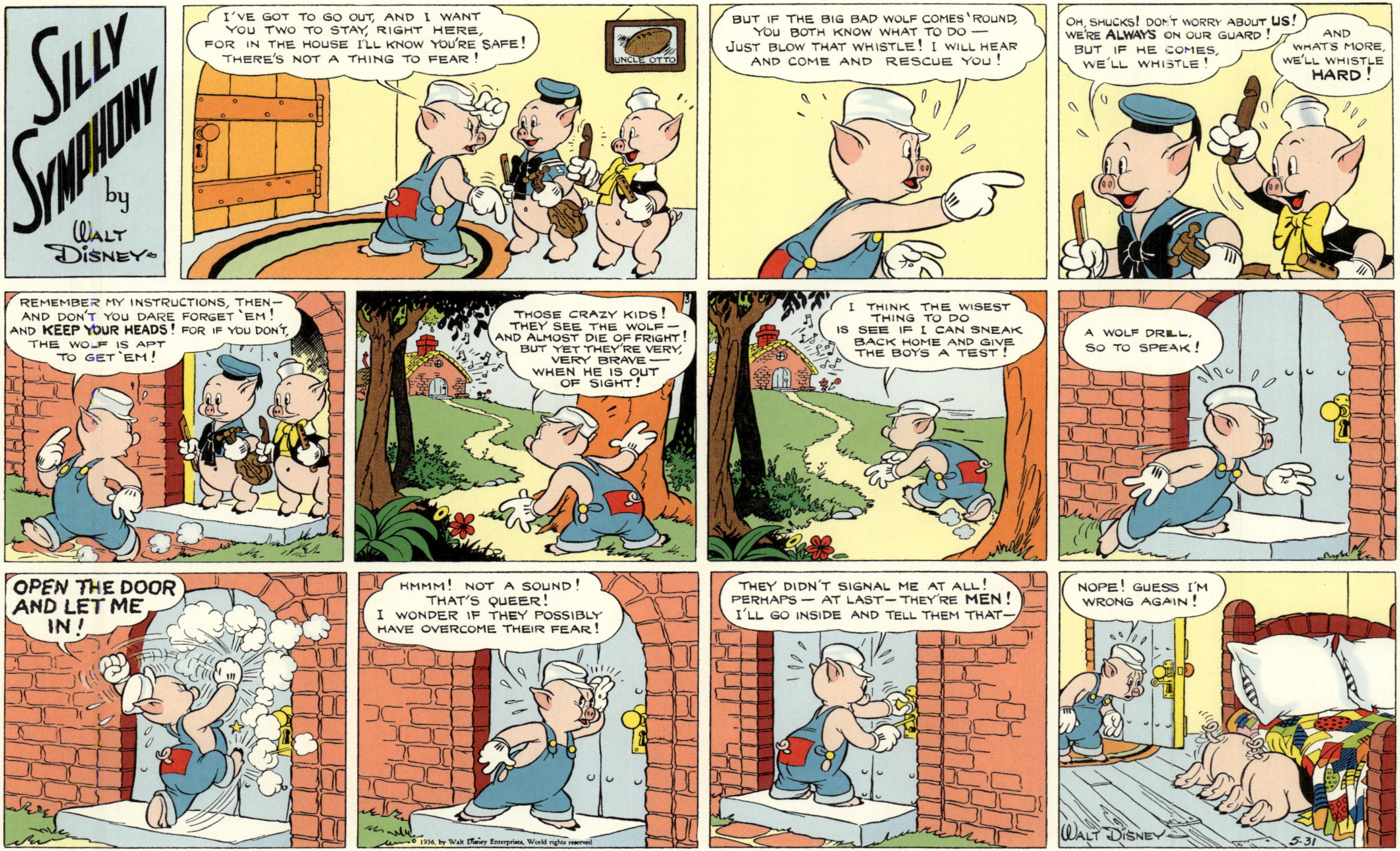

SILLY SYMPHONY by WALT DISNEY
I'VE GOT TO GO OUT, AND I WANT YOU TWO TO STAY RIGHT HERE, FOR IN THE HOUSE I'LL KNOW YOU'RE SAFE! THERE'S NOT A THING TO FEAR!
UNCLE OTTO
BUT IF THE BIG BAD WOLF COMES 'ROUND, YOU BOTH KNOW WHAT TO DO — JUST BLOW THAT WHISTLE! I WILL HEAR AND COME AND RESCUE YOU!
OH, SHUCKS! DON'T WORRY ABOUT US! WE'RE ALWAYS ON OUR GUARD! BUT IF HE COMES, WE'LL WHISTLE!
AND WHAT'S MORE, WE'LL WHISTLE HARD!
REMEMBER MY INSTRUCTIONS, THEN— AND DON'T YOU DARE FORGET 'EM! AND KEEP YOUR HEADS! FOR IF YOU DON'T, THE WOLF IS APT TO GET 'EM!
THOSE CRAZY KIDS! THEY SEE THE WOLF— AND ALMOST DIE OF FRIGHT! BUT YET THEY'RE VERY, VERY BRAVE— WHEN HE IS OUT OF SIGHT!
I THINK THE WISEST THING TO DO IS SEE IF I CAN SNEAK BACK HOME AND GIVE THE BOYS A TEST!
A WOLF DRILL, SO TO SPEAK!
OPEN THE DOOR AND LET ME IN!
HMMM! NOT A SOUND! THAT'S QUEER! I WONDER IF THEY POSSIBLY HAVE OVERCOME THEIR FEAR!
THEY DIDN'T SIGNAL ME AT ALL! PERHAPS — AT LAST — THEY'RE MEN! I'LL GO INSIDE AND TELL THEM THAT—
NOPE! GUESS I'M WRONG AGAIN!
© 1936, by Walt Disney Enterprises, World rights reserved
WALT DISNEY 5-31

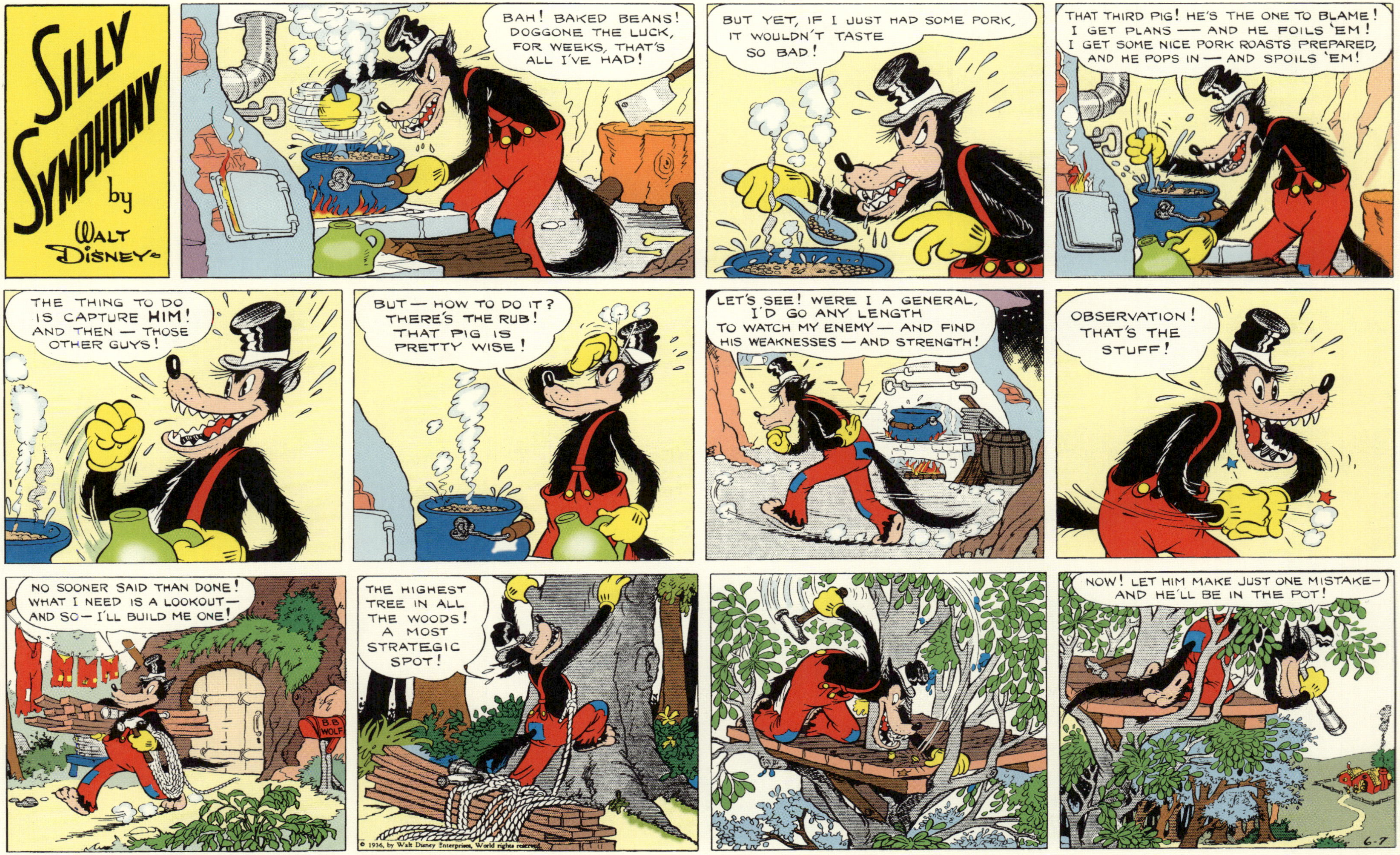
SILLY SYMPHONY by WALT DISNEY
BAH! BAKED BEANS! DOGGONE THE LUCK, FOR WEEKS, THAT'S ALL I'VE HAD!
BUT YET, IF I JUST HAD SOME PORK, IT WOULDN'T TASTE SO BAD!
THAT THIRD PIG! HE'S THE ONE TO BLAME! I GET PLANS — AND HE FOILS 'EM! I GET SOME NICE PORK ROASTS PREPARED, AND HE POPS IN — AND SPOILS 'EM!
THE THING TO DO IS CAPTURE HIM! AND THEN — THOSE OTHER GUYS!
BUT — HOW TO DO IT? THERE'S THE RUB! THAT PIG IS PRETTY WISE!
LET'S SEE! WERE I A GENERAL, I'D GO ANY LENGTH TO WATCH MY ENEMY — AND FIND HIS WEAKNESSES — AND STRENGTH!
OBSERVATION! THAT'S THE STUFF!
NO SOONER SAID THAN DONE! WHAT I NEED IS A LOOKOUT— AND SO— I'LL BUILD ME ONE!
B.B. WOLF
THE HIGHEST TREE IN ALL THE WOODS! A MOST STRATEGIC SPOT!
© 1936, by Walt Disney Enterprises, World rights reserved.
NOW! LET HIM MAKE JUST ONE MISTAKE— AND HE'LL BE IN THE POT!
6-7

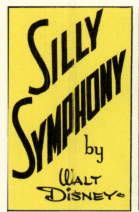

62 • June 14, 1936

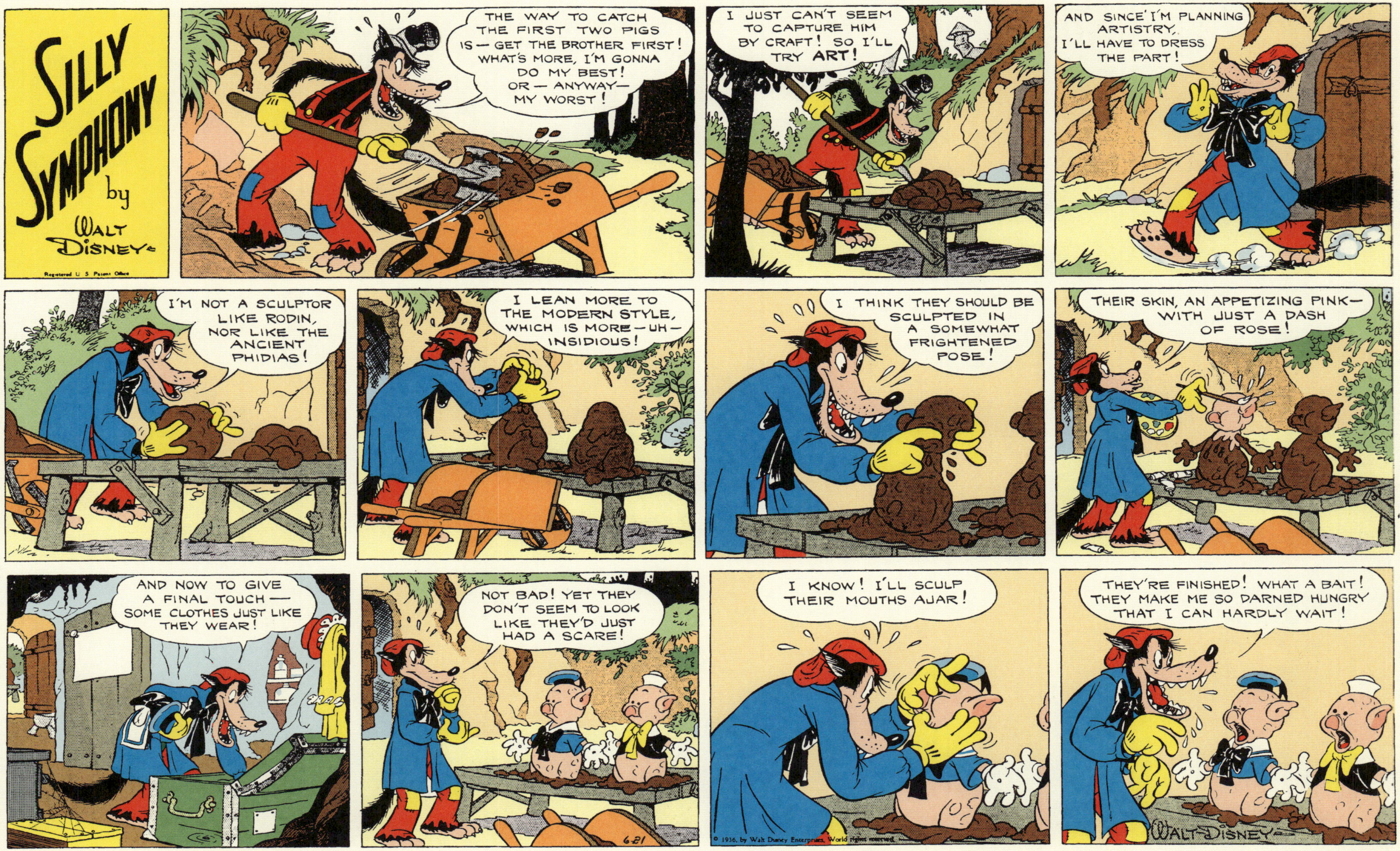
SILLY SYMPHONY
by
WALT DISNEY
Registered U. S. Patent Office
THE WAY TO CATCH THE FIRST TWO PIGS IS — GET THE BROTHER FIRST! WHAT'S MORE, I'M GONNA DO MY BEST! OR — ANYWAY— MY WORST!
I JUST CAN'T SEEM TO CAPTURE HIM BY CRAFT! SO I'LL TRY ART!
AND SINCE I'M PLANNING ARTISTRY, I'LL HAVE TO DRESS THE PART!
I'M NOT A SCULPTOR LIKE RODIN, NOR LIKE THE ANCIENT PHIDIAS!
I LEAN MORE TO THE MODERN STYLE, WHICH IS MORE — UH — INSIDIOUS!
I THINK THEY SHOULD BE SCULPTED IN A SOMEWHAT FRIGHTENED POSE!
THEIR SKIN, AN APPETIZING PINK— WITH JUST A DASH OF ROSE!
AND NOW TO GIVE A FINAL TOUCH — SOME CLOTHES JUST LIKE THEY WEAR!
NOT BAD! YET THEY DON'T SEEM TO LOOK LIKE THEY'D JUST HAD A SCARE!
6-21
I KNOW! I'LL SCULP THEIR MOUTHS AJAR!
THEY'RE FINISHED! WHAT A BAIT! THEY MAKE ME SO DARNED HUNGRY THAT I CAN HARDLY WAIT!
WALT DISNEY

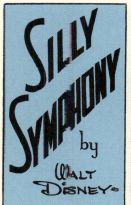

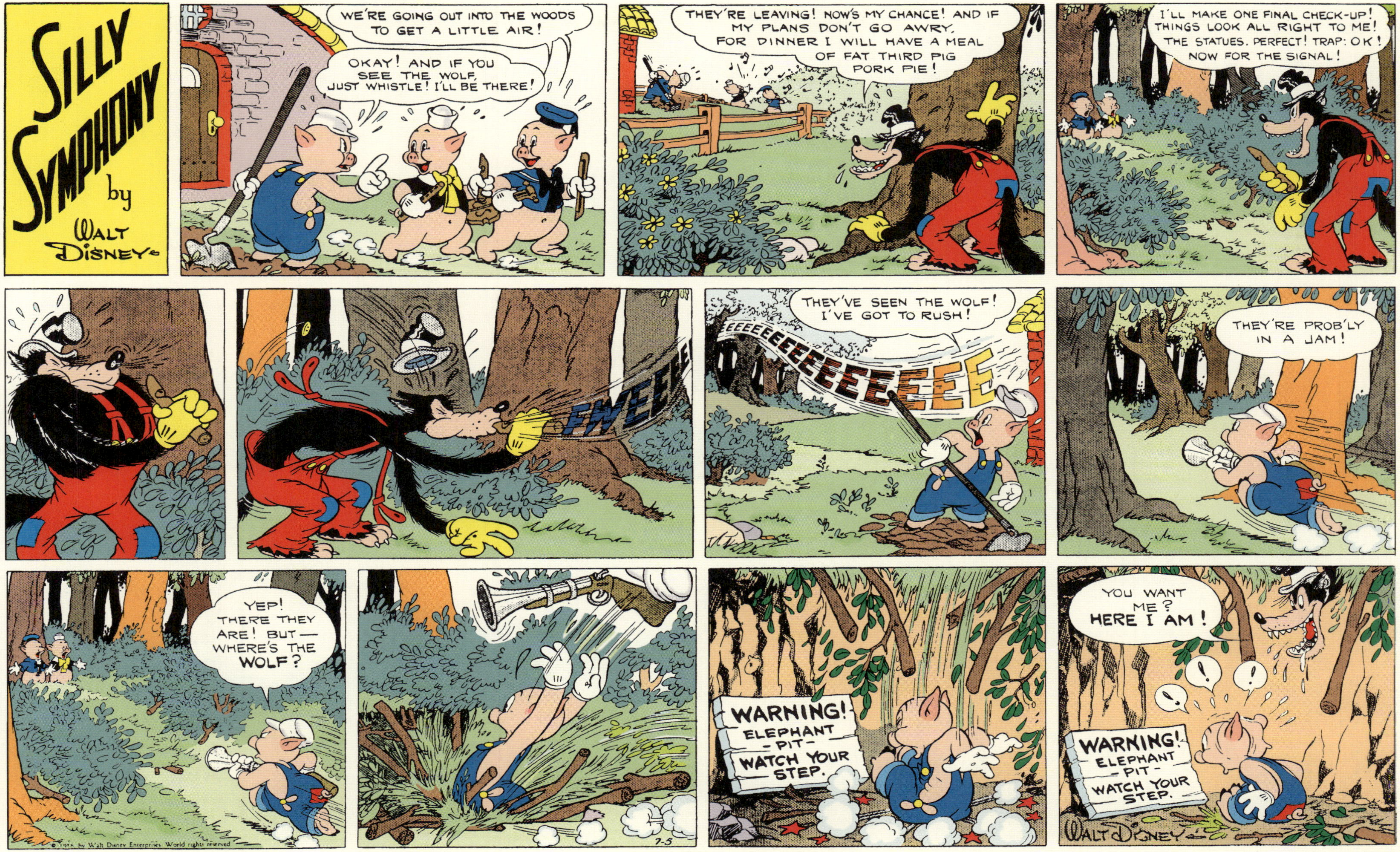
SILLY SYMPHONY
by
WALT DISNEY
WE'RE GOING OUT INTO THE WOODS TO GET A LITTLE AIR!
OKAY! AND IF YOU SEE THE WOLF, JUST WHISTLE! I'LL BE THERE!
THEY'RE LEAVING! NOW'S MY CHANCE! AND IF MY PLANS DON'T GO AWRY, FOR DINNER I WILL HAVE A MEAL OF FAT THIRD PIG PORK PIE!
I'LL MAKE ONE FINAL CHECK-UP! THINGS LOOK ALL RIGHT TO ME! THE STATUES. PERFECT! TRAP: OK! NOW FOR THE SIGNAL!
FWEEE
EEEEEEEEEEEEEEEE
THEY'VE SEEN THE WOLF! I'VE GOT TO RUSH!
THEY'RE PROB'LY IN A JAM!
YEP! THERE THEY ARE! BUT— WHERE'S THE WOLF?
© 1936 by Walt Disney Enterprises World rights reserved
WARNING! ELEPHANT -PIT- WATCH YOUR STEP.
YOU WANT ME? HERE I AM!
WARNING! ELEPHANT -PIT- WATCH YOUR STEP.
WALT DISNEY

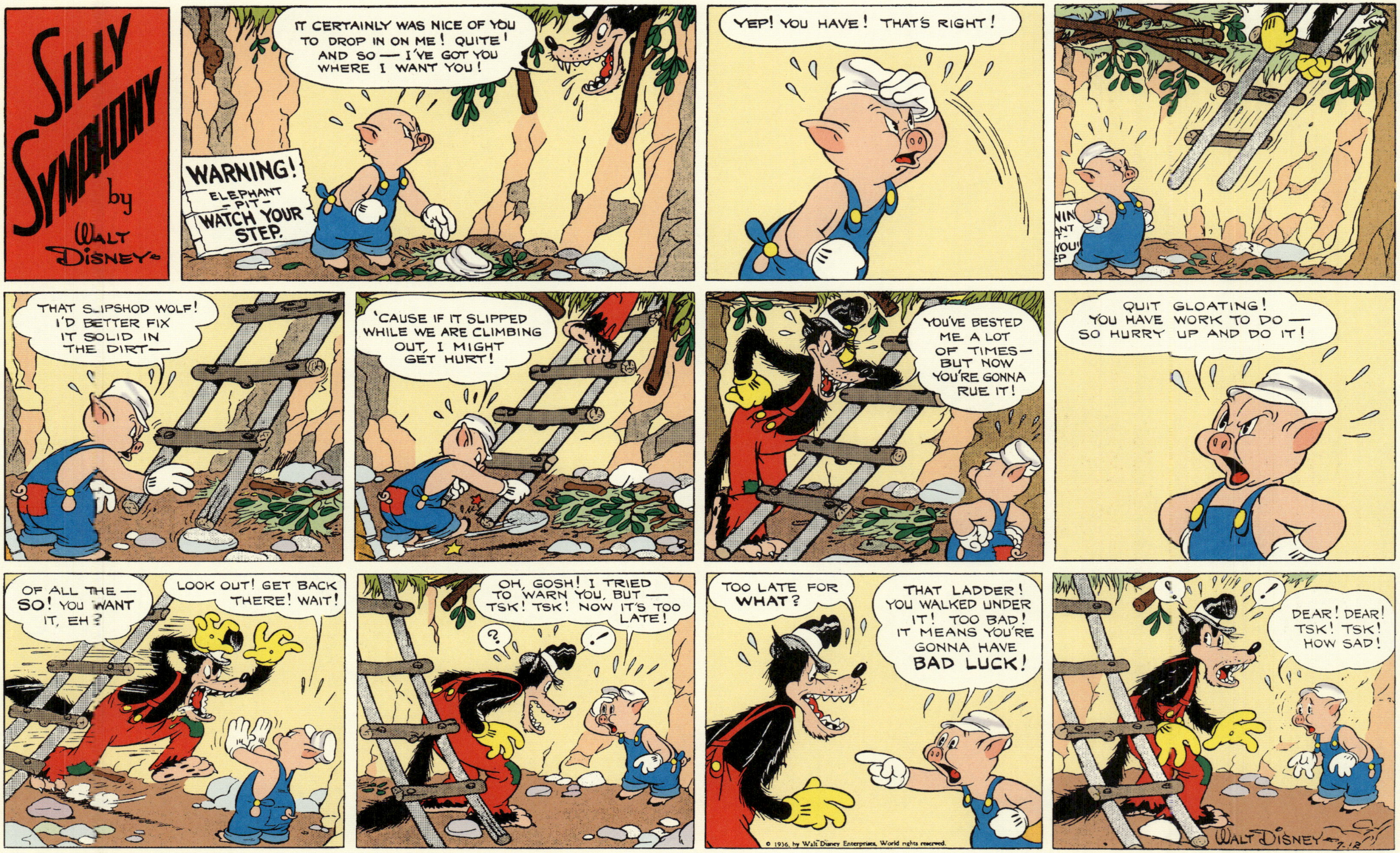
SILLY SYMPHONY
by
WALT DISNEY
IT CERTAINLY WAS NICE OF YOU TO DROP IN ON ME! QUITE! AND SO — I'VE GOT YOU WHERE I WANT YOU!
WARNING! ELEPHANT -PIT- WATCH YOUR STEP.
YEP! YOU HAVE! THAT'S RIGHT!
THAT SLIPSHOD WOLF! I'D BETTER FIX IT SOLID IN THE DIRT—
'CAUSE IF IT SLIPPED WHILE WE ARE CLIMBING OUT, I MIGHT GET HURT!
YOU'VE BESTED ME A LOT OF TIMES— BUT NOW YOU'RE GONNA RUE IT!
QUIT GLOATING! YOU HAVE WORK TO DO — SO HURRY UP AND DO IT!
OF ALL THE — SO! YOU WANT IT, EH?
LOOK OUT! GET BACK THERE! WAIT!
OH, GOSH! I TRIED TO WARN YOU, BUT — TSK! TSK! NOW IT'S TOO LATE!
TOO LATE FOR WHAT?
THAT LADDER! YOU WALKED UNDER IT! TOO BAD! IT MEANS YOU'RE GONNA HAVE BAD LUCK!
DEAR! DEAR! TSK! TSK! HOW SAD!
© 1936, by Walt Disney Enterprises. World rights reserved.
WALT DISNEY 7-12

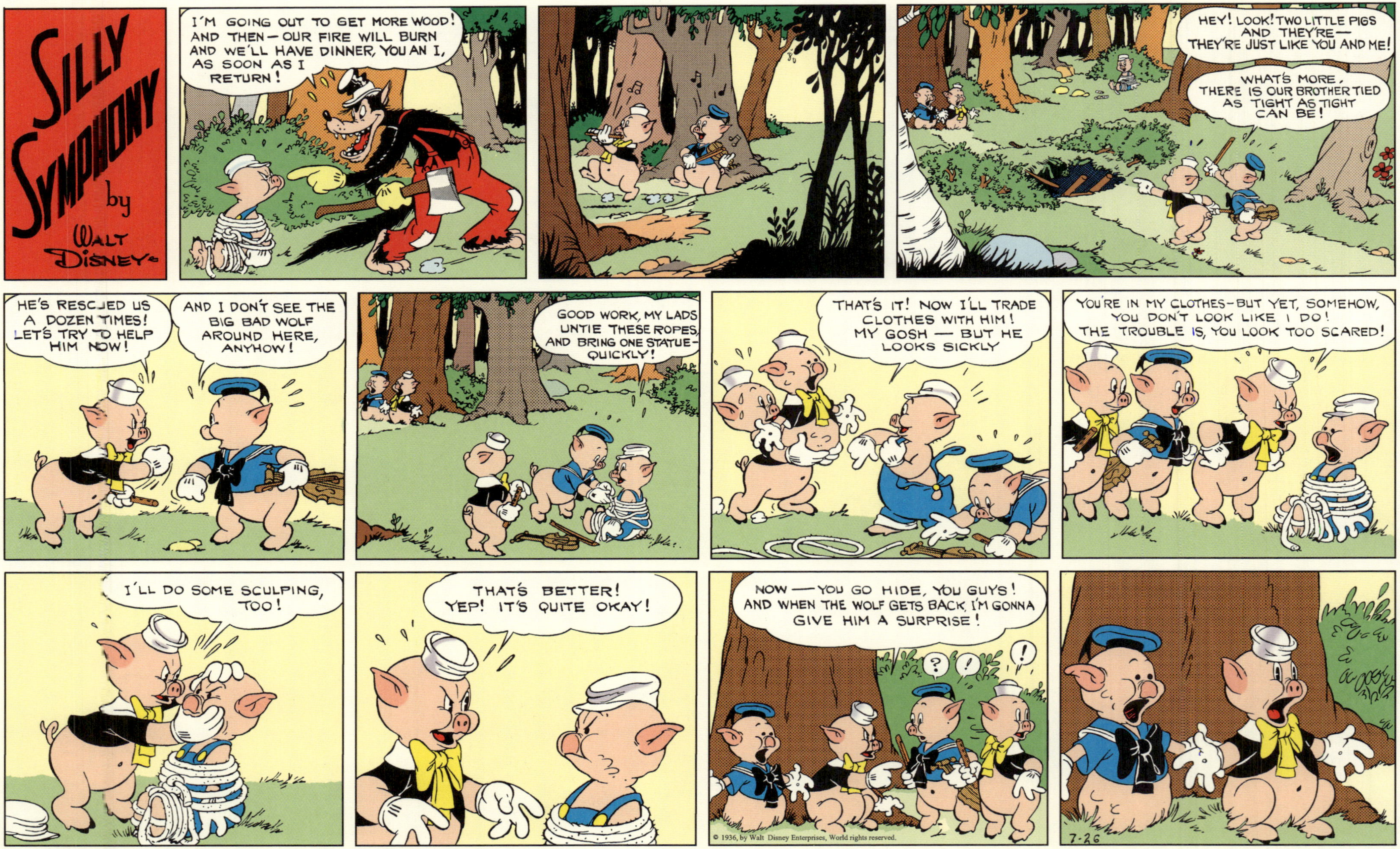
SILLY SYMPHONY by WALT DISNEY
I'M GOING OUT TO GET MORE WOOD! AND THEN — OUR FIRE WILL BURN AND WE'LL HAVE DINNER, YOU AN I, AS SOON AS I RETURN!
HEY! LOOK! TWO LITTLE PIGS AND THEY'RE — THEY'RE JUST LIKE YOU AND ME!
WHAT'S MORE, THERE IS OUR BROTHER TIED AS TIGHT AS TIGHT CAN BE!
HE'S RESCUED US A DOZEN TIMES! LET'S TRY TO HELP HIM NOW!
AND I DON'T SEE THE BIG BAD WOLF AROUND HERE, ANYHOW!
GOOD WORK, MY LADS UNTIE THESE ROPES, AND BRING ONE STATUE — QUICKLY!
THAT'S IT! NOW I'LL TRADE CLOTHES WITH HIM! MY GOSH — BUT HE LOOKS SICKLY
YOU'RE IN MY CLOTHES — BUT YET, SOMEHOW, YOU DON'T LOOK LIKE I DO! THE TROUBLE IS, YOU LOOK TOO SCARED!
I'LL DO SOME SCULPING, TOO!
THAT'S BETTER! YEP! IT'S QUITE OKAY!
NOW — YOU GO HIDE, YOU GUYS! AND WHEN THE WOLF GETS BACK, I'M GONNA GIVE HIM A SURPRISE!
?
!
!
© 1936, by Walt Disney Enterprises, World rights reserved.
7-26

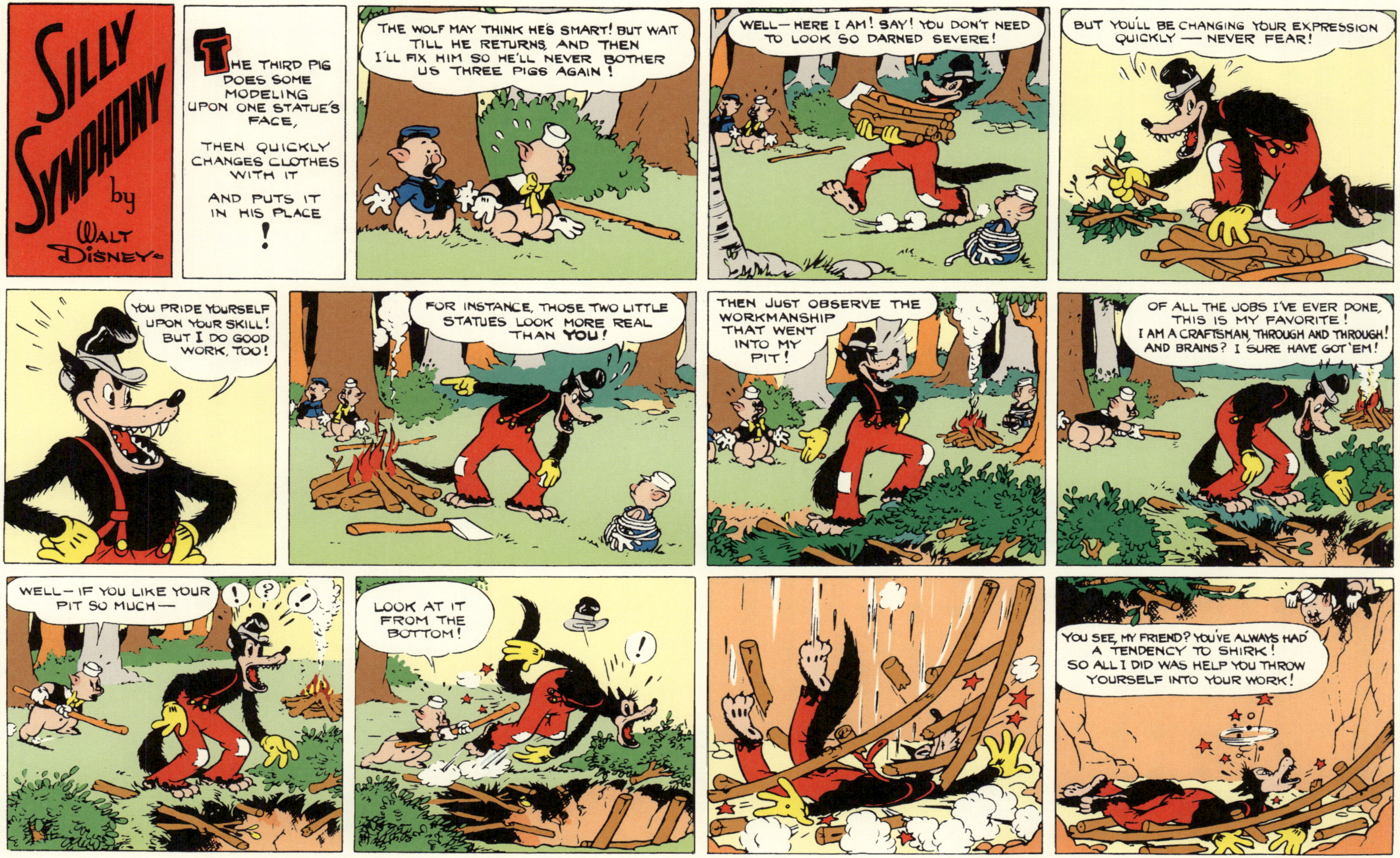
SILLY SYMPHONY by WALT DISNEY
THE THIRD PIG DOES SOME MODELING UPON ONE STATUE'S FACE, THEN QUICKLY CHANGES CLOTHES WITH IT AND PUTS IT IN HIS PLACE !
THE WOLF MAY THINK HE'S SMART! BUT WAIT TILL HE RETURNS, AND THEN I'LL FIX HIM SO HE'LL NEVER BOTHER US THREE PIGS AGAIN !
WELL— HERE I AM! SAY! YOU DON'T NEED TO LOOK SO DARNED SEVERE!
BUT YOU'LL BE CHANGING YOUR EXPRESSION QUICKLY — NEVER FEAR!
YOU PRIDE YOURSELF UPON YOUR SKILL! BUT I DO GOOD WORK, TOO!
FOR INSTANCE, THOSE TWO LITTLE STATUES LOOK MORE REAL THAN **YOU**!
THEN JUST OBSERVE THE WORKMANSHIP THAT WENT INTO MY PIT!
OF ALL THE JOBS I'VE EVER DONE, THIS IS MY FAVORITE! I AM A CRAFTSMAN, THROUGH AND THROUGH! AND BRAINS? I SURE HAVE GOT 'EM!
WELL— IF YOU LIKE YOUR PIT SO MUCH—
! ? !
LOOK AT IT FROM THE BOTTOM!
!
YOU SEE, MY FRIEND? YOU'VE ALWAYS HAD A TENDENCY TO SHIRK! SO ALL I DID WAS HELP YOU THROW YOURSELF INTO YOUR WORK!

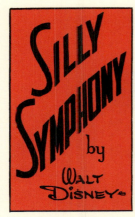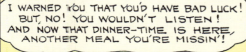

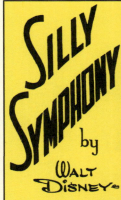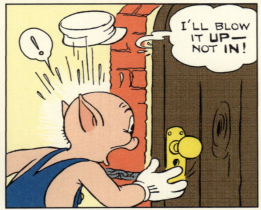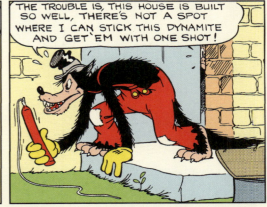

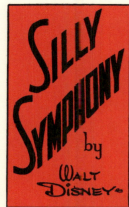

WALT DISNEY'S
SILLY SYMPHONY
'THE BIG BAD WOLF'
SS21-2

MICKEY MOUSE
PRESENTS A
WALT DISNEY
SILLY SYMPHONY
THREE LITTLE WOLVES
CHOICE CUTS OF PIG
PORK CHOPS
BACON
SPARE RIBS
HAM
PIG'S KNUCKLES
LARD
UNITED ARTISTS PICTURE
IN TECHNICOLOR !

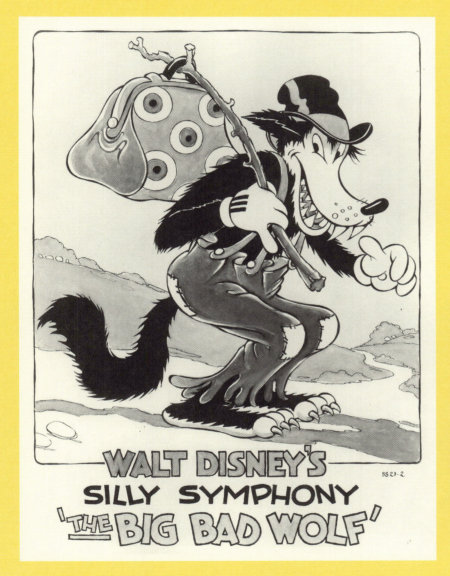

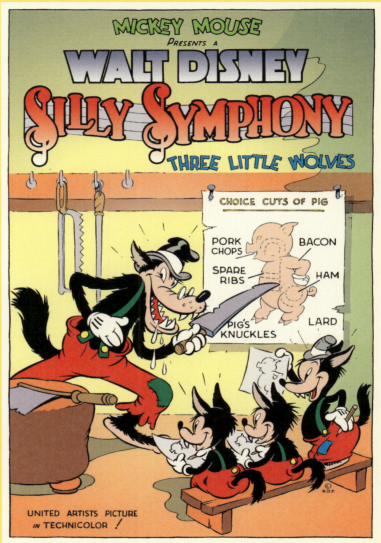

LEFT: Publicity drawing by Tom Wood for *The Big Bad Wolf* (1934), an earlier pigs-and-wolf Silly Symphony from which Ted Osborne and Al Taliaferro borrowed plot elements for the comics. Image courtesy Walt Disney Photo Library.

RIGHT: The original 1936 poster art for *Three Little Wolves*, the cartoon that appeared concurrently with Osborne's and Taliaferro's strips—and from which the pair took most of their inspiration. Image courtesy Walt Disney Archives, color by David Gerstein.

DONALD DUCK

August 30, 1936 - December 5, 1937
Written by Ted Osborne, penciled by Floyd Gottfredson (October 3 and 10, 1937)
and Al Taliaferro (all others), inked by Al Taliaferro

A SIGNIFICANT SLICE OF DISNEY HISTORY is captured in these pages. The fifteen months of this run marked a critical phase in Donald Duck's rise to superstardom. Originally a one-shot performer, then a regular in Mickey Mouse's circle of friends, Donald had always been seen as a supporting character, his irritable nature a refreshingly comic change of pace. But one can't keep an angry duck down, and the more disagreeable Donald became, the more audiences wanted to see him in the spotlight. Early in the autumn of 1936, as this comic continuity was getting underway, the studio released *Donald and Pluto*—a short in which, as the title implied, Donald shared top billing with Pluto the pup, and Mickey Mouse was never seen at all. Clearly the Duck was being groomed for top stardom and the Sunday comics would play a key role in his campaign.

Seen through this historical lens, the Duck series becomes doubly fascinating. The attentive Disney fan will notice that Donald's graphic design, both on the screen and in the comics, had undergone a marked change since his introduction in 1934. By August 1936 his evolution was still not quite complete, and as the strips continue one can observe subtle changes in his appearance. In other ways, too, the comics reflect the movies. In one September 1936 strip Donald is chased by an angry bull, one who unmistakably resembles the same bull that had menaced Mickey and Minnie on the screen in *Mickey's Rival*. In the 1935 short *On Ice* Donald had been seen singing "Hi-Le, Hi-Lo," a traditional novelty waltz; in the latter months of 1936 the comic strip makes a concerted attempt to turn this into a theme song for him. And other movie references crop up throughout the run of this series. As late as the closing weeks of the continuity in 1937, we can see the little burro who had appeared earlier in the year in *Don Donald*, a key early starring vehicle for the Duck.

Equally interesting is Donald's character development. In the early months, building on his irascible nature, Osborne and Taliaferro present a Duck who is not only misanthropic but downright sociopathic. Later he begins to curb his temperament. In the summer of 1937 there's even a fascinating subseries in which Donald tries to reform, restraining his violent impulses and attempting good deeds. Of course this effort doesn't last long, but while it does, readers are treated to a glimpse of his psychology. This in turn leads the strip in new and unpredictable directions—including a minor feud between Donald and Clarabelle Cow, an unlikely development that never occurs in the movies.

For many Disney enthusiasts, the big news in this Sunday series is the introduction of Donald's nephews, Huey, Dewey, and Louie, in October 1937. The three little hellions made such a hit with newspaper readers that they were introduced into the animated cartoons as well. Their first screen vehicle, *Donald's Nephews* (1938), was a loose adaptation of the October-November 1937 comic pages, and a new trio of Disney stars was born.

—J.B. KAUFMAN

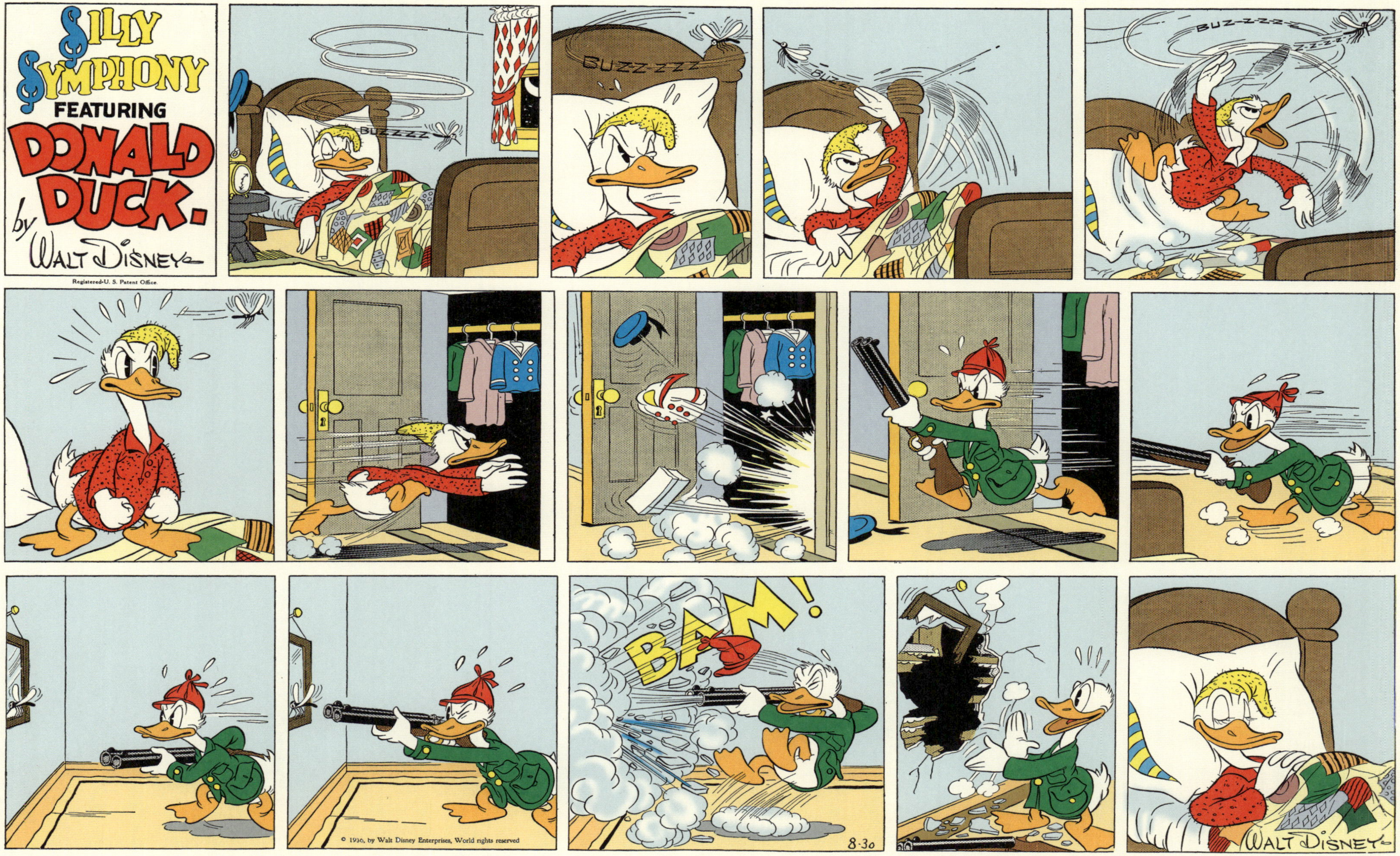
SILLY SYMPHONY
FEATURING
DONALD DUCK
by
WALT DISNEY
Registered-U. S. Patent Office
BUZZZZZ
BUZZ-ZZZZ
BUZZ
BUZ-ZZZZ
Z-Z-Z
BAM!
© 1936, by Walt Disney Enterprises, World rights reserved
8-30
WALT DISNEY

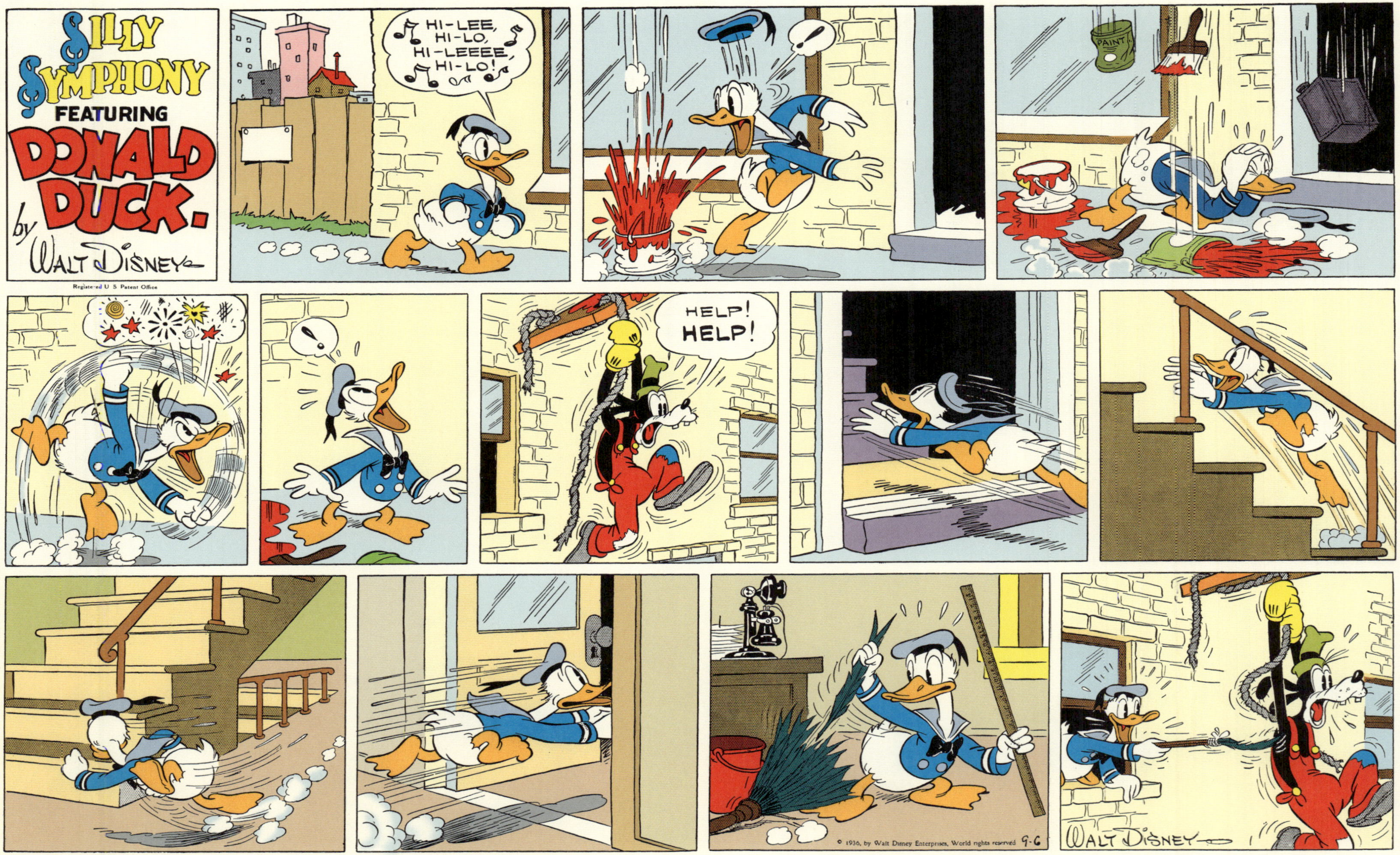
SILLY SYMPHONY
FEATURING
DONALD DUCK.
by WALT DISNEY
Registered U S Patent Office
HI-LEE, HI-LO, HI-LEEEE, HI-LO!
!
PAINT
!
HELP! HELP!
© 1936, by Walt Disney Enterprises, World rights reserved 9-6
WALT DISNEY

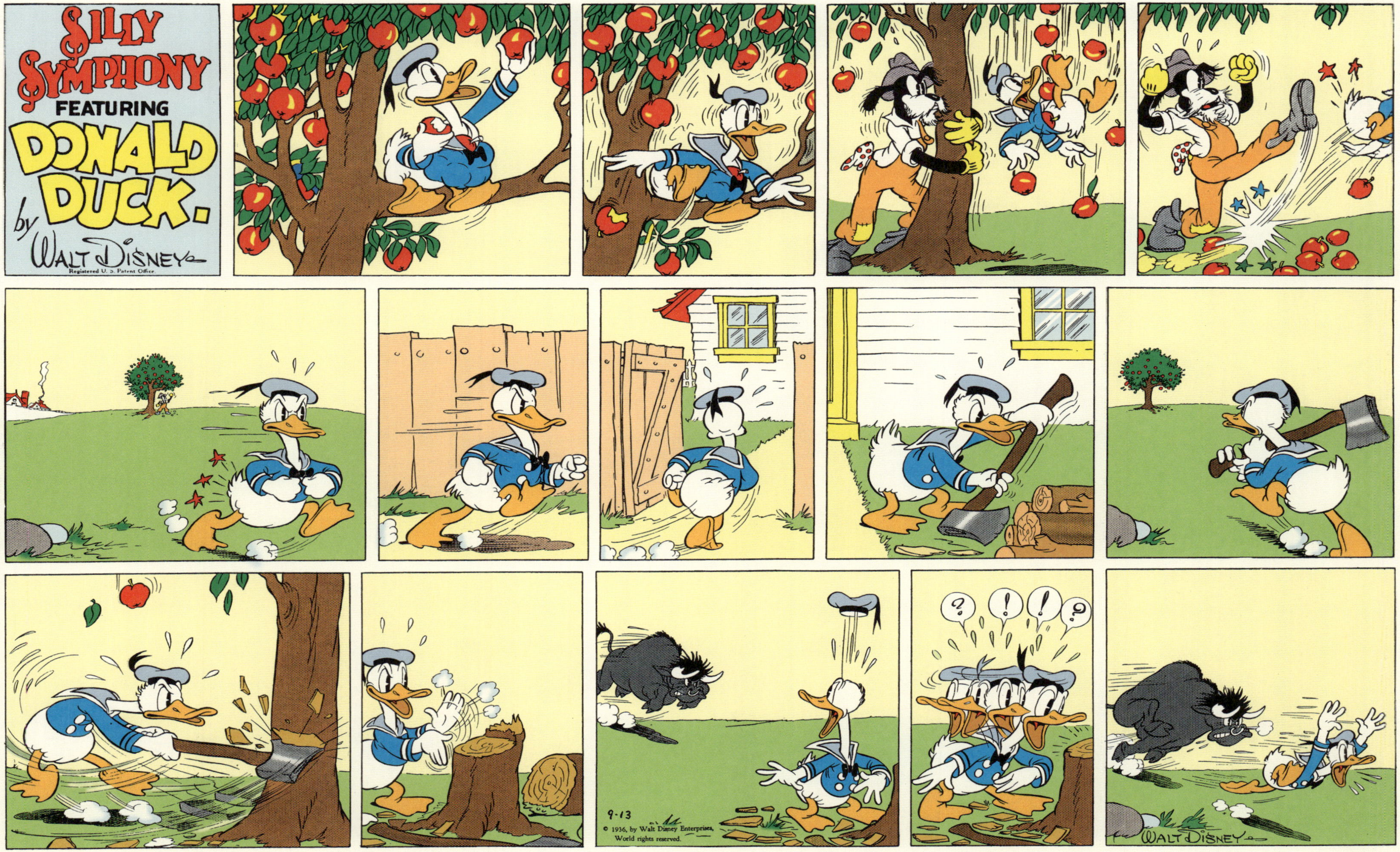
SILLY SYMPHONY
FEATURING
DONALD DUCK.
by WALT DISNEY
Registered U. S. Patent Office.
?
!
!
?
9-13
© 1936, by Walt Disney Enterprises, World rights reserved.
WALT DISNEY

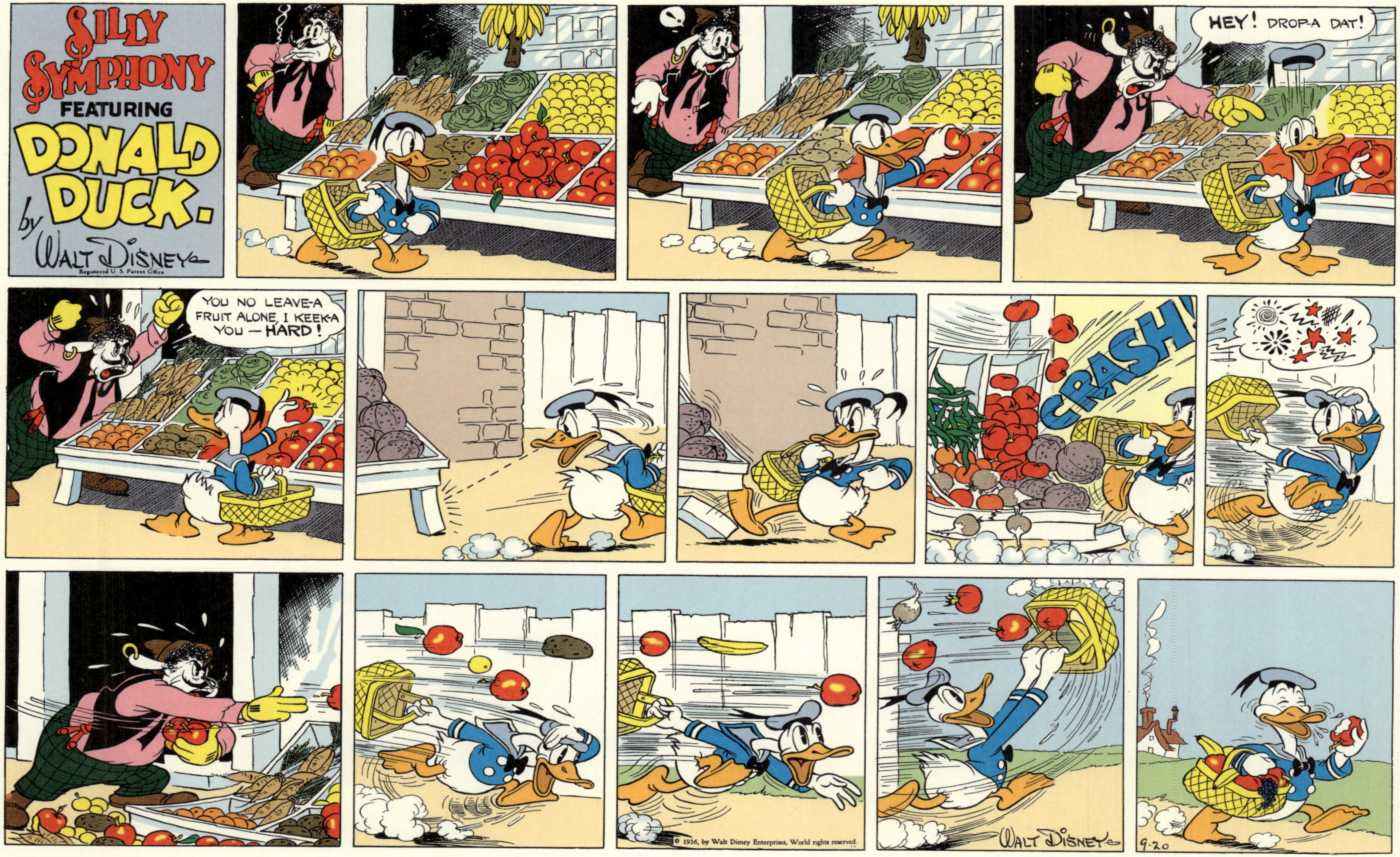
SILLY SYMPHONY
FEATURING
DONALD DUCK.
by
WALT DISNEY
Registered U.S. Patent Office
HEY! DROP-A DAT!
YOU NO LEAVE-A FRUIT ALONE, I KEEK-A YOU — HARD!
CRASH!
© 1936, by Walt Disney Enterprises. World rights reserved.
WALT DISNEY
9-20

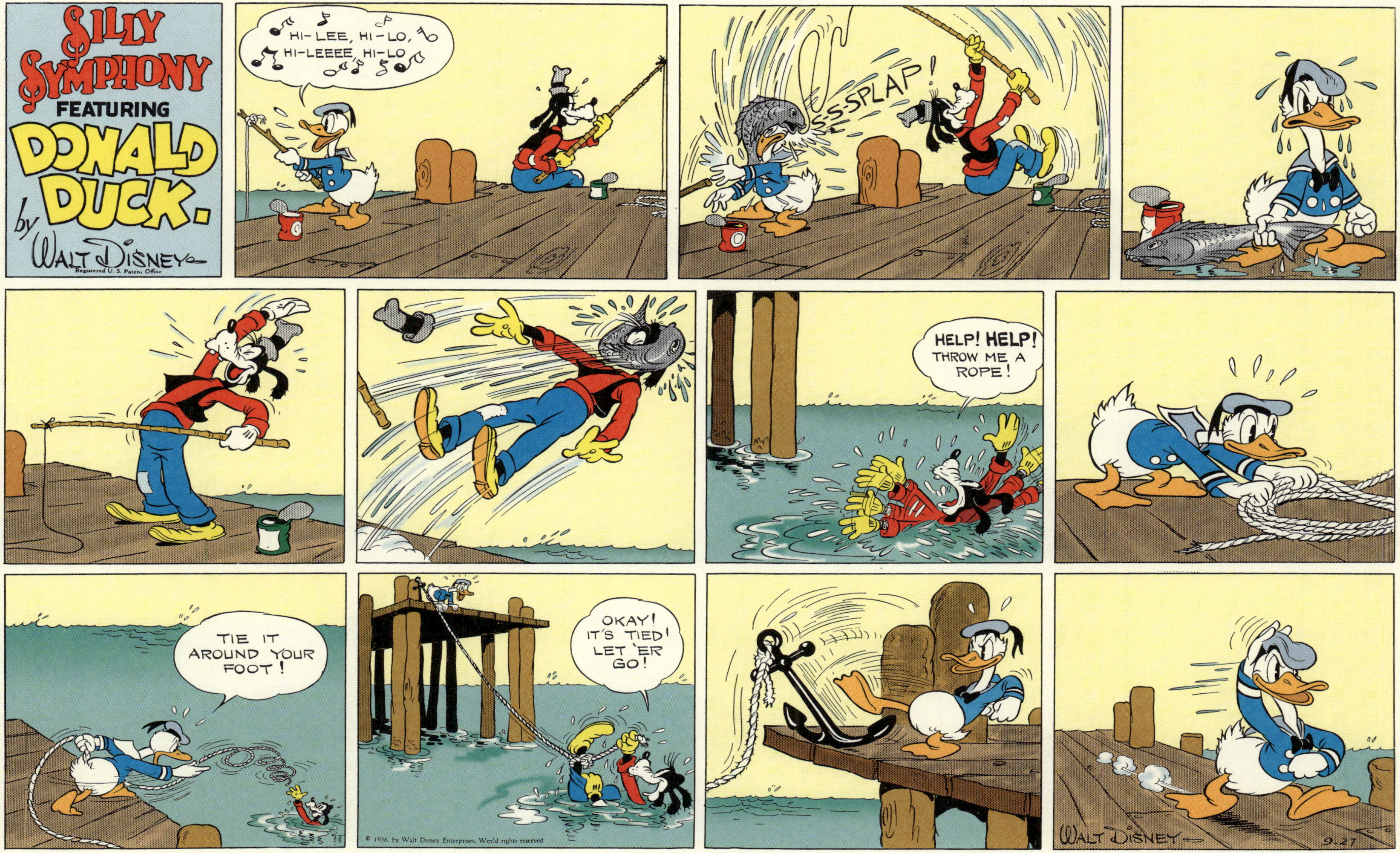
SILLY SYMPHONY
FEATURING
DONALD DUCK.
by WALT DISNEY
Registered U. S. Patent Office
HI-LEE, HI-LO,
HI-LEEEE, HI-LO
S-S-SPLAP!
HELP! HELP! THROW ME A ROPE!
TIE IT AROUND YOUR FOOT!
OKAY! IT'S TIED! LET 'ER GO!
© 1936, by Walt Disney Enterprises. World rights reserved
WALT DISNEY
9-27

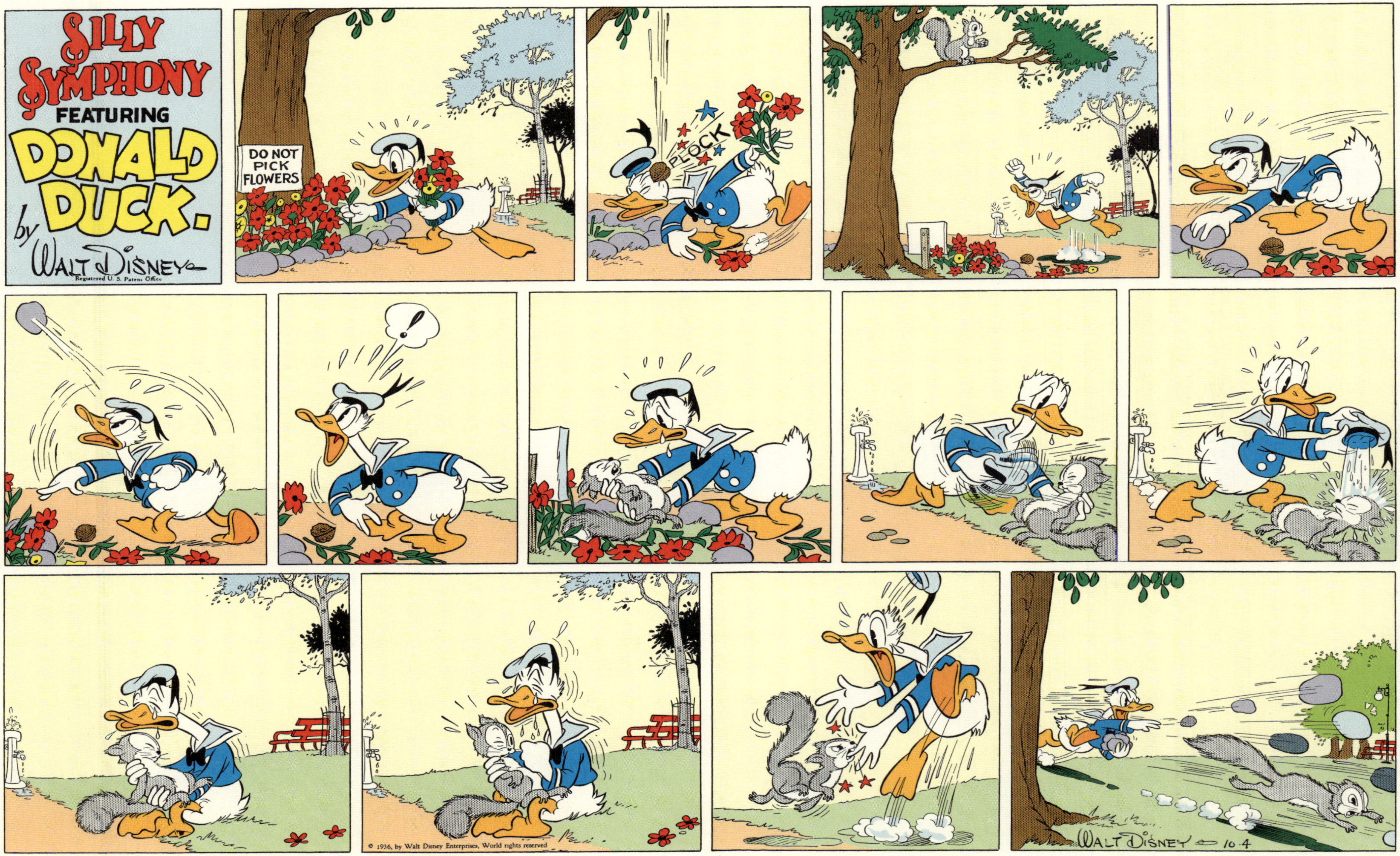

SILLY SYMPHONY
FEATURING
DONALD DUCK.
by WALT DISNEY
Registered U. S. Patent Office
DO NOT PICK FLOWERS
PLOCK
!
© 1936, by Walt Disney Enterprises, World rights reserved
WALT DISNEY 10-4

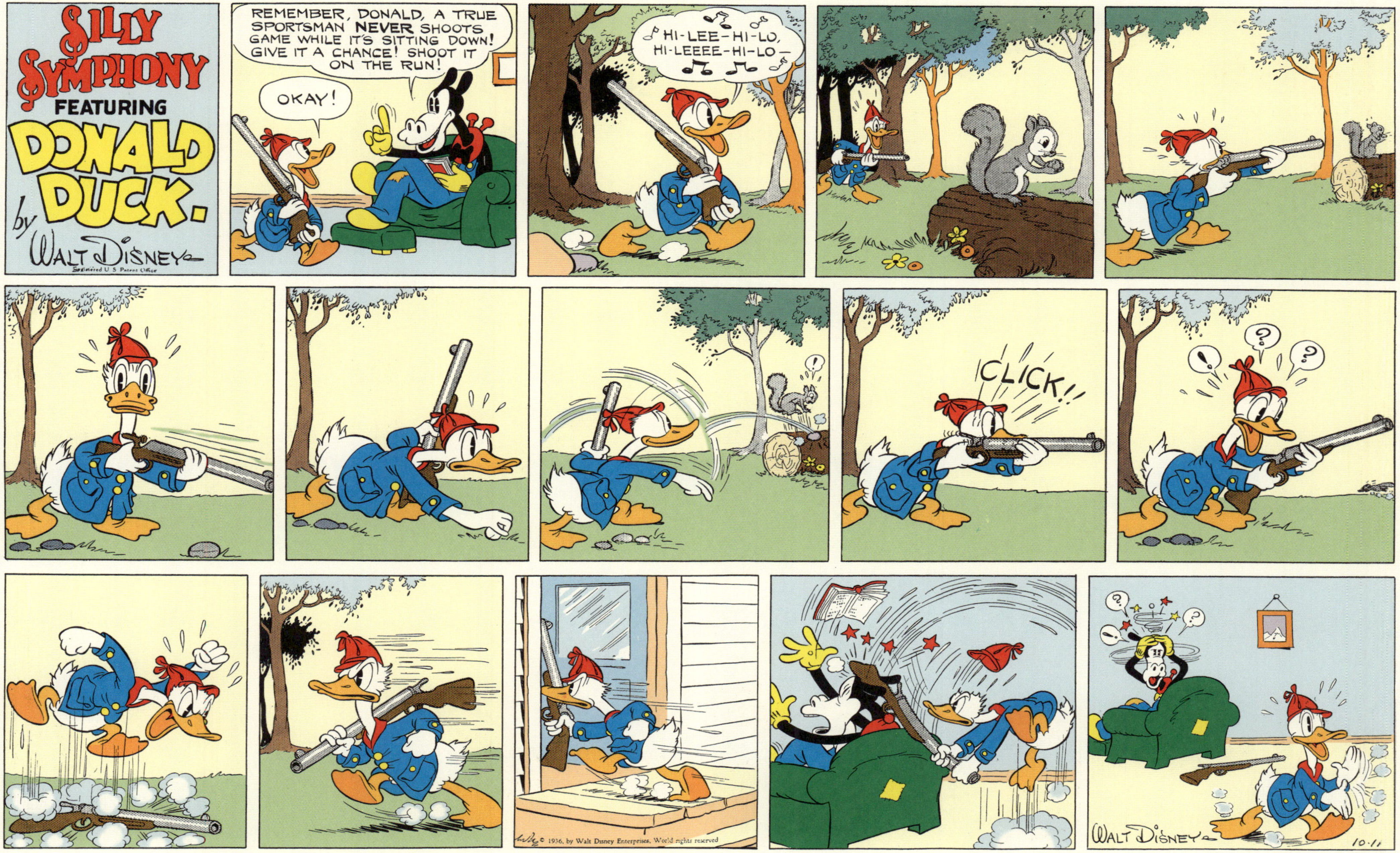
SILLY SYMPHONY
FEATURING
DONALD DUCK
by WALT DISNEY
Registered U S Patent Office
REMEMBER, DONALD, A TRUE SPORTSMAN NEVER SHOOTS GAME WHILE IT'S SITTING DOWN! GIVE IT A CHANCE! SHOOT IT ON THE RUN!
OKAY!
HI-LEE-HI-LO, HI-LEEEE-HI-LO —
!
CLICK!!
! ? ?
? ?
© 1936, by Walt Disney Enterprises. World rights reserved
WALT DISNEY
10-11

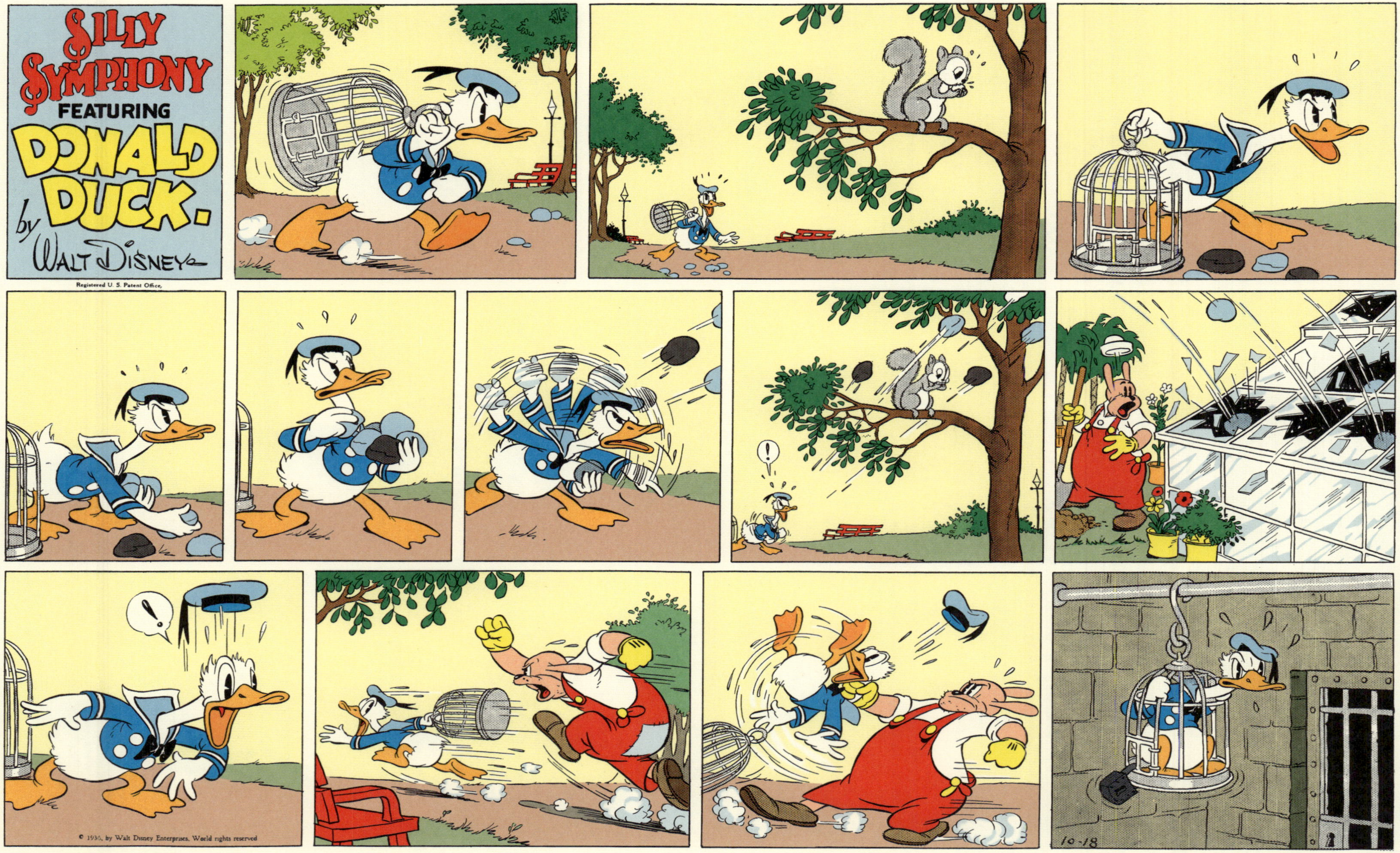
SILLY SYMPHONY
FEATURING
DONALD DUCK.
by WALT DISNEY
Registered U. S. Patent Office.
!
!
© 1936, by Walt Disney Enterprises. World rights reserved
10-18

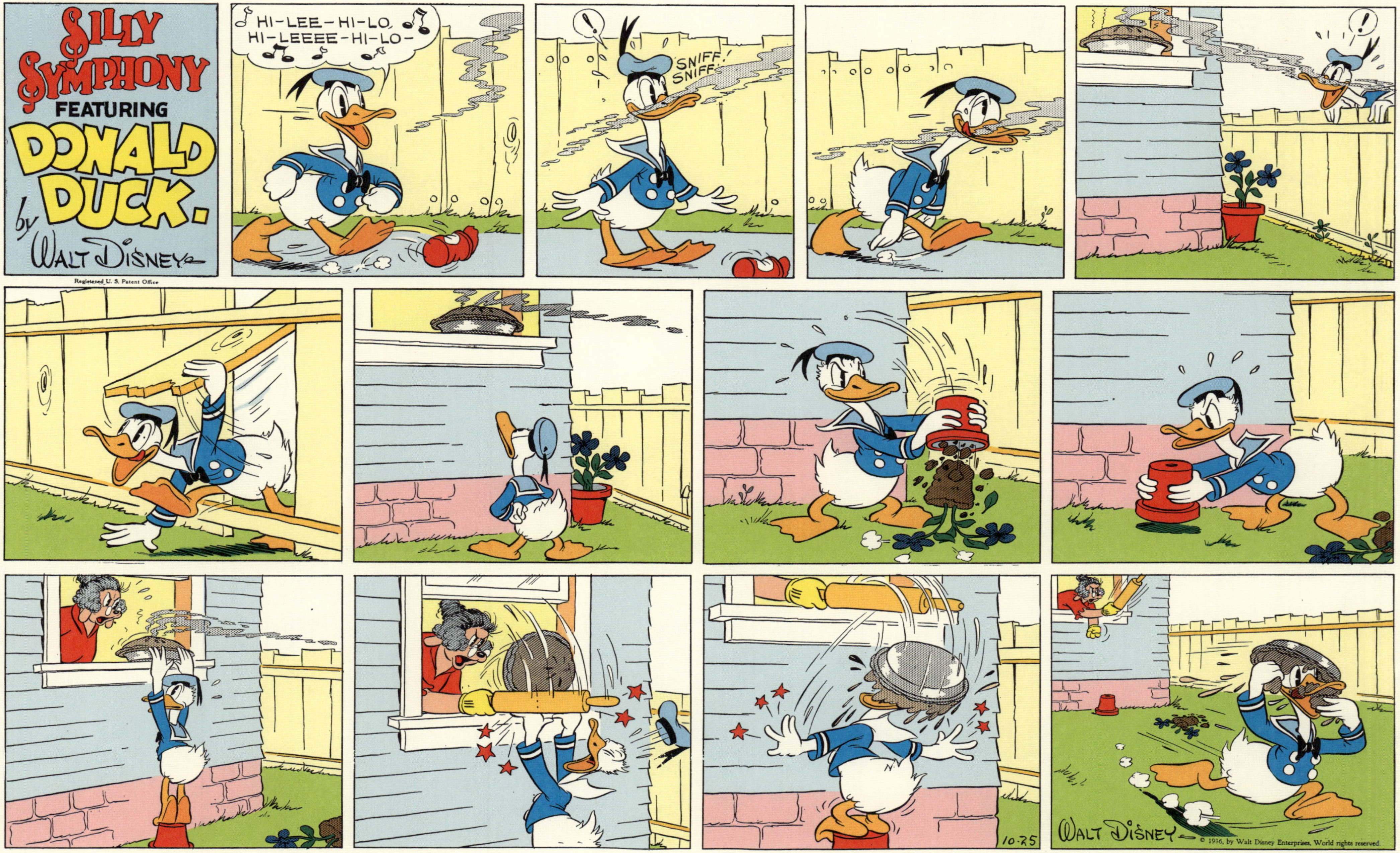

SILLY SYMPHONY
FEATURING
DONALD DUCK.
by WALT DISNEY
Registered U. S. Patent Office
HI-LEE-HI-LO
HI-LEEEE-HI-LO-
!
SNIFF! SNIFF!
!
10-25
WALT DISNEY
© 1936, by Walt Disney Enterprises. World rights reserved.

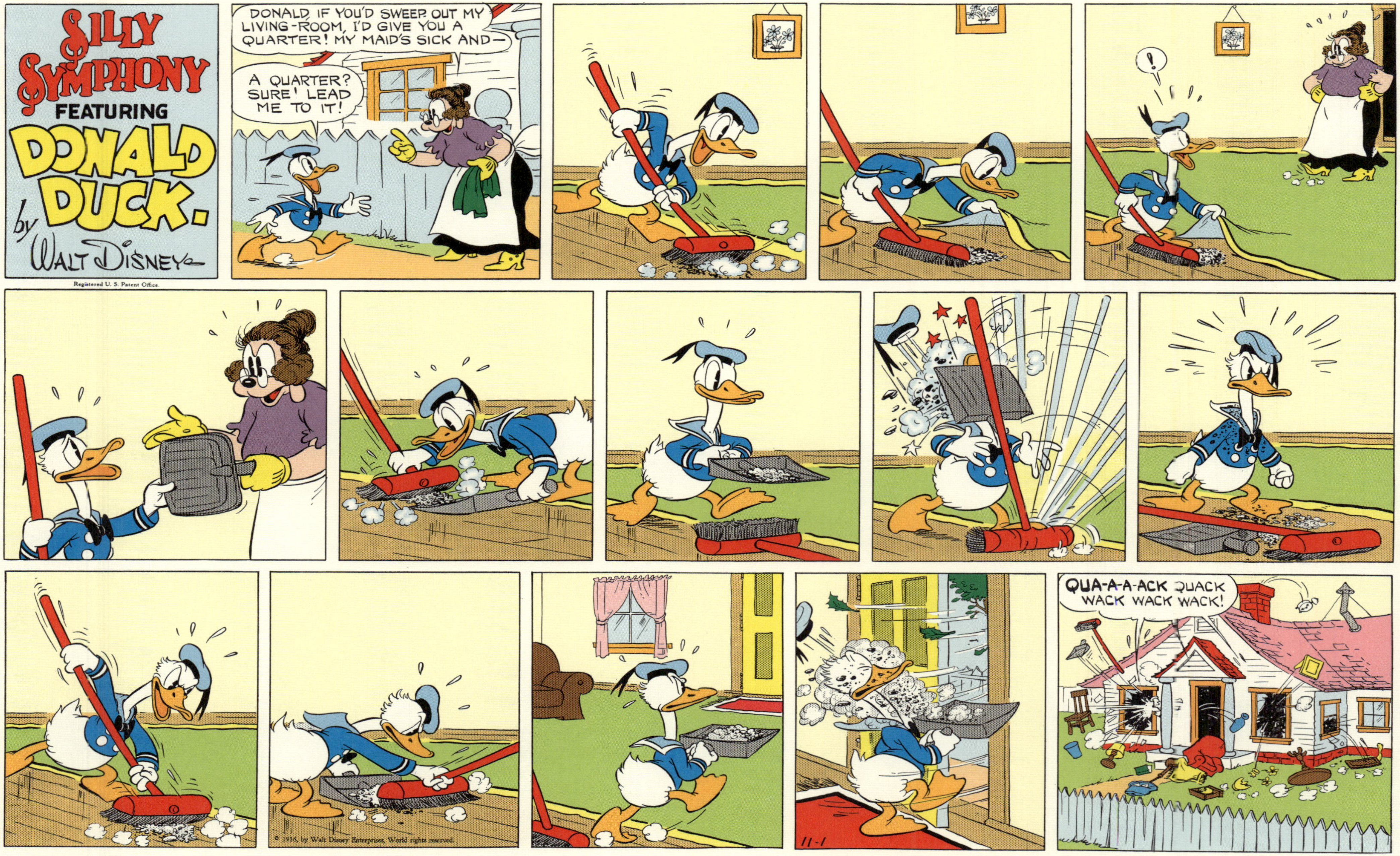
SILLY SYMPHONY
FEATURING
DONALD DUCK.
by WALT DISNEY
Registered U. S. Patent Office.
DONALD, IF YOU'D SWEEP OUT MY LIVING-ROOM, I'D GIVE YOU A QUARTER! MY MAID'S SICK AND—
A QUARTER? SURE! LEAD ME TO IT!
!
© 1936, by Walt Disney Enterprises, World rights reserved.
11-1
QUA-A-A-ACK QUACK WACK WACK WACK!

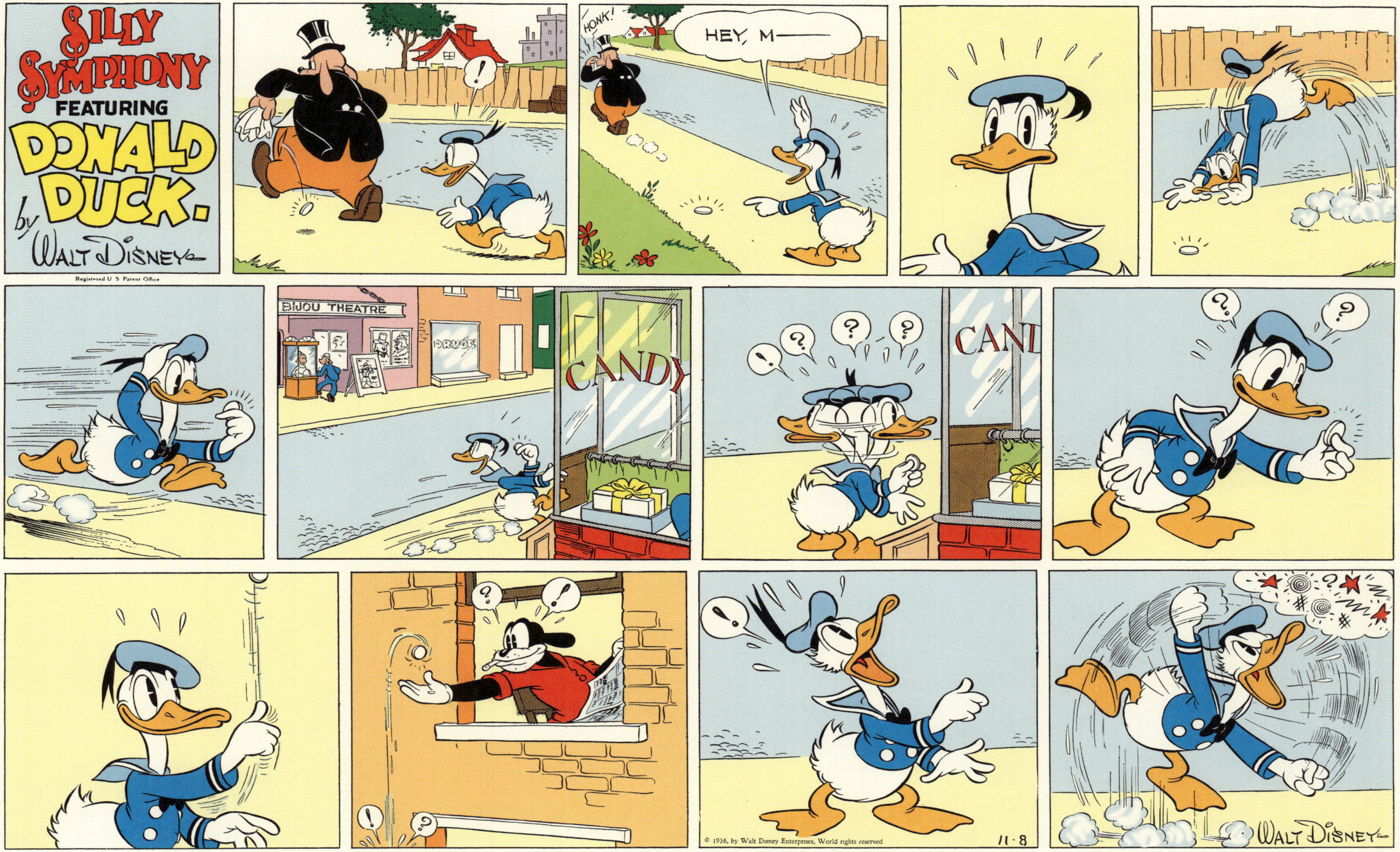
SILLY SYMPHONY
FEATURING
DONALD DUCK.
by WALT DISNEY
Registered U. S. Patent Office
HONK!
HEY, M——
BIJOU THEATRE
DRUGS
CANDY
CAND
© 1936, by Walt Disney Enterprises, World rights reserved
11·8
WALT DISNEY

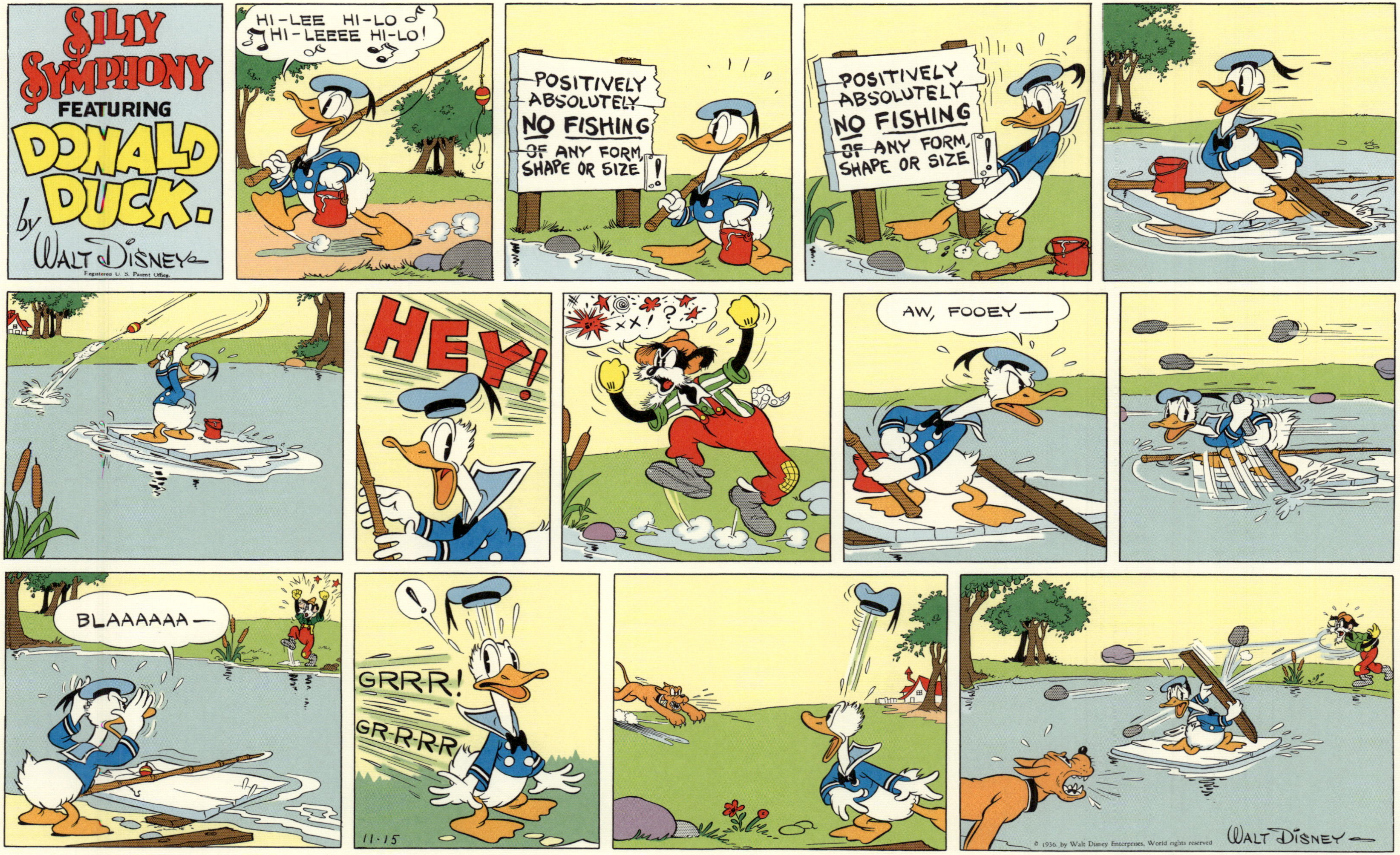

SILLY SYMPHONY
FEATURING
DONALD DUCK.
by WALT DISNEY
Registered U. S. Patent Office.
HI-LEE HI-LO HI-LEEEE HI-LO!
POSITIVELY ABSOLUTELY NO FISHING OF ANY FORM, SHAPE OR SIZE!
POSITIVELY ABSOLUTELY NO FISHING OF ANY FORM, SHAPE OR SIZE!
HEY!
AW, FOOEY—
BLAAAAAA—
!
GRR-R!
GR-R-R-R
11-15
© 1936, by Walt Disney Enterprises. World rights reserved
WALT DISNEY

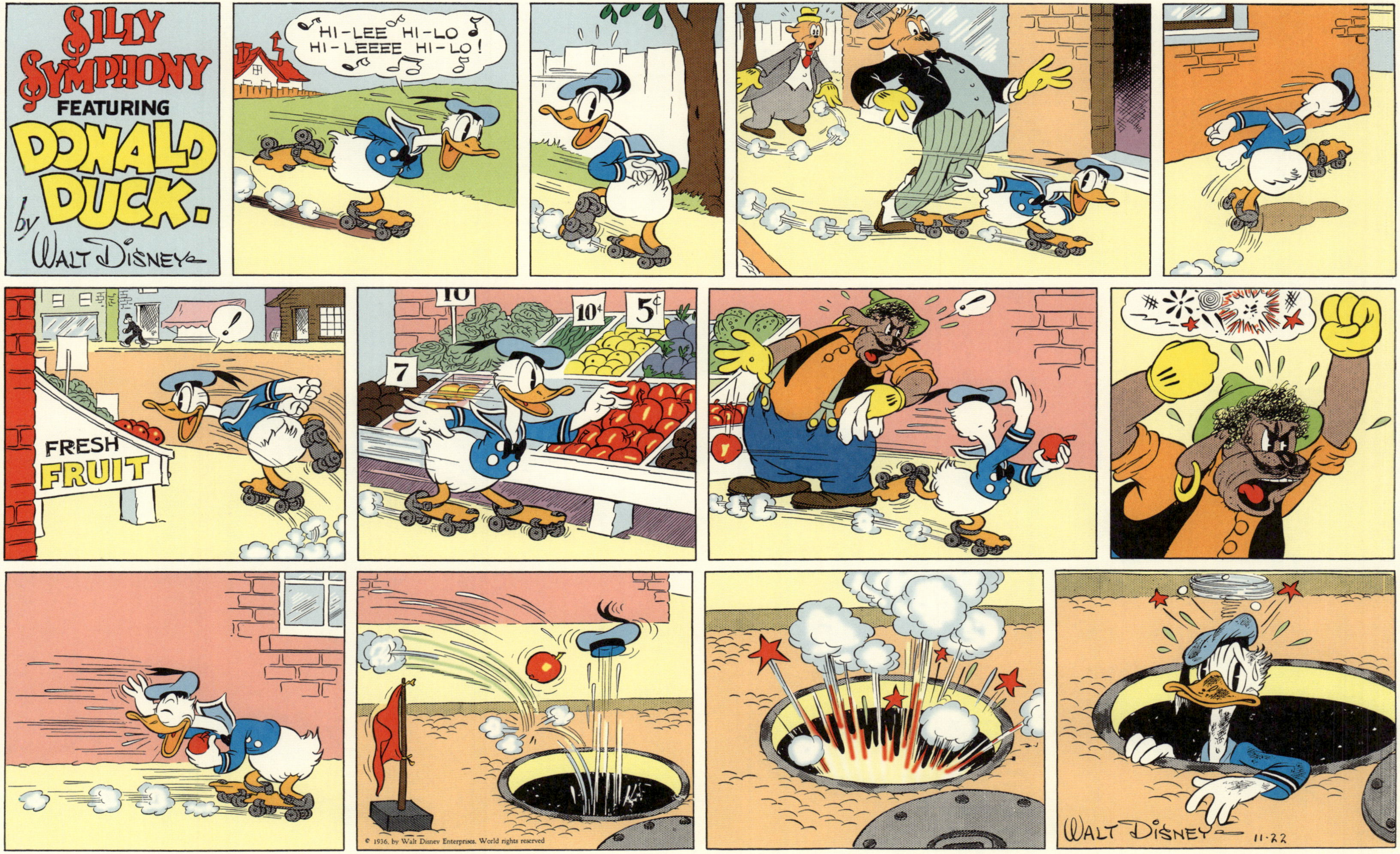
SILLY SYMPHONY
FEATURING
DONALD DUCK.
by WALT DISNEY
HI-LEE HI-LO
HI-LEEEE HI-LO!
!
10
10¢
5¢
7
FRESH
FRUIT
!
© 1936, by Walt Disney Enterprises. World rights reserved
WALT DISNEY 11-22

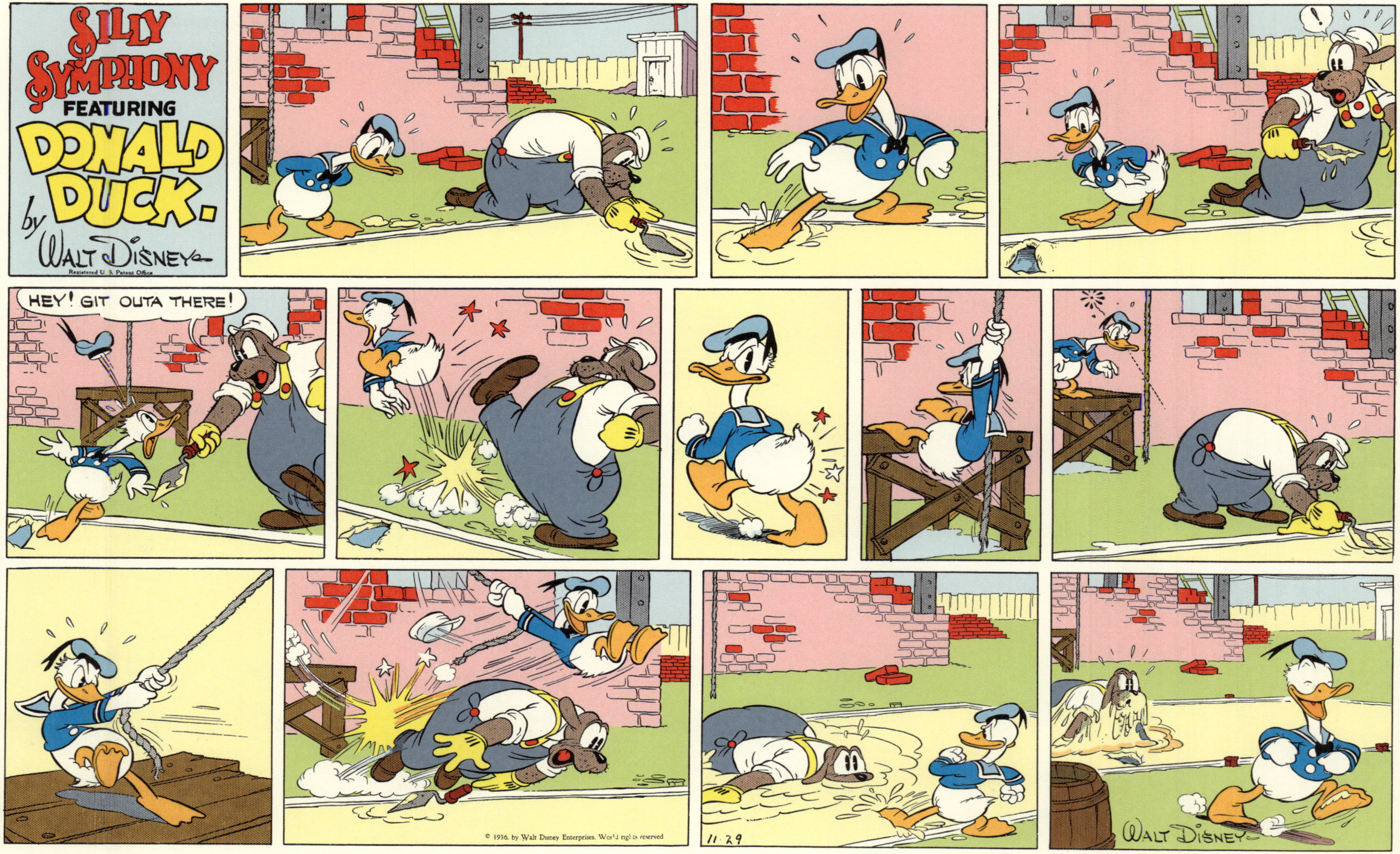

SILLY SYMPHONY
FEATURING
DONALD DUCK.
by WALT DISNEY
Registered U.S. Patent Office
HEY! GIT OUTA THERE!
© 1936, by Walt Disney Enterprises. World rights reserved
11-29
WALT DISNEY

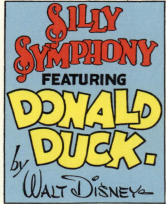

89 • December 6, 1936

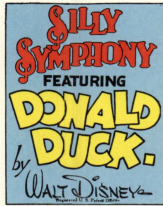

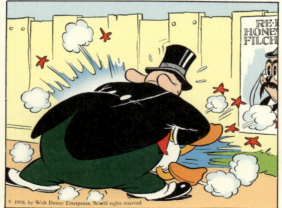

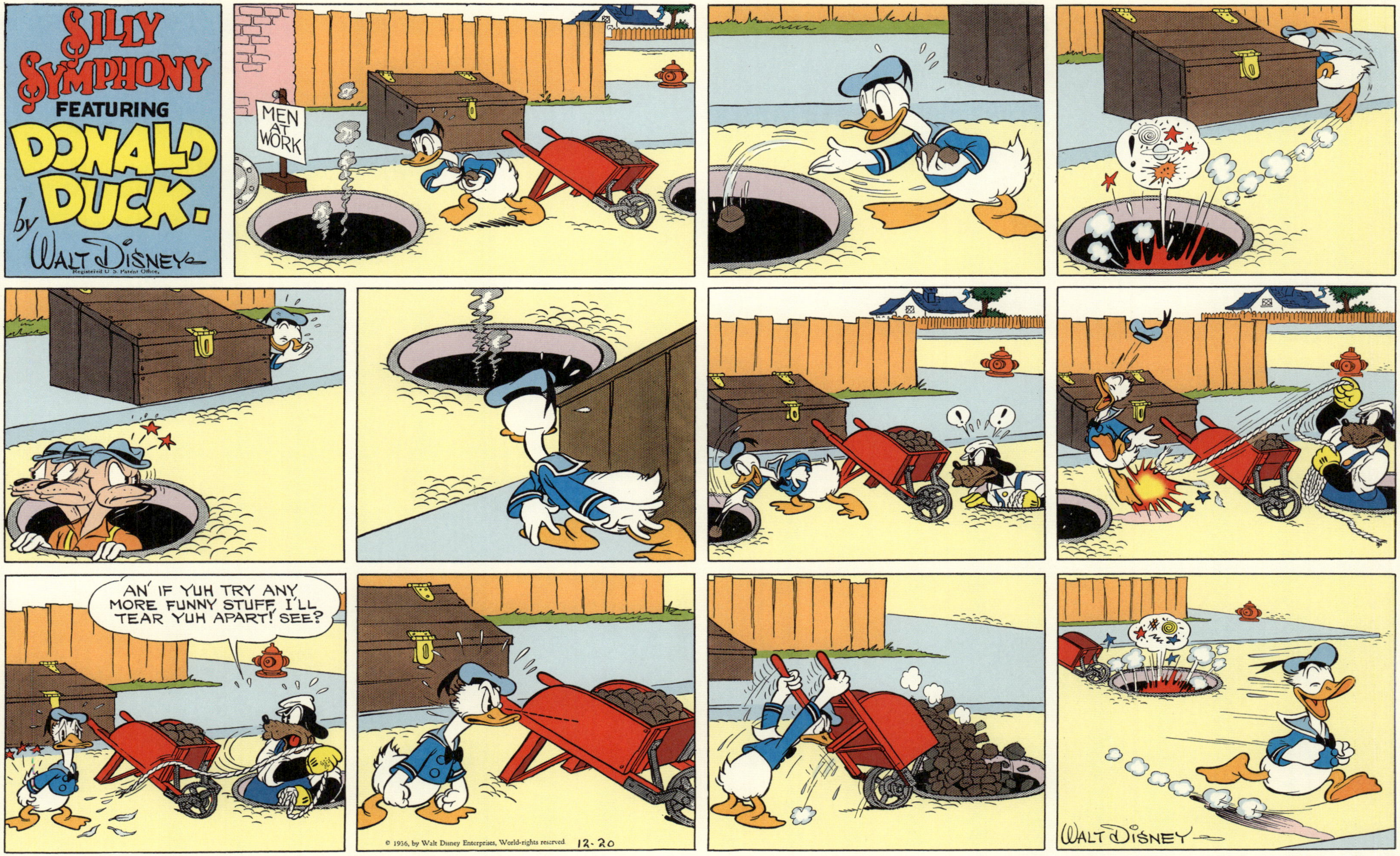
SILLY SYMPHONY
FEATURING
DONALD DUCK.
by WALT DISNEY
Registered U. S. Patent Office.
MEN AT WORK
!
! !
AN' IF YUH TRY ANY MORE FUNNY STUFF, I'LL TEAR YUH APART! SEE?
© 1936, by Walt Disney Enterprises, World-rights reserved 12-20
WALT DISNEY

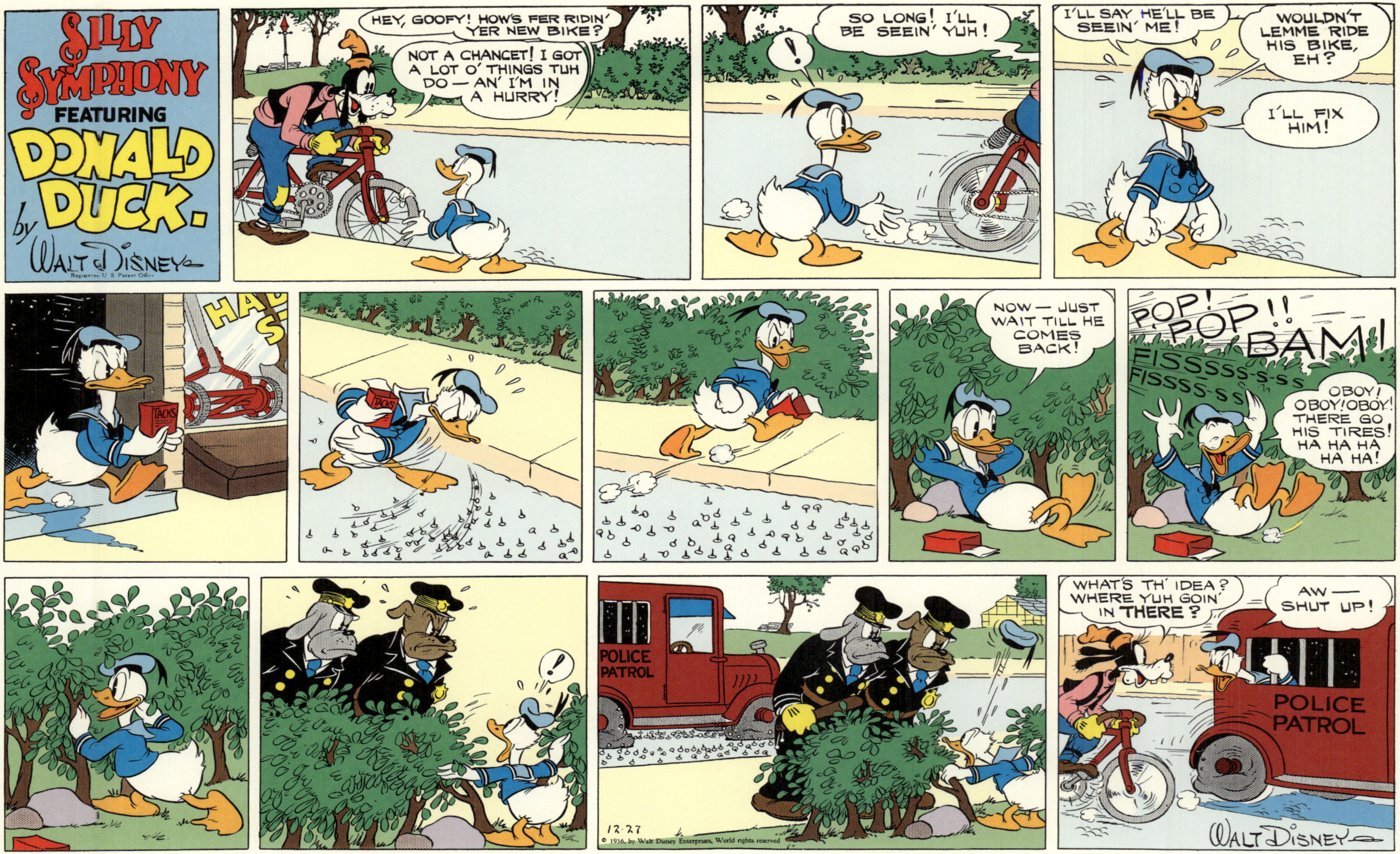

SILLY SYMPHONY
FEATURING
DONALD DUCK.
by WALT DISNEY
Registered U S Patent Office
HEY, GOOFY! HOW'S FER RIDIN' YER NEW BIKE?
NOT A CHANCET! I GOT A LOT O' THINGS TUH DO — AN' I'M IN A HURRY!
SO LONG! I'LL BE SEEIN' YUH!
!
I'LL SAY HE'LL BE SEEIN' ME!
WOULDN'T LEMME RIDE HIS BIKE, EH?
I'LL FIX HIM!
TACKS
TACKS
NOW — JUST WAIT TILL HE COMES BACK!
POP! POP!! BAM!
FISSSSS-S-SS
FISSSS-SS
OBOY! OBOY! OBOY! THERE GO HIS TIRES! HA HA HA HA HA!
!
POLICE PATROL
12-27
© 1936, by Walt Disney Enterprises, World rights reserved
WHAT'S TH' IDEA? WHERE YUH GOIN' IN THERE?
AW — SHUT UP!
POLICE PATROL
WALT DISNEY

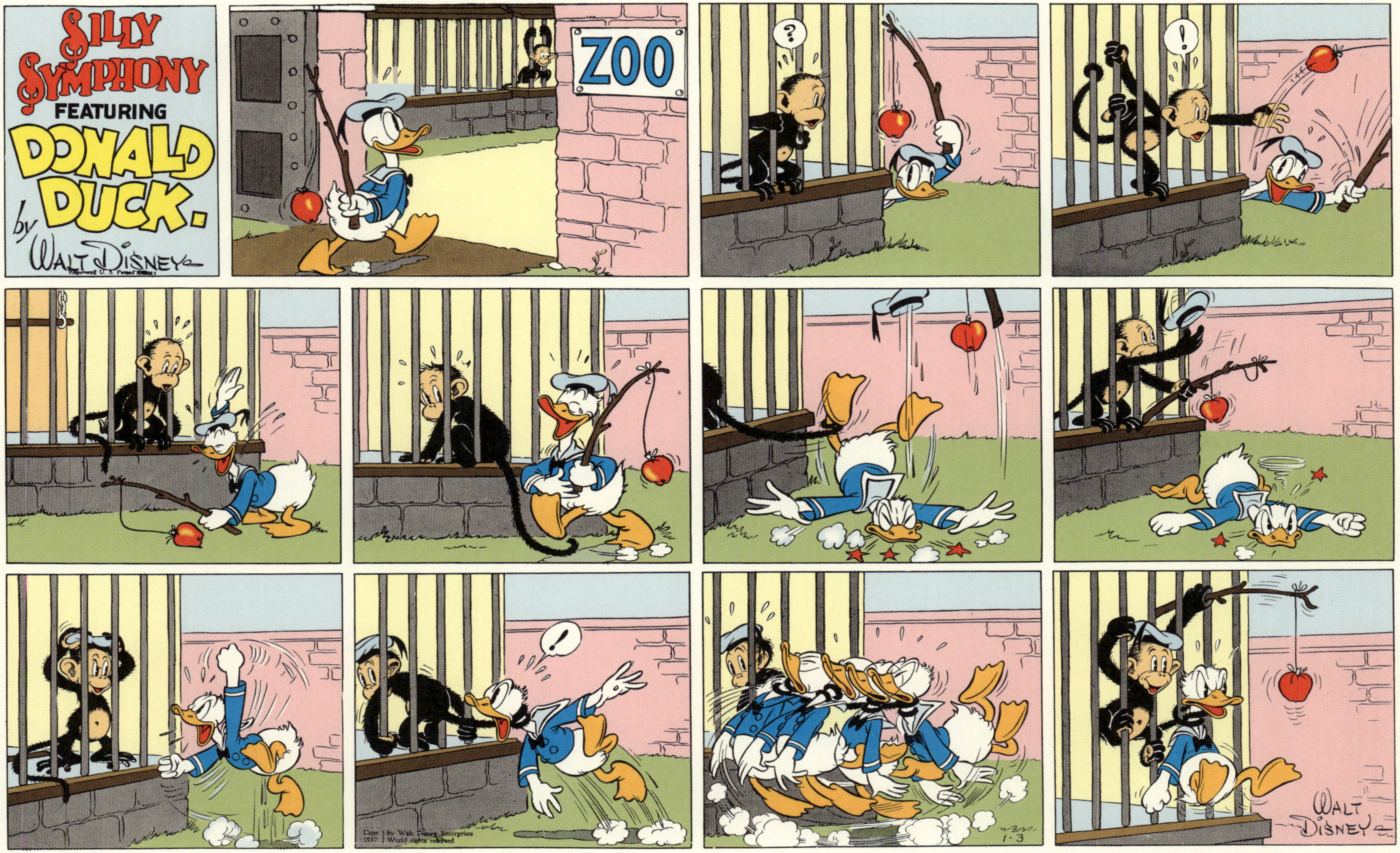
SILLY SYMPHONY
FEATURING
DONALD DUCK.
by WALT DISNEY
ZOO
?
!
!
Copr. 1937 by Walt Disney Enterprises World rights reserved
1-3
WALT DISNEY

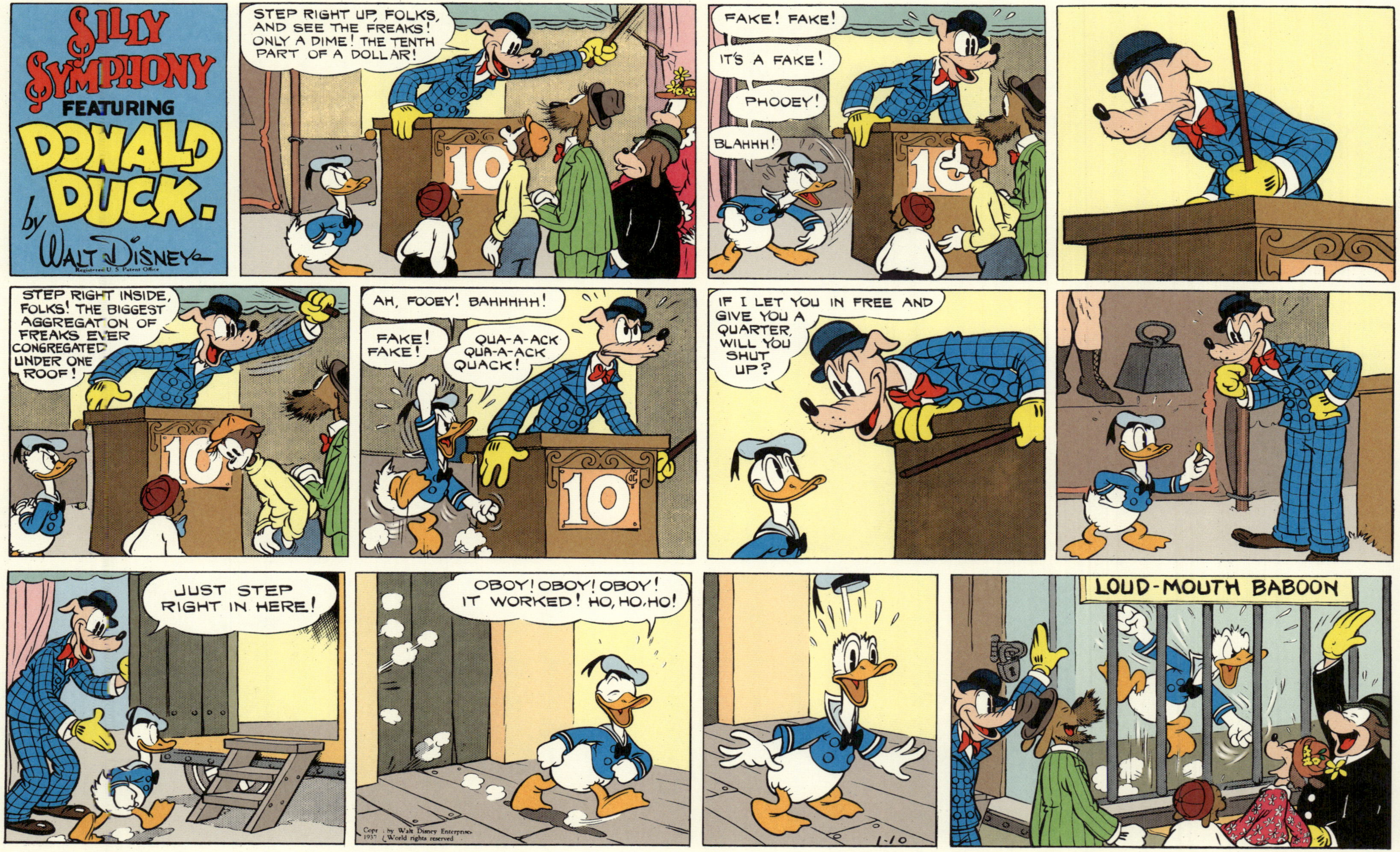
SILLY SYMPHONY
FEATURING
DONALD DUCK.
by WALT DISNEY
Registered U.S. Patent Office
STEP RIGHT UP, FOLKS, AND SEE THE FREAKS! ONLY A DIME! THE TENTH PART OF A DOLLAR!
10
FAKE! FAKE!
IT'S A FAKE!
PHOOEY!
BLAHHH!
STEP RIGHT INSIDE, FOLKS! THE BIGGEST AGGREGATION OF FREAKS EVER CONGREGATED UNDER ONE ROOF!
AH, FOOEY! BAHHHHH!
FAKE! FAKE!
QUA-A-ACK QUA-A-ACK QUACK!
IF I LET YOU IN FREE AND GIVE YOU A QUARTER, WILL YOU SHUT UP?
JUST STEP RIGHT IN HERE!
OBOY! OBOY! OBOY! IT WORKED! HO, HO, HO!
Copr. by Walt Disney Enterprises 1937 World rights reserved
1-10
LOUD-MOUTH BABOON

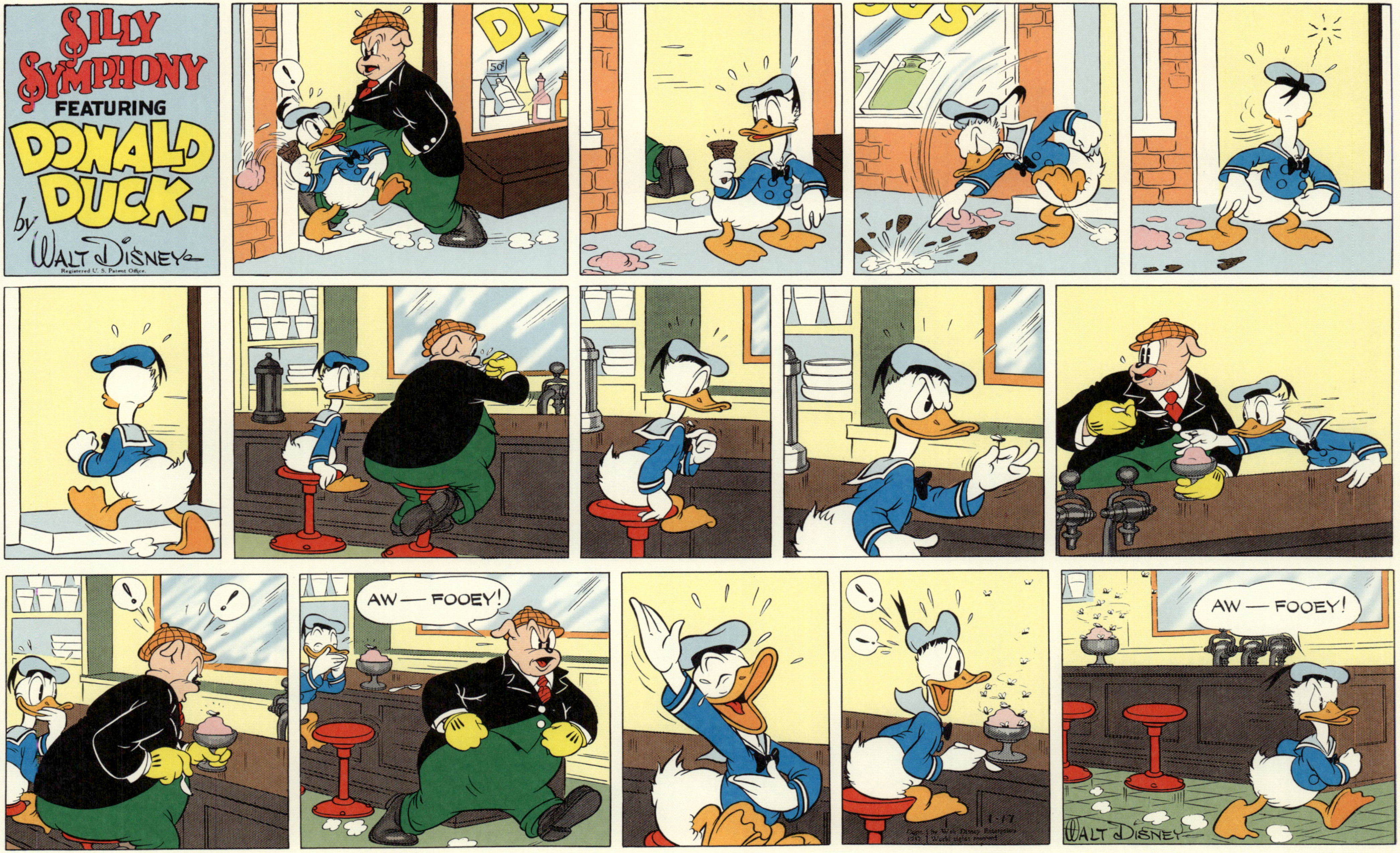
SILLY SYMPHONY
FEATURING
DONALD DUCK.
by WALT DISNEY
Registered U. S. Patent Office.
AW — FOOEY!
AW — FOOEY!
WALT DISNEY

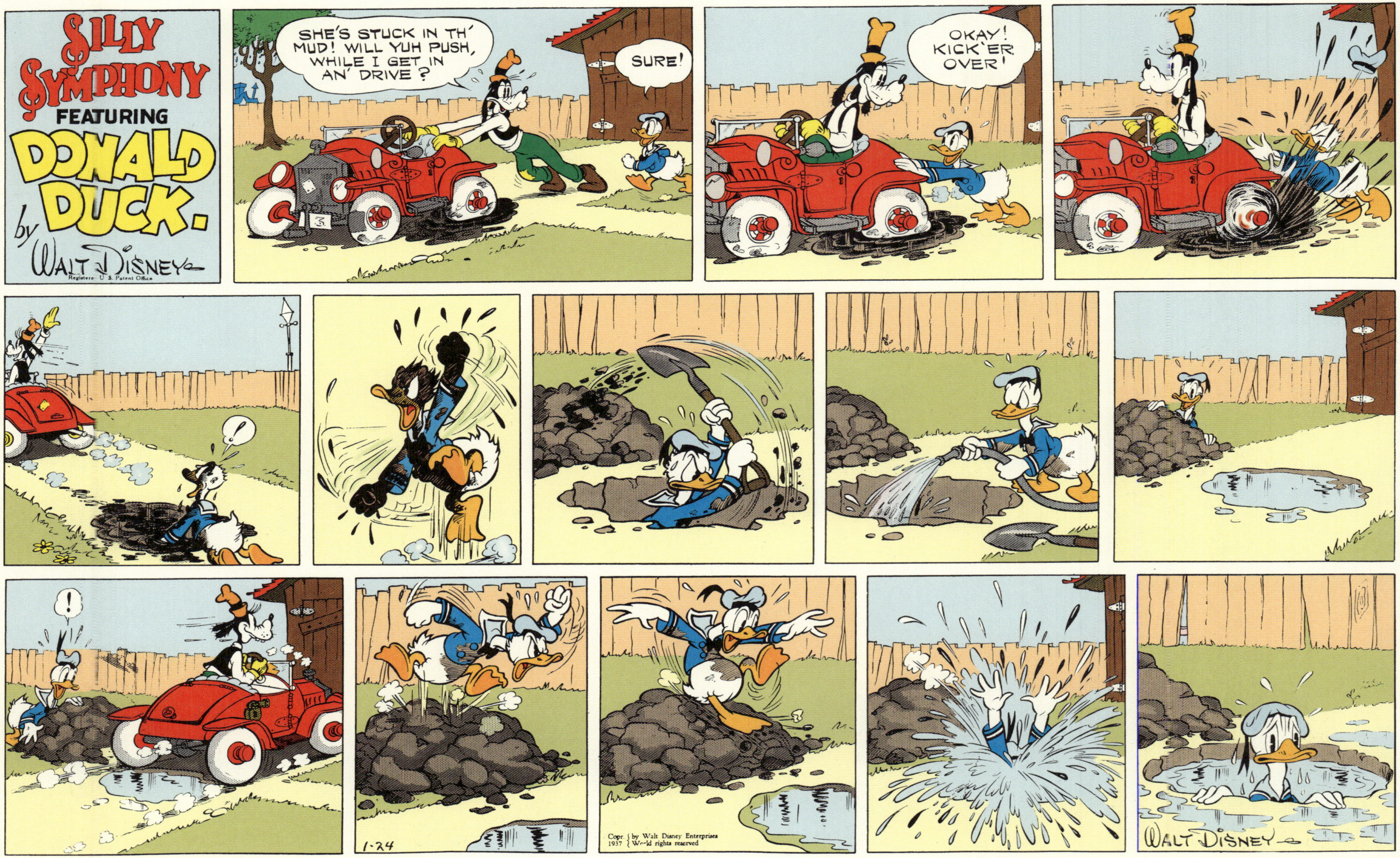

SILLY SYMPHONY
FEATURING
DONALD DUCK.
by WALT DISNEY
Registered U. S. Patent Office
SHE'S STUCK IN TH' MUD! WILL YUH PUSH, WHILE I GET IN AN' DRIVE?
SURE!
OKAY! KICK 'ER OVER!
!
!
1-24
Copr. by Walt Disney Enterprises 1937 World rights reserved
WALT DISNEY

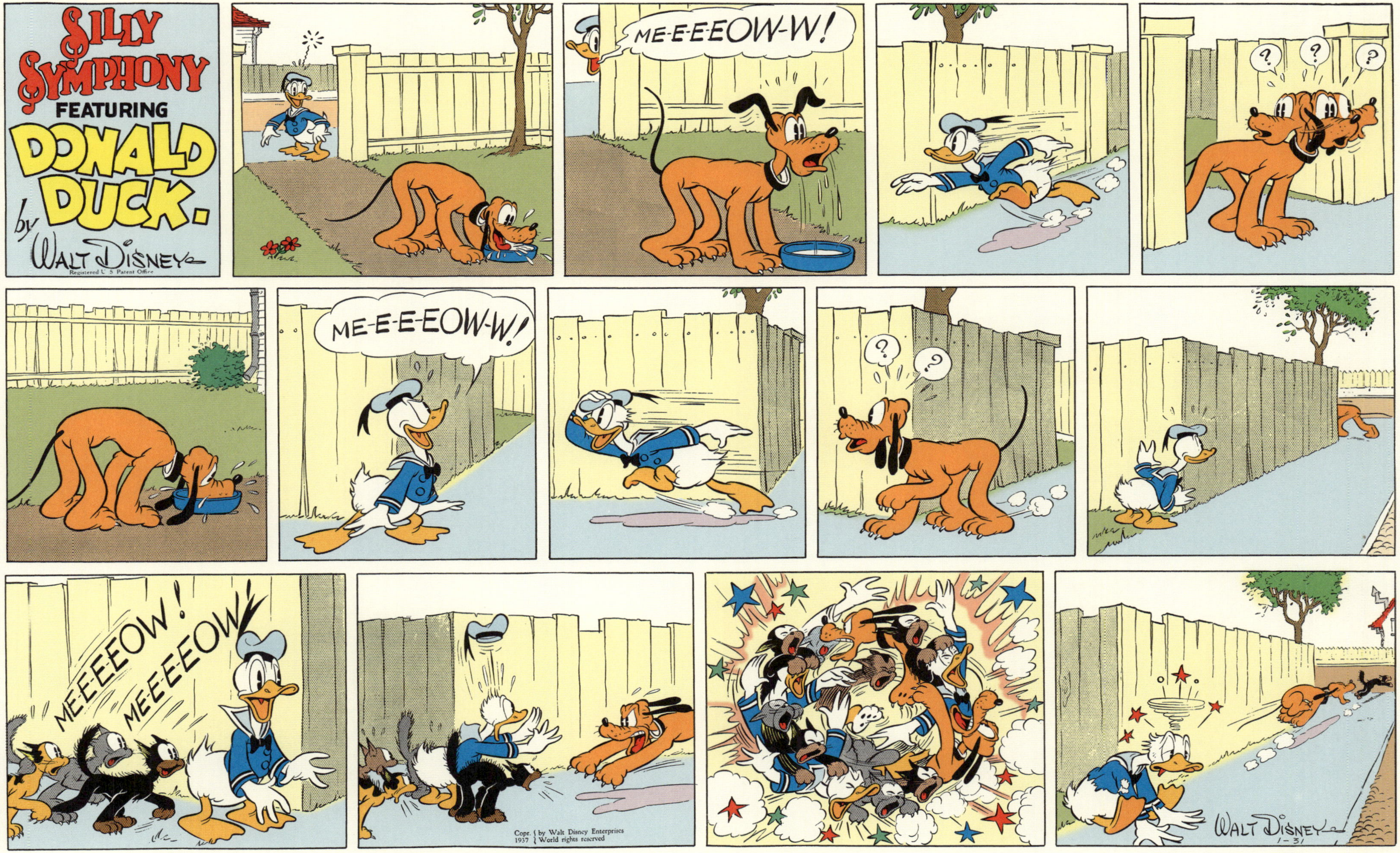

SILLY SYMPHONY
FEATURING
DONALD DUCK.
by WALT DISNEY
Registered U.S. Patent Office
ME-E-E-EOW-W!
ME-E-E-EOW-W!
ME-E-EEOW!
ME-E-E-EOW!
Copr. 1937 by Walt Disney Enterprises World rights reserved
WALT DISNEY
1-31

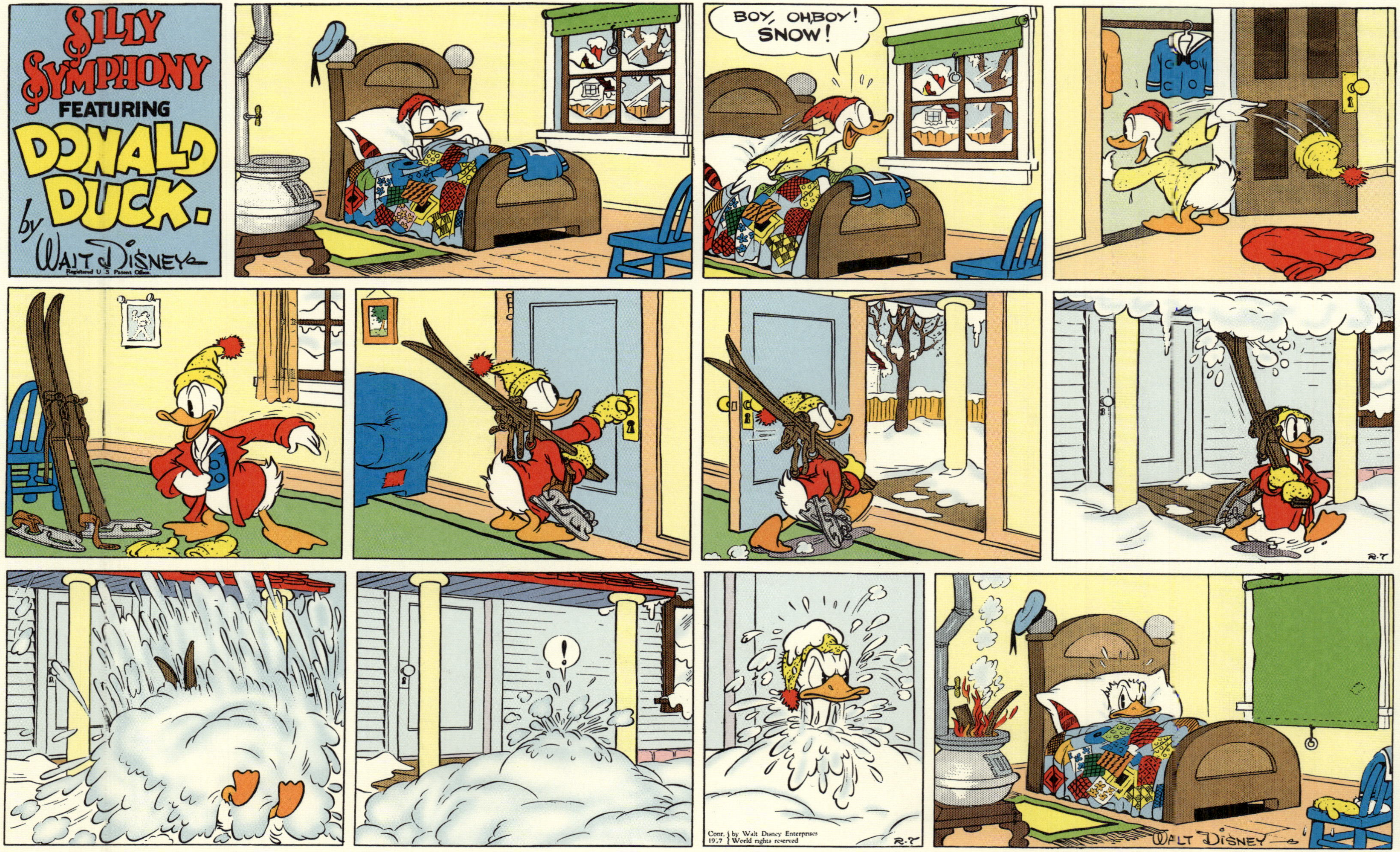
SILLY SYMPHONY
FEATURING
DONALD DUCK.
by
WALT DISNEY
Registered U. S. Patent Office.
BOY, OH BOY! SNOW!
!
Copr. 1937 by Walt Disney Enterprises World rights reserved
WALT DISNEY

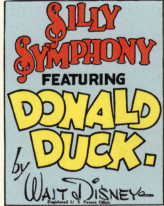

99 • February 14, 1937

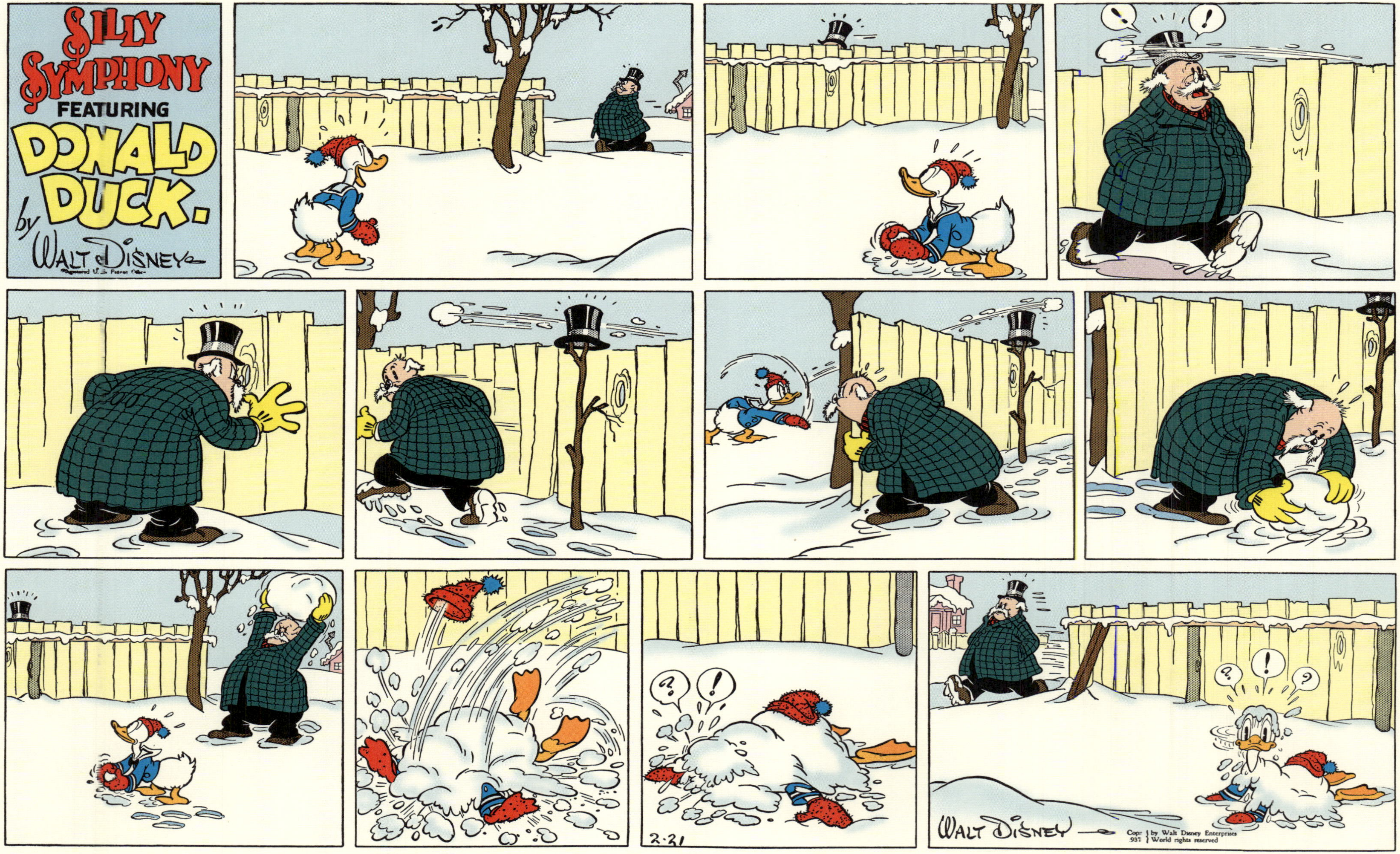
SILLY SYMPHONY
FEATURING
DONALD DUCK.
by WALT DISNEY
!
!
?
!
?
!
?
2-21
WALT DISNEY
by Walt Disney Enterprises
World rights reserved

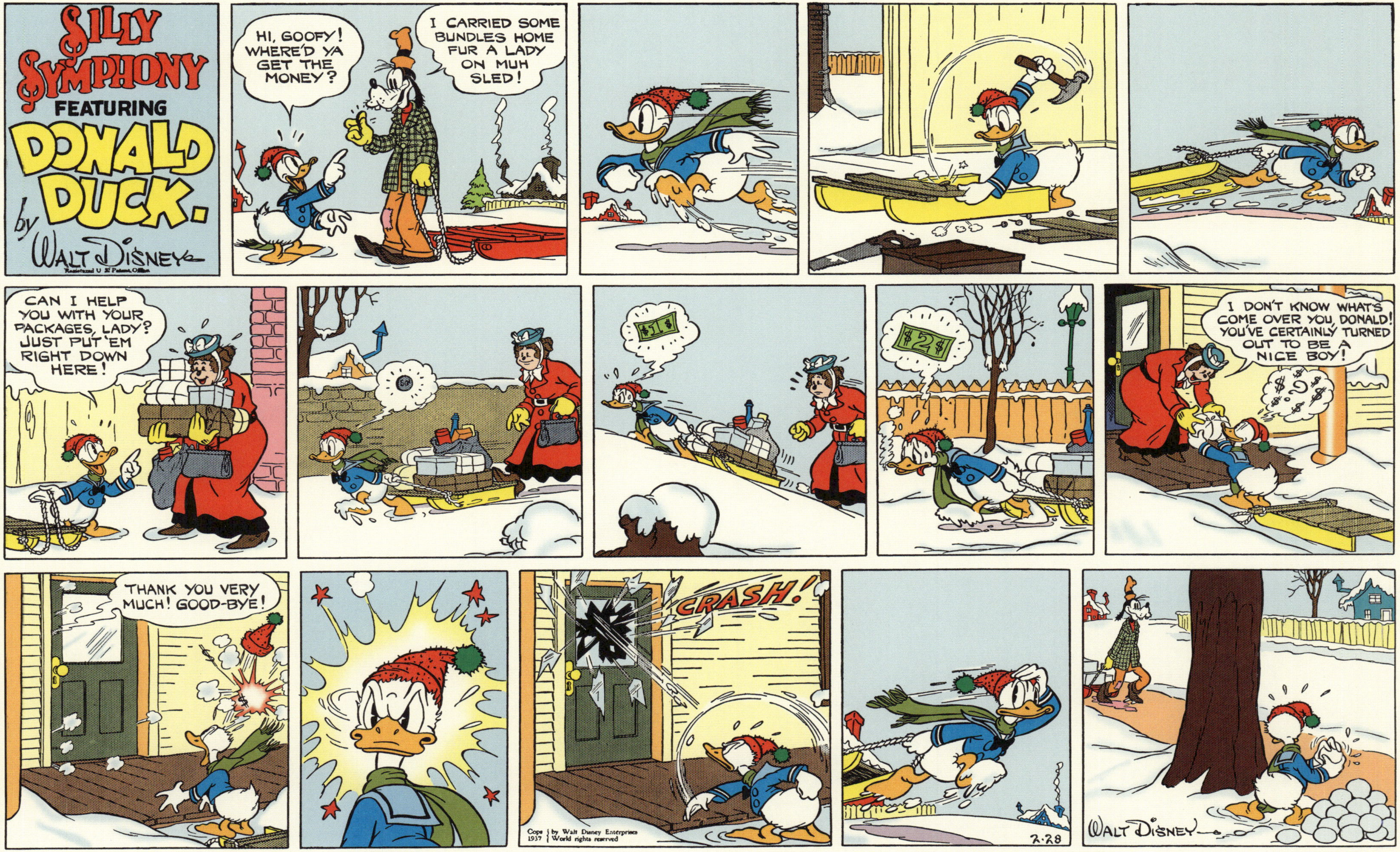
SILLY SYMPHONY
FEATURING
DONALD DUCK.
by WALT DISNEY
HI, GOOFY! WHERE'D YA GET THE MONEY?
I CARRIED SOME BUNDLES HOME FUR A LADY ON MUH SLED!
CAN I HELP YOU WITH YOUR PACKAGES, LADY? JUST PUT 'EM RIGHT DOWN HERE!
I DON'T KNOW WHAT'S COME OVER YOU, DONALD! YOU'VE CERTAINLY TURNED OUT TO BE A NICE BOY!
THANK YOU VERY MUCH! GOOD-BYE!
CRASH!
Copr. 1937 by Walt Disney Enterprises World rights reserved
2-28
WALT DISNEY

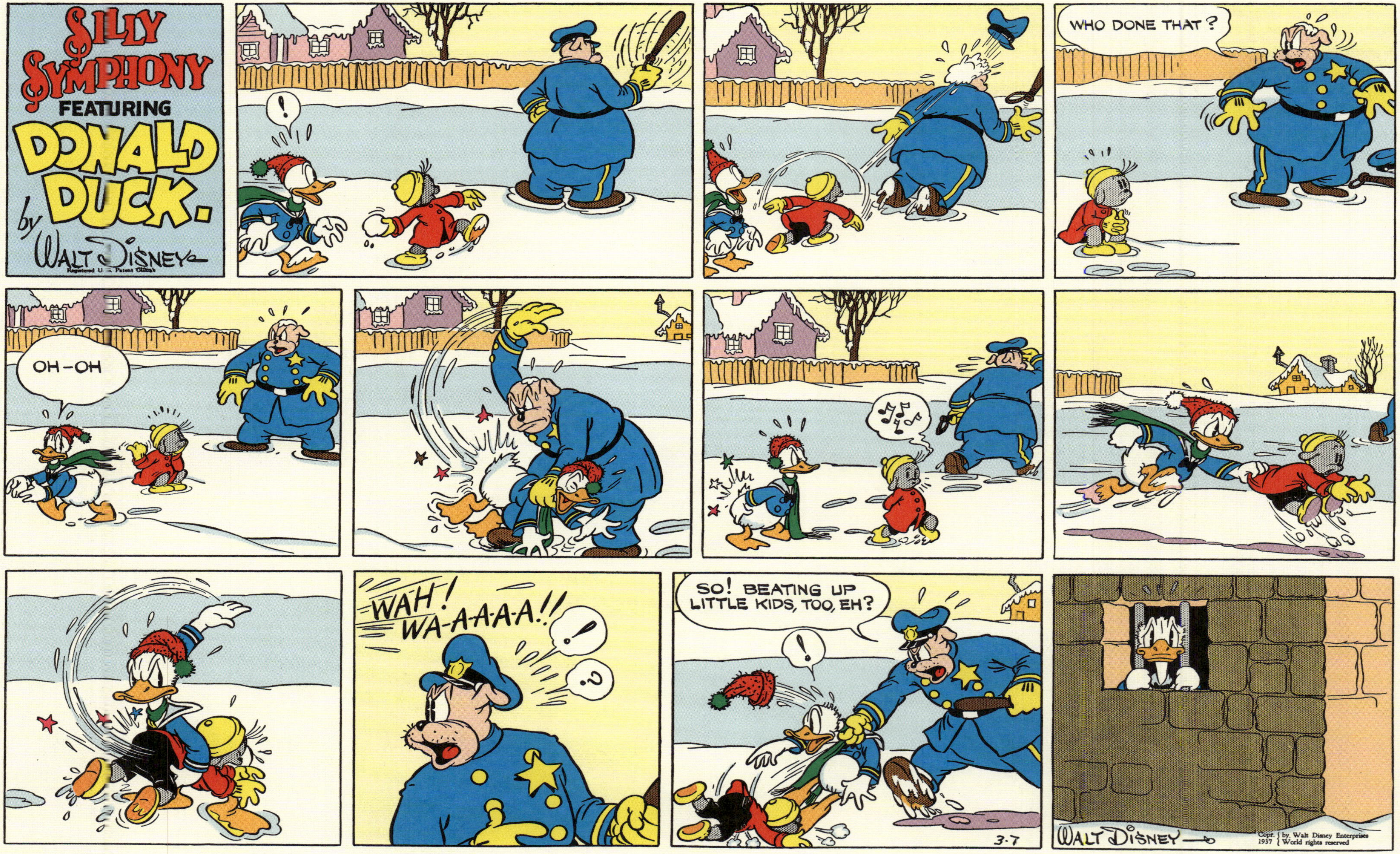
SILLY SYMPHONY
FEATURING
DONALD DUCK.
by WALT DISNEY
!
WHO DONE THAT?
OH-OH
WAH! WA-A-A-A-A!!
!
?
SO! BEATING UP LITTLE KIDS, TOO, EH?
!
3-7
WALT DISNEY
Copr. 1937 by Walt Disney Enterprises World rights reserved

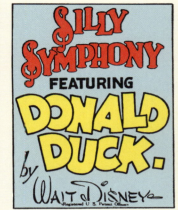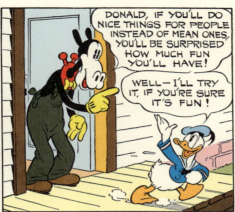

103 • March 14, 1937

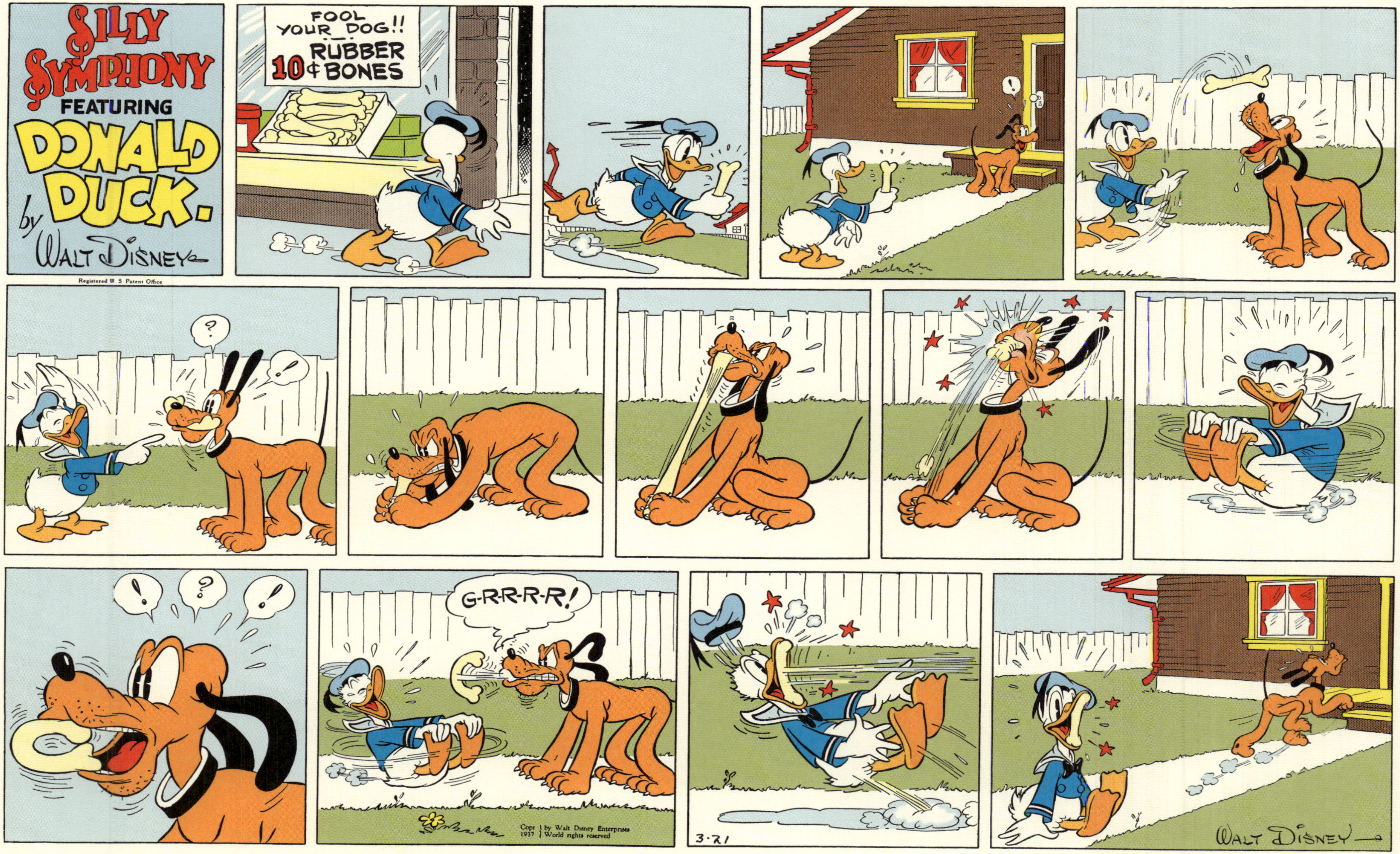
SILLY SYMPHONY
FEATURING
DONALD DUCK.
by WALT DISNEY
Registered U S Patent Office
FOOL YOUR DOG!!
10¢ RUBBER BONES
G-R-R-R-R!
Copr 1937 by Walt Disney Enterprises World rights reserved
3-21
WALT DISNEY

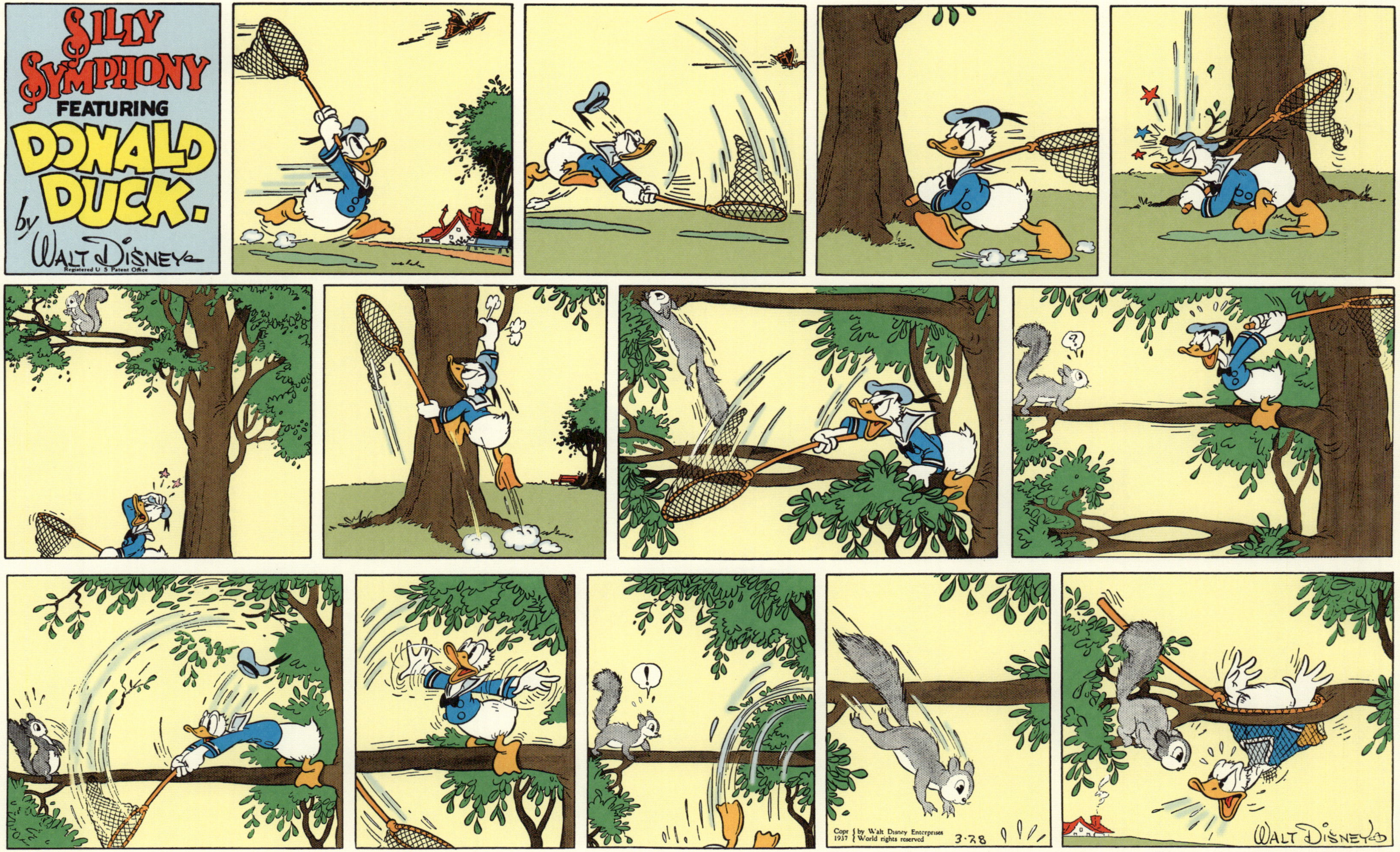
SILLY SYMPHONY
FEATURING
DONALD DUCK.
by WALT DISNEY
Registered U S Patent Office
Copr 1937 by Walt Disney Enterprises World rights reserved
3-28
WALT DISNEY

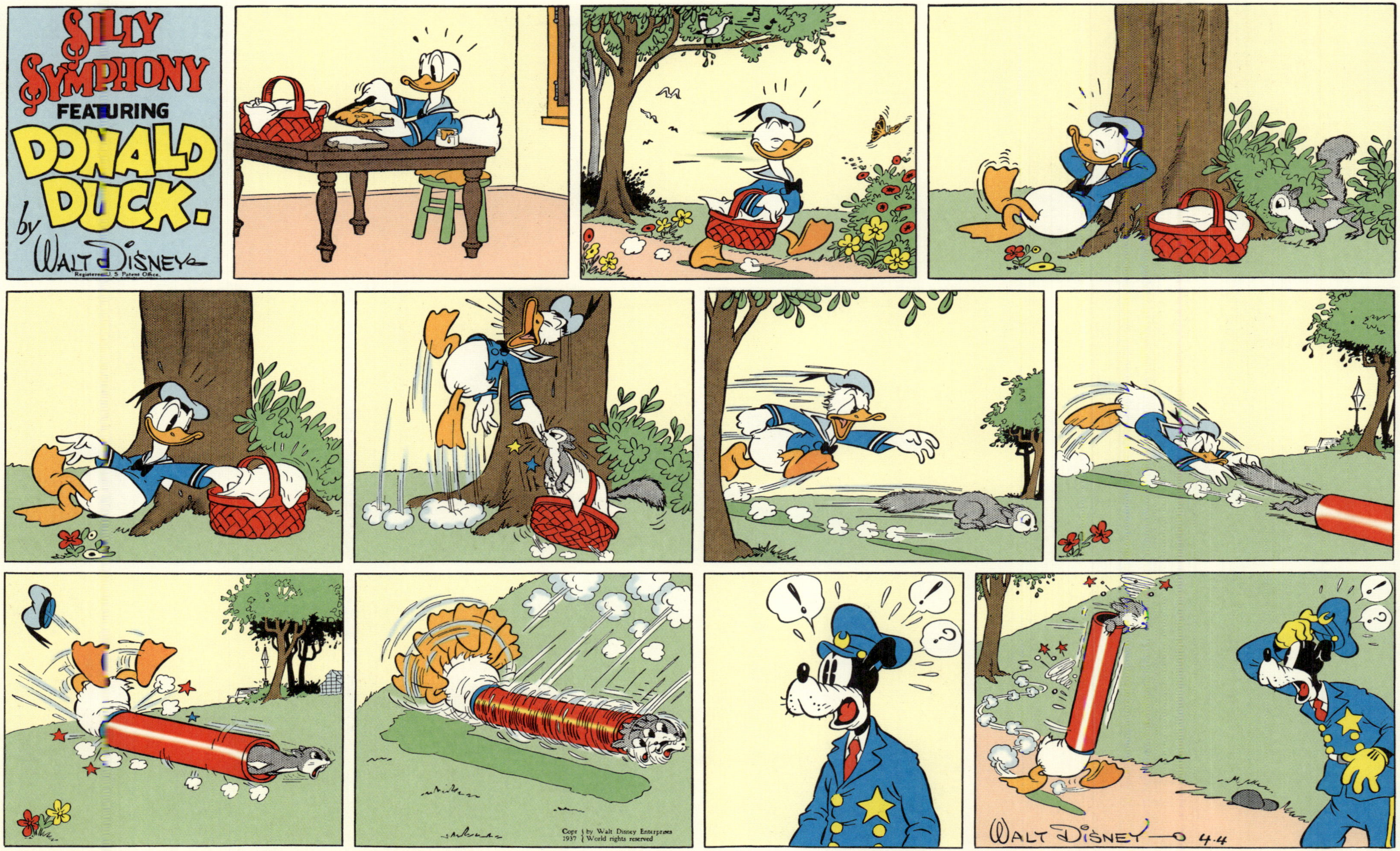
SILLY SYMPHONY
FEATURING
DONALD DUCK.
by WALT DISNEY
Registered U.S. Patent Office.
!
!
?
!
?
Copr by Walt Disney Enterprises 1937 World rights reserved
WALT DISNEY 4.4

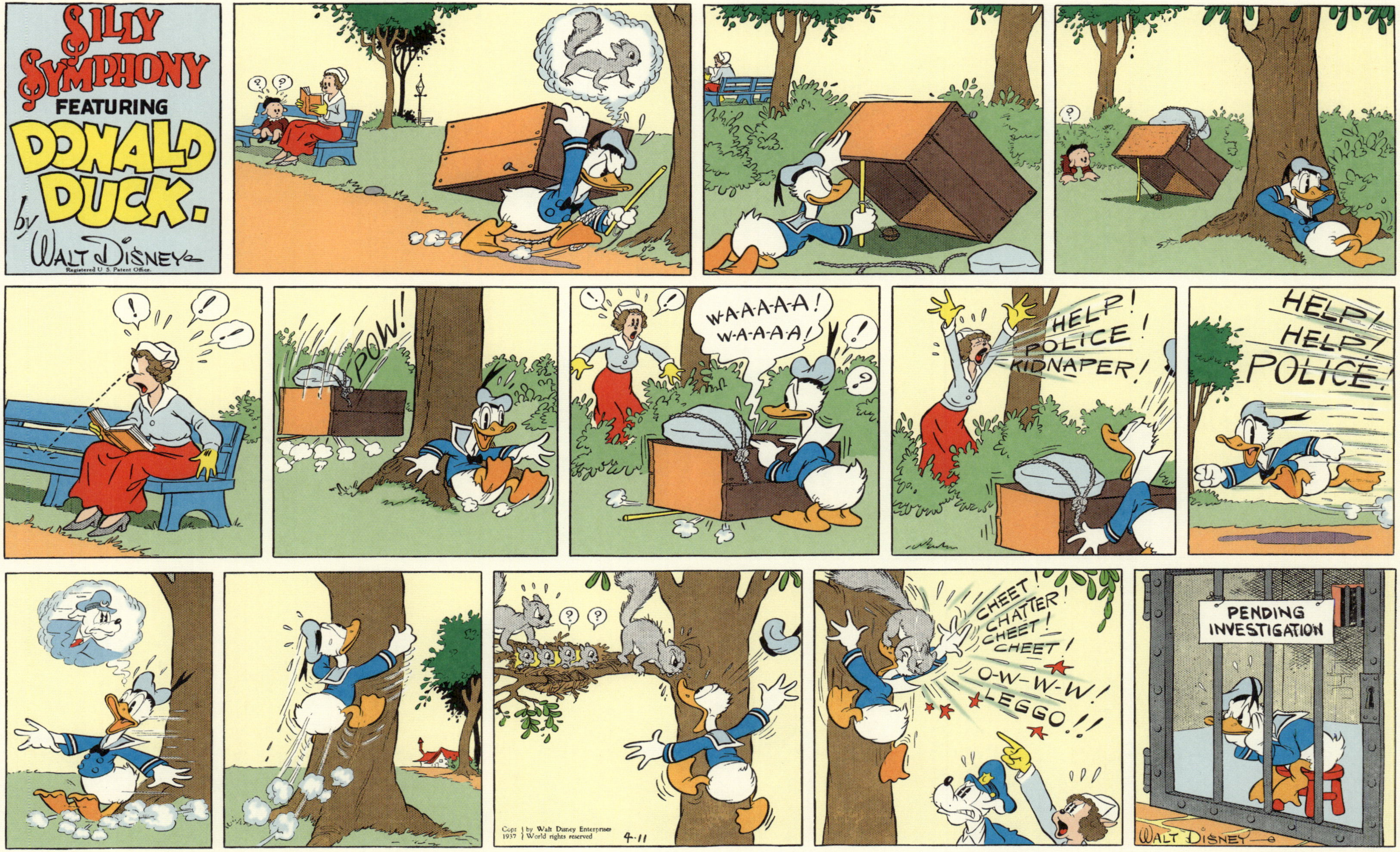
SILLY SYMPHONY
FEATURING
DONALD DUCK.
by WALT DISNEY
Registered U. S. Patent Office.
POW!
W-A-A-A-A-A!
W-A-A-A-A!
HELP!
POLICE!
KIDNAPER!
HELP!
HELP!
POLICE!
Copr. 1937 by Walt Disney Enterprises World rights reserved
4-11
CHEET!
CHATTER!
CHEET!
CHEET!
O-W-W-W!
LEGGO!!
PENDING INVESTIGATION
WALT DISNEY

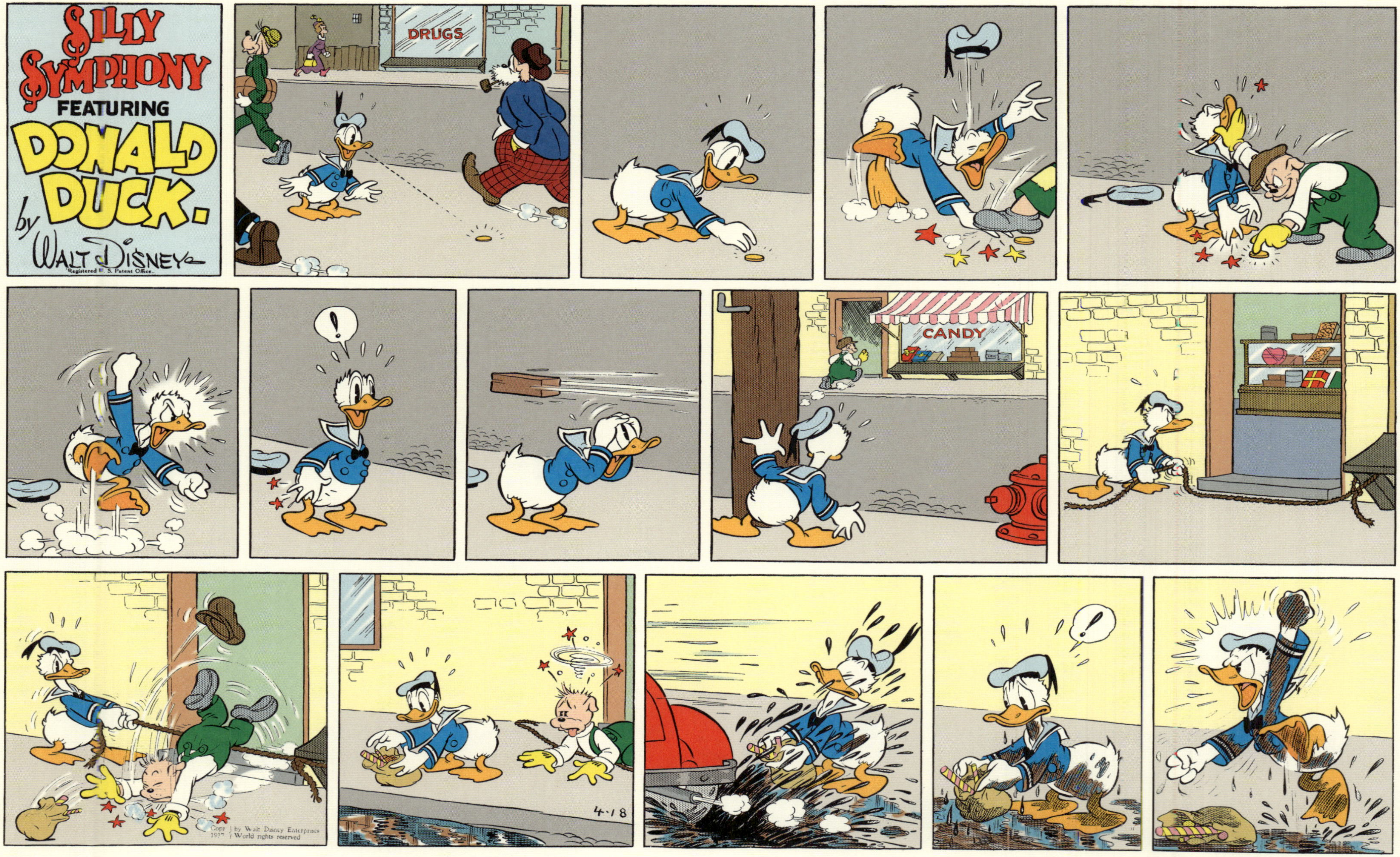
SILLY SYMPHONY
FEATURING
DONALD DUCK.
by
WALT DISNEY
Registered U. S. Patent Office.
DRUGS
!
CANDY
Copr. 1937 by Walt Disney Enterprises World rights reserved
4-18
!

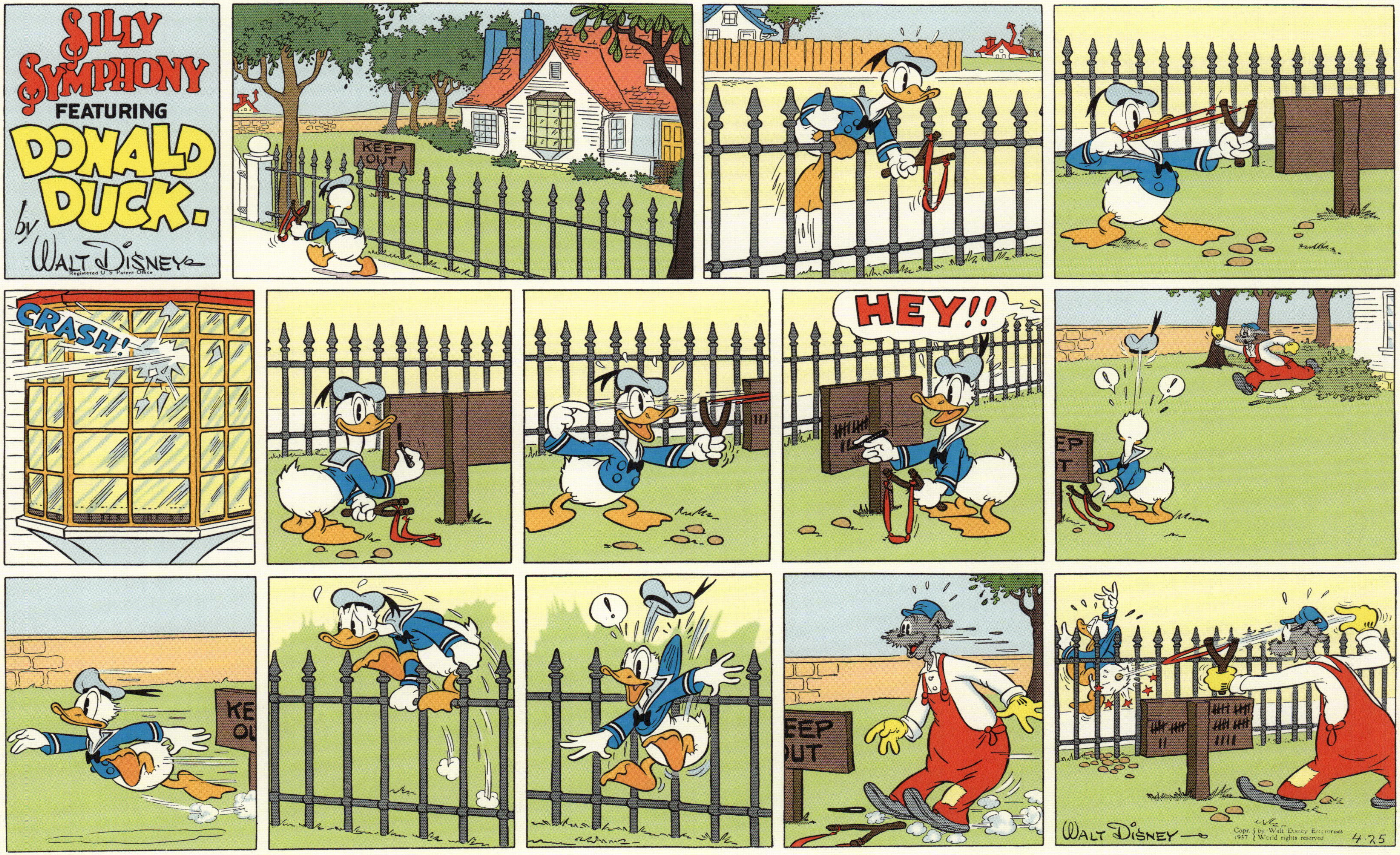
SILLY SYMPHONY
FEATURING
DONALD DUCK.
by
WALT DISNEY
Registered U. S. Patent Office
KEEP OUT
CRASH!
HEY!!
KEEP OUT
WALT DISNEY
Copr. 1937 by Walt Disney Enterprises World rights reserved
4·25

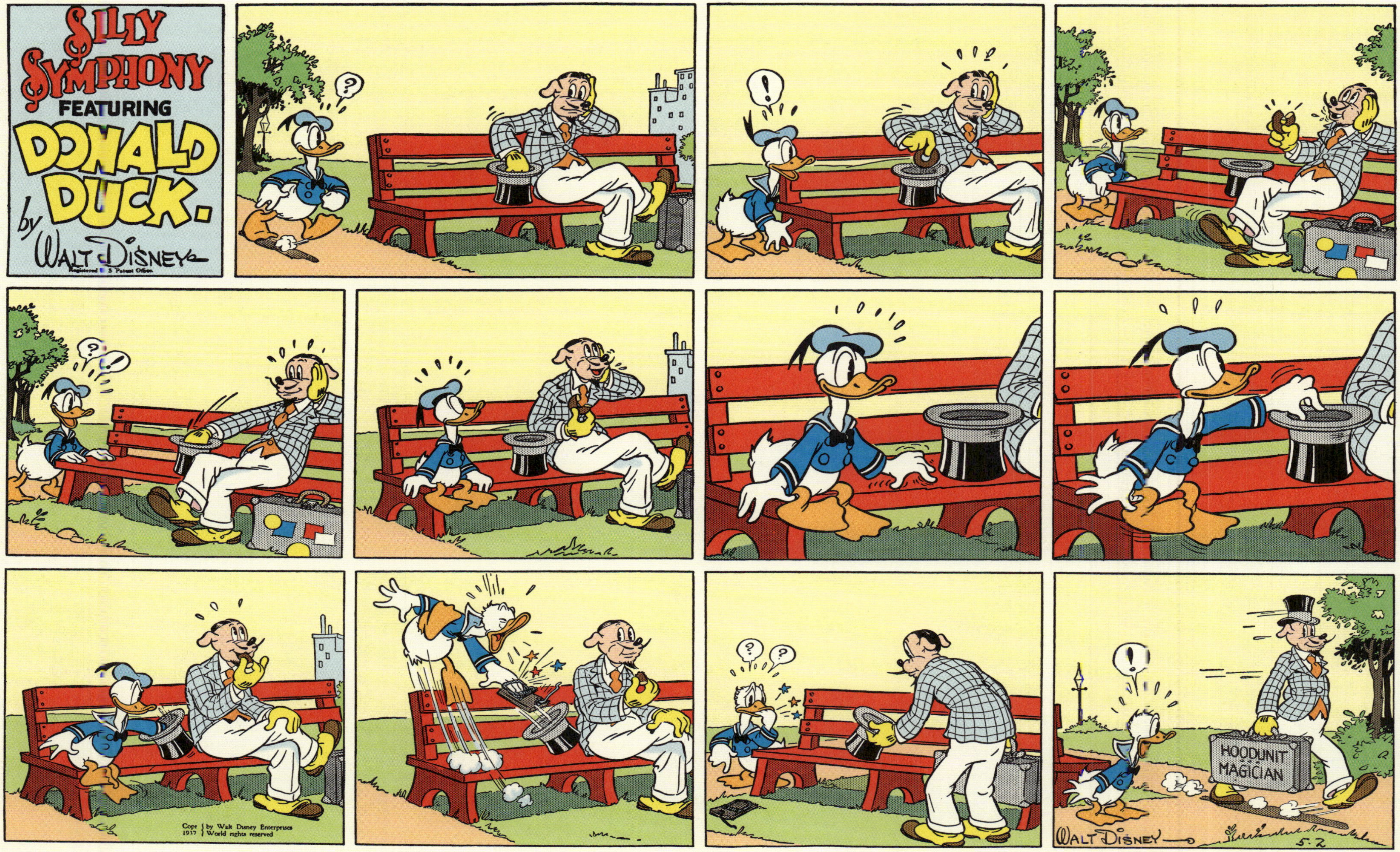
SILLY SYMPHONY
FEATURING
DONALD DUCK.
by WALT DISNEY
Copr 1937 by Walt Disney Enterprises World rights reserved
HOODUNIT MAGICIAN
WALT DISNEY
5-2

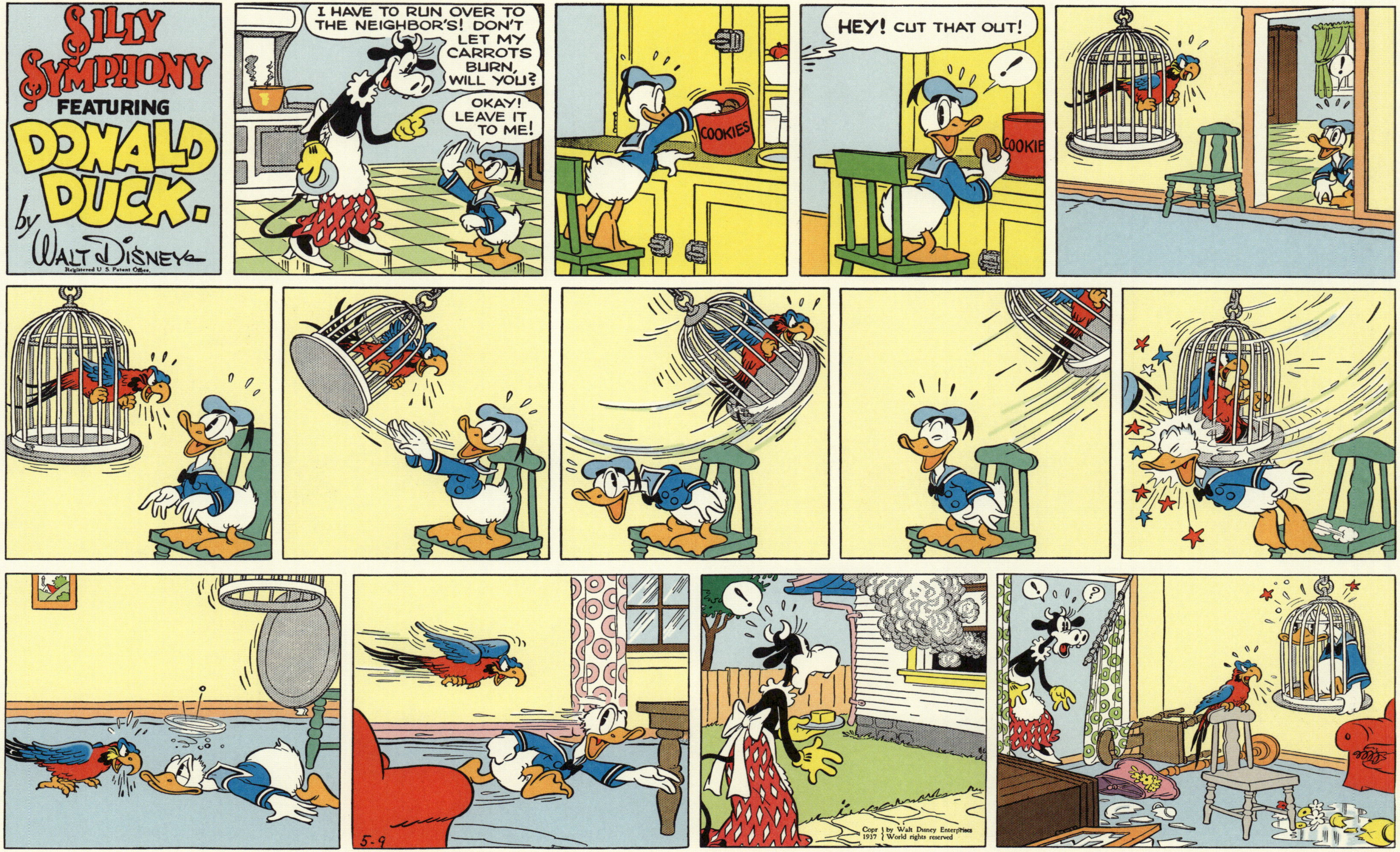
SILLY SYMPHONY
FEATURING
DONALD DUCK.
by WALT DISNEY
Registered U S. Patent Office.
I HAVE TO RUN OVER TO THE NEIGHBOR'S! DON'T LET MY CARROTS BURN, WILL YOU?
OKAY! LEAVE IT TO ME!
COOKIES
HEY! CUT THAT OUT!
!
COOKIE
!
5-9
!
Copr 1937 by Walt Disney Enterprises World rights reserved
!
?

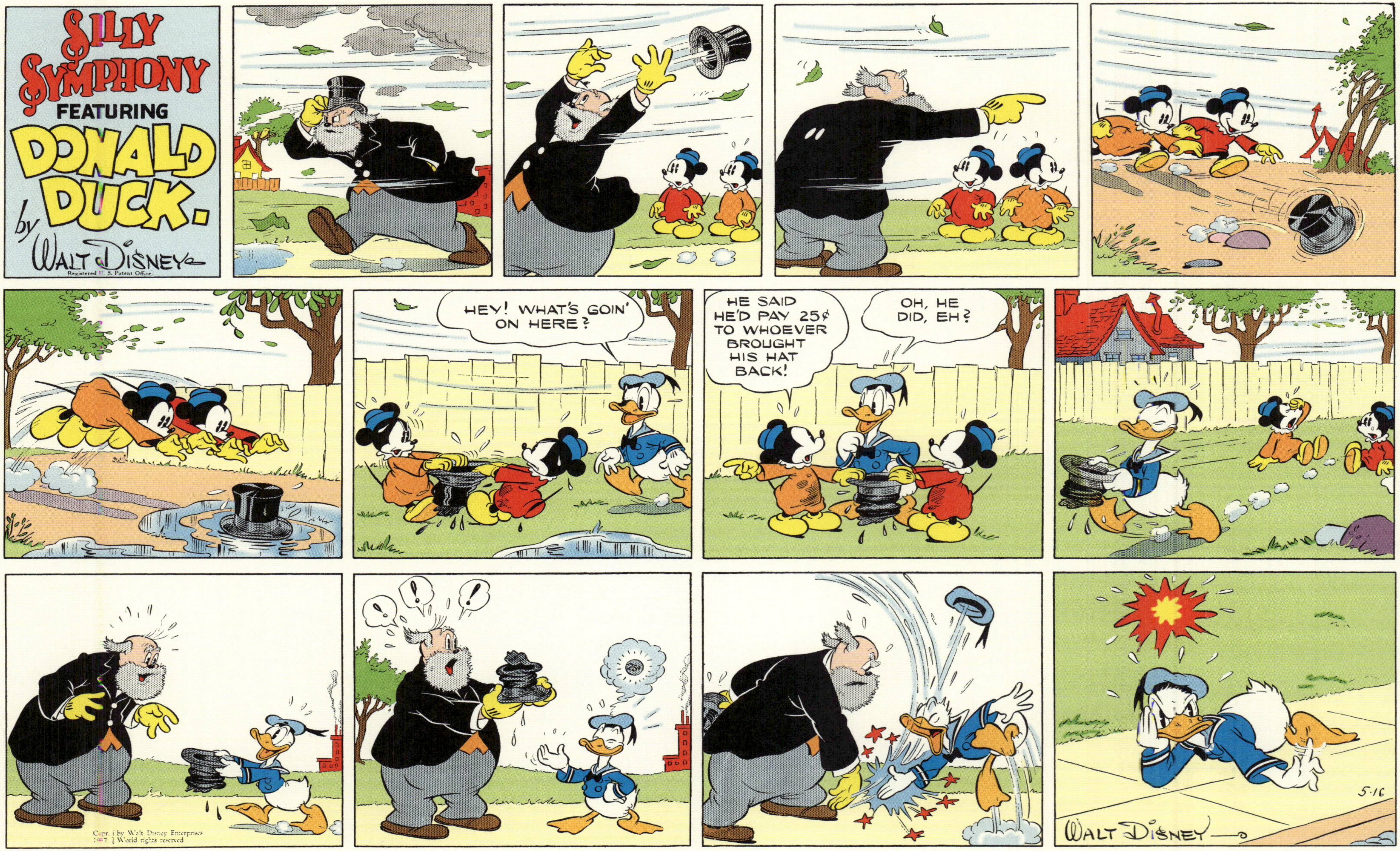
SILLY SYMPHONY
FEATURING
DONALD DUCK.
by WALT DISNEY
Registered U. S. Patent Office.
HEY! WHAT'S GOIN' ON HERE?
HE SAID HE'D PAY 25¢ TO WHOEVER BROUGHT HIS HAT BACK!
OH, HE DID, EH?
Copr. by Walt Disney Enterprises
World rights reserved
5·16
WALT DISNEY

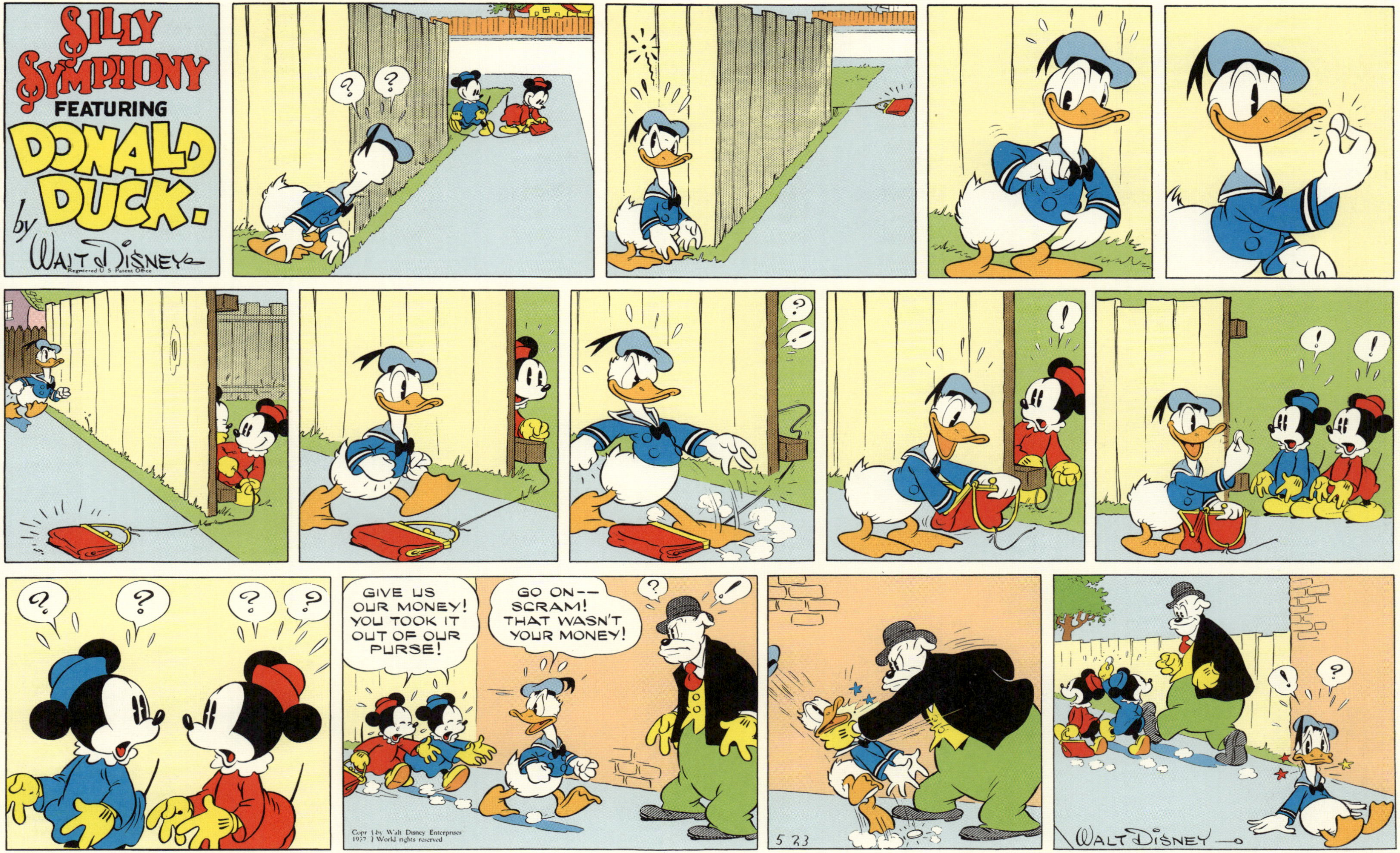
SILLY SYMPHONY
FEATURING
DONALD DUCK.
by WALT DISNEY
Registered U S Patent Office
GIVE US OUR MONEY! YOU TOOK IT OUT OF OUR PURSE!
GO ON-- SCRAM! THAT WASN'T YOUR MONEY!
Copr 1937 by Walt Disney Enterprises World rights reserved
5 23
WALT DISNEY

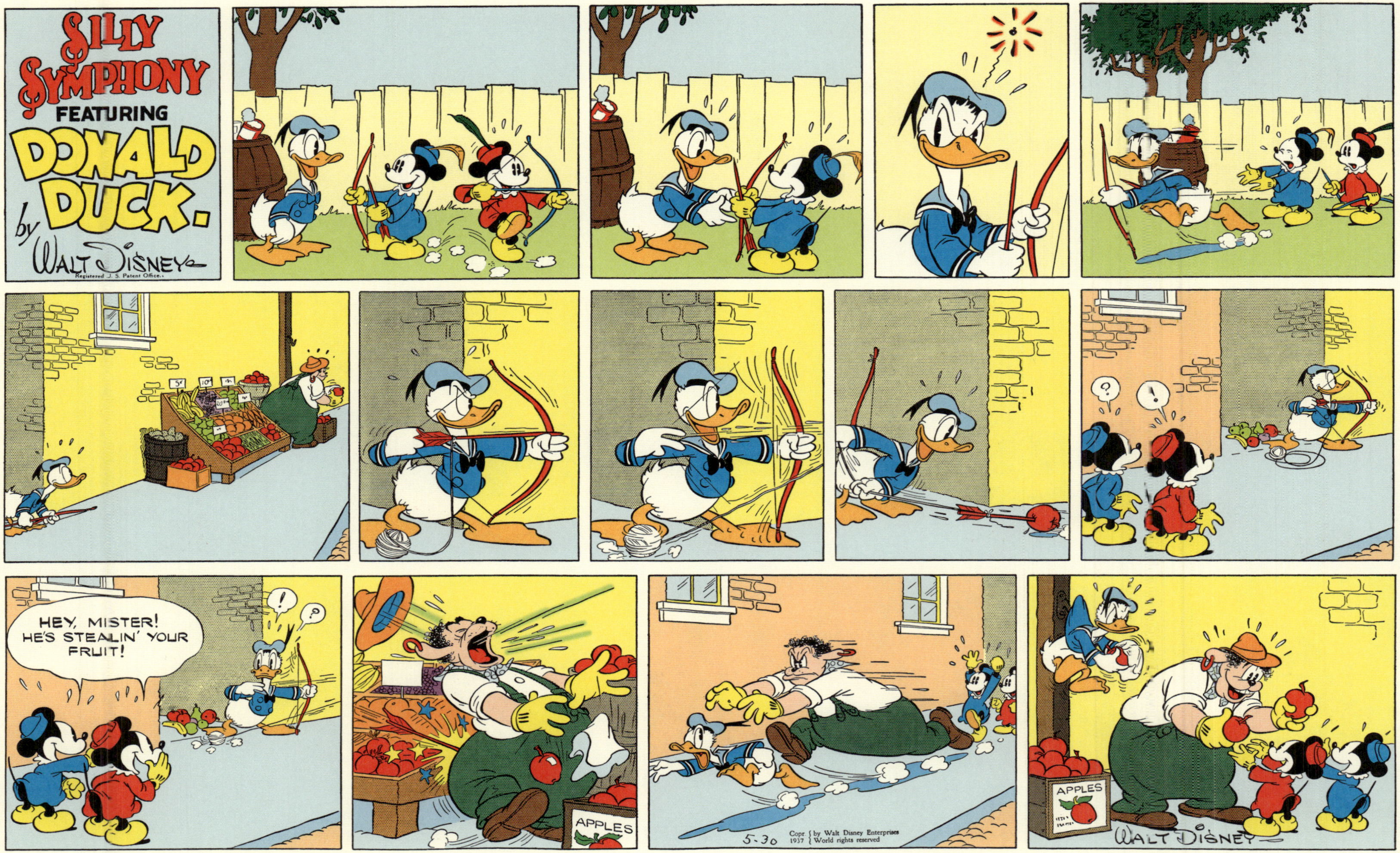
SILLY SYMPHONY
FEATURING
DONALD DUCK.
by WALT DISNEY
Registered U.S. Patent Office.
HEY, MISTER! HE'S STEALIN' YOUR FRUIT!
APPLES
5-30
Copr 1937 by Walt Disney Enterprises World rights reserved
APPLES
WALT DISNEY

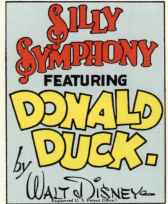

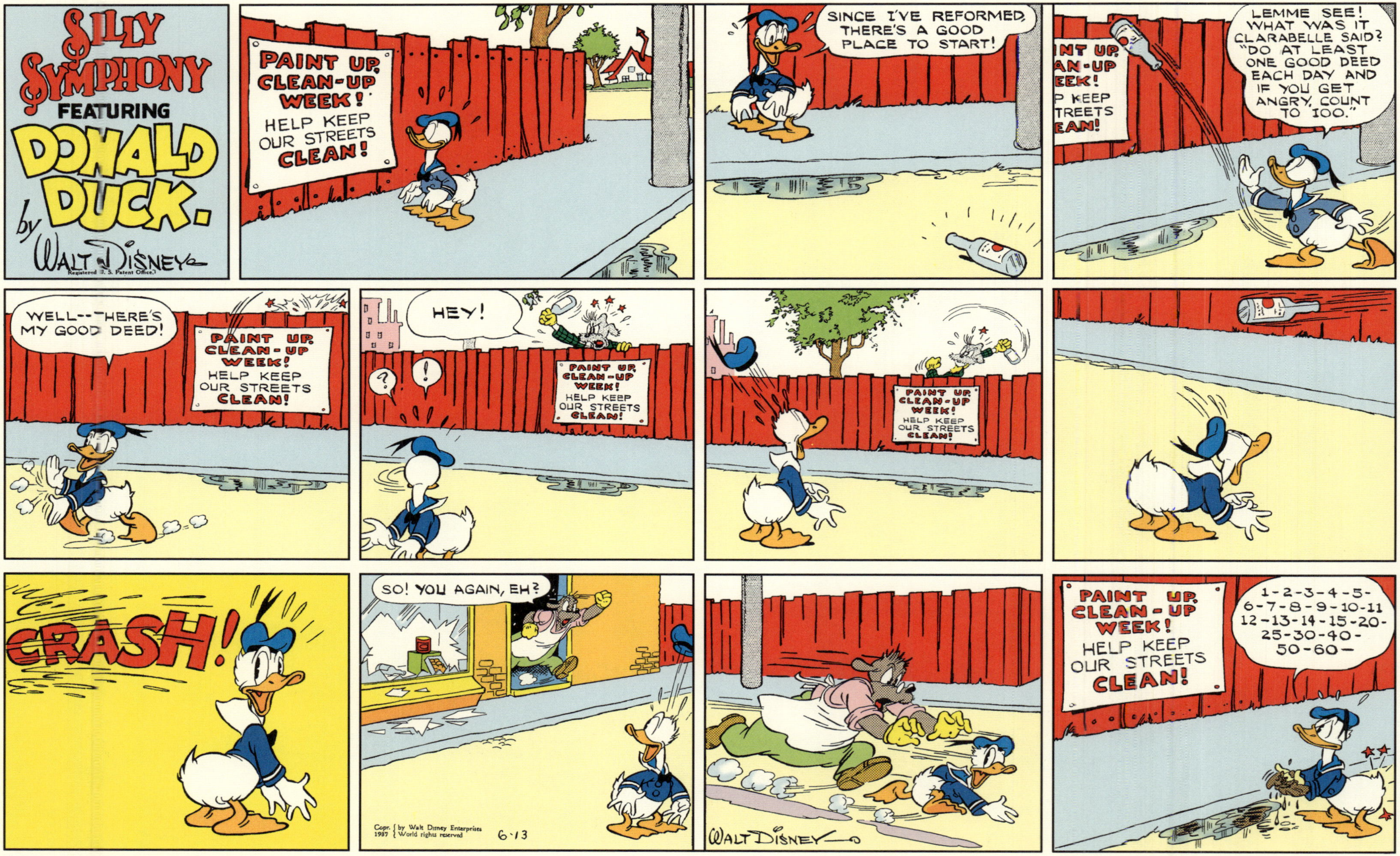
SILLY SYMPHONY FEATURING DONALD DUCK. by WALT DISNEY
Registered U. S. Patent Office.
PAINT UP, CLEAN-UP WEEK! HELP KEEP OUR STREETS CLEAN!
SINCE I'VE REFORMED, THERE'S A GOOD PLACE TO START!
LEMME SEE! WHAT WAS IT CLARABELLE SAID? "DO AT LEAST ONE GOOD DEED EACH DAY AND IF YOU GET ANGRY, COUNT TO 100."
WELL--THERE'S MY GOOD DEED!
HEY!
?
!
CRASH!
SO! YOU AGAIN, EH?
Copr. 1937 by Walt Disney Enterprises World rights reserved
6-13
WALT DISNEY
1-2-3-4-5-6-7-8-9-10-11 12-13-14-15-20-25-30-40-50-60-

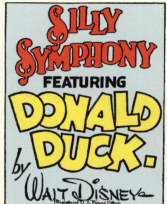

117 • June 20, 1937

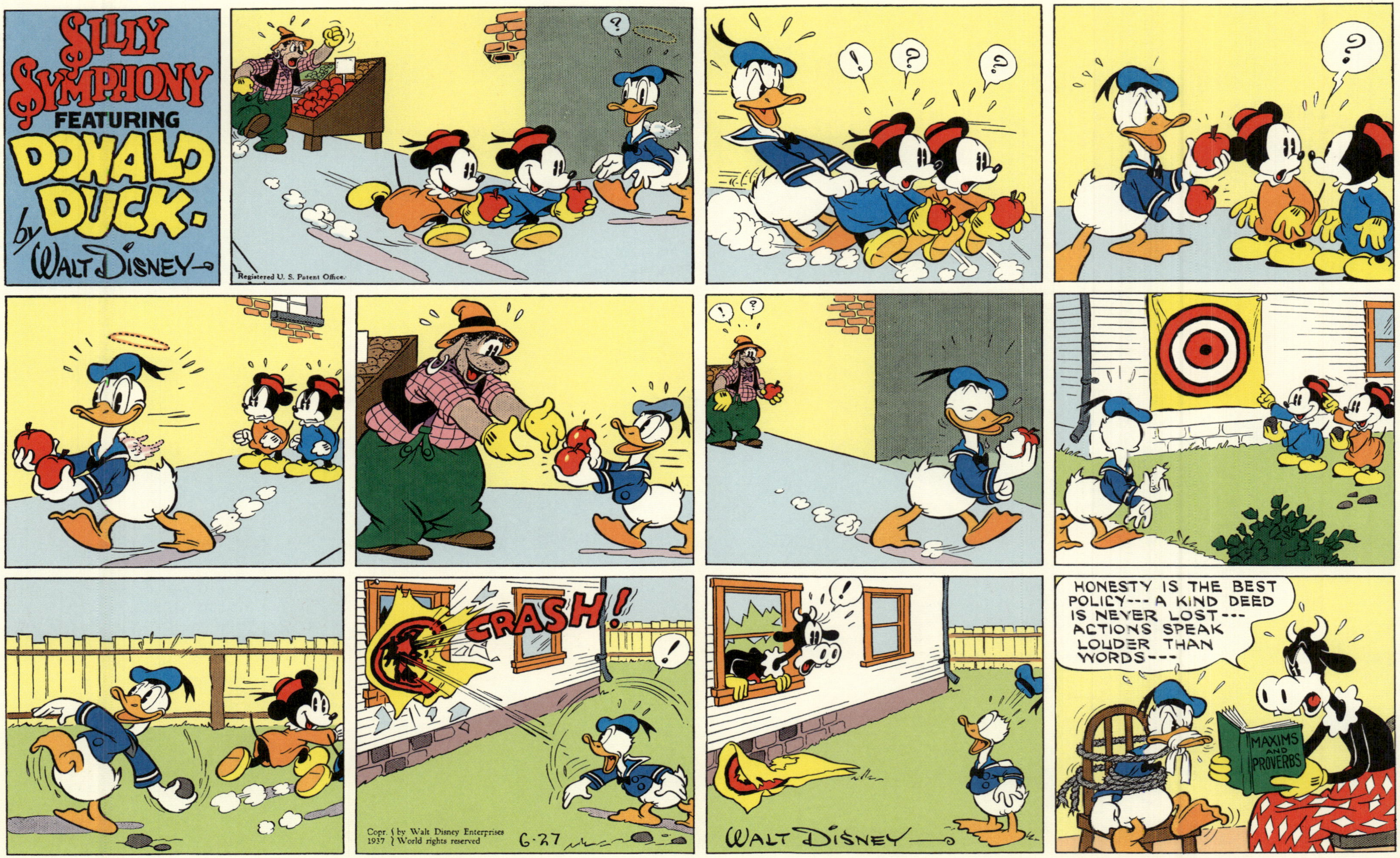
SILLY SYMPHONY
FEATURING
DONALD DUCK.
by WALT DISNEY
Registered U. S. Patent Office.
?
! ? ?
?
! ?
CRASH!
!
!
Copr. 1937 { by Walt Disney Enterprises } World rights reserved
6-27
WALT DISNEY
HONESTY IS THE BEST POLICY--- A KIND DEED IS NEVER LOST--- ACTIONS SPEAK LOUDER THAN WORDS---
MAXIMS AND PROVERBS

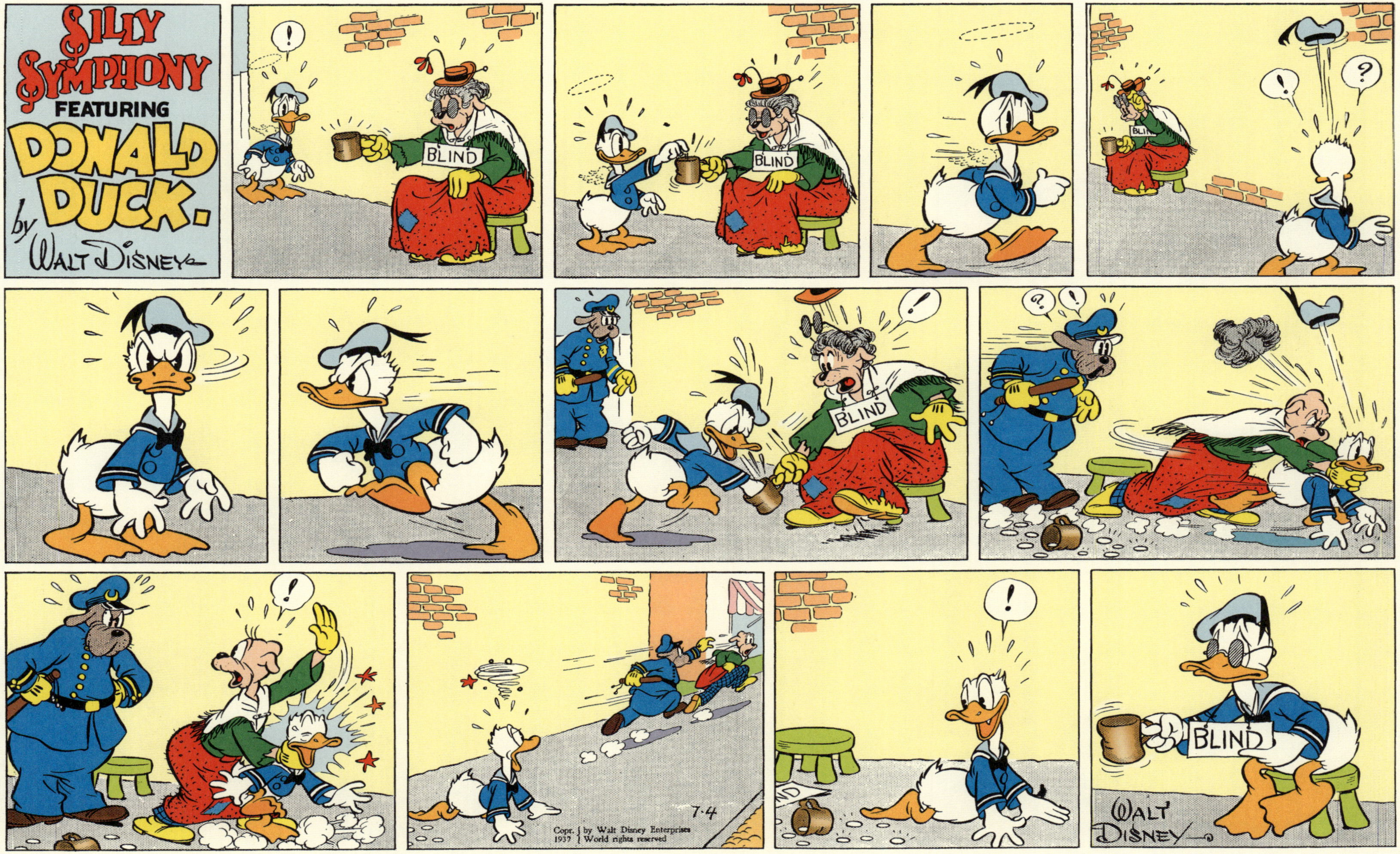

SILLY SYMPHONY
FEATURING
DONALD DUCK.
by WALT DISNEY
!
BLIND
BLIND
!
?
BLIND
?
!
!
7·4
Copr. 1937 by Walt Disney Enterprises World rights reserved
!
BLIND
WALT DISNEY

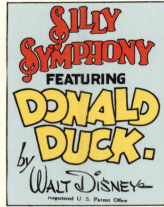

120 • July 11, 1937

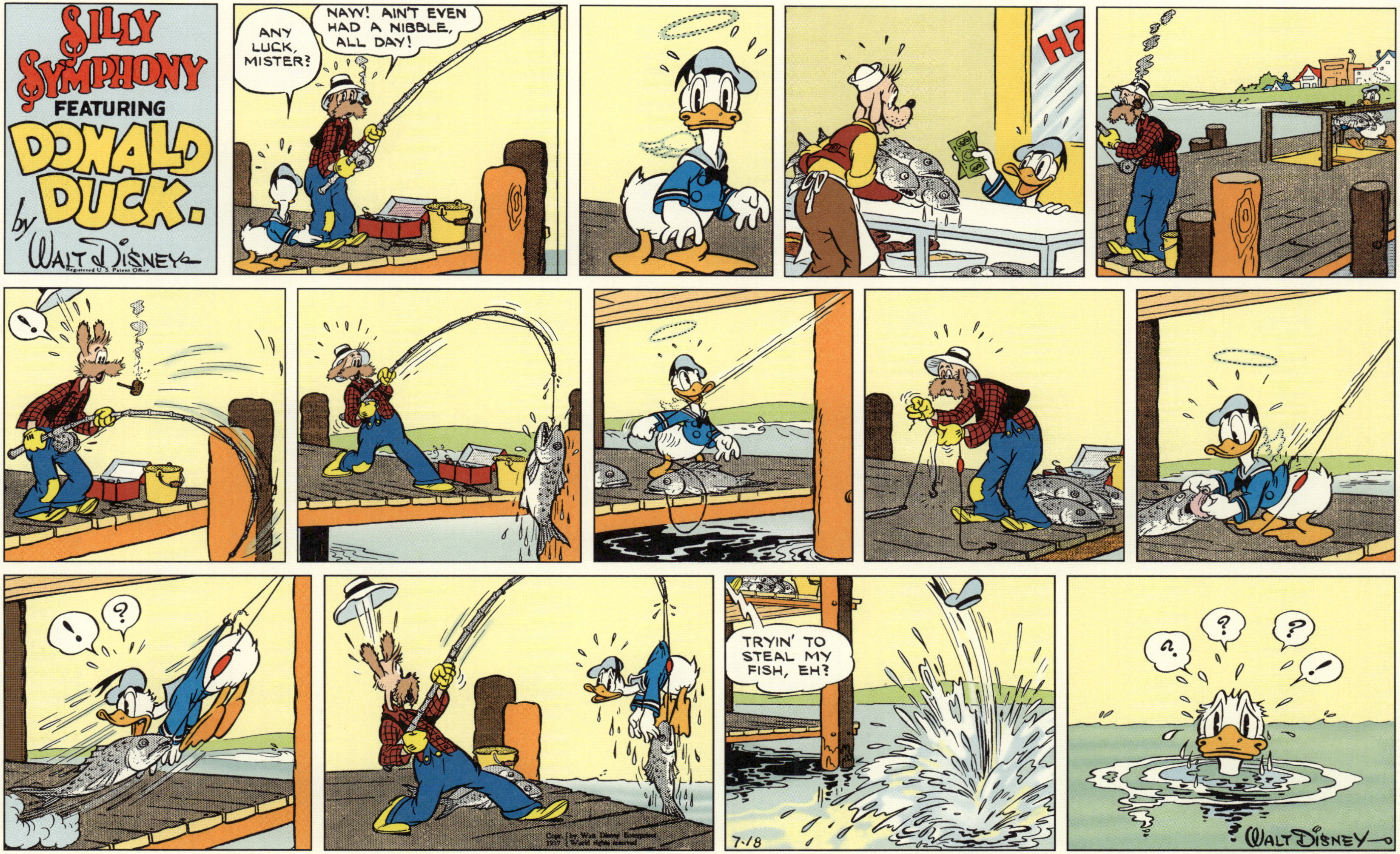
SILLY SYMPHONY
FEATURING
DONALD DUCK.
by WALT DISNEY
ANY LUCK, MISTER?
NAW! AIN'T EVEN HAD A NIBBLE, ALL DAY!
TRYIN' TO STEAL MY FISH, EH?
7-18
WALT DISNEY

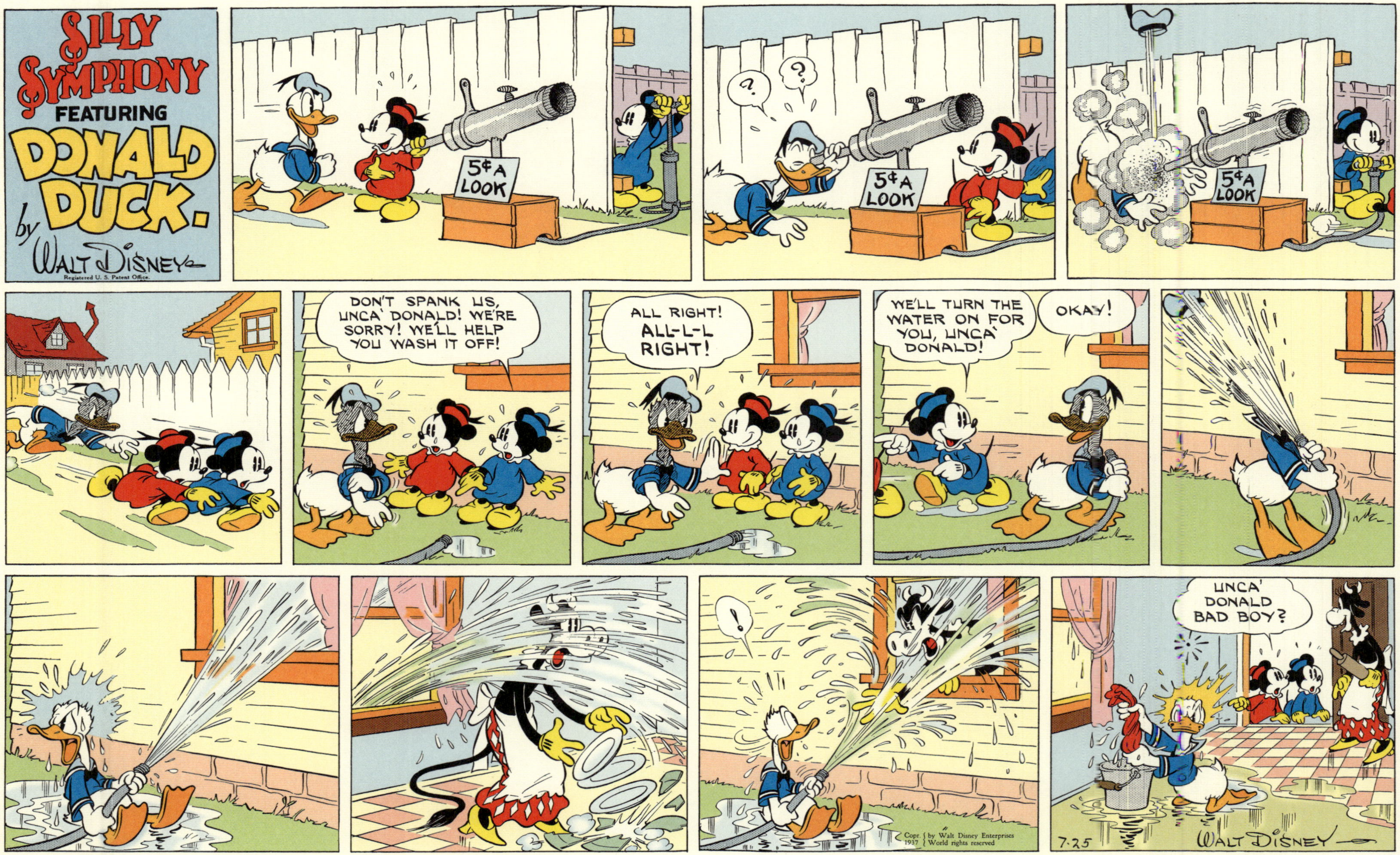

SILLY SYMPHONY
FEATURING
DONALD DUCK.
by WALT DISNEY
Registered U. S. Patent Office.
5¢ A LOOK
?
?
5¢ A LOOK
5¢ A LOOK
DON'T SPANK US, UNCA' DONALD! WE'RE SORRY! WE'LL HELP YOU WASH IT OFF!
ALL RIGHT! ALL-L-L RIGHT!
WE'LL TURN THE WATER ON FOR YOU, UNCA' DONALD!
OKAY!
!
UNCA' DONALD BAD BOY?
Copr. 1937 by Walt Disney Enterprises World rights reserved
7-25
WALT DISNEY

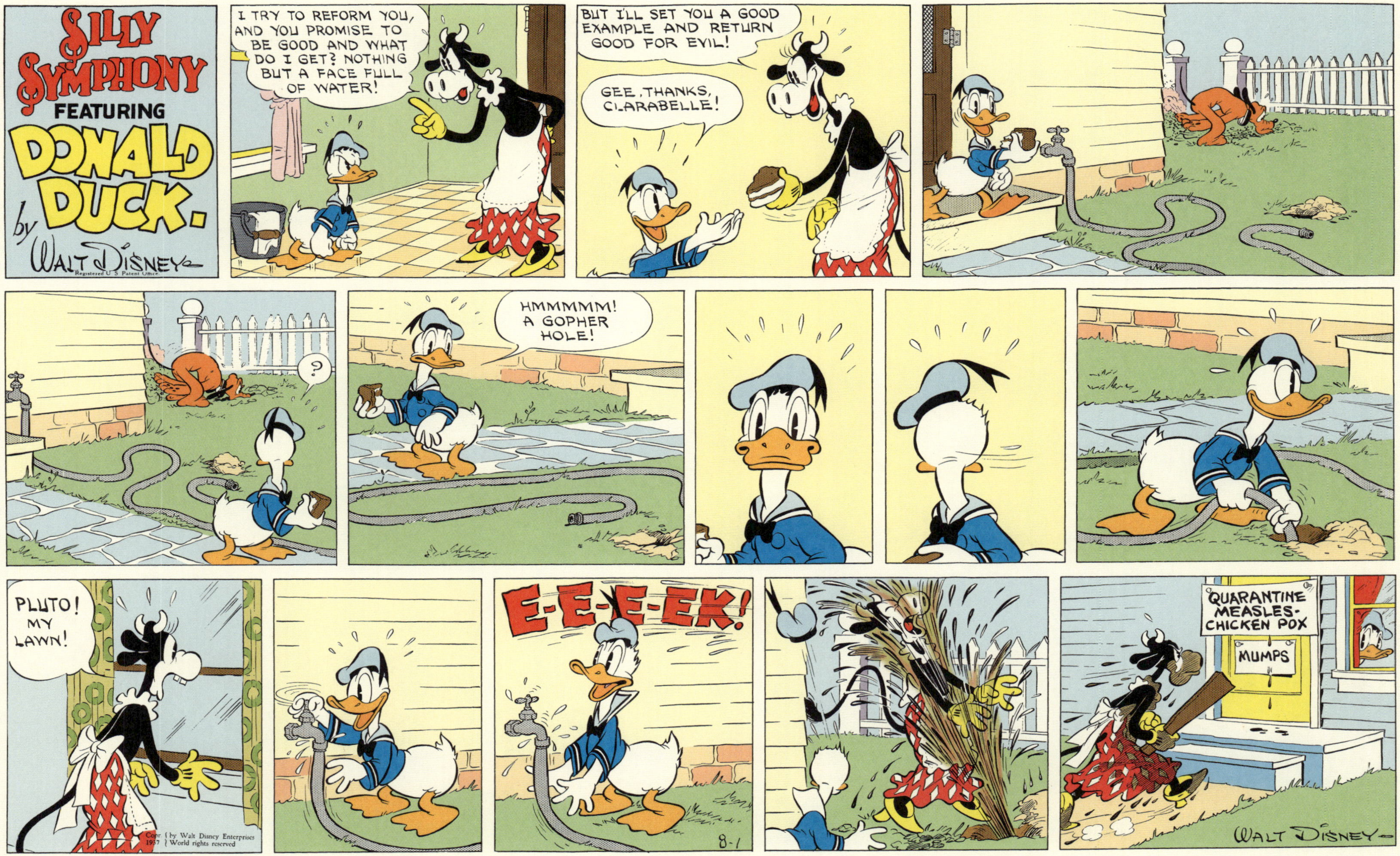
SILLY SYMPHONY
FEATURING
DONALD DUCK.
by WALT DISNEY
Registered U. S. Patent Office
I TRY TO REFORM YOU, AND YOU PROMISE TO BE GOOD AND WHAT DO I GET? NOTHING BUT A FACE FULL OF WATER!
BUT I'LL SET YOU A GOOD EXAMPLE AND RETURN GOOD FOR EVIL!
GEE, THANKS, CLARABELLE!
?
HMMMMM! A GOPHER HOLE!
PLUTO! MY LAWN!
Copr. 1937 by Walt Disney Enterprises World rights reserved
E-E-E-EK!
8-1
QUARANTINE MEASLES-CHICKEN POX
MUMPS
WALT DISNEY

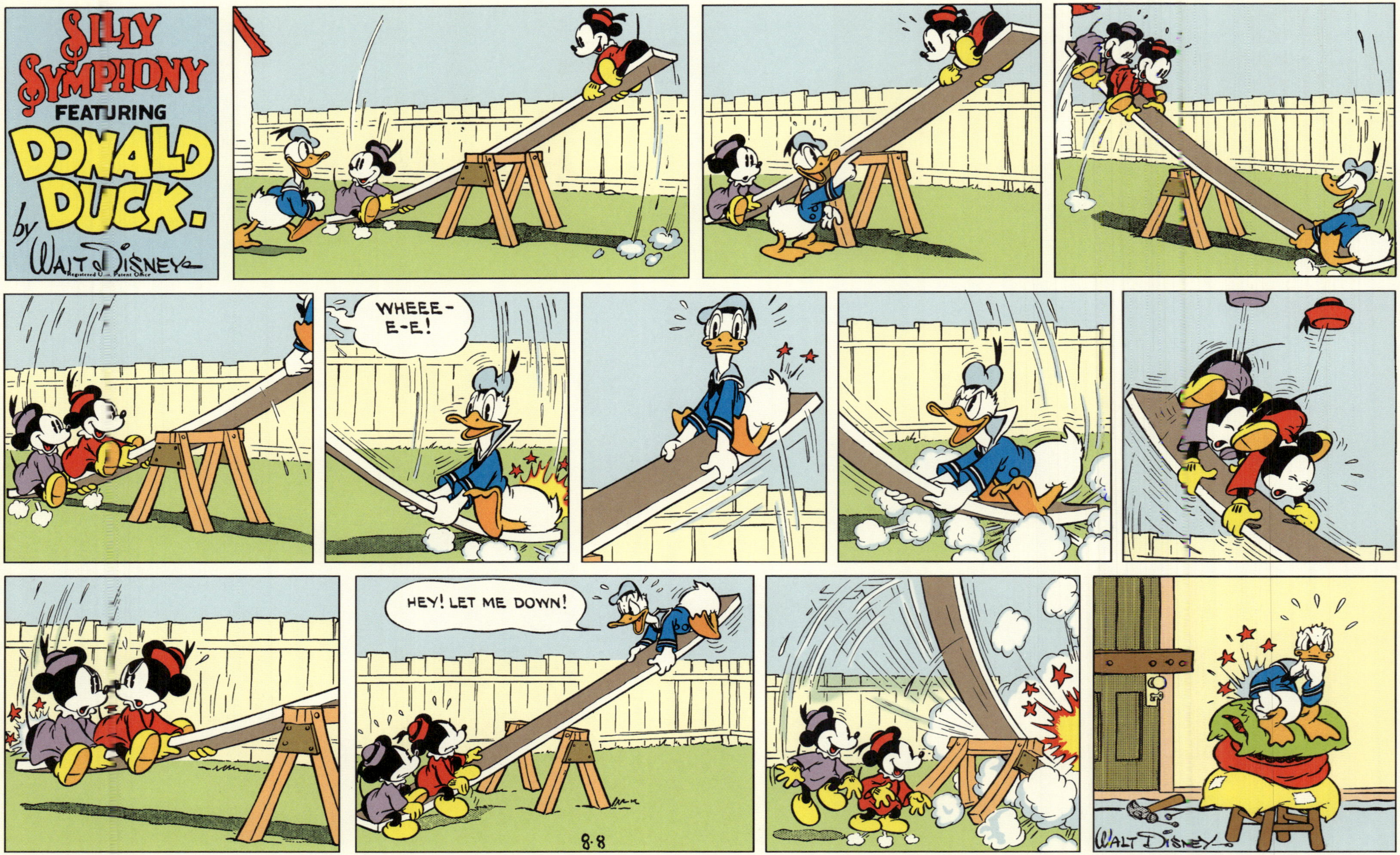
SILLY SYMPHONY
FEATURING
DONALD DUCK.
by WALT DISNEY
WHEEE-
E-E!
HEY! LET ME DOWN!
8-8
WALT DISNEY

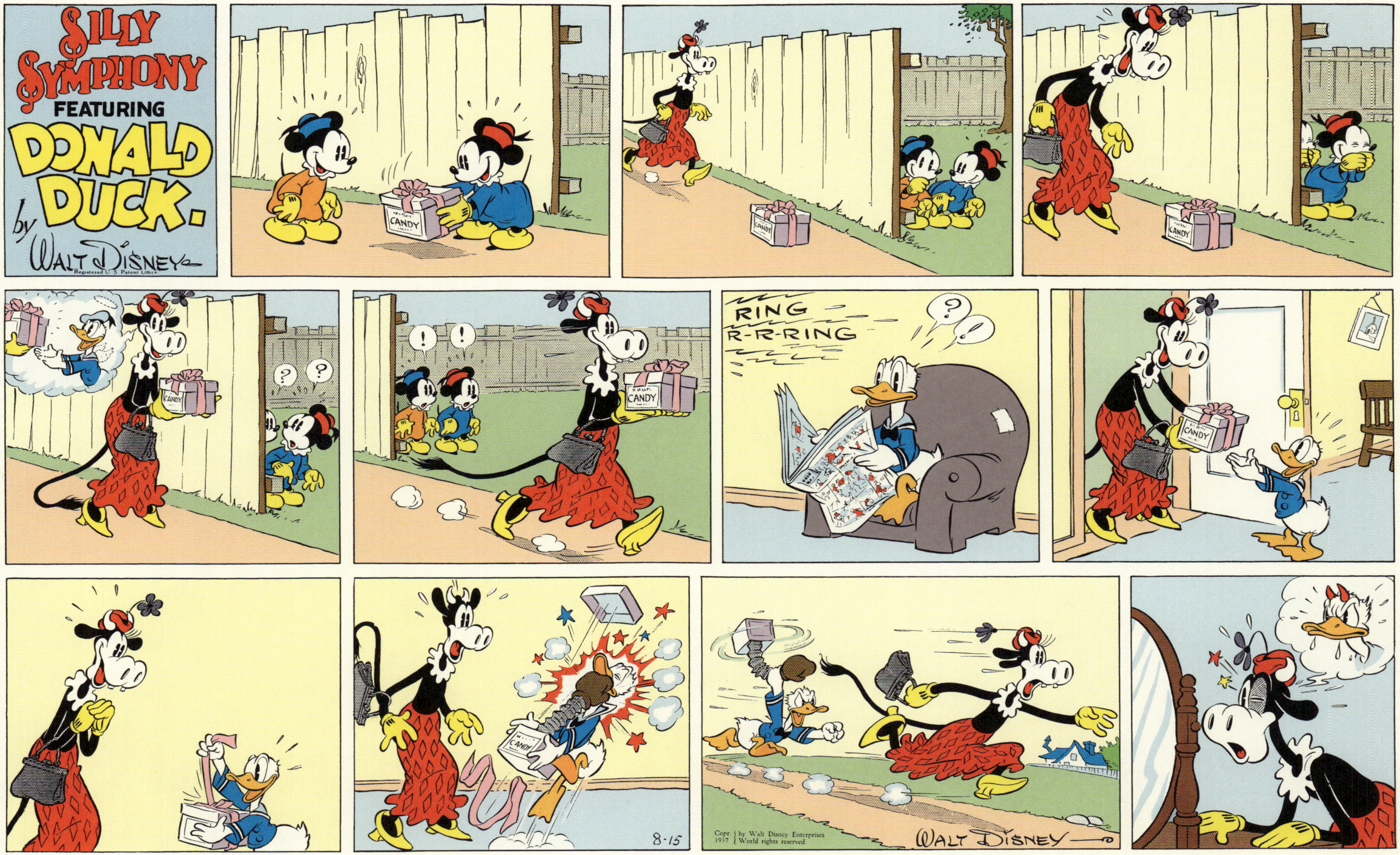
SILLY SYMPHONY
FEATURING
DONALD DUCK.
by WALT DISNEY
Registered U S Patent Office
CANDY
? ?
! !
RING
R-R-RING
? !
8-15
Copr. 1937 by Walt Disney Enterprises World rights reserved
WALT DISNEY

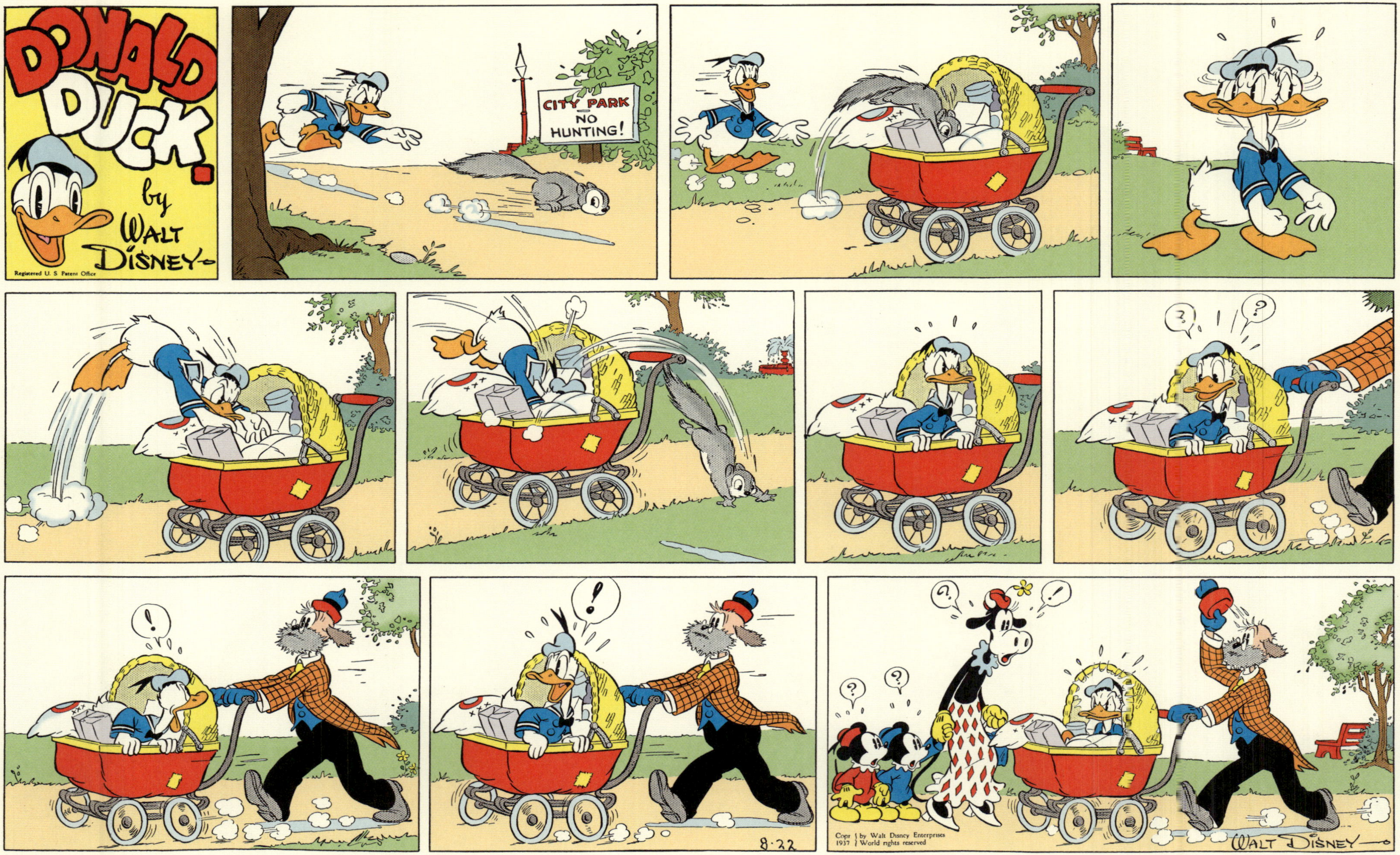
DONALD DUCK
by WALT DISNEY
Registered U. S. Patent Office
CITY PARK
NO HUNTING!
?
?
!
!
?
?
?
?
!
8·22
Copr 1937 by Walt Disney Enterprises World rights reserved
WALT DISNEY

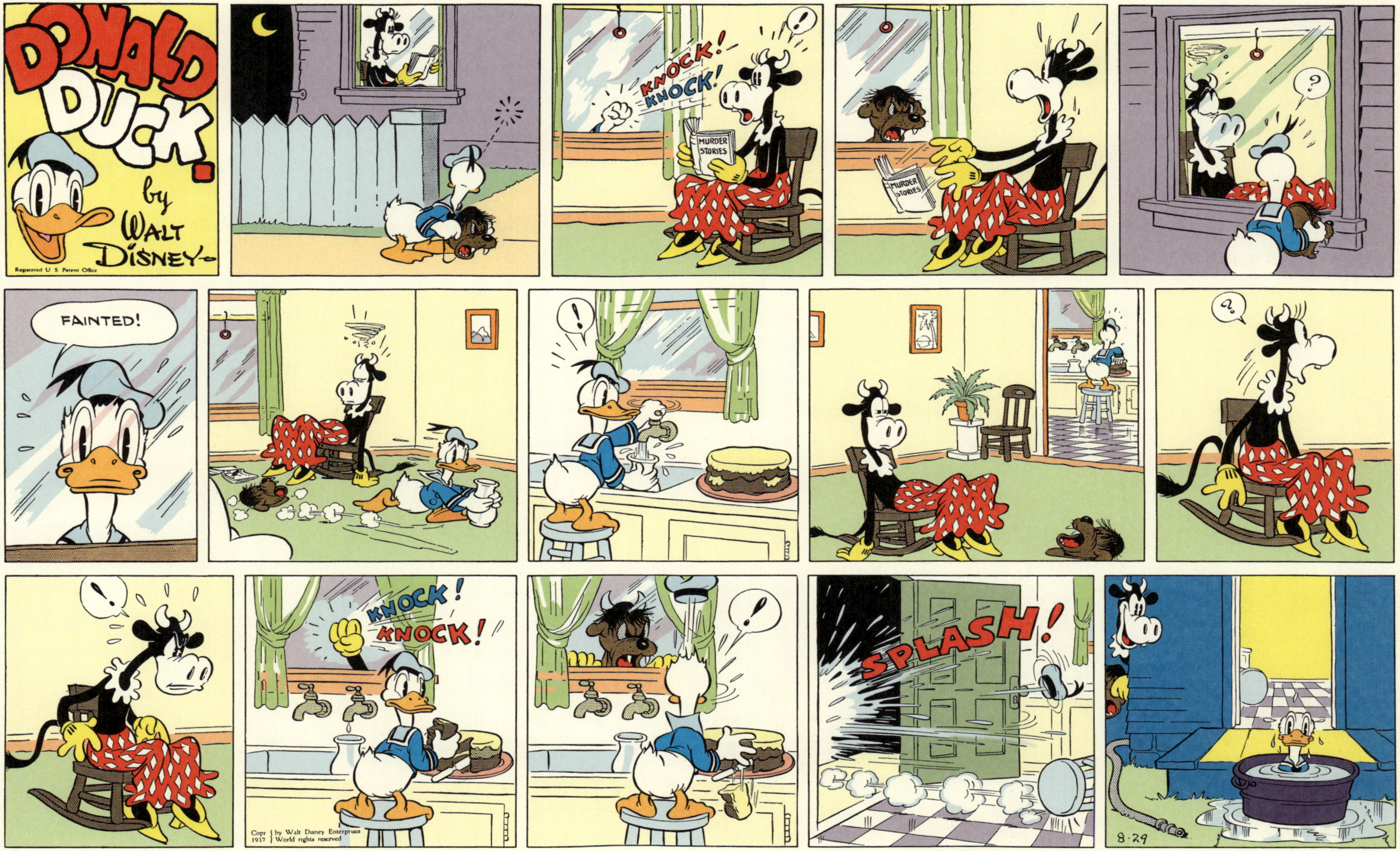
DONALD DUCK
by WALT DISNEY
Registered U S Patent Office
KNOCK! KNOCK!
!
MURDER STORIES
MURDER STORIES
?
FAINTED!
!
?
!
KNOCK! KNOCK!
Copr 1937 by Walt Disney Enterprises World rights reserved
!
SPLASH!
8-29

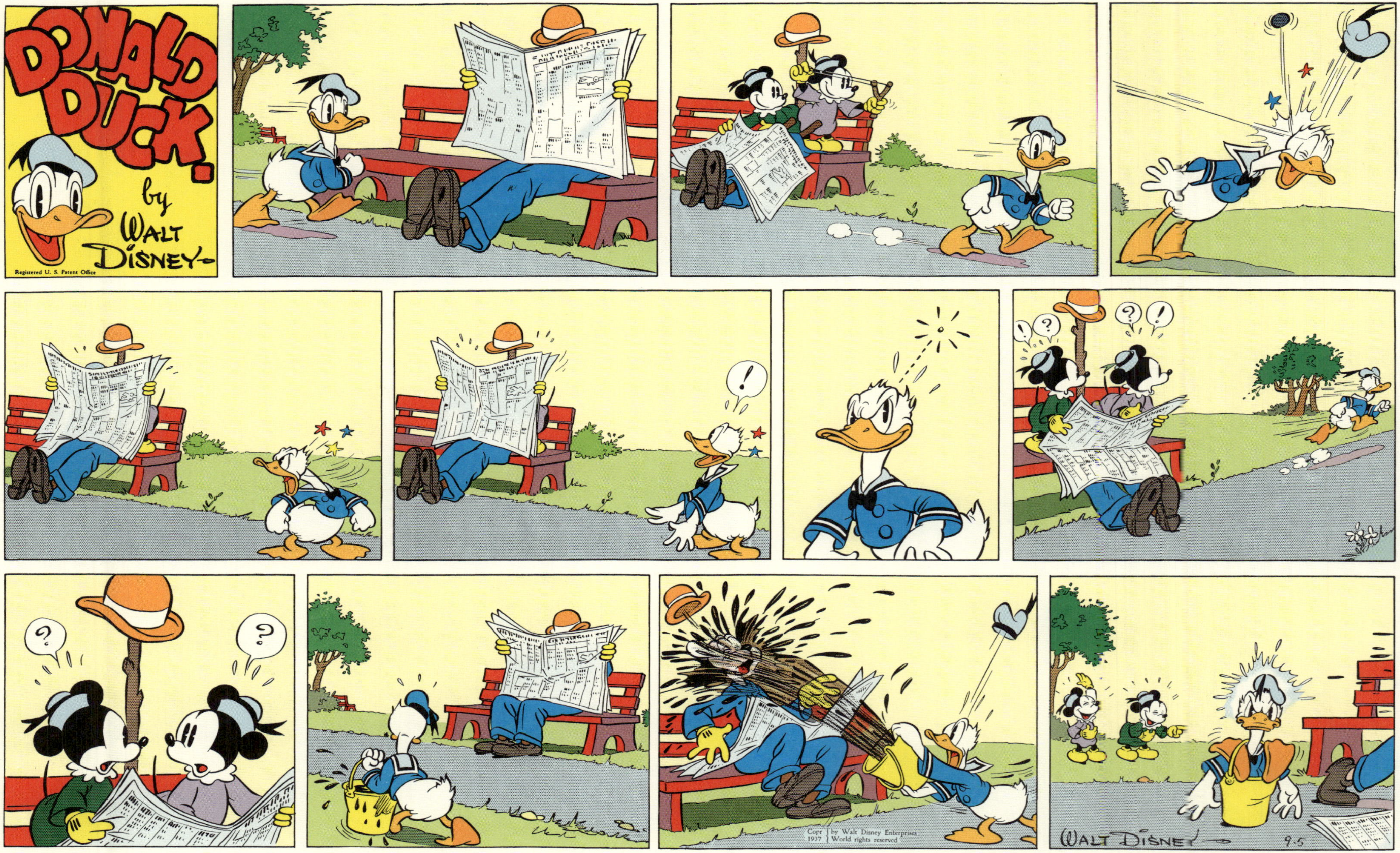
DONALD DUCK
by
WALT DISNEY
Registered U. S. Patent Office
!
!?
?!
?
?
Copr 1937 by Walt Disney Enterprises World rights reserved
WALT DISNEY
9-5

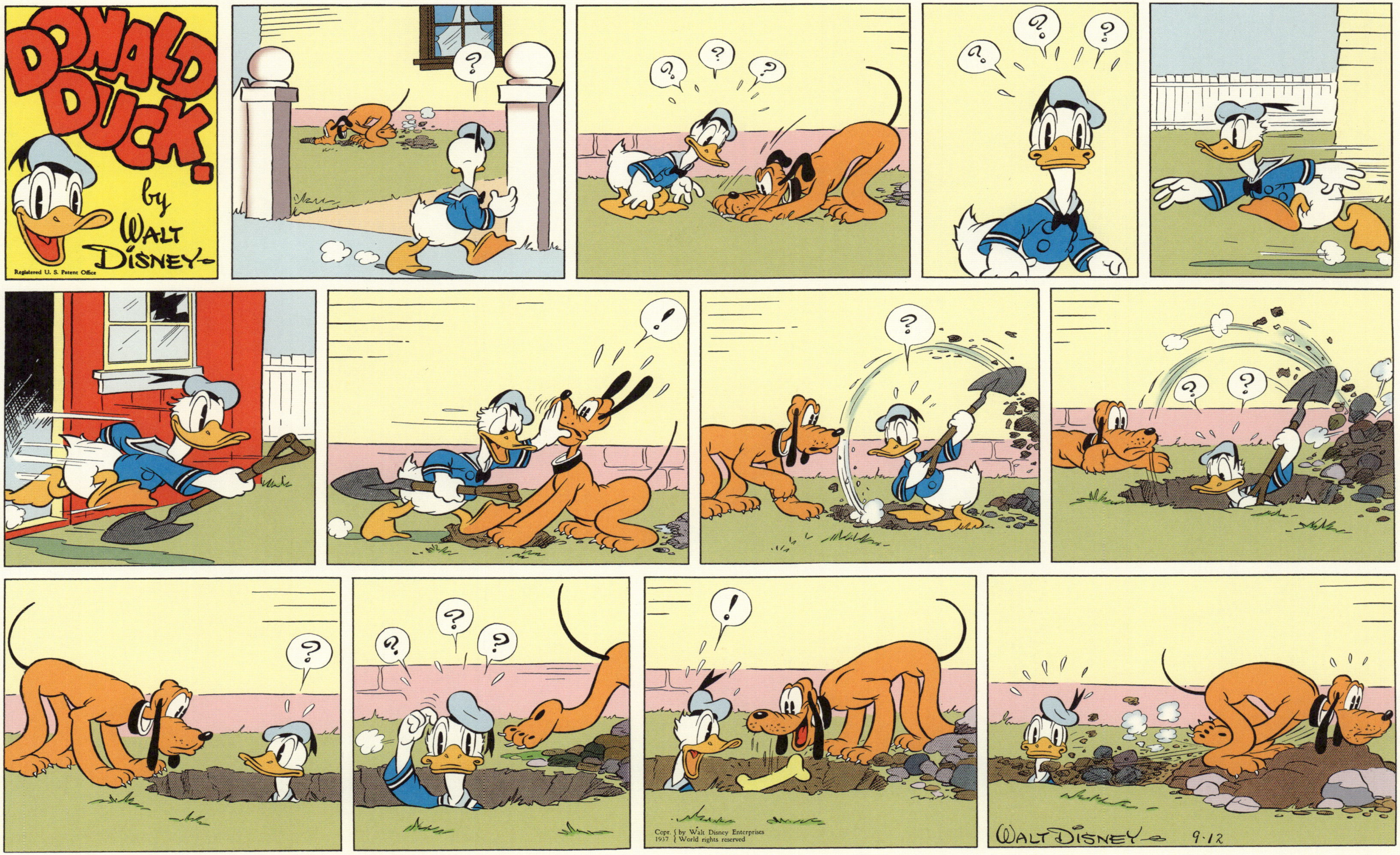
DONALD DUCK
by WALT DISNEY
Registered U. S. Patent Office
?
? ? ?
? ? ?
!
?
? ?
?
? ? ?
!
Copr. 1937 by Walt Disney Enterprises World rights reserved
WALT DISNEY 9-12

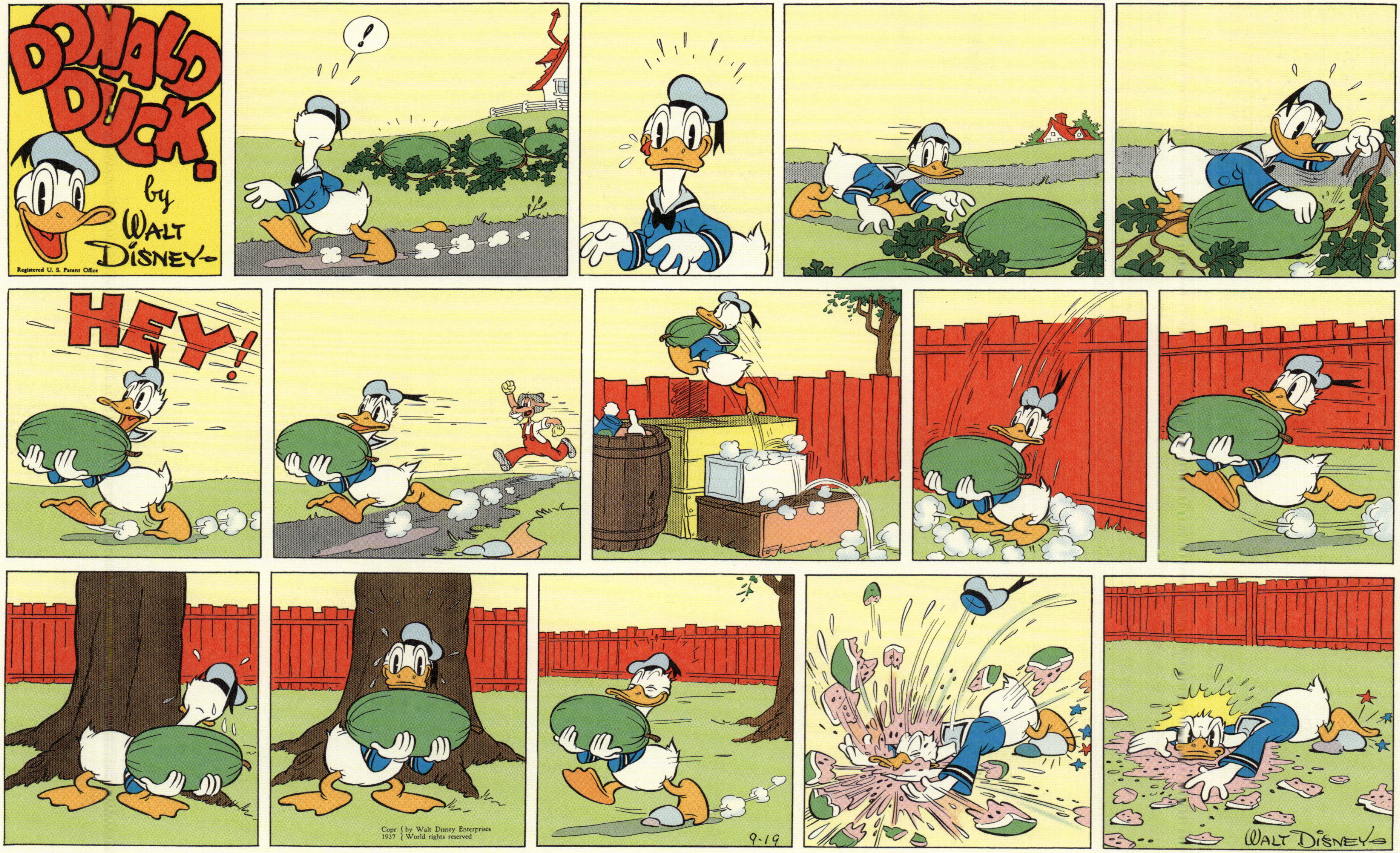
DONALD DUCK
by WALT DISNEY
Registered U. S. Patent Office
!
HEY!
Copr 1937 by Walt Disney Enterprises World rights reserved
9-19
WALT DISNEY

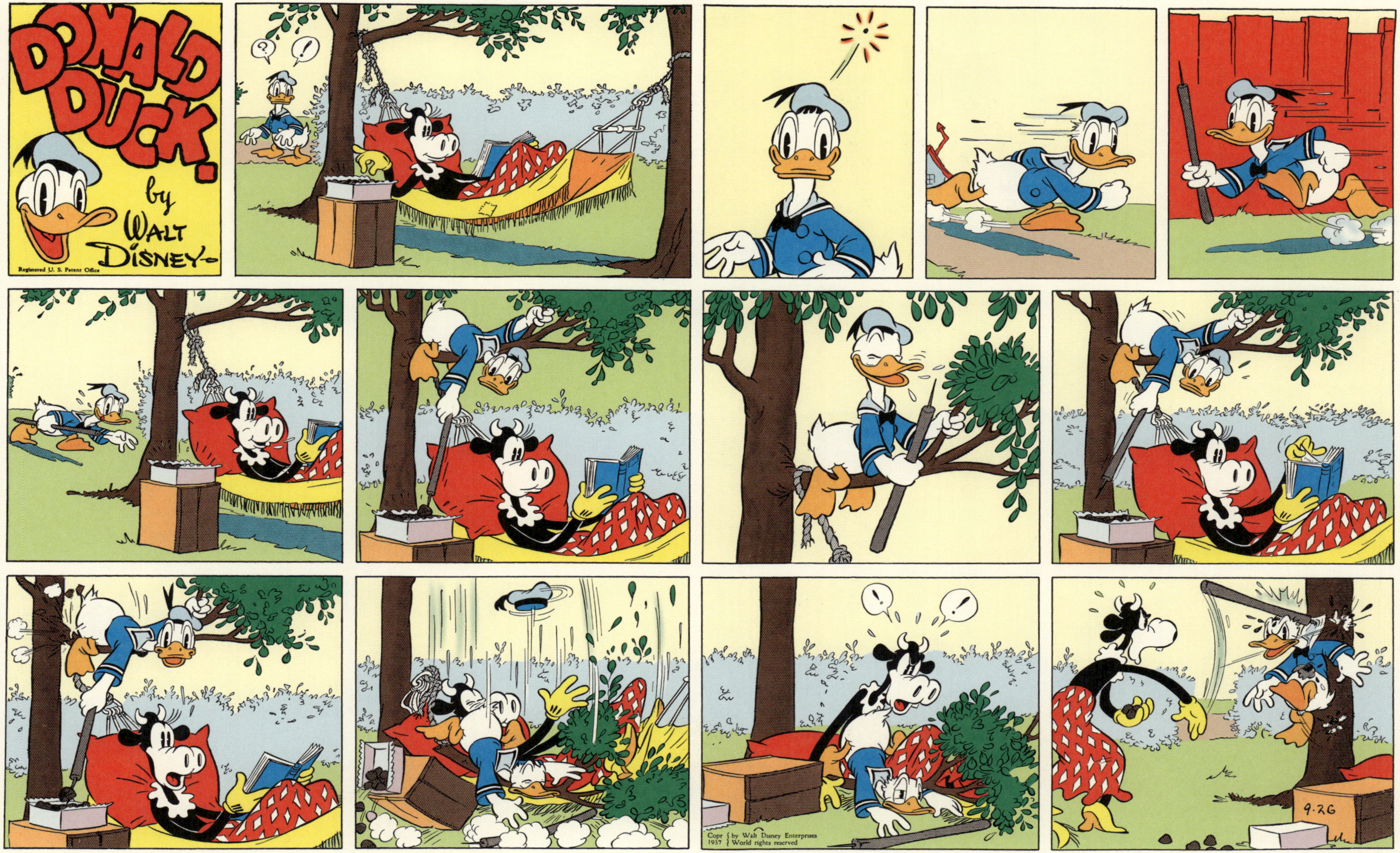
DONALD DUCK
by WALT DISNEY
Registered U. S. Patent Office
?
!
!
!
Copr 1937 by Walt Disney Enterprises World rights reserved
9.26

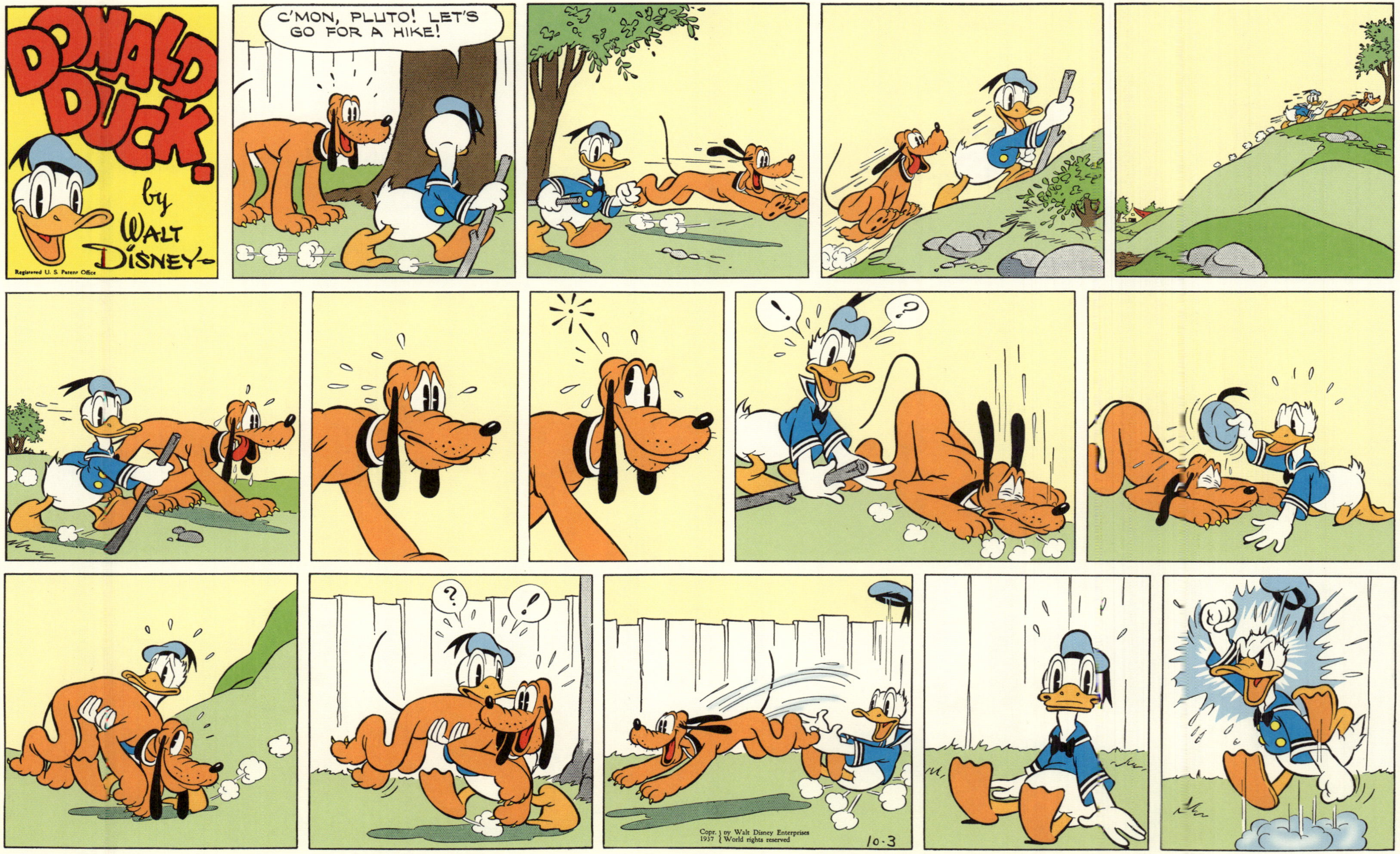
DONALD DUCK.
by WALT DISNEY
Registered U. S. Patent Office
C'MON, PLUTO! LET'S GO FOR A HIKE!
!
?
?
!
Copr. 1937 by Walt Disney Enterprises World rights reserved
10-3

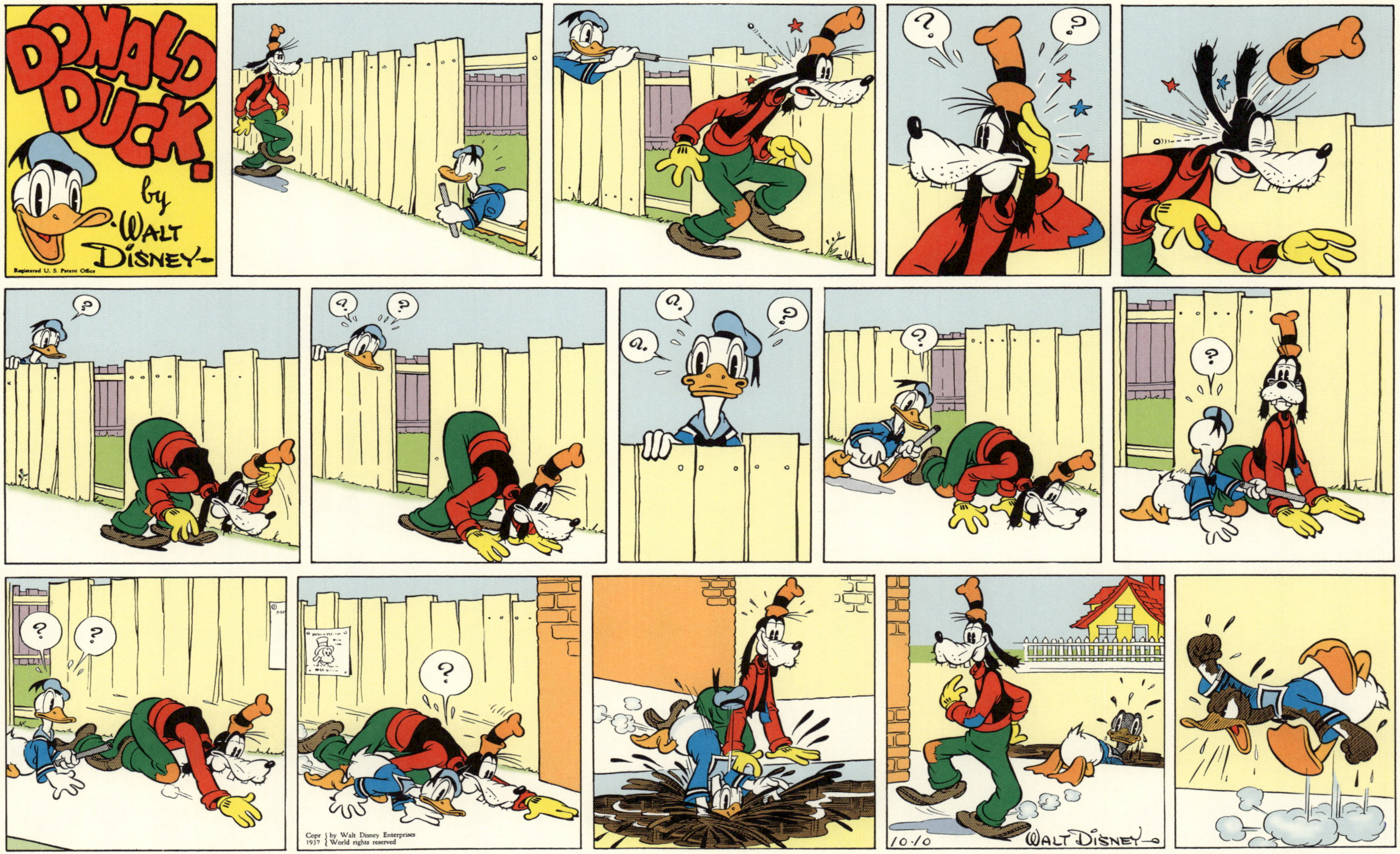
DONALD DUCK
by
WALT DISNEY
Registered U. S. Patent Office
?
?
?
?
?
?
?
?
?
?
?
?
?
Copr 1937 by Walt Disney Enterprises World rights reserved
10-10
WALT DISNEY

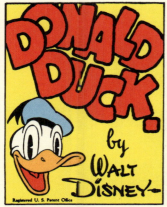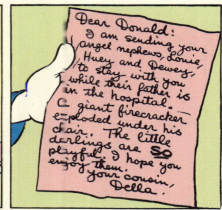

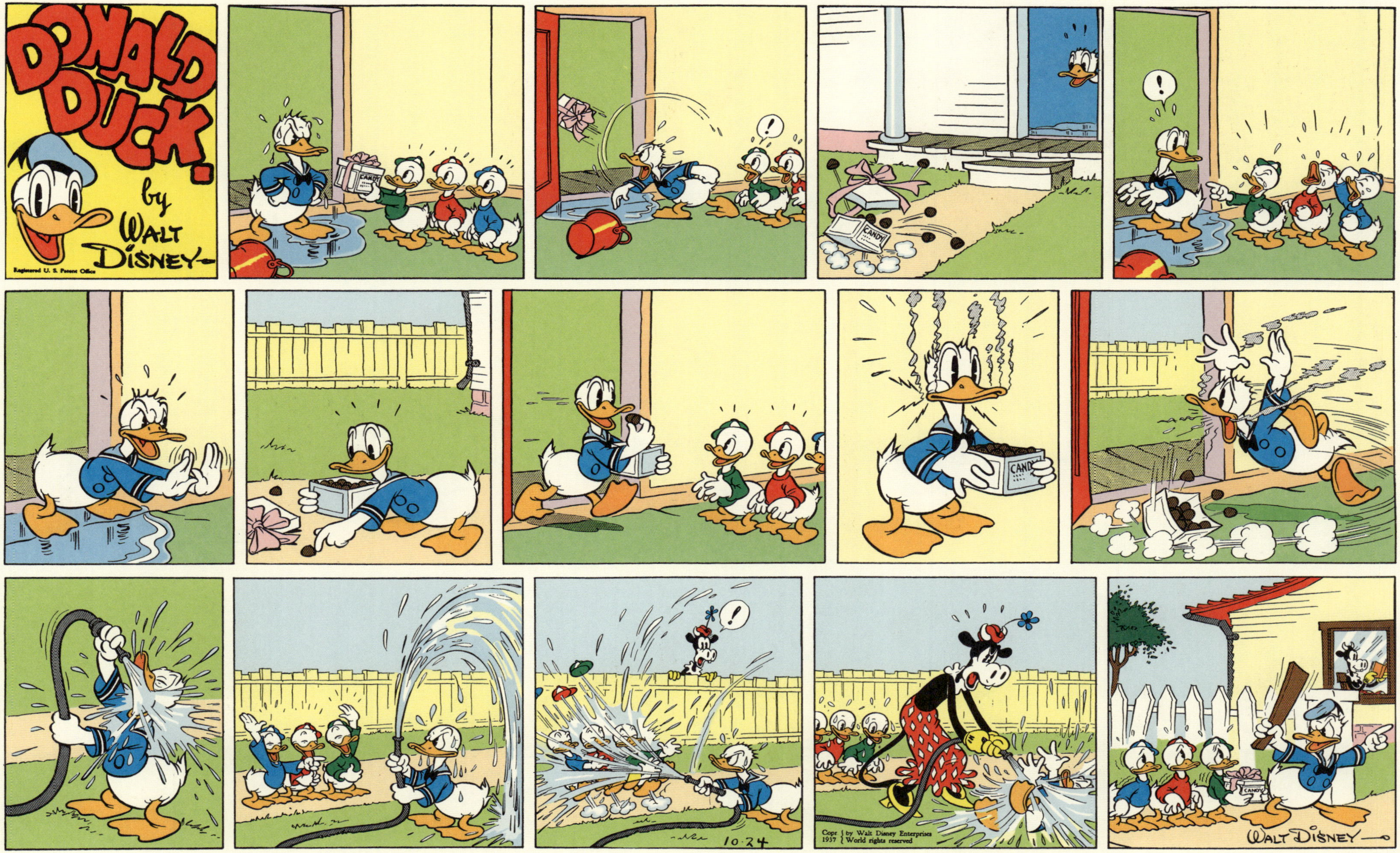
DONALD DUCK
by WALT DISNEY
Registered U. S. Patent Office
CANDY
!
CANDY
!
CANDY
!
!
10·24
Copr 1937 by Walt Disney Enterprises World rights reserved
CANDY
WALT DISNEY

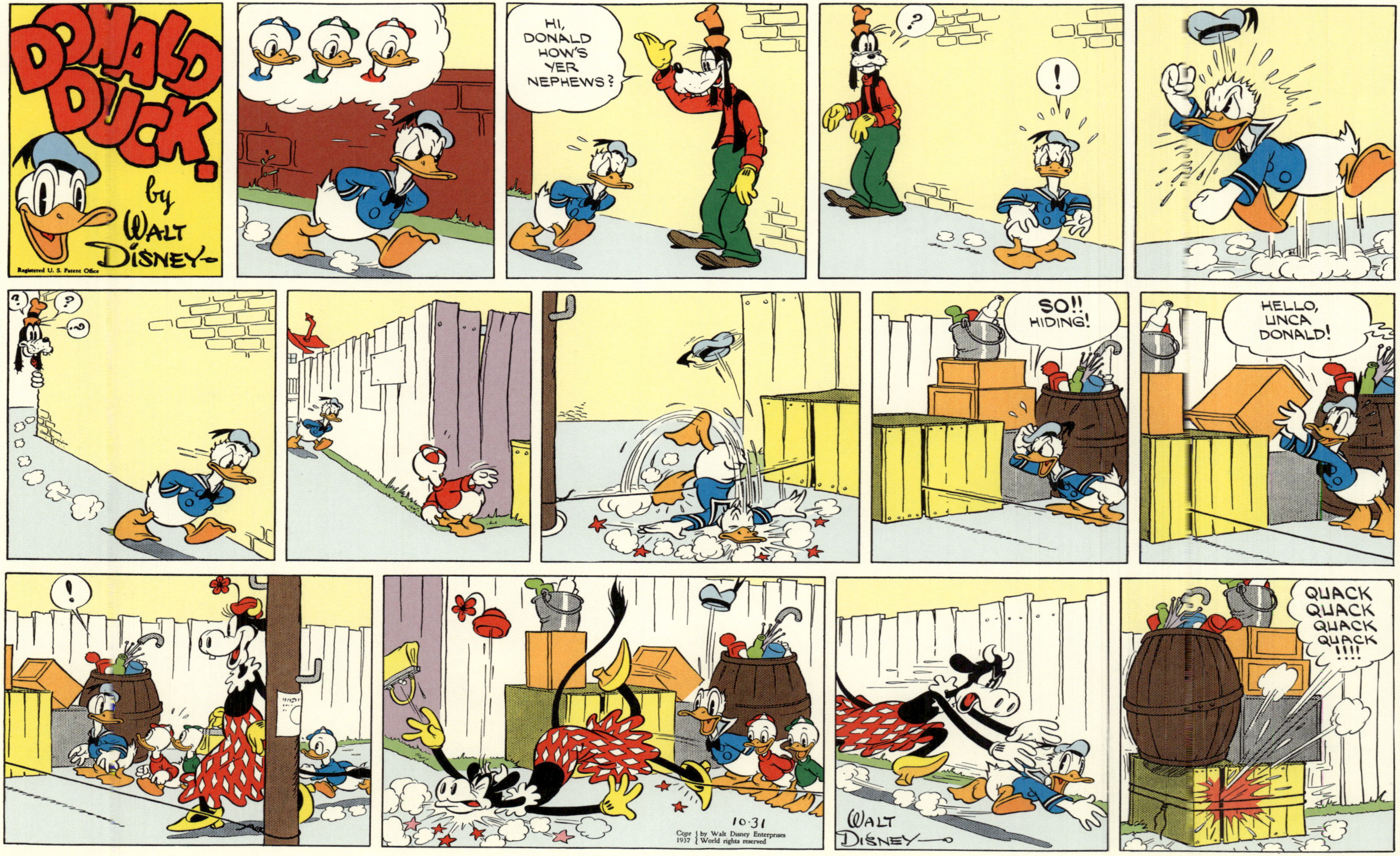
DONALD DUCK
by WALT DISNEY
Registered U. S. Patent Office
HI, DONALD HOW'S YER NEPHEWS?
?
!
?
SO!! HIDING!
HELLO, UNCA DONALD!
!
10-31
Copr 1937 by Walt Disney Enterprises World rights reserved
WALT DISNEY
QUACK QUACK QUACK QUACK !!!!

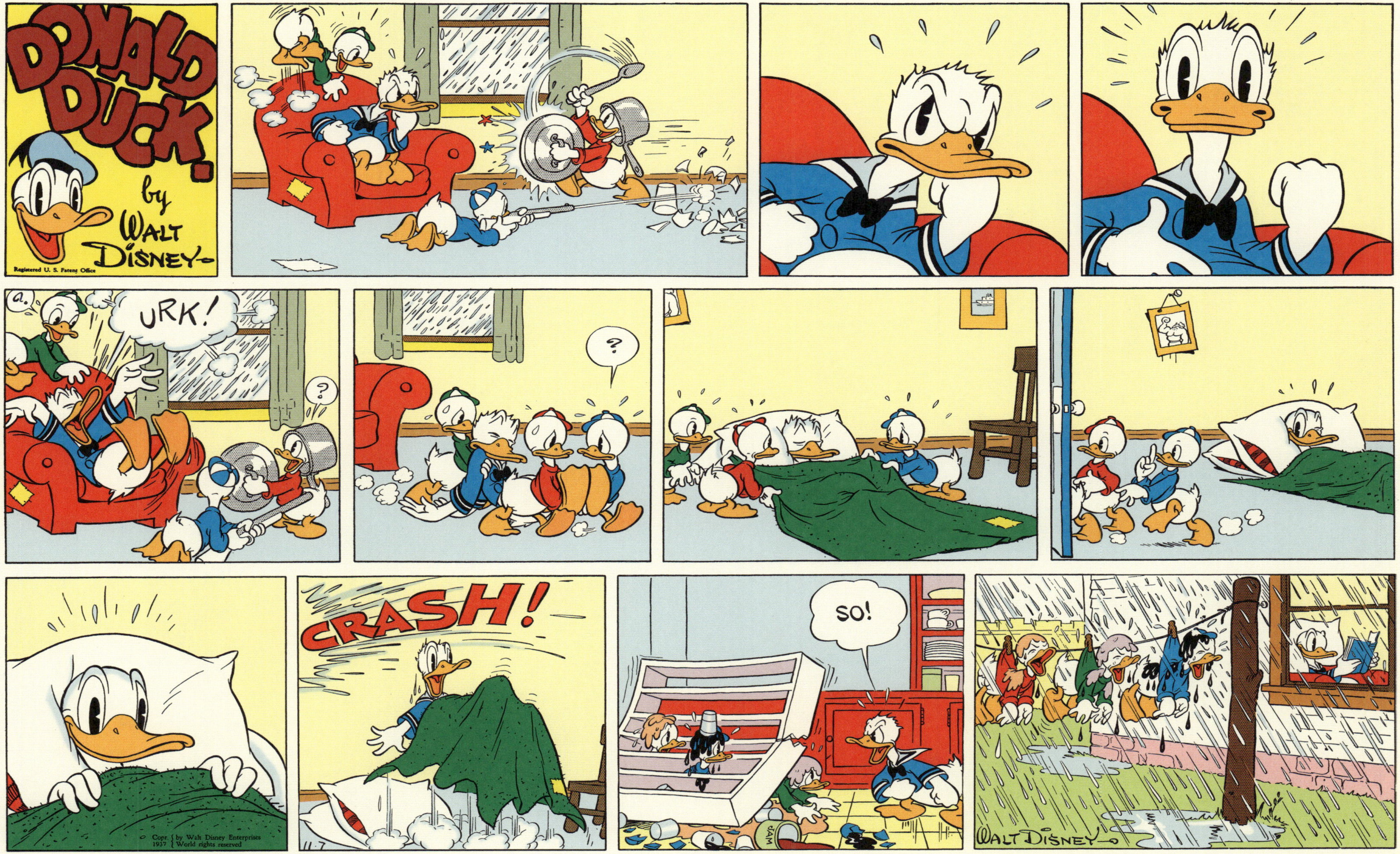
DONALD DUCK
by
WALT DISNEY
Registered U. S. Patent Office
URK!
?
?
CRASH!
SO!
WALT DISNEY
Copr. 1937 by Walt Disney Enterprises World rights reserved

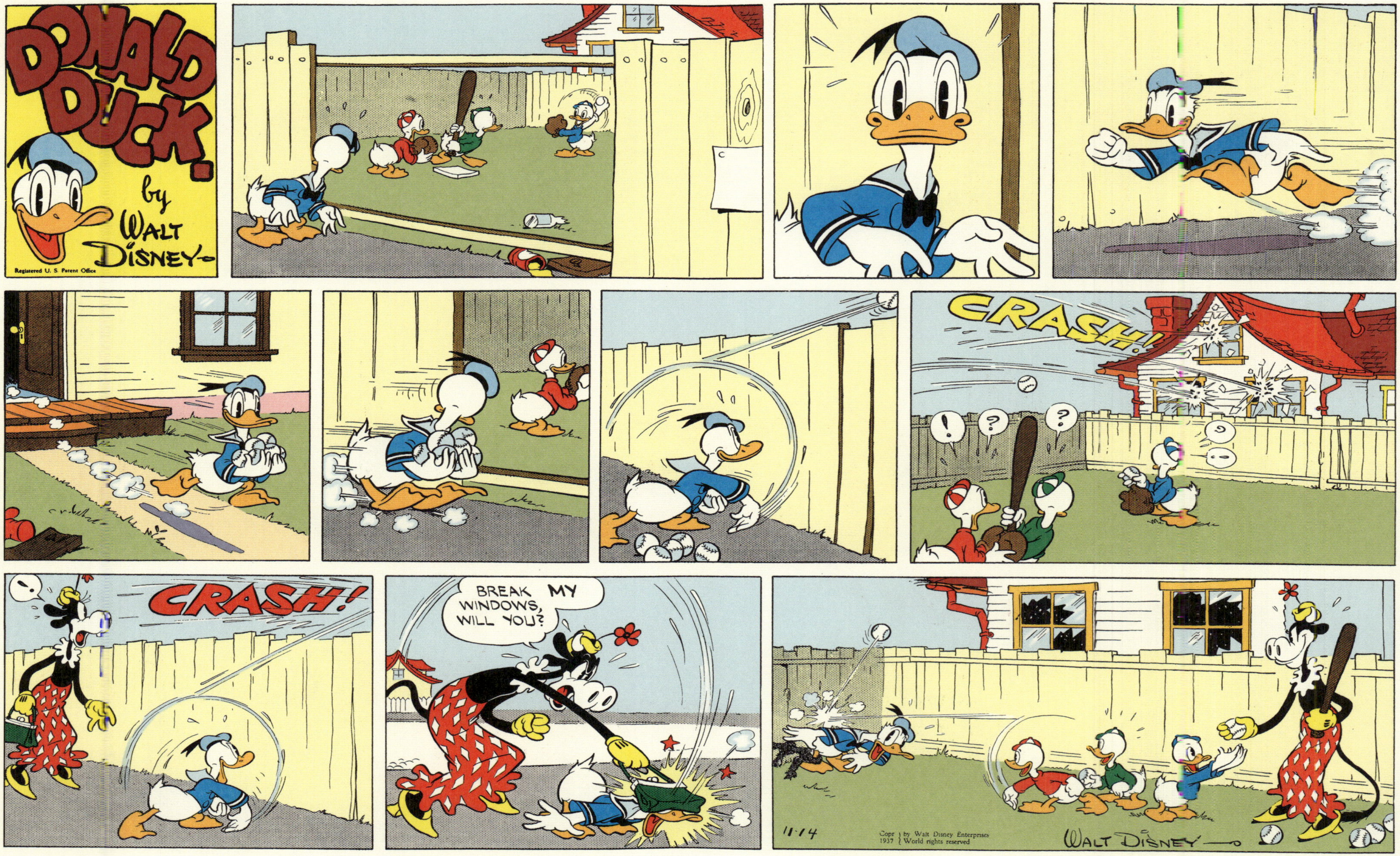
DONALD DUCK
by
WALT DISNEY
Registered U. S. Patent Office
CRASH!
CRASH!
BREAK MY WINDOWS, WILL YOU?
11-14
Copr 1937 by Walt Disney Enterprises World rights reserved
WALT DISNEY

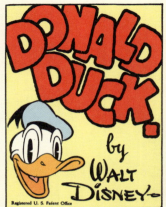

November 21, 1937

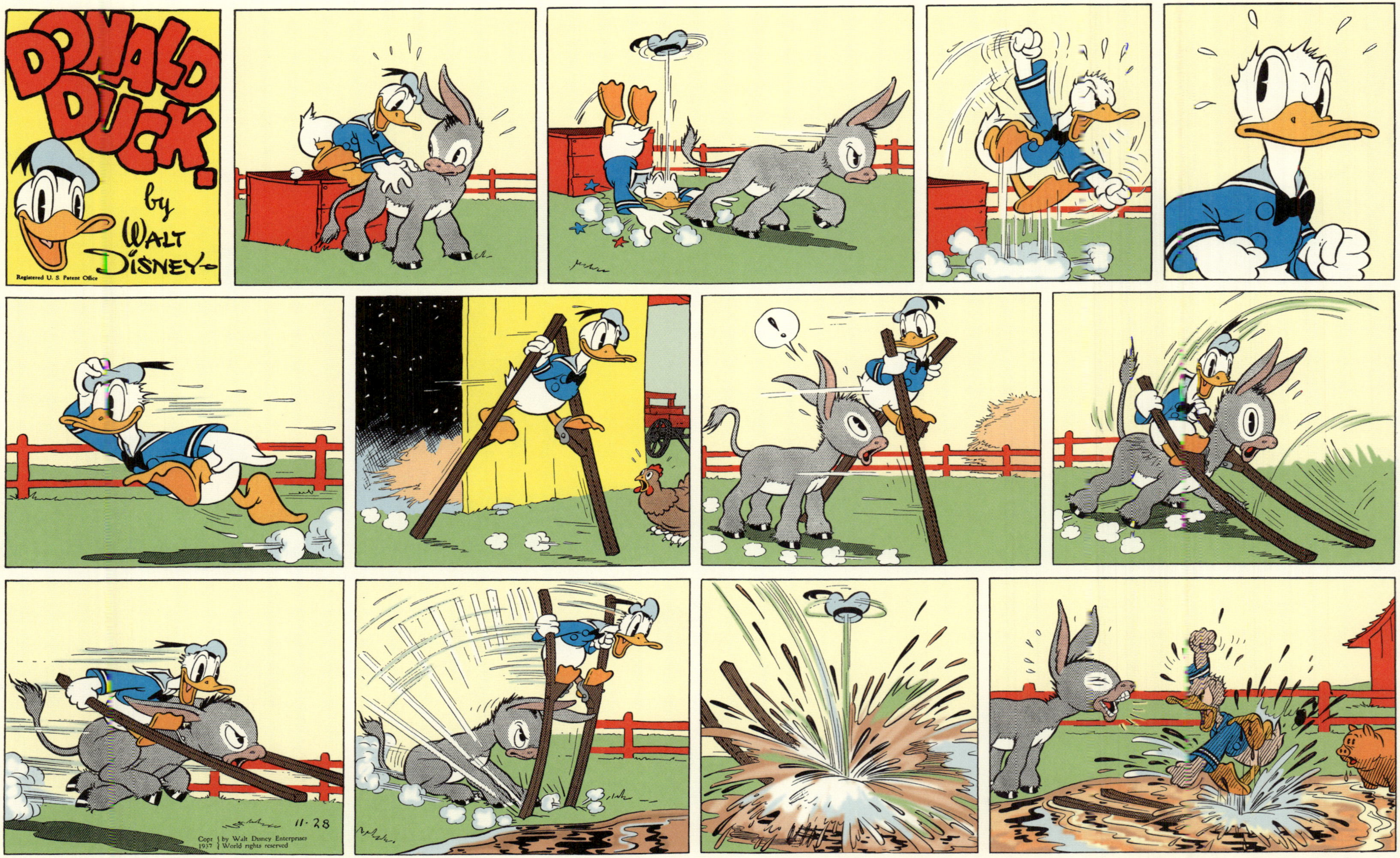
DONALD DUCK
by WALT DISNEY
Registered U. S. Patent Office
!
11·28
Copr 1937 by Walt Disney Enterprises World rights reserved

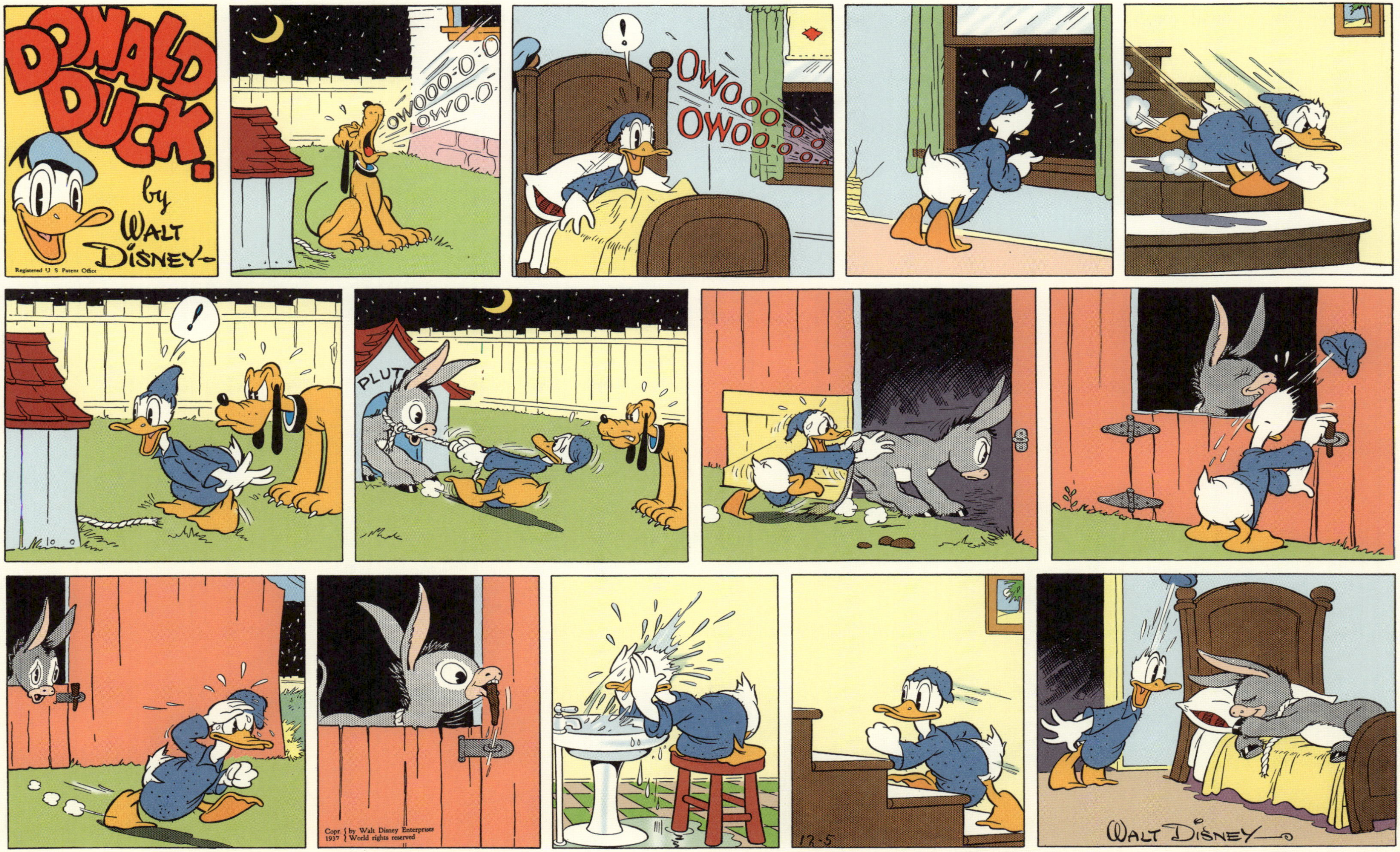
DONALD DUCK
by
WALT DISNEY
Registered U S Patent Office
OWOOO-O-O
OWO-O
!
OWOOO-O-O
OWOO-O-O-O
!
PLUT
Copr 1937 { by Walt Disney Enterprises World rights reserved
12-5
WALT DISNEY

SNOW WHITE AND THE SEVEN DWARFS

December 12, 1937 - April 24, 1938
Written by Merrill de Maris, drawn by Hank Porter, assisted by Bob Grant

AFTER FIVE YEARS, the *Silly Symphony* comic strip had become a flexible arena in which the Disney studio could display a variety of artistic wares. Now it was pressed into service to help promote the studio's historic feature-length film. By the time the movie began to open in theaters, readers were already getting to know Snow White, the Dwarfs, and the rest of the cast in weekly comic installments. Carefully coordinated with the rest of the *Snow White* promotional campaign, the strip retold the story in a more or less faithful adaptation. Here, as in the film, Snow White fell in love with her Prince, fled into the forest to escape the Queen's murderous jealousy, and was sheltered by the Dwarfs; here the Queen disguised herself, attempted to dispatch her victim with a poisoned apple and met her own demise, clearing the way for a happy ending for Snow White and the Prince.

But the *similarities* between strip and film serve to make the *differences* even more interesting. Some variations were dictated by the medium. In the film, the frightened Dwarfs search their house for the monster they think is hiding inside—a scene ideally suited for an extended set-piece of expressive character animation, but less adaptable to static comic panels. Here it's skimmed over quickly. Later in the film, confined downstairs after giving up their bedroom for Snow White's use, the Dwarfs fight over the one available pillow in a slapstick episode, then find comically uncomfortable ways to bed down for the night. In the comic page, again, each of these scenes is disposed of in a single panel.

The film's songs, several of which became standards in the popular-music market, similarly were of little use in the comics. In this continuity, only "Heigh-Ho," the Dwarfs' marching song (here rendered "Hi Ho"), was repeated; all the other songs in the score were eliminated. One of the highlights of the film is the sequence in which the Dwarfs ask Snow White to tell them a story; she responds by singing the romantic ballad "Some Day My Prince Will Come." In the comics, not only the song but the storytelling scene were cut altogether.

On the other hand, the comic strip offers intriguing plot elements that did *not* appear on the screen. Early in story development of the film, the writers had suggested an opening scene in which Snow White might construct an imaginary prince from garden implements, dub the effigy "Prince Buckethead," and play a mock-romantic scene with it until the real Prince overheard her and made a surprise appearance. This idea was soon dropped from the film, but it reappears in the comics version. Even more strikingly, the Disney story crew had considered an elaborate plot thread in which the jealous Queen had the Prince seized and imprisoned in a dungeon, from which he later made a heroic escape. These scenes, too, were cut from the film but survived intact on the comic page.

Thus discarding some elements from the film and adding some new ones of its own, this continuity stands as a distinct *Snow White* adaptation in its own right. Note, too, the marked shift in graphic style that appears in this story. In place of Al Taliaferro's clean, uncluttered line, previously the standard in the *Silly Symphony* comics, Hank Porter and Bob Grant introduce a quaint, shadowy storybook atmosphere—translating the rich texture of the film's visuals into the terms of the newspaper comic page.

—J.B. KAUFMAN

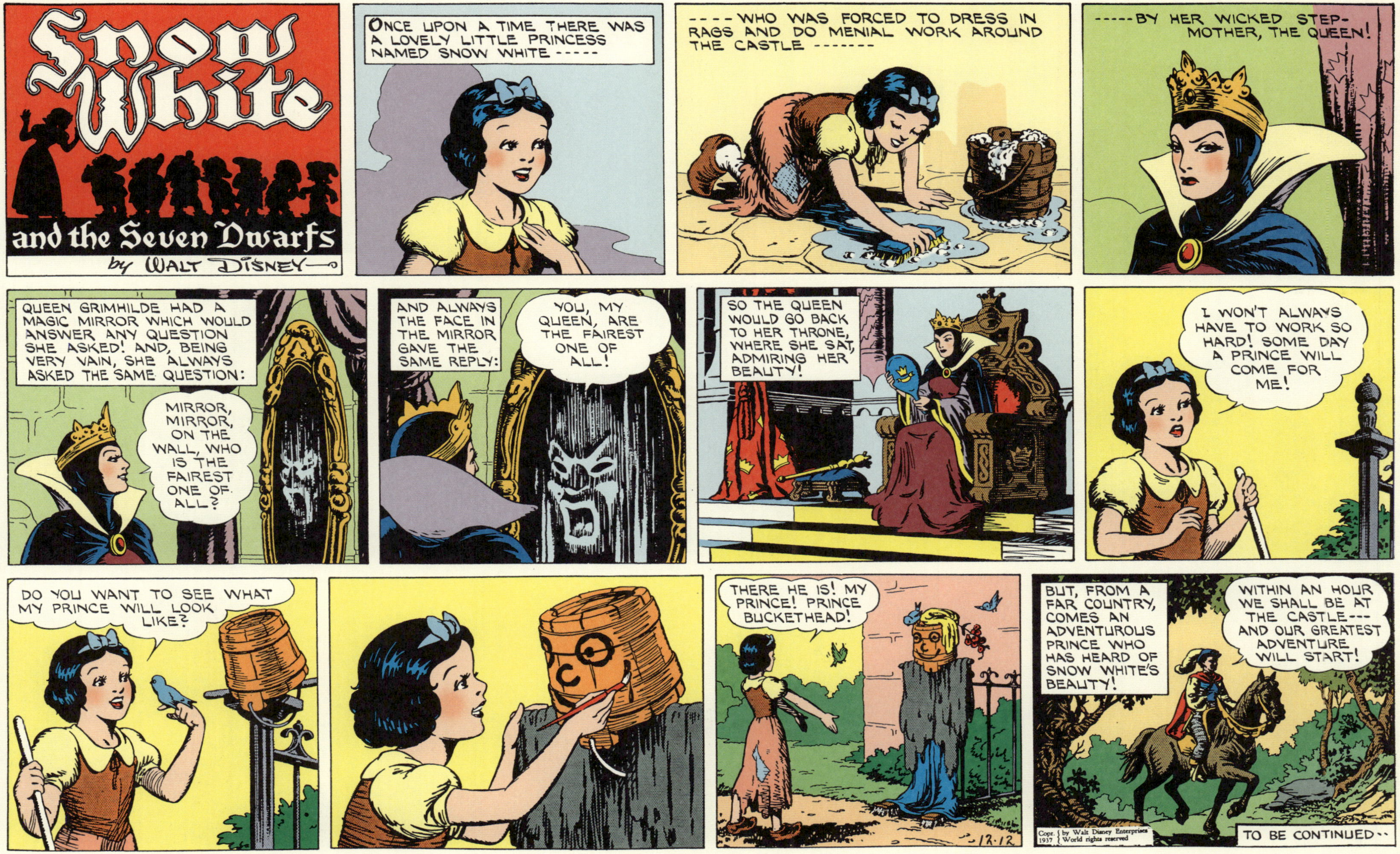
Snow White
and the Seven Dwarfs
by Walt Disney
ONCE UPON A TIME THERE WAS A LOVELY LITTLE PRINCESS NAMED SNOW WHITE -----
---- WHO WAS FORCED TO DRESS IN RAGS AND DO MENIAL WORK AROUND THE CASTLE -------
-----BY HER WICKED STEP-MOTHER, THE QUEEN!
QUEEN GRIMHILDE HAD A MAGIC MIRROR WHICH WOULD ANSWER ANY QUESTION SHE ASKED! AND, BEING VERY VAIN, SHE ALWAYS ASKED THE SAME QUESTION:
MIRROR, MIRROR, ON THE WALL, WHO IS THE FAIREST ONE OF ALL?
AND ALWAYS THE FACE IN THE MIRROR GAVE THE SAME REPLY:
YOU, MY QUEEN, ARE THE FAIREST ONE OF ALL!
SO THE QUEEN WOULD GO BACK TO HER THRONE, WHERE SHE SAT, ADMIRING HER BEAUTY!
I WON'T ALWAYS HAVE TO WORK SO HARD! SOME DAY A PRINCE WILL COME FOR ME!
DO YOU WANT TO SEE WHAT MY PRINCE WILL LOOK LIKE?
THERE HE IS! MY PRINCE! PRINCE BUCKETHEAD!
12-12
BUT, FROM A FAR COUNTRY, COMES AN ADVENTUROUS PRINCE WHO HAS HEARD OF SNOW WHITE'S BEAUTY!
WITHIN AN HOUR WE SHALL BE AT THE CASTLE--- AND OUR GREATEST ADVENTURE WILL START!
Copr. 1937 by Walt Disney Enterprises World rights reserved
TO BE CONTINUED--

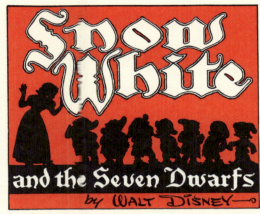

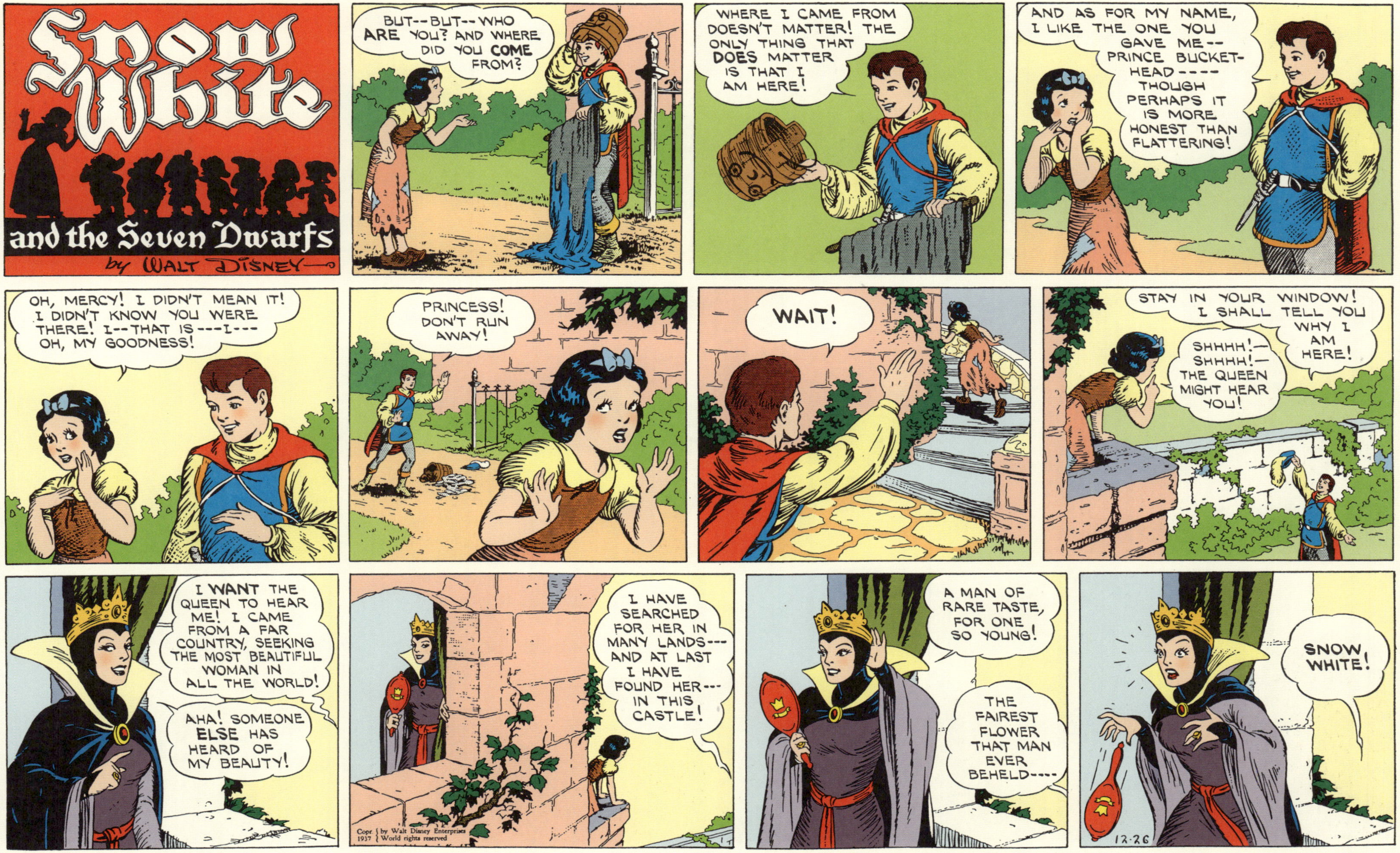

Snow White
and the Seven Dwarfs
by WALT DISNEY
BUT--BUT--WHO ARE YOU? AND WHERE DID YOU COME FROM?
WHERE I CAME FROM DOESN'T MATTER! THE ONLY THING THAT DOES MATTER IS THAT I AM HERE!
AND AS FOR MY NAME, I LIKE THE ONE YOU GAVE ME-- PRINCE BUCKET-HEAD---- THOUGH PERHAPS IT IS MORE HONEST THAN FLATTERING!
OH, MERCY! I DIDN'T MEAN IT! I DIDN'T KNOW YOU WERE THERE! I--THAT IS---I--- OH, MY GOODNESS!
PRINCESS! DON'T RUN AWAY!
WAIT!
STAY IN YOUR WINDOW! I SHALL TELL YOU WHY I AM HERE!
SHHHH!— SHHHH!— THE QUEEN MIGHT HEAR YOU!
I WANT THE QUEEN TO HEAR ME! I CAME FROM A FAR COUNTRY, SEEKING THE MOST BEAUTIFUL WOMAN IN ALL THE WORLD!
AHA! SOMEONE ELSE HAS HEARD OF MY BEAUTY!
I HAVE SEARCHED FOR HER IN MANY LANDS--- AND AT LAST I HAVE FOUND HER--- IN THIS CASTLE!
Copr 1937 by Walt Disney Enterprises World rights reserved
A MAN OF RARE TASTE, FOR ONE SO YOUNG!
THE FAIREST FLOWER THAT MAN EVER BEHELD----
SNOW WHITE!
12-26

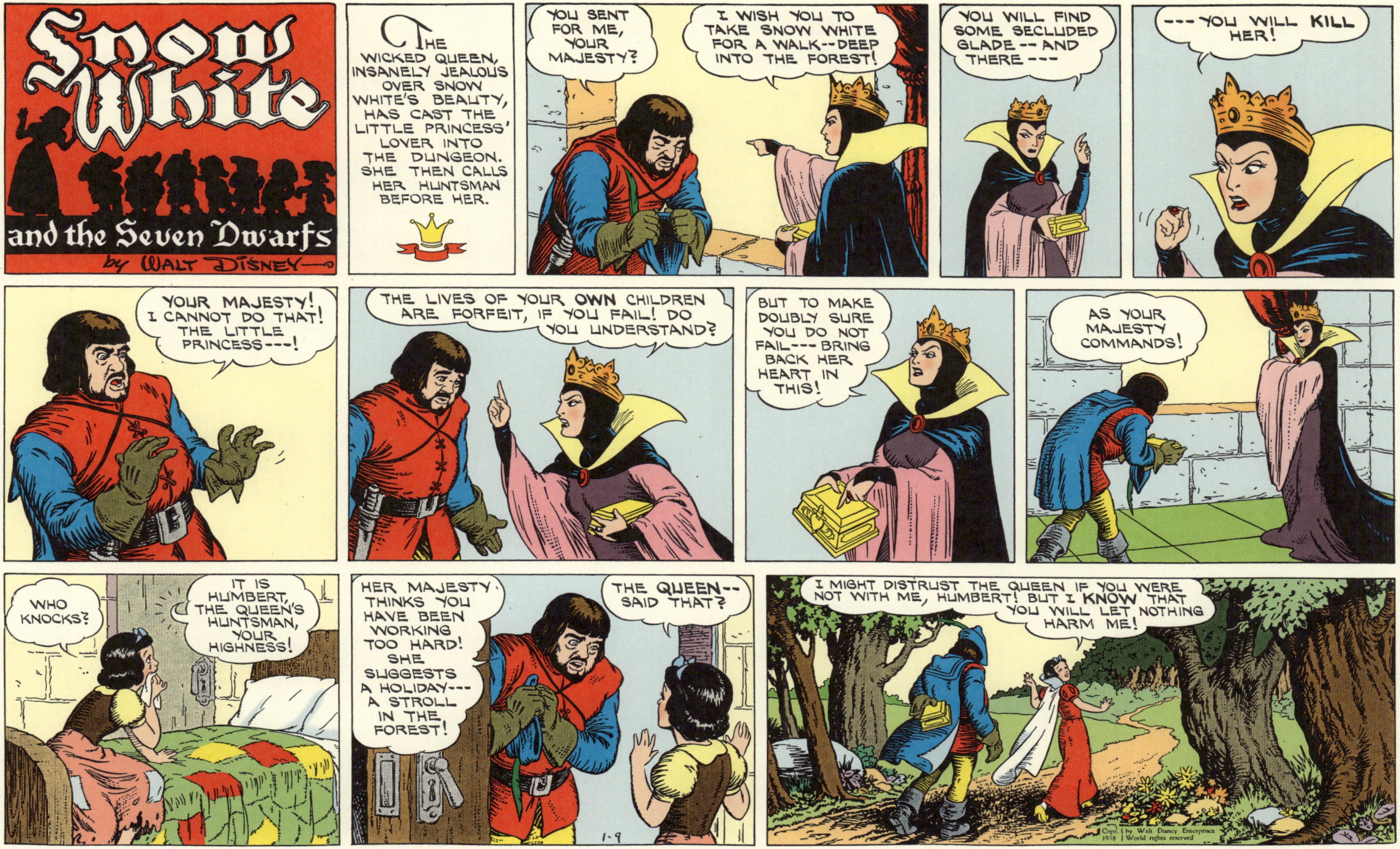
Snow White and the Seven Dwarfs
by Walt Disney
The wicked queen, insanely jealous over Snow White's beauty, has cast the little princess' lover into the dungeon. She then calls her huntsman before her.
YOU SENT FOR ME, YOUR MAJESTY?
I WISH YOU TO TAKE SNOW WHITE FOR A WALK--DEEP INTO THE FOREST!
YOU WILL FIND SOME SECLUDED GLADE -- AND THERE ---
--- YOU WILL KILL HER!
YOUR MAJESTY! I CANNOT DO THAT! THE LITTLE PRINCESS---!
THE LIVES OF YOUR OWN CHILDREN ARE FORFEIT, IF YOU FAIL! DO YOU UNDERSTAND?
BUT TO MAKE DOUBLY SURE YOU DO NOT FAIL--- BRING BACK HER HEART IN THIS!
AS YOUR MAJESTY COMMANDS!
WHO KNOCKS?
IT IS HUMBERT, THE QUEEN'S HUNTSMAN, YOUR HIGHNESS!
HER MAJESTY THINKS YOU HAVE BEEN WORKING TOO HARD! SHE SUGGESTS A HOLIDAY--- A STROLL IN THE FOREST!
THE QUEEN-- SAID THAT?
1-9
I MIGHT DISTRUST THE QUEEN IF YOU WERE NOT WITH ME, HUMBERT! BUT I KNOW THAT YOU WILL LET NOTHING HARM ME!
Copr. 1938 by Walt Disney Enterprises World rights reserved

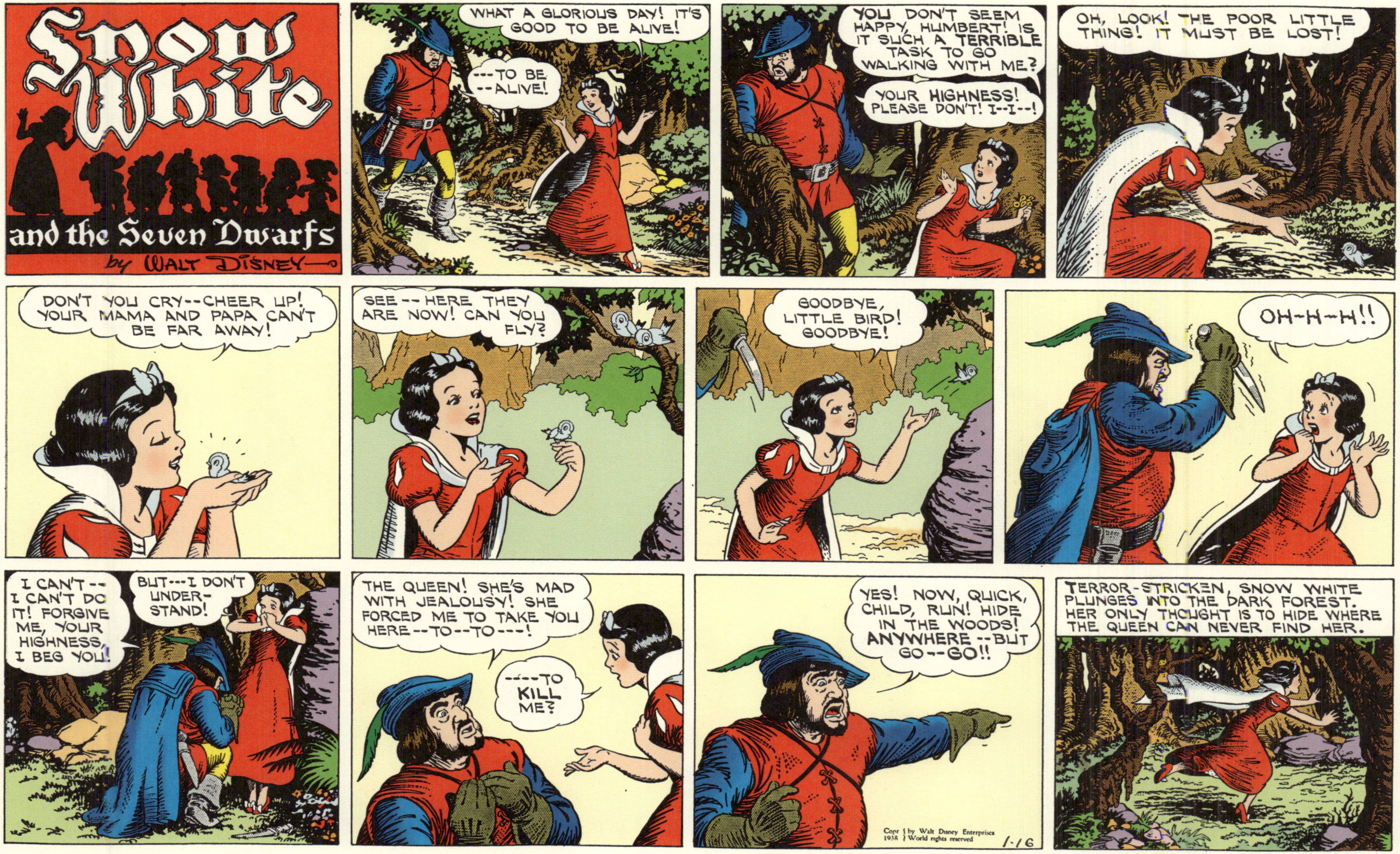
Snow White
and the Seven Dwarfs
by Walt Disney
WHAT A GLORIOUS DAY! IT'S GOOD TO BE ALIVE!
---TO BE --ALIVE!
YOU DON'T SEEM HAPPY, HUMBERT! IS IT SUCH A TERRIBLE TASK TO GO WALKING WITH ME?
YOUR HIGHNESS! PLEASE DON'T! I--I--!
OH, LOOK! THE POOR LITTLE THING! IT MUST BE LOST!
DON'T YOU CRY--CHEER UP! YOUR MAMA AND PAPA CAN'T BE FAR AWAY!
SEE--HERE THEY ARE NOW! CAN YOU FLY?
GOODBYE, LITTLE BIRD! GOODBYE!
OH-H-H!!
I CAN'T-- I CAN'T DO IT! FORGIVE ME, YOUR HIGHNESS, I BEG YOU!
BUT---I DON'T UNDER-STAND!
THE QUEEN! SHE'S MAD WITH JEALOUSY! SHE FORCED ME TO TAKE YOU HERE--TO--TO---!
----TO KILL ME?
YES! NOW, QUICK, CHILD, RUN! HIDE IN THE WOODS! ANYWHERE--BUT GO--GO!!
Copr 1938 by Walt Disney Enterprises World rights reserved
1-16
TERROR-STRICKEN, SNOW WHITE PLUNGES INTO THE DARK FOREST. HER ONLY THOUGHT IS TO HIDE WHERE THE QUEEN CAN NEVER FIND HER.

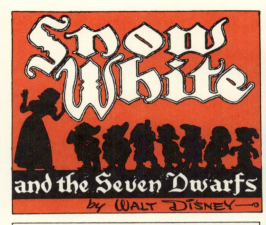

Frightened by her narrow escape from death, Snow White flees, terrified, into the woods.

Blinded with fear, she trips and falls.

In her great fright, Snow White's imagination causes her to see fearful monsters surrounding her.

Harmless bushes take the form of clutching hands....

....gnarled tree trunks appear as gigantic ogres. The eyes of owls and bats are magnified in her mind to the eyes of horrible demons.

Running blindly, she stumbles into a shallow pond.

As she scrambles out, the little princess thinks she has barely escaped the gaping mouths of crocodiles.

Overcome by fear, her strength exhausted....

....Snow White falls, sobbing, to the ground.

149 • January 23, 1938

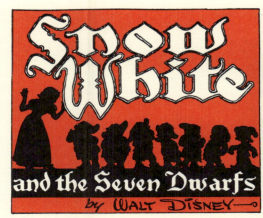

150 • January 30, 1938

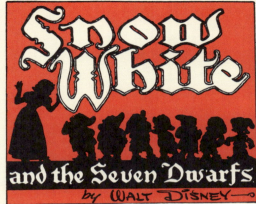

February 6, 1938

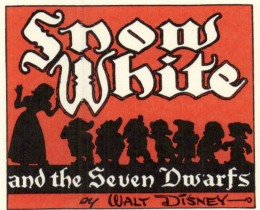

152 • February 13, 1938

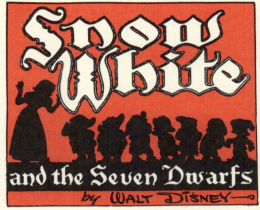

153 • February 20, 1938

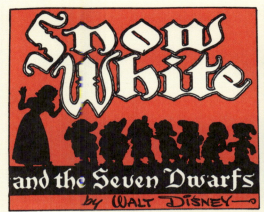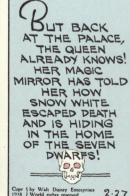

154 • February 27, 1938

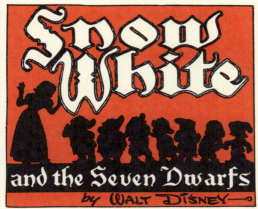

March 6, 1938

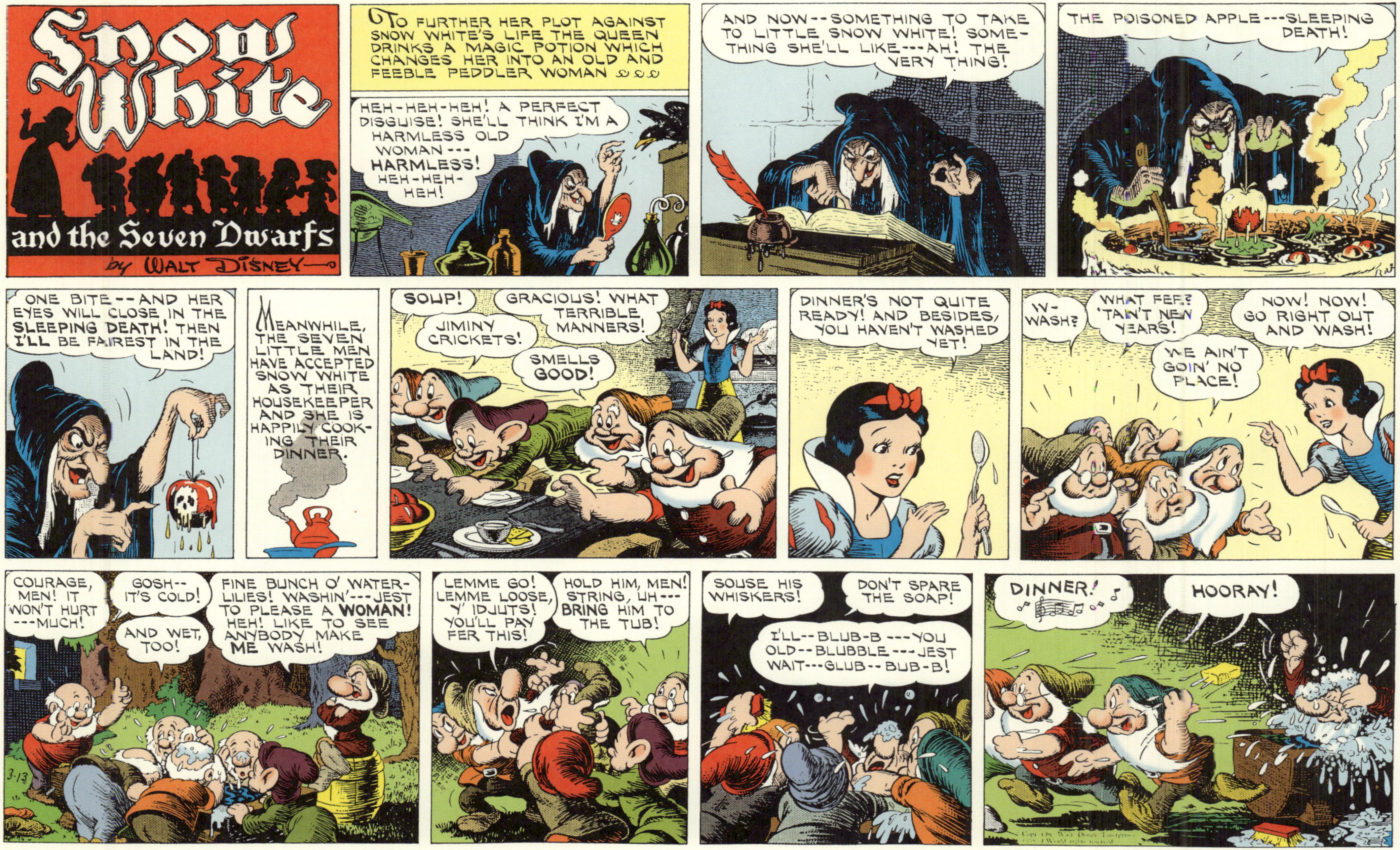

Snow White and the Seven Dwarfs
by Walt Disney
TO FURTHER HER PLOT AGAINST SNOW WHITE'S LIFE THE QUEEN DRINKS A MAGIC POTION WHICH CHANGES HER INTO AN OLD AND FEEBLE PEDDLER WOMAN
HEH-HEH-HEH! A PERFECT DISGUISE! SHE'LL THINK I'M A HARMLESS OLD WOMAN--- HARMLESS! HEH-HEH-HEH!
AND NOW--SOMETHING TO TAKE TO LITTLE SNOW WHITE! SOMETHING SHE'LL LIKE---AH! THE VERY THING!
THE POISONED APPLE---SLEEPING DEATH!
ONE BITE--AND HER EYES WILL CLOSE IN THE SLEEPING DEATH! THEN I'LL BE FAIREST IN THE LAND!
MEANWHILE, THE SEVEN LITTLE MEN HAVE ACCEPTED SNOW WHITE AS THEIR HOUSEKEEPER AND SHE IS HAPPILY COOKING THEIR DINNER.
SOUP!
GRACIOUS! WHAT TERRIBLE MANNERS!
JIMINY CRICKETS!
SMELLS GOOD!
DINNER'S NOT QUITE READY! AND BESIDES, YOU HAVEN'T WASHED YET!
W-WASH?
WHAT FER? 'TAIN'T NEW YEARS!
NOW! NOW! GO RIGHT OUT AND WASH!
WE AIN'T GOIN' NO PLACE!
COURAGE, MEN! IT WON'T HURT ---MUCH!
GOSH-- IT'S COLD!
AND WET, TOO!
FINE BUNCH O' WATER-LILIES! WASHIN'---JEST TO PLEASE A WOMAN! HEH! LIKE TO SEE ANYBODY MAKE ME WASH!
LEMME GO! LEMME LOOSE, Y' IDJUTS! YOU'LL PAY FER THIS!
HOLD HIM, MEN! STRING, UH--- BRING HIM TO THE TUB!
SOUSE HIS WHISKERS!
DON'T SPARE THE SOAP!
I'LL--BLUB-B---YOU OLD--BLUBBLE---JEST WAIT---GLUB--BUB-B!
DINNER!
HOORAY!

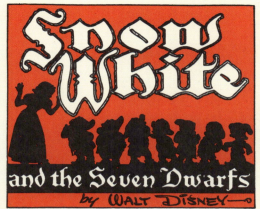

157 • March 20, 1938

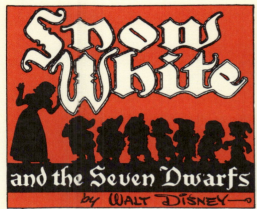

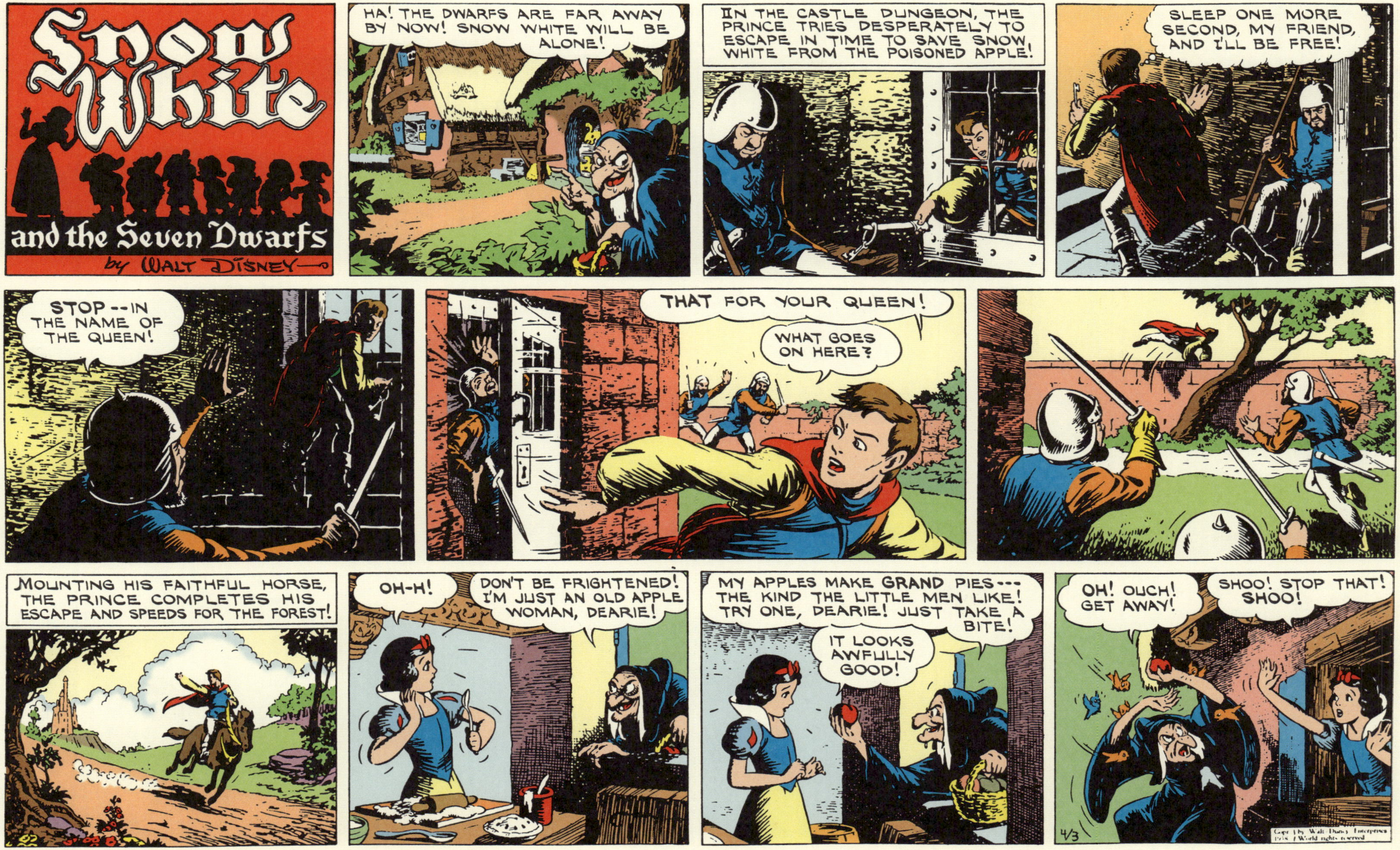
Snow White
and the Seven Dwarfs
by WALT DISNEY
HA! THE DWARFS ARE FAR AWAY BY NOW! SNOW WHITE WILL BE ALONE!
IN THE CASTLE DUNGEON, THE PRINCE TRIES DESPERATELY TO ESCAPE IN TIME TO SAVE SNOW WHITE FROM THE POISONED APPLE!
SLEEP ONE MORE SECOND, MY FRIEND, AND I'LL BE FREE!
STOP --IN THE NAME OF THE QUEEN!
THAT FOR YOUR QUEEN!
WHAT GOES ON HERE?
MOUNTING HIS FAITHFUL HORSE, THE PRINCE COMPLETES HIS ESCAPE AND SPEEDS FOR THE FOREST!
OH-H!
DON'T BE FRIGHTENED! I'M JUST AN OLD APPLE WOMAN, DEARIE!
MY APPLES MAKE GRAND PIES--- THE KIND THE LITTLE MEN LIKE! TRY ONE, DEARIE! JUST TAKE A BITE!
IT LOOKS AWFULLY GOOD!
OH! OUCH! GET AWAY!
SHOO! STOP THAT! SHOO!
4/3

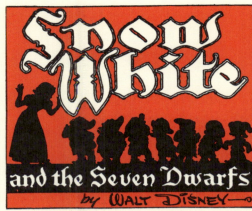

160 • April 10, 1938

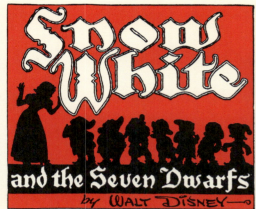
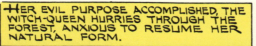

161 • April 17, 1938

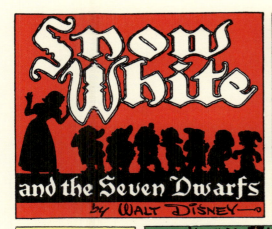

Walt Disney's
FIRST FULL LENGTH FEATURE PRODUCTION
Snow White
and the
Seven Dwarfs
in the Marvelous
MULTIPLANE TECHNICOLOR
Distributed by R K O Radio Pictures Inc.

I HEAR A VOICE! WHO--?
IT'S ME, DARLING! PRINCE CHARMING! I'M IN THE CELL NEXT TO YOURS!
OH! I'VE FINALLY FOUND YOU! LET ME TOUCH YOUR HAND!
DON'T BE AFRAID, MY SWEET...
Meanwhile, at the cottage...
JUST STOLE HER AWAY...
WE GOTTA FIND HER! WE GOTTA!
YES! WE MUST PLINK UP A THAN... THINK UP A PLAN!
LET'S SLEEP ON IT.
WAIT... WHERE'S DOPEY?
"HE'S AT THE WINDOW, STARING AT THE SKY. PROBABLY TRYING TO COME UP WITH AN..."
IDEA!

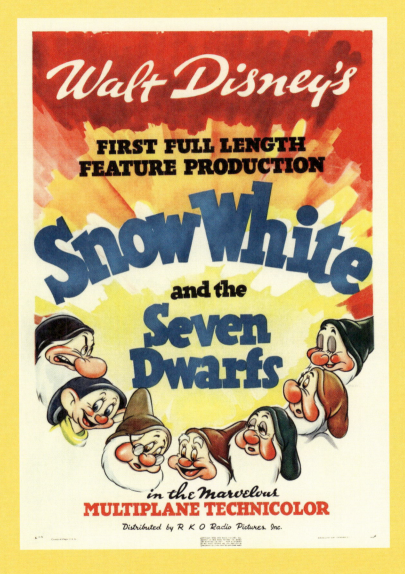

LEFT: A 1937 one-sheet poster for *Snow White and the Seven Dwarfs*. Image courtesy Heritage Auctions.

RIGHT: The Sunday strip version of *Snow White*, collected in comic book form around the world, was popular enough in Italy to inspire an ongoing series of follow-ups, many by the fan-favorite team of writer Guido Martina and artist Romano Scarpa. In this excerpt from Martina's and Scarpa's "Peril of the Witch of Potions" (1954), we find Snow White and Prince Charming imprisoned by the titular sorceress—but their seven friends always find a way to save them. Translation by Alberto Becattini and Jonathan H. Gray.

THE PRACTICAL PIG

May 1 - August 7, 1938
Written by Merrill de Maris, drawn by Al Taliaferro

FOR THE FIRST TIME IN NEARLY TWO YEARS—after detouring into unfamiliar territory with *Donald Duck* and *Snow White*—the Sunday comic feature returned in May 1938 to its original mission: adapting and retelling stories from the Silly Symphonies. The last previous *Symphony* continuity in 1936 had been based on a story featuring the Three Little Pigs and the Big Bad Wolf; now, fittingly, the strip picked up where it had left off. Production of *The Practical Pig*, the studio's latest Pig sequel, was essentially complete by May 1938, but most movie audiences would not see it until the following year.

By 1938 Al Taliaferro was installed as the artist behind the new Donald Duck daily strip, but he returned to his *Silly Symphony* post and carried a double workload, continuing to draw both strips. Merrill de Maris, who had written the *Snow White* continuity, remained in place as the Sunday page's writer when the *Silly Symphony* stories resumed. It's worth noting that he did not revive the convention of rhyming dialogue, previously a regular practice in the strip. Otherwise de Maris and Taliaferro proceeded along familiar lines, loosely adapting the film's story but also introducing some new ideas of their own. Practical Pig's latest invention, an intricately designed "lie detector," is a highlight of the film and survives in the comic adaptation. So does the Wolf's disguise as a comically lisping messenger boy. On the other hand, the Wolf's most preposterous disguise yet—as a mermaid, complete with portable island—does *not* reappear in the strip. Instead he masquerades as a fortune-teller, his advice to the pigs laced with double-entendres that telegraph his true intentions.

Like the earlier Pig story, this one includes a bonus for Disney enthusiasts: the continuity is primarily based on *The Practical Pig* but is also sprinkled with images and gags from the earlier films. Not least among these is an appearance by the Three Little Wolves, who had made their debut in the 1936 short of the same title.

—J.B. KAUFMAN

165 • May 1, 1938

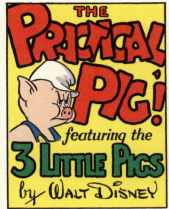

167 • May 15, 1938

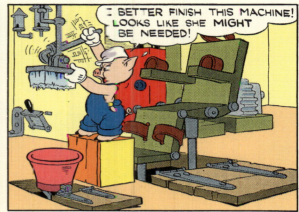

May 22, 1938

   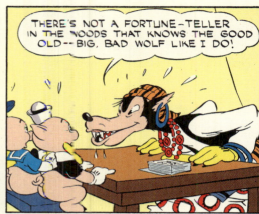

 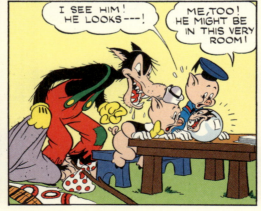  

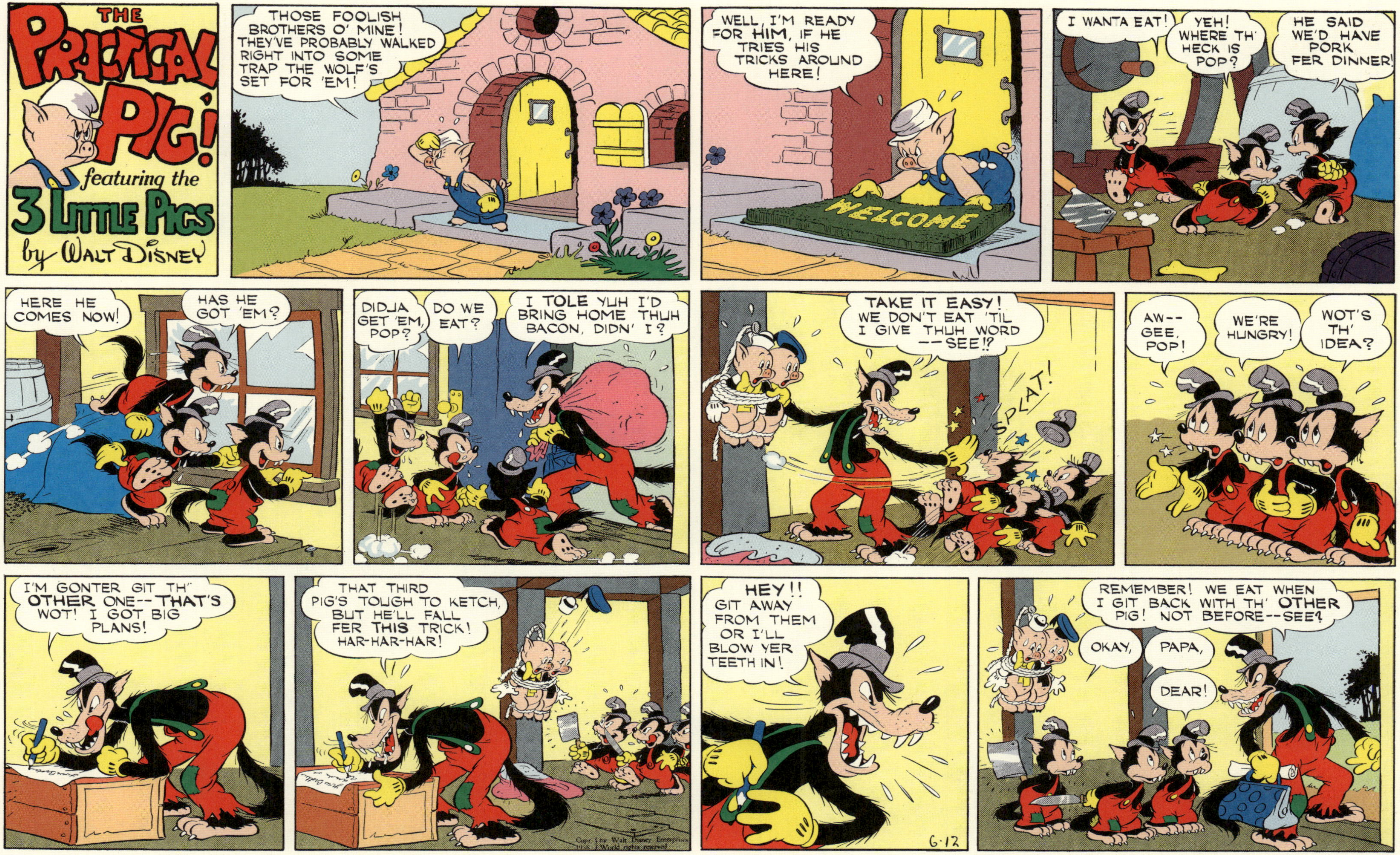

THE PRACTICAL PIG!
featuring the 3 LITTLE PIGS
by WALT DISNEY
THOSE FOOLISH BROTHERS O' MINE! THEY'VE PROBABLY WALKED RIGHT INTO SOME TRAP THE WOLF'S SET FOR 'EM!
WELL, I'M READY FOR HIM, IF HE TRIES HIS TRICKS AROUND HERE!
WELCOME
I WANTA EAT!
YEH! WHERE TH' HECK IS POP?
HE SAID WE'D HAVE PORK FER DINNER!
HERE HE COMES NOW!
HAS HE GOT 'EM?
DIDJA GET 'EM, POP?
DO WE EAT?
I TOLE YUH I'D BRING HOME THUH BACON, DIDN' I?
TAKE IT EASY! WE DON'T EAT 'TIL I GIVE THUH WORD --SEE!?
SPLAT!
AW-- GEE, POP!
WE'RE HUNGRY!
WOT'S TH' IDEA?
I'M GONTER GIT TH' OTHER ONE--THAT'S WOT! I GOT BIG PLANS!
THAT THIRD PIG'S TOUGH TO KETCH, BUT HE'LL FALL FER THIS TRICK! HAR-HAR-HAR!
HEY!! GIT AWAY FROM THEM OR I'LL BLOW YER TEETH IN!
6-12
REMEMBER! WE EAT WHEN I GIT BACK WITH TH' OTHER PIG! NOT BEFORE--SEE?
OKAY,
PAPA,
DEAR!

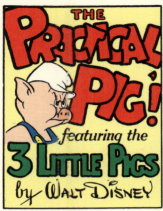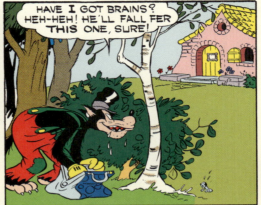

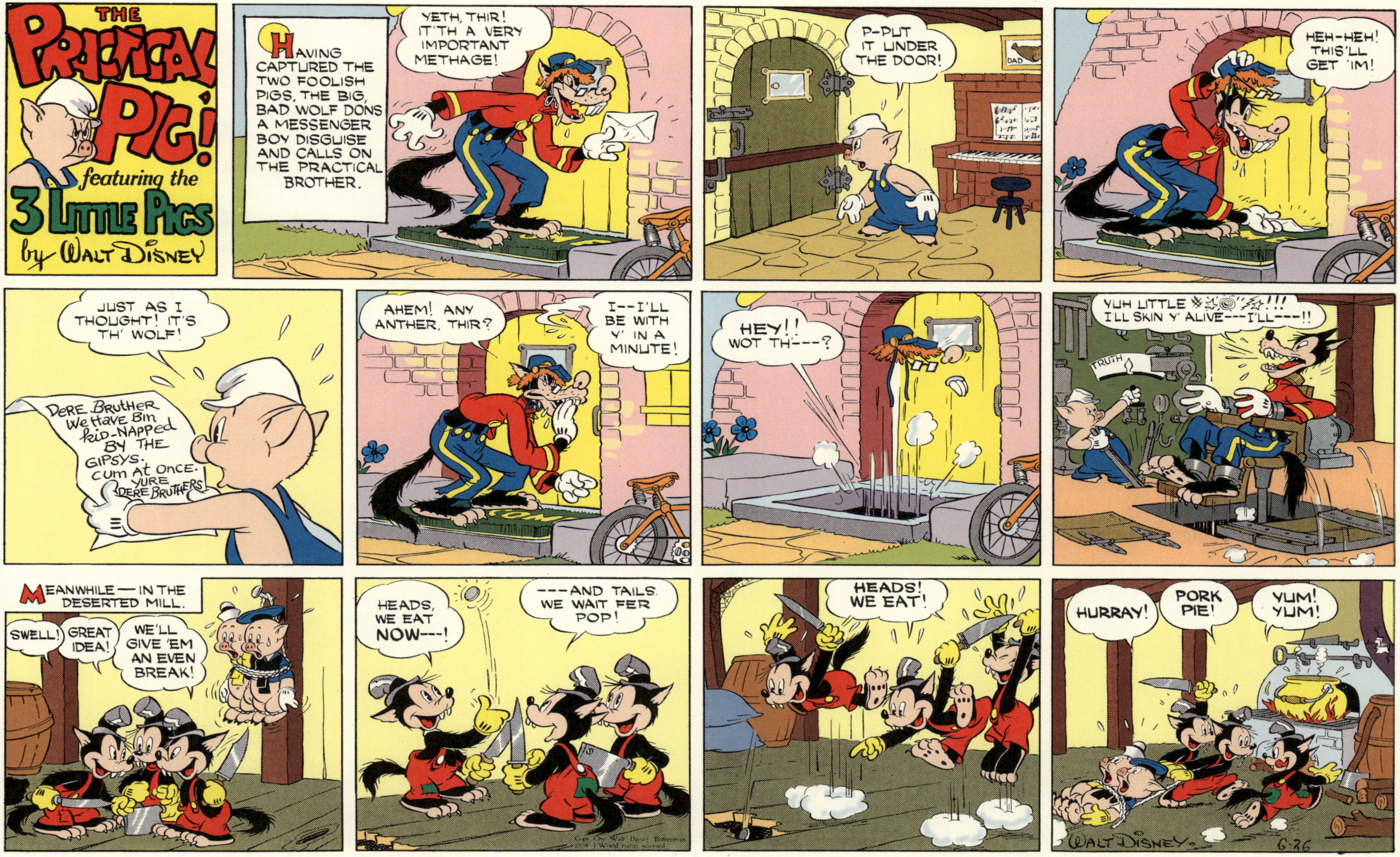
THE PRACTICAL PIG!
featuring the
3 LITTLE PIGS
by WALT DISNEY
HAVING CAPTURED THE TWO FOOLISH PIGS, THE BIG, BAD WOLF DONS A MESSENGER BOY DISGUISE AND CALLS ON THE PRACTICAL BROTHER.
YETH, THIR! IT'TH A VERY IMPORTANT METHAGE!
P-PUT IT UNDER THE DOOR!
HEH-HEH! THIS'LL GET 'IM!
JUST AS I THOUGHT! IT'S TH' WOLF!
DERE BRUTHER WE HAVE BIN KID-NAPPED BY THE GIPSYS. CUM AT ONCE. YURE DERE BRUTHERS
AHEM! ANY ANTHER, THIR?
I--I'LL BE WITH Y' IN A MINUTE!
HEY!! WOT TH'---?
YUH LITTLE ※☆◎⚡!!! I'LL SKIN Y' ALIVE---I'LL---!!
TRUTH
MEANWHILE — IN THE DESERTED MILL.
SWELL!
GREAT IDEA!
WE'LL GIVE 'EM AN EVEN BREAK!
HEADS, WE EAT NOW---!
---AND TAILS, WE WAIT FER POP!
HEADS! WE EAT!
HURRAY!
PORK PIE!
YUM! YUM!
WALT DISNEY
6-26

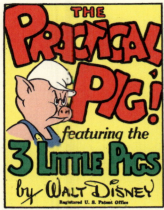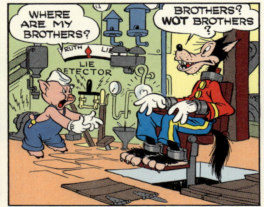

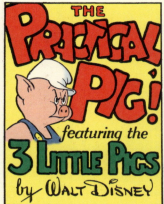

175 • July 10, 1938

THE PRACTICAL PIG!
featuring the 3 LITTLE PIGS
by WALT DISNEY
BOY-OH-BOY!
PORK PIE!
WITH ALL TH' TRIMMIN'S!
GIVE IT PLENTY O' HEAT!
COOK IT FAST!
I KIN HARDLY WAIT!
BLUB! BLUB!
YEE-OW-W!
I'M ON FIRE!!
HEY!
CATCH 'EM!
DON'T LOSE OUR PORK PIE!
WE GOTTA CATCH 'EM!
OR POP'LL MURDER US!
BUT "POP" ISN'T SITTING SO PRETTY, HIMSELF!
C'MON NOW! Y' CAN'T FOOL THIS MACHINE! WHERE ARE MY BROTHERS?
NOW LISSEN! YUH GOT ME ALL WRONG--BUDDY!
I'M YER PAL, SEE? I WOULDN'T HARM THEM LI'L GUYS! WHY, THEY'RE LIKE ME OWN BRUDDERS, THEY ARE!
Copr. 1938 by Walt Disney Enterprises World rights reserved
TOOT TOO-OOT TOOT!
LIE
LIE ETECTOR
RING! RR-RING
BONG! BONG!
7-24
HALP! QUIT! STOP! I'LL TELL THE TRUTH! LET UP! I'LL TELL!
BANG!
SMACKO
SOAP
WALT DISNEY

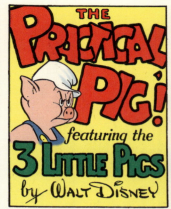

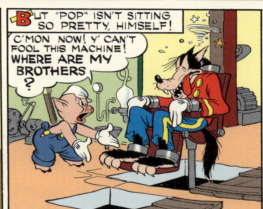

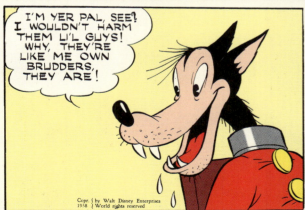

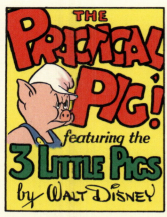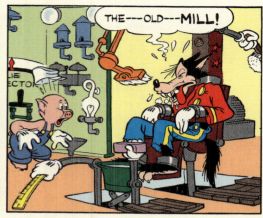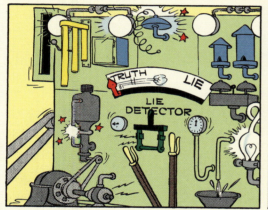

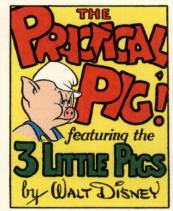

MOTHER PLUTO

August 14 - October 16, 1938
Written by Merrill de Maris, drawn by Al Taliaferro

RELEASED IN 1936, *Mother Pluto* was a charming film and a gem of the animator's art. Today it is sometimes overlooked, but in the 1930s its story had a quiet staying power. It turned up again in Disney storybook adaptations, and, in 1938—nearly two years after the film's release—in the comics.

The *Silly Symphony* comic strip routinely took creative liberties with its source stories, so it's not surprising that de Maris adapted this one for the purposes of the strip. Perhaps most strikingly, one of the baby chicks is isolated as a distinct character. In the film, the chicks are simply a gaggle of little interchangeable creatures; here the black chick wanders away, gets himself lost, and motivates a plot thread that doesn't appear in the film. In fact, if there's a precedent for this thread, it's in the Symphony comic page itself. Readers of *Silly Symphonies* Volume 1 may recall a 1934 continuity based on *The Wise Little Hen*, in which another little black runaway chick prompts an anxious search—also not reflecting anything in the film! Here, too, the end of the "Mother Pluto" strip resolves the story more or less as in the film, but discards the warmth of the film's ending and substitutes a gag finish in its place.

—J.B. KAUFMAN

181 • August 14, 1938

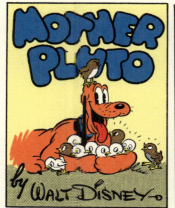

182 • August 21, 1938

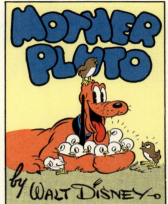

183 • August 28, 1938

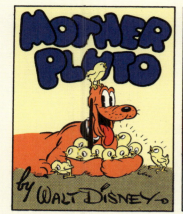

184 • September 4, 1938

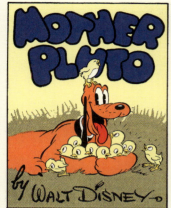

185 • September 11, 1938

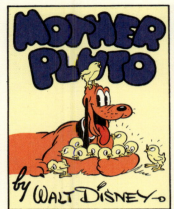

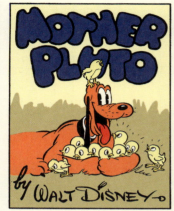

187 • September 25, 1938

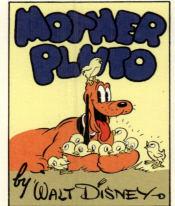

188 • October 2, 1938

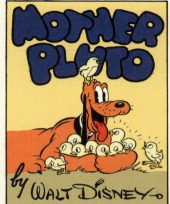
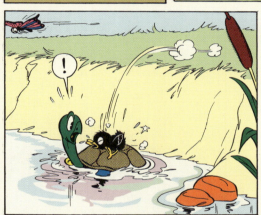

189 • October 9, 1938

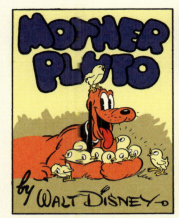

October 16, 1938

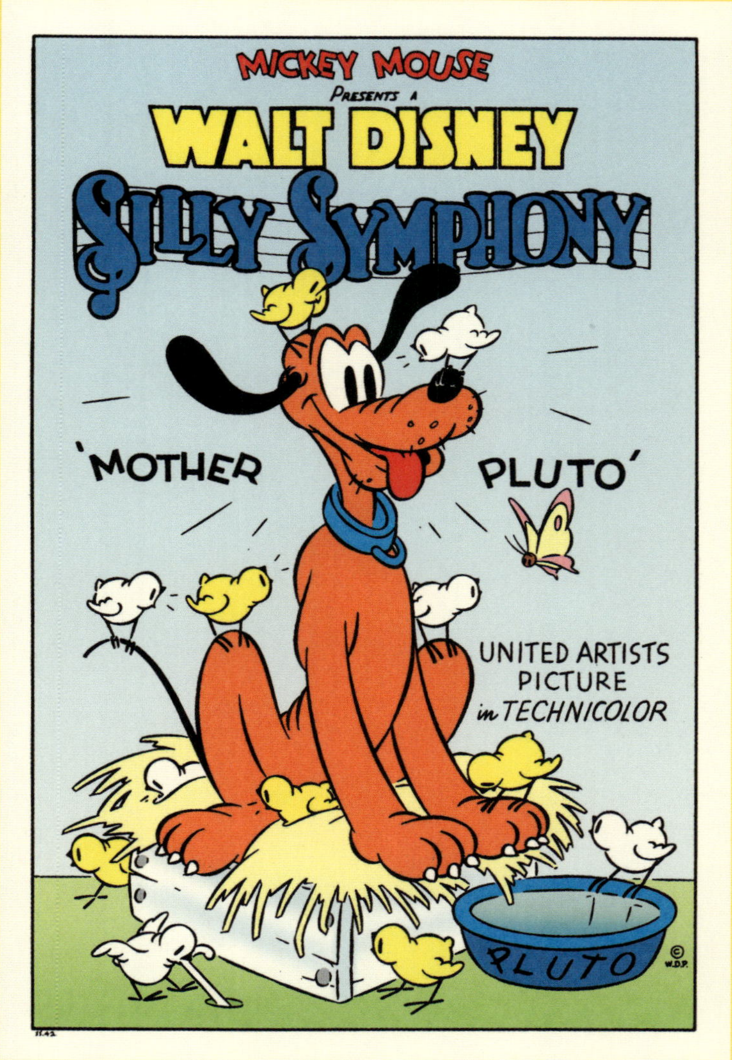
MICKEY MOUSE
PRESENTS A
WALT DISNEY
SILLY SYMPHONY
'MOTHER PLUTO'
UNITED ARTISTS
PICTURE
in TECHNICOLOR
PLUTO
© W.D.P.

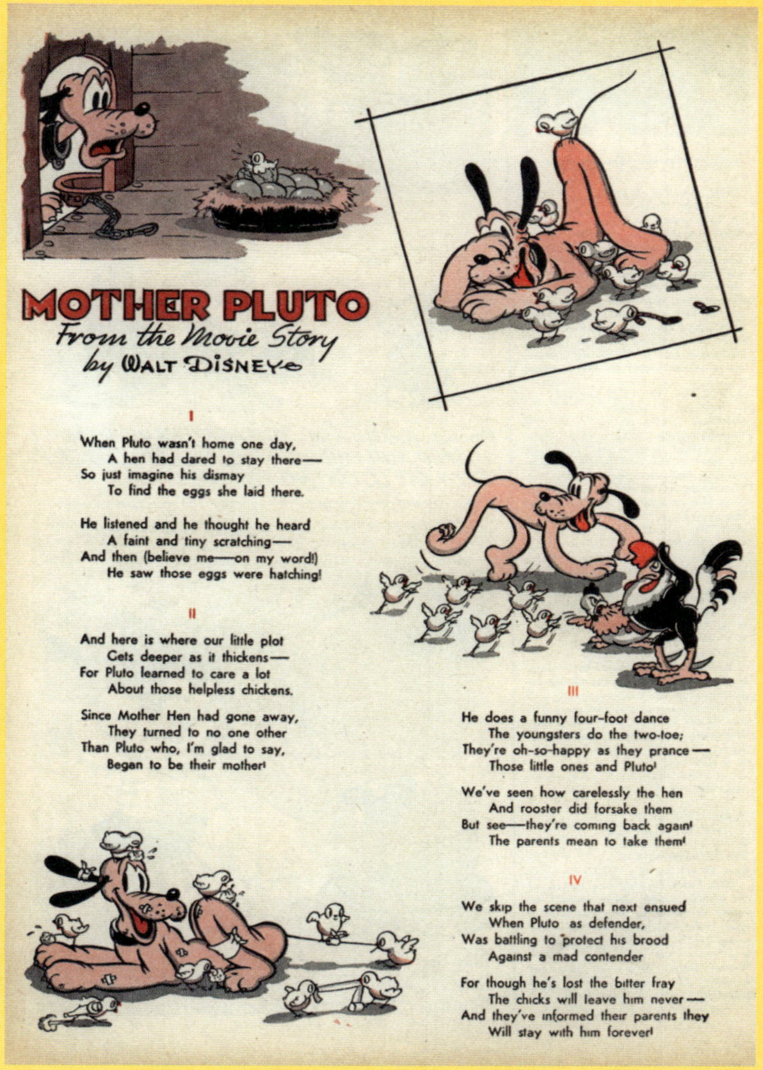

MOTHER PLUTO

From the Movie Story
by Walt Disney

I

When Pluto wasn't home one day,
A hen had dared to stay there—
So just imagine his dismay
To find the eggs she laid there.

He listened and he thought he heard
A faint and tiny scratching—
And then (believe me—on my word!)
He saw those eggs were hatching!

II

And here is where our little plot
Gets deeper as it thickens—
For Pluto learned to care a lot
About those helpless chickens.

Since Mother Hen had gone away,
They turned to no one other
Than Pluto who, I'm glad to say,
Began to be their mother!

III

He does a funny four-foot dance
The youngsters do the two-toe;
They're oh-so-happy as they prance—
Those little ones and Pluto!

We've seen how carelessly the hen
And rooster did forsake them
But see—they're coming back again!
The parents mean to take them!

IV

We skip the scene that next ensued
When Pluto as defender,
Was battling to protect his brood
Against a mad contender

For though he's lost the bitter fray
The chicks will leave him never—
And they've informed their parents they
Will stay with him forever!

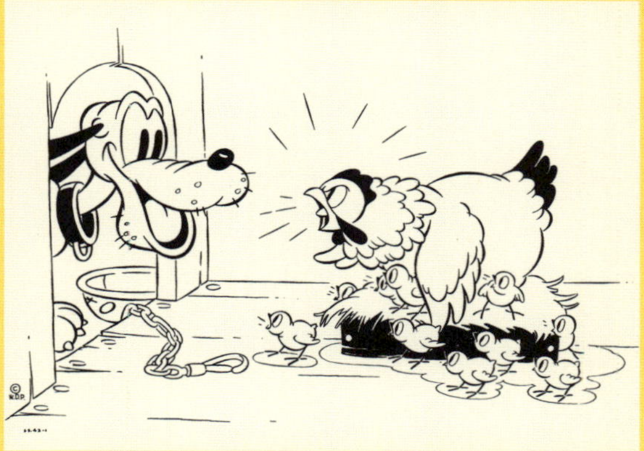

LEFT: The original 1936 poster art for *Mother Pluto*. Image courtesy Walt Disney Archives, color by Digikore Studios.

MIDDLE: This rhyming adaptation of the *Mother Pluto* storyline appeared in *Mickey Mouse Magazine* 20 (1937). Image courtesy Hake's Americana.

RIGHT: A 1936 publicity drawing for *Mother Pluto*; art by Manuel Gonzales, image courtesy Walt Disney Photo Library.

THE FARMYARD SYMPHONY

October 23 - November 27, 1938
Written by Merrill de Maris, drawn by Al Taliaferro

FARMYARD SYMPHONY, one of the last entries in the *Silly Symphony* series, is a lovely film with practically no plot. Its premise is simple: the animals and people on a farm go about their daily routines while vocalizing, and accompanied by, classical music and operatic themes—a charming cinematic device, but unpromising material for a comic strip. Writer Merrill de Maris seizes on a running gag from the film, a hungry piglet's search for food, and expands it into a short (only six weeks) comic continuity, published concurrently with the film's release. Here the piglet is given distinctive markings and a name, and becomes the protagonist of the story.

By 1938 the Disney animation studio had grown so proficient that there was no single "Disney style"—each new film displayed a visual and storytelling approach tailored to the specific story and characters at hand. The *Silly Symphony* comics reflected the same versatility: the narrative style of one story might be discarded and replaced for the next one. Here the graphic format of "Mother Pluto"—predominantly visual, with only an occasional narrative comment or thought balloon—gives way to a quasi-storybook, with explanatory, and heavily moralizing, text in every panel. Al Taliaferro, too, maintains the impressive facility of his draftsmanship. *Farmyard Symphony*, the film, is distinguished partly by the lifelike appearance and movement of its animal characters; some of the same artists who would soon be working on *Bambi* sharpened their skills by animating the farmyard animals. Here Taliaferro keeps pace, rendering not only the pigs, but the other animals and the farmer, as they appear on the screen.

—J.B. KAUFMAN

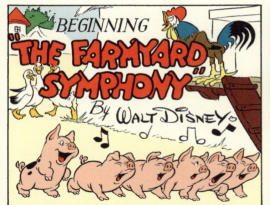

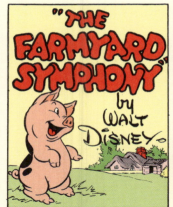

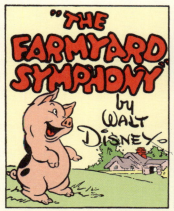

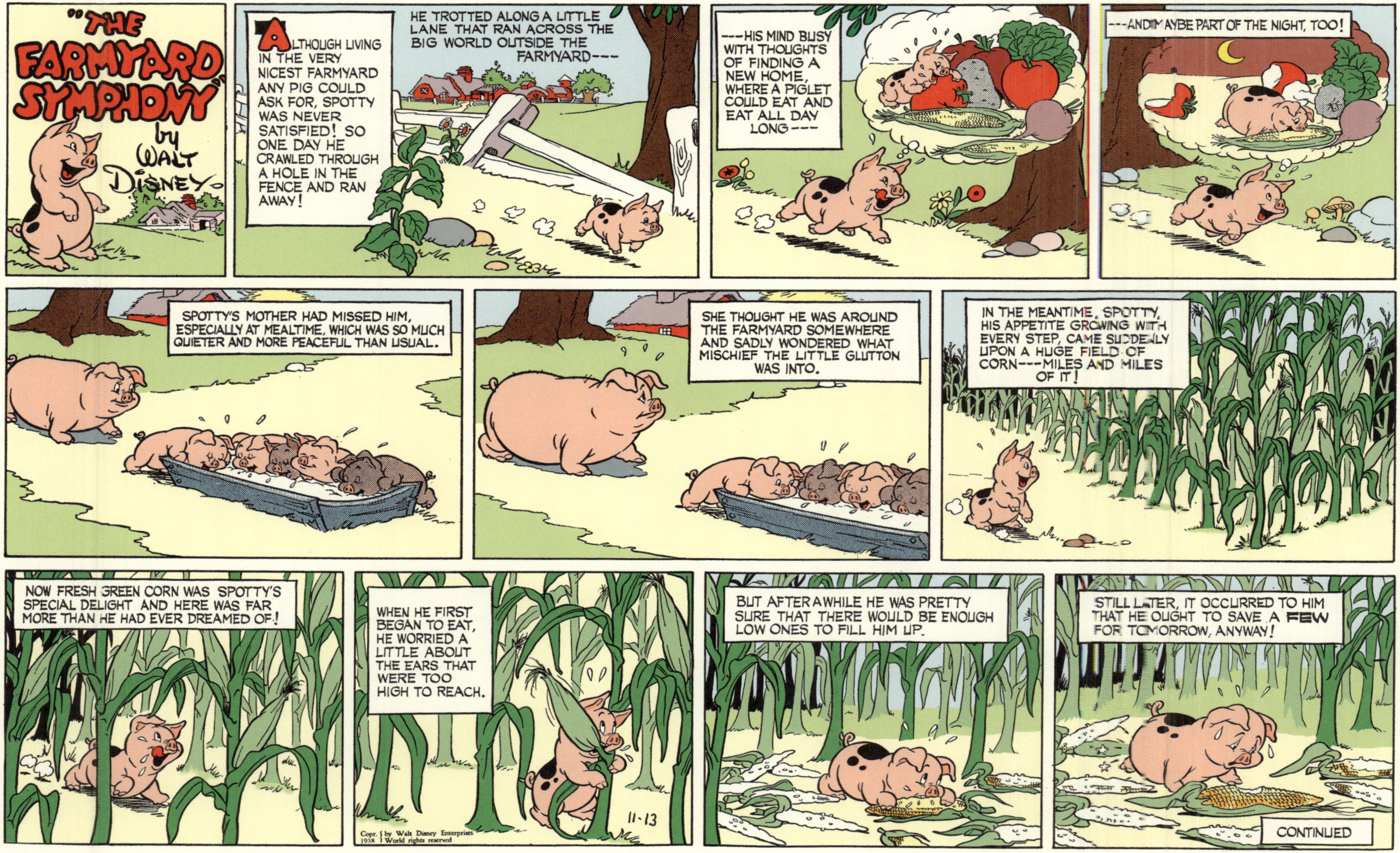
"THE FARMYARD SYMPHONY"
by WALT DISNEY
ALTHOUGH LIVING IN THE VERY NICEST FARMYARD ANY PIG COULD ASK FOR, SPOTTY WAS NEVER SATISFIED! SO ONE DAY HE CRAWLED THROUGH A HOLE IN THE FENCE AND RAN AWAY!
HE TROTTED ALONG A LITTLE LANE THAT RAN ACROSS THE BIG WORLD OUTSIDE THE FARMYARD---
---HIS MIND BUSY WITH THOUGHTS OF FINDING A NEW HOME, WHERE A PIGLET COULD EAT AND EAT ALL DAY LONG---
---AND MAYBE PART OF THE NIGHT, TOO!
SPOTTY'S MOTHER HAD MISSED HIM, ESPECIALLY AT MEALTIME, WHICH WAS SO MUCH QUIETER AND MORE PEACEFUL THAN USUAL.
SHE THOUGHT HE WAS AROUND THE FARMYARD SOMEWHERE AND SADLY WONDERED WHAT MISCHIEF THE LITTLE GLUTTON WAS INTO.
IN THE MEANTIME, SPOTTY, HIS APPETITE GROWING WITH EVERY STEP, CAME SUDDENLY UPON A HUGE FIELD OF CORN---MILES AND MILES OF IT!
NOW FRESH GREEN CORN WAS SPOTTY'S SPECIAL DELIGHT AND HERE WAS FAR MORE THAN HE HAD EVER DREAMED OF!
WHEN HE FIRST BEGAN TO EAT, HE WORRIED A LITTLE ABOUT THE EARS THAT WERE TOO HIGH TO REACH.
Copr. 1938 by Walt Disney Enterprises World rights reserved
11-13
BUT AFTER A WHILE HE WAS PRETTY SURE THAT THERE WOULD BE ENOUGH LOW ONES TO FILL HIM UP.
STILL LATER, IT OCCURRED TO HIM THAT HE OUGHT TO SAVE A FEW FOR TOMORROW, ANYWAY!
CONTINUED

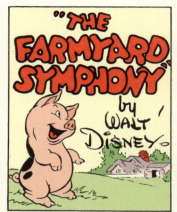

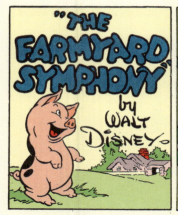

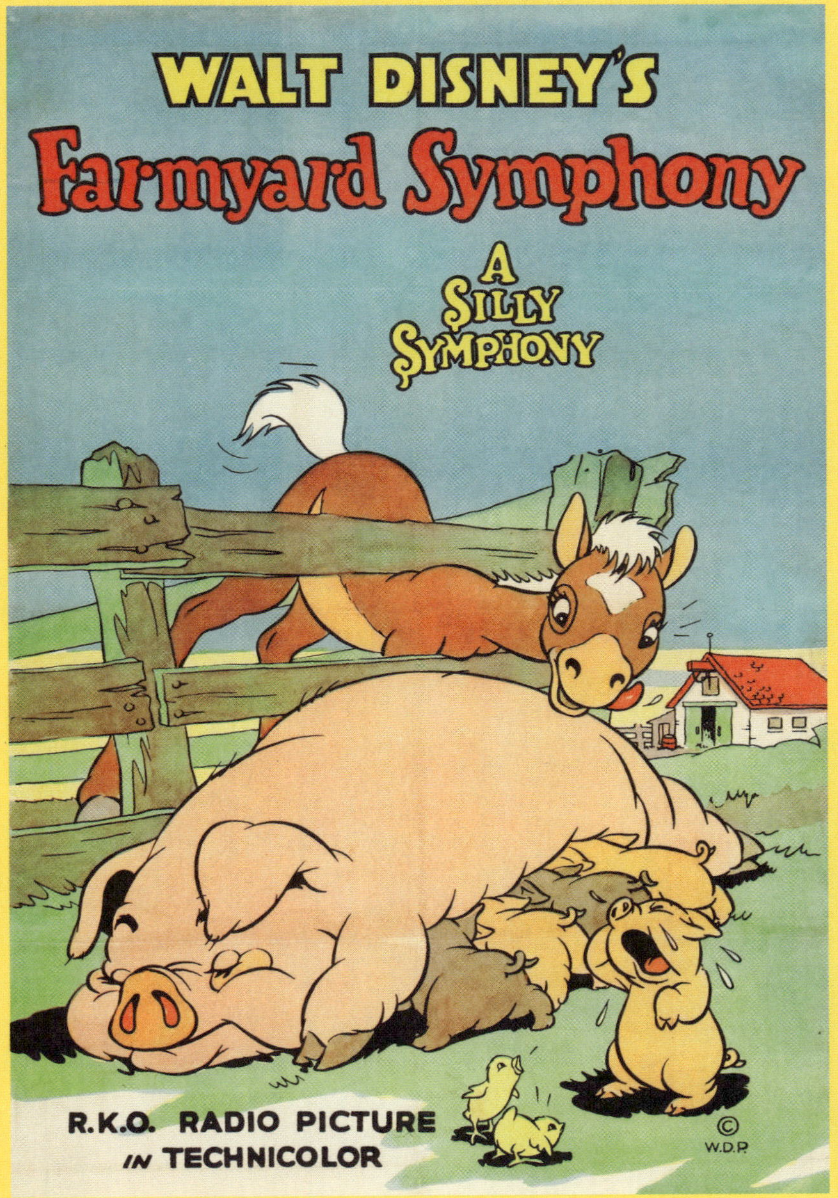
WALT DISNEY'S
Farmyard Symphony
A SILLY SYMPHONY
R.K.O. RADIO PICTURE
IN TECHNICOLOR
© W.D.P.

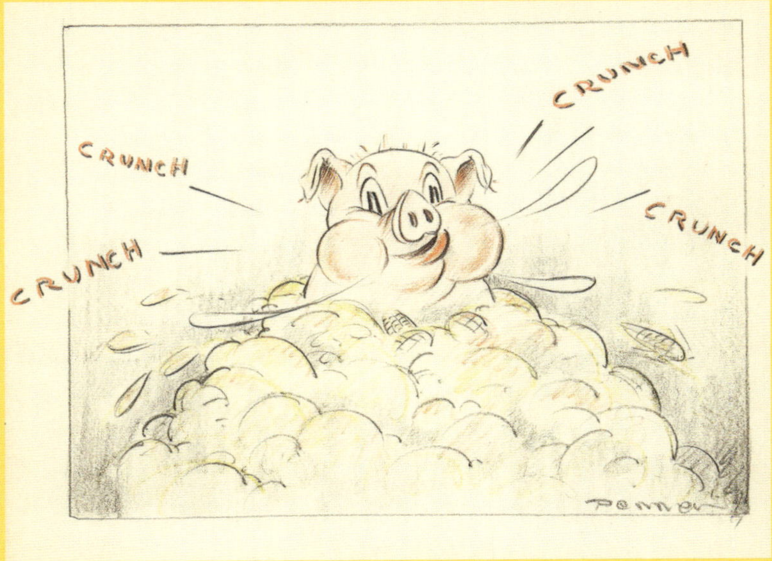
CRUNCH
CRUNCH
CRUNCH
CRUNCH

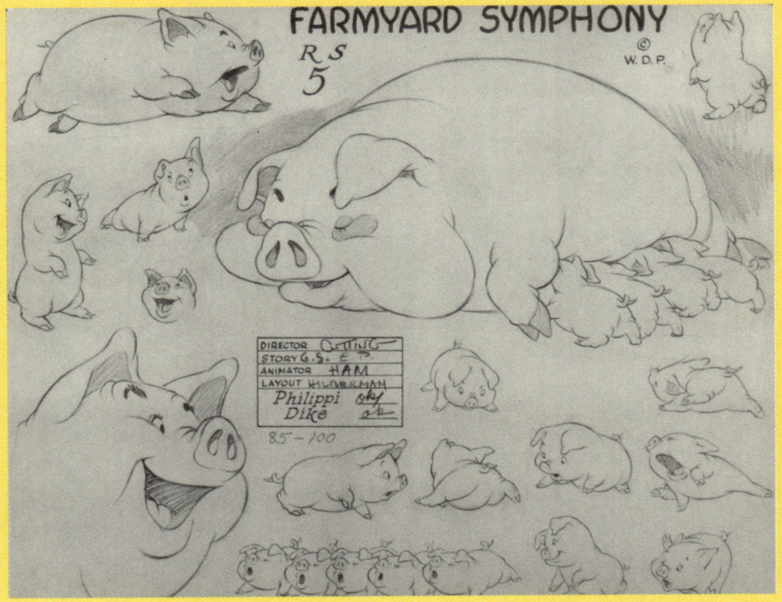
FARMYARD SYMPHONY
R S
5
© W.D.P.
DIRECTOR
STORY
ANIMATOR
LAYOUT
Philippi
Dike
85-100

LEFT: The original 1938 poster for *Farmyard Symphony*; image courtesy Heritage Auctions.

RIGHT: Early stages of *Farmyard Symphony*'s Spotty Pig: a story sketch by writer Ed Penner (top), and a model sheet showing the gluttonous hog with his family (bottom). Images courtesy Heritage Auctions.

TIMID ELMER

December 4, 1938 - February 12, 1939
Plotted by Bianca Majolie, Ferdinand Horvath, Carl Barks, and Walt Kelly,
scripted by Merrill de Maris, drawn by Al Taliaferro

THE CONCLUDING STORY in this volume is an historical treasure, based on a film that was planned but unfinished. Three years had passed since Disney fans had enjoyed *Elmer Elephant* and its comic adaptation, reproduced earlier in this volume. Now the studio story department planned to continue the little elephant's story in a sequel, "Timid Elmer." The film project was abandoned before completion, but its story, as adapted for the comics, is presented in the following pages.

"Adapted" is a key word here. The writing of a Disney cartoon story involved constant refining and revision—and, as we've seen, the finished story might still be radically altered when transferred to the comics. Story outlines and sketches survive for the unmade *Timid Elmer* film. A set by Carl Barks suggested a story in which Tillie Tiger, tiring of oafish Elmer, set her sights on a romantic, ballet-dancing goat. But when Tillie was threatened by a huge gorilla, the goat beat a hasty retreat, while Elmer—motivated by his love for Tillie—took on the bullying gorilla and prevailed. Sketches by another future comics great, Walt Kelly, established the gorilla fight as a proper wrestling match staged for a roaring crowd. Then an outline by Bianca Majolie and Ferdinand Horvath eliminated the goat and expanded the gorilla's role: now *he* became the romantic rival, doubly motivating Elmer to overcome his timidity and stand up to the bully.

Merrill de Maris' comic-strip script incorporates elements from Barks, Kelly, Majolie, and Horvath. Al Taliaferro's art depicts the world of *Elmer Elephant* with seemingly effortless ease, even to reproducing specific poses that suggest scenes in the original film. In addition to Elmer and Tillie, the bullying kids are back again, and the gorilla—now named Gooch—is adapted from a Horvath model sheet. There's also an appearance by the kindly old giraffe who had figured in the 1936 film. The giraffe had not appeared in the first comic continuity, but he takes a key role here.

What's perhaps even more interesting is the device introduced by the giraffe: the "magic acorn," a talisman that makes Elmer invincible because he *believes* it gives him special powers. This device—first suggested for "The Shy Little Bear," another unmade cartoon—was brought into the story by Majolie and would prove an enduring concept. Elmer never did return to the screen, but another little elephant did: in June 1939—a few months after the "Timid Elmer" continuity appeared in newspapers—the Disney studio secured the rights to the story that would be produced as *Dumbo.* As developed for the screen, a key plot element in *Dumbo* is the "magic feather," an object that convinces Dumbo of his ability to fly. In the end, of course, both Elmer and Dumbo learn that those "magic" charms were only psychological props and that they had those powers all along. Historically fascinating in itself, Timid Elmer's story is also notable for its connections in the larger picture of Disney history.

—J.B. KAUFMAN AND DAVID GERSTEIN

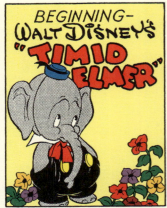

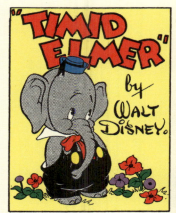

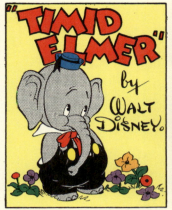

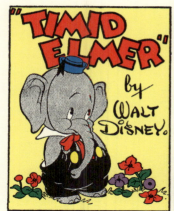

December 25, 1938

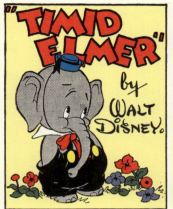

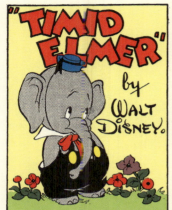

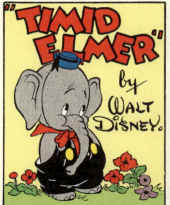

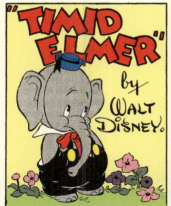

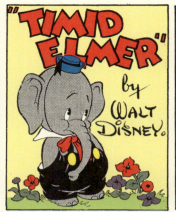

209 • January 29, 1939

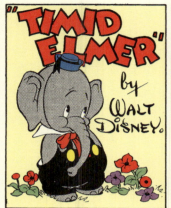

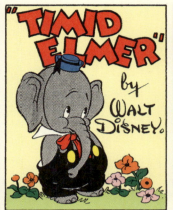

211 • February 12, 1939

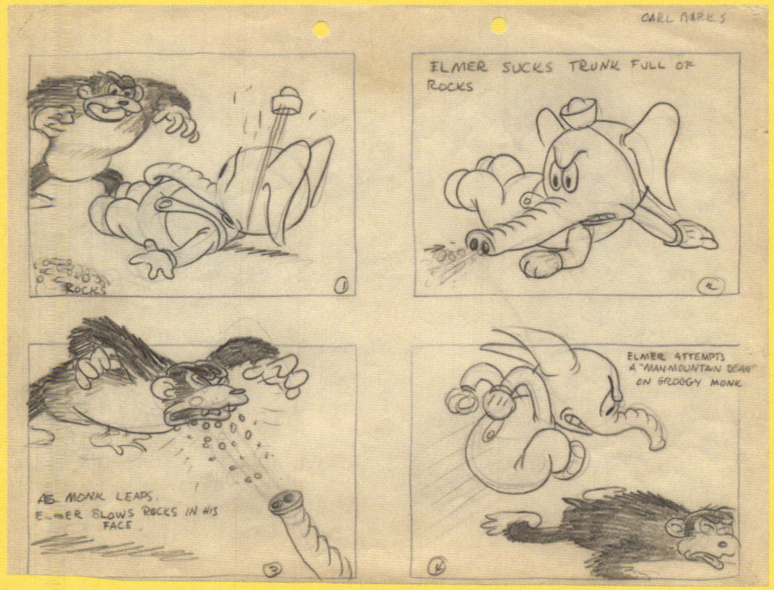
CARL BARKS
ELMER SUCKS TRUNK FULL OF ROCKS
ELMER ATTEMPTS A "MAN-MOUNTAIN DEAN" ON GROOGY MONK
AS MONK LEAPS. ELMER BLOWS ROCKS IN HIS FACE.

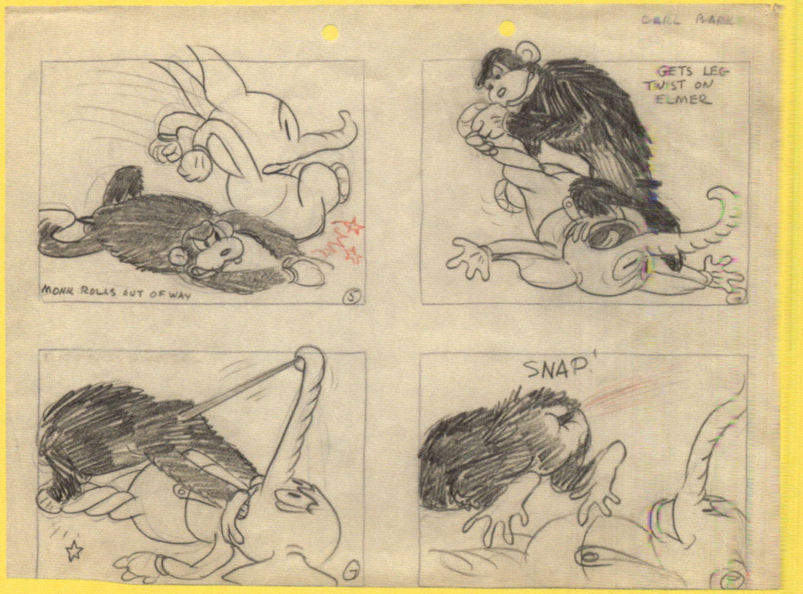
GETS LEG TWIST ON ELMER
MONK ROLLS OUT OF WAY
SNAP!

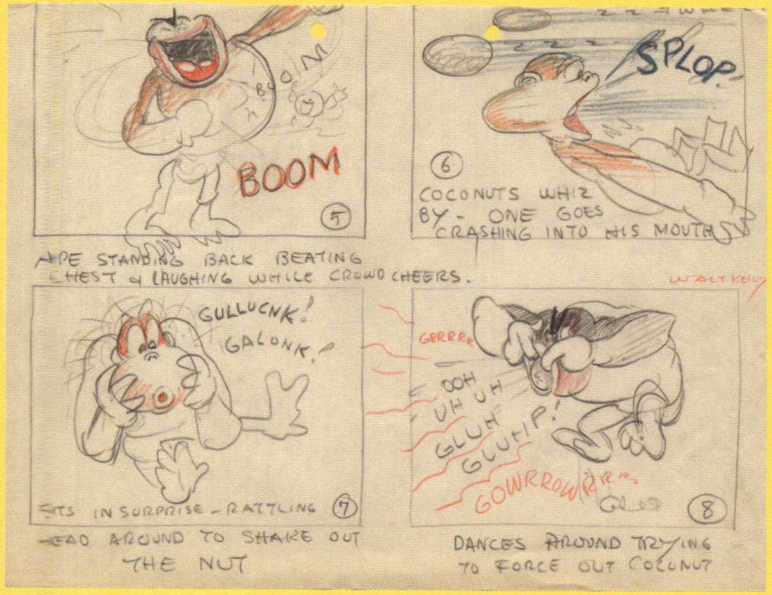
BOOM
SPLOP
COCONUTS WHIZ BY - ONE GOES CRASHING INTO HIS MOUTH
APE STANDING BACK BEATING CHEST & LAUGHING WHILE CROWD CHEERS.
GULLUCNK!
GALONK!
GRRRR
OOH UH UH GLUH GLUHP!
GOWRROWRR
SITS IN SURPRISE - RATTLING
AROUND TO SHAKE OUT THE NUT
DANCES AROUND TRYING TO FORCE OUT COCONUT

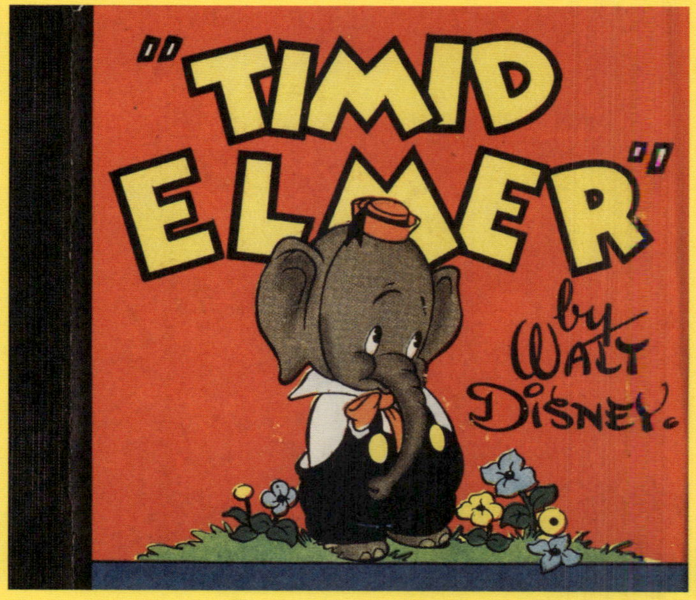
"TIMID ELMER"
by WALT DISNEY

TOP TWO AND BOTTOM LEFT: Story sketches by Carl Barks (top two) and Walt Kelly (bottom) show Elmer's slapstick battle with Gooch Gorilla in "Timid Elmer," as originally planned for animation. While Barks and Kelly both drew Gooch as quite an uncivilized ape, suggesting his portrayal in Barks' original story outline (see page 39), the battle was by now a knockabout spectacle staged for the other jungle children, just as in Taliaferro's comic. Images courtesy Disney Publishing Worldwide.

BOTTOM RIGHT: A small-size black-and-white storybook reprint of Taliaferro's *Timid Elmer* (1939) ended up being the only dedicated spinoff of the story. (See page 9 for a larger book that didn't end up being published as a standalone.) Image courtesy Heritage Auctions.

OPPOSITE: Elmer made few appearances in comics after "Timid Elmer"—but Tillie and Tuffy Tiger got a sequel of their own in *Walt Disney's Comics and Stories* 51 (1944). Art and lettering by Carl Buettner, color restoration by Digikore Studios.

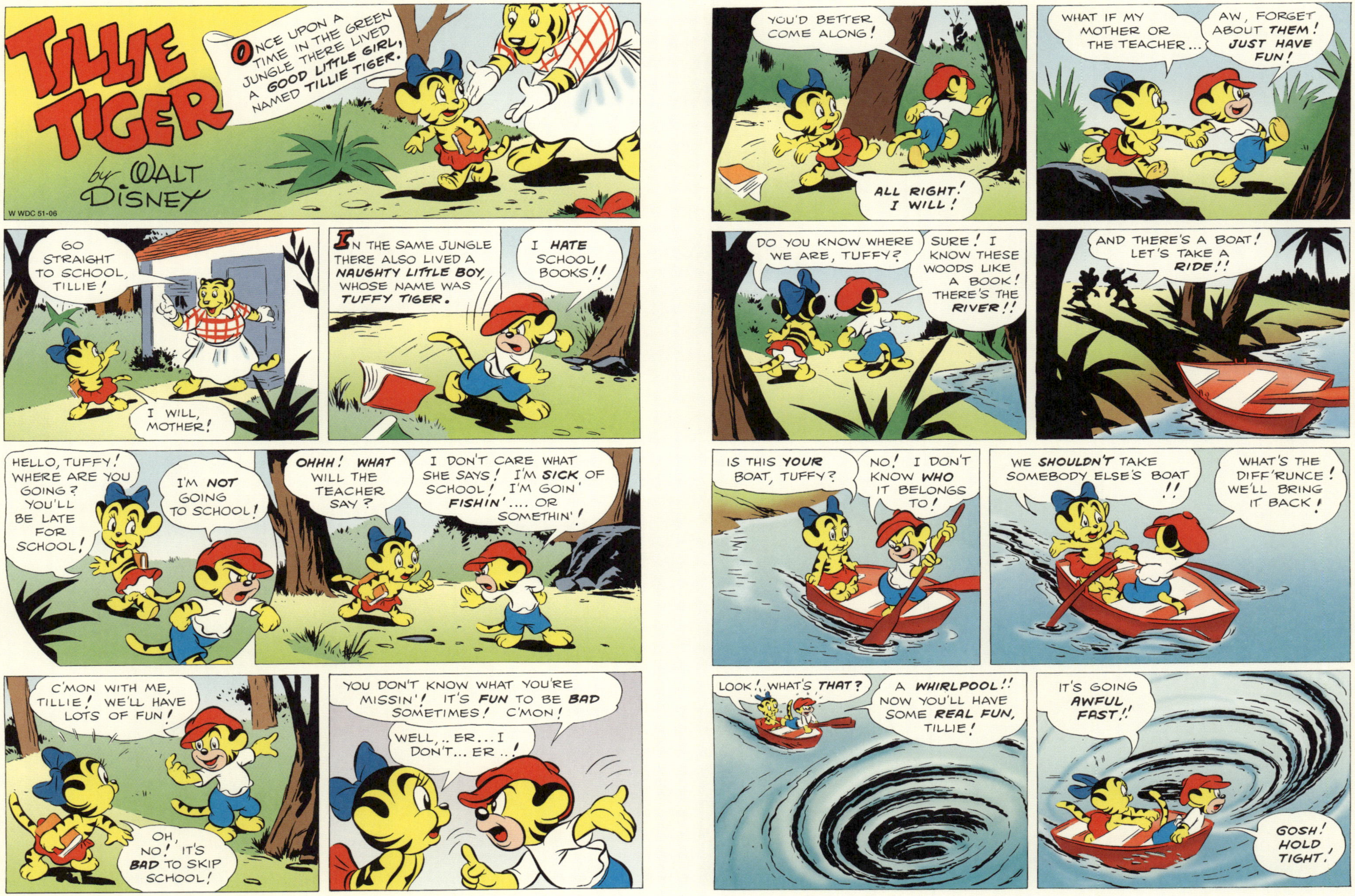
TILLIE TIGER
by WALT DISNEY
W WDC 51-06
ONCE UPON A TIME IN THE GREEN JUNGLE THERE LIVED A GOOD LITTLE GIRL, NAMED TILLIE TIGER.
GO STRAIGHT TO SCHOOL, TILLIE!
I WILL, MOTHER!
IN THE SAME JUNGLE THERE ALSO LIVED A NAUGHTY LITTLE BOY, WHOSE NAME WAS TUFFY TIGER.
I HATE SCHOOL BOOKS!!
HELLO, TUFFY! WHERE ARE YOU GOING? YOU'LL BE LATE FOR SCHOOL!
I'M NOT GOING TO SCHOOL!
OHHH! WHAT WILL THE TEACHER SAY?
I DON'T CARE WHAT SHE SAYS! I'M SICK OF SCHOOL! I'M GOIN' FISHIN'.... OR SOMETHIN'!
C'MON WITH ME, TILLIE! WE'LL HAVE LOTS OF FUN!
OH, NO! IT'S BAD TO SKIP SCHOOL!
YOU DON'T KNOW WHAT YOU'RE MISSIN'! IT'S FUN TO BE BAD SOMETIMES! C'MON!
WELL,.. ER... I DON'T... ER..!
YOU'D BETTER COME ALONG!
ALL RIGHT! I WILL!
WHAT IF MY MOTHER OR THE TEACHER...
AW, FORGET ABOUT THEM! JUST HAVE FUN!
DO YOU KNOW WHERE WE ARE, TUFFY?
SURE! I KNOW THESE WOODS LIKE A BOOK! THERE'S THE RIVER!!
AND THERE'S A BOAT! LET'S TAKE A RIDE!!
IS THIS YOUR BOAT, TUFFY?
NO! I DON'T KNOW WHO IT BELONGS TO!
WE SHOULDN'T TAKE SOMEBODY ELSE'S BOAT!!
WHAT'S THE DIFF'RUNCE! WE'LL BRING IT BACK!
LOOK! WHAT'S THAT?
A WHIRLPOOL!! NOW YOU'LL HAVE SOME REAL FUN, TILLIE!
IT'S GOING AWFUL FAST!!
GOSH! HOLD TIGHT!

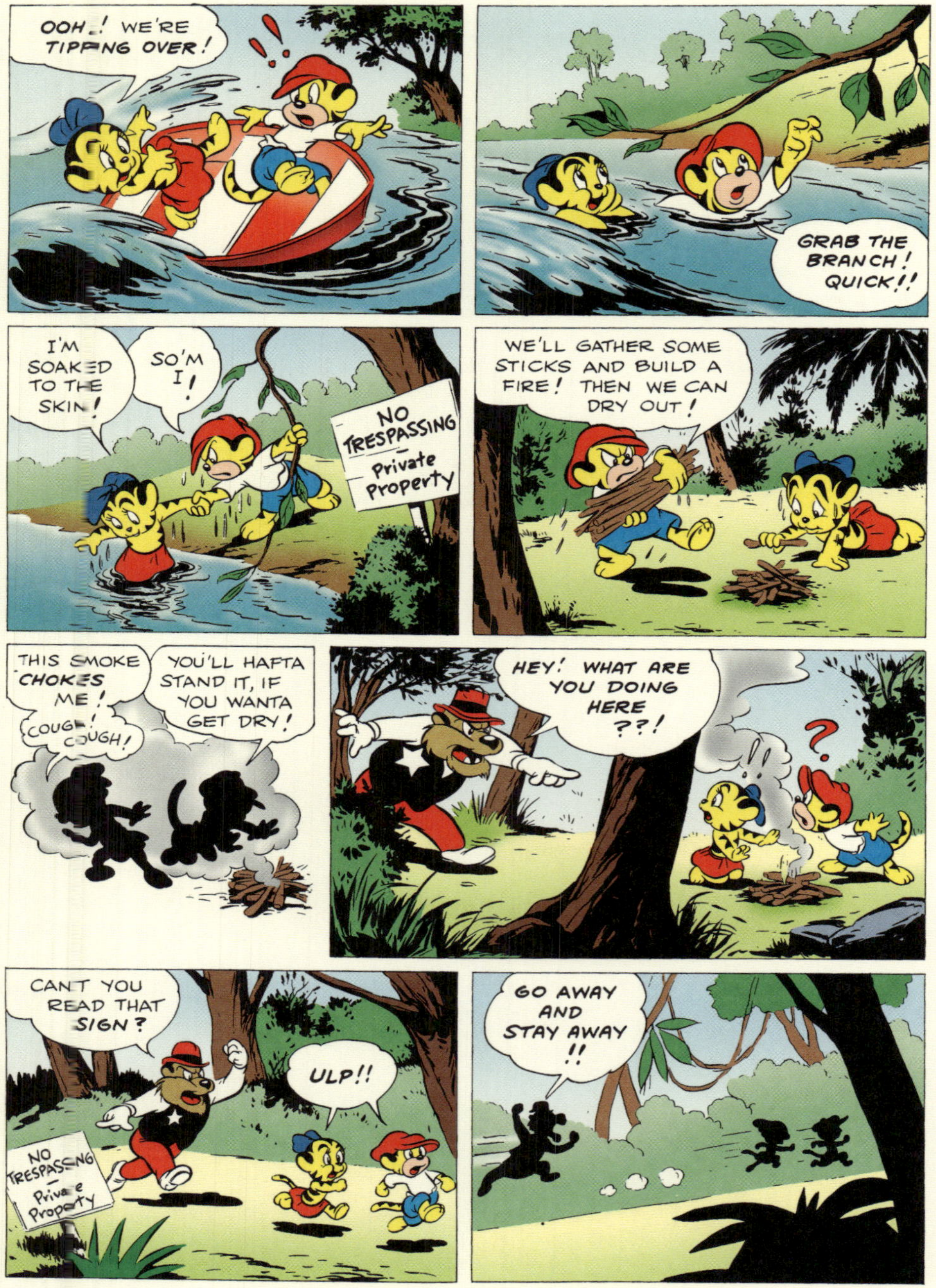
OOH..! WE'RE TIPPING OVER!
GRAB THE BRANCH! QUICK!!
I'M SOAKED TO THE SKIN!
SO'M I!
NO TRESPASSING
Private Property
WE'LL GATHER SOME STICKS AND BUILD A FIRE! THEN WE CAN DRY OUT!
THIS SMOKE CHOKES ME!
COUGH! COUGH!
YOU'LL HAFTA STAND IT, IF YOU WANTA GET DRY!
HEY! WHAT ARE YOU DOING HERE??!
CAN'T YOU READ THAT SIGN?
ULP!!
NO TRESPASSING
Private Property
GO AWAY AND STAY AWAY!!

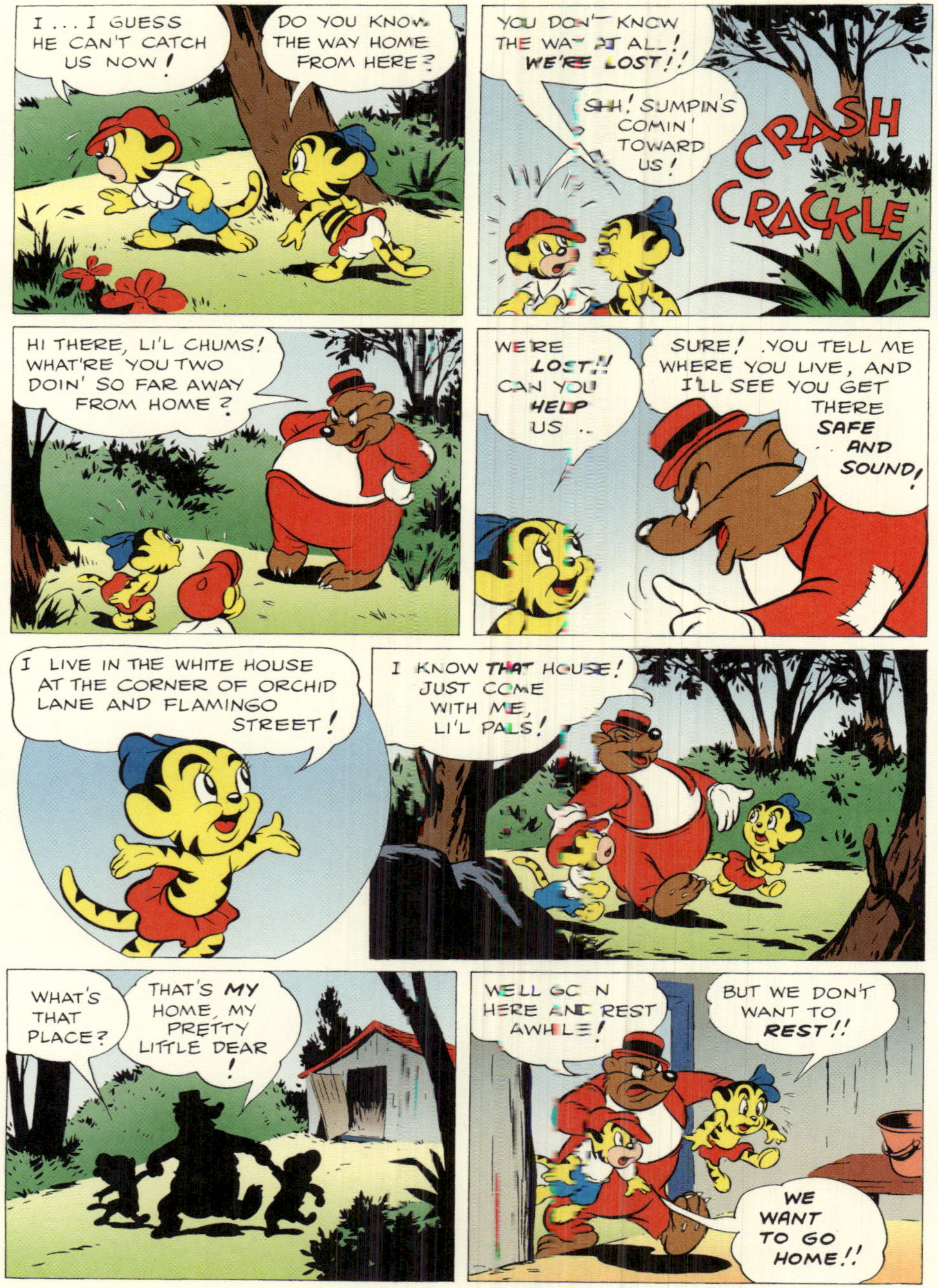
I... I GUESS HE CAN'T CATCH US NOW!
DO YOU KNOW THE WAY HOME FROM HERE?
YOU DON'T KNOW THE WAY AT ALL! WE'RE LOST!!
SHH! SUMPIN'S COMIN' TOWARD US!
CRASH
CRACKLE
HI THERE, LI'L CHUMS! WHAT'RE YOU TWO DOIN' SO FAR AWAY FROM HOME?
WE'RE LOST!! CAN YOU HELP US..
SURE! YOU TELL ME WHERE YOU LIVE, AND I'LL SEE YOU GET THERE SAFE AND SOUND!
I LIVE IN THE WHITE HOUSE AT THE CORNER OF ORCHID LANE AND FLAMINGO STREET!
I KNOW THAT HOUSE! JUST COME WITH ME, LI'L PALS!
WHAT'S THAT PLACE?
THAT'S MY HOME, MY PRETTY LITTLE DEAR!
WE'LL GO IN HERE AND REST AWHILE!
BUT WE DON'T WANT TO REST!!
WE WANT TO GO HOME!!

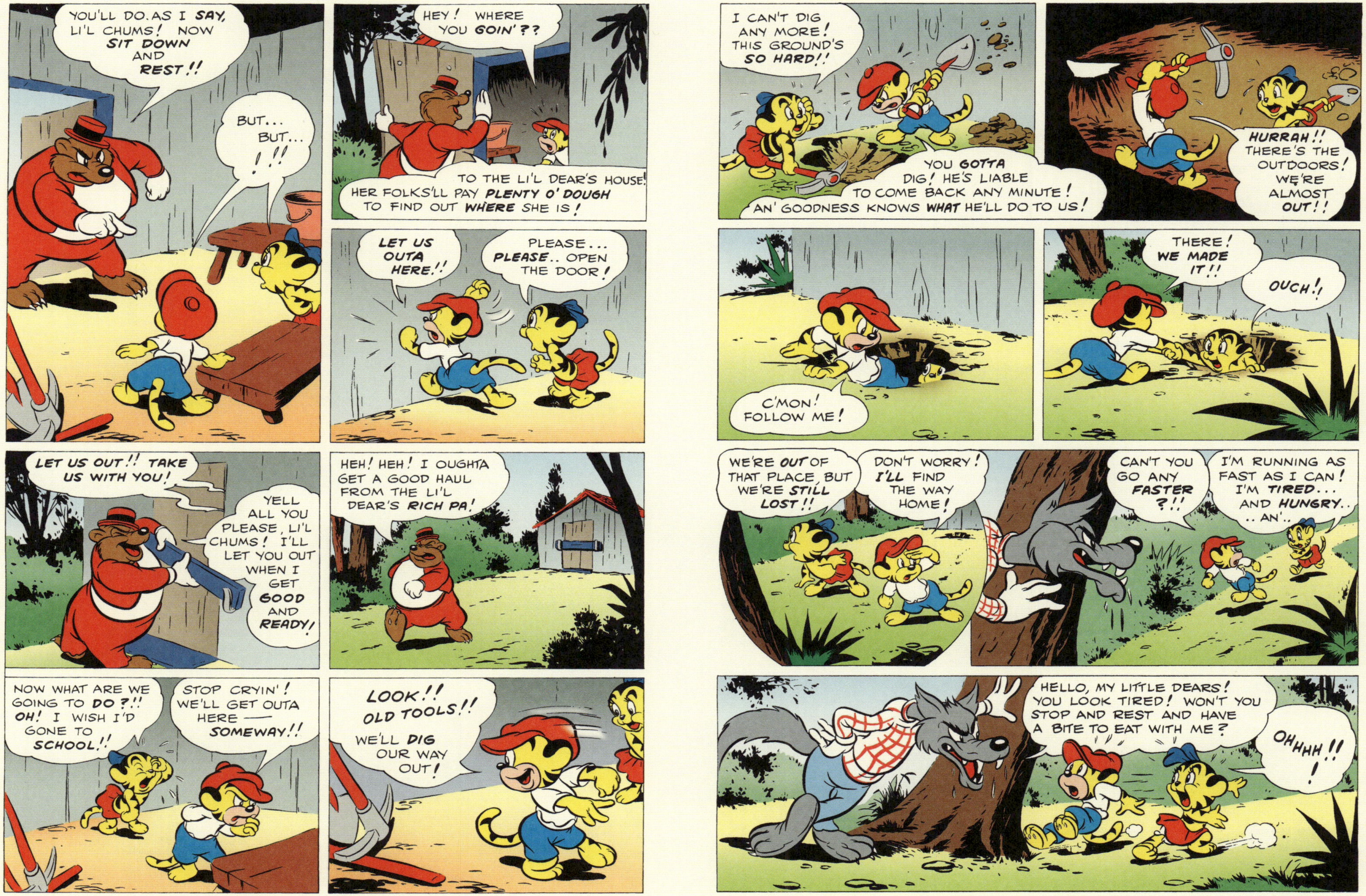

YOU'LL DO AS I SAY, LI'L CHUMS! NOW SIT DOWN AND REST!!
BUT... BUT... !!!
HEY! WHERE YOU GOIN'??
TO THE LI'L DEAR'S HOUSE! HER FOLKS'LL PAY PLENTY O' DOUGH TO FIND OUT WHERE SHE IS!
LET US OUTA HERE!!
PLEASE... PLEASE.. OPEN THE DOOR!
LET US OUT!! TAKE US WITH YOU!
YELL ALL YOU PLEASE, LI'L CHUMS! I'LL LET YOU OUT WHEN I GET GOOD AND READY!
HEH! HEH! I OUGHTA GET A GOOD HAUL FROM THE LI'L DEAR'S RICH PA!
NOW WHAT ARE WE GOING TO DO?!! OH! I WISH I'D GONE TO SCHOOL!!
STOP CRYIN'! WE'LL GET OUTA HERE — SOMEWAY!!
LOOK!! OLD TOOLS!!
WE'LL DIG OUR WAY OUT!
I CAN'T DIG ANY MORE! THIS GROUND'S SO HARD!!
YOU GOTTA DIG! HE'S LIABLE TO COME BACK ANY MINUTE! AN' GOODNESS KNOWS WHAT HE'LL DO TO US!
HURRAH!! THERE'S THE OUTDOORS! WE'RE ALMOST OUT!!
C'MON! FOLLOW ME!
THERE! WE MADE IT!!
OUCH!!
WE'RE OUT OF THAT PLACE, BUT WE'RE STILL LOST!!
DON'T WORRY! I'LL FIND THE WAY HOME!
CAN'T YOU GO ANY FASTER?!!
I'M RUNNING AS FAST AS I CAN! I'M TIRED... AND HUNGRY.. .. AN'..
HELLO, MY LITTLE DEARS! YOU LOOK TIRED! WON'T YOU STOP AND REST AND HAVE A BITE TO EAT WITH ME?
OHHHH!!!

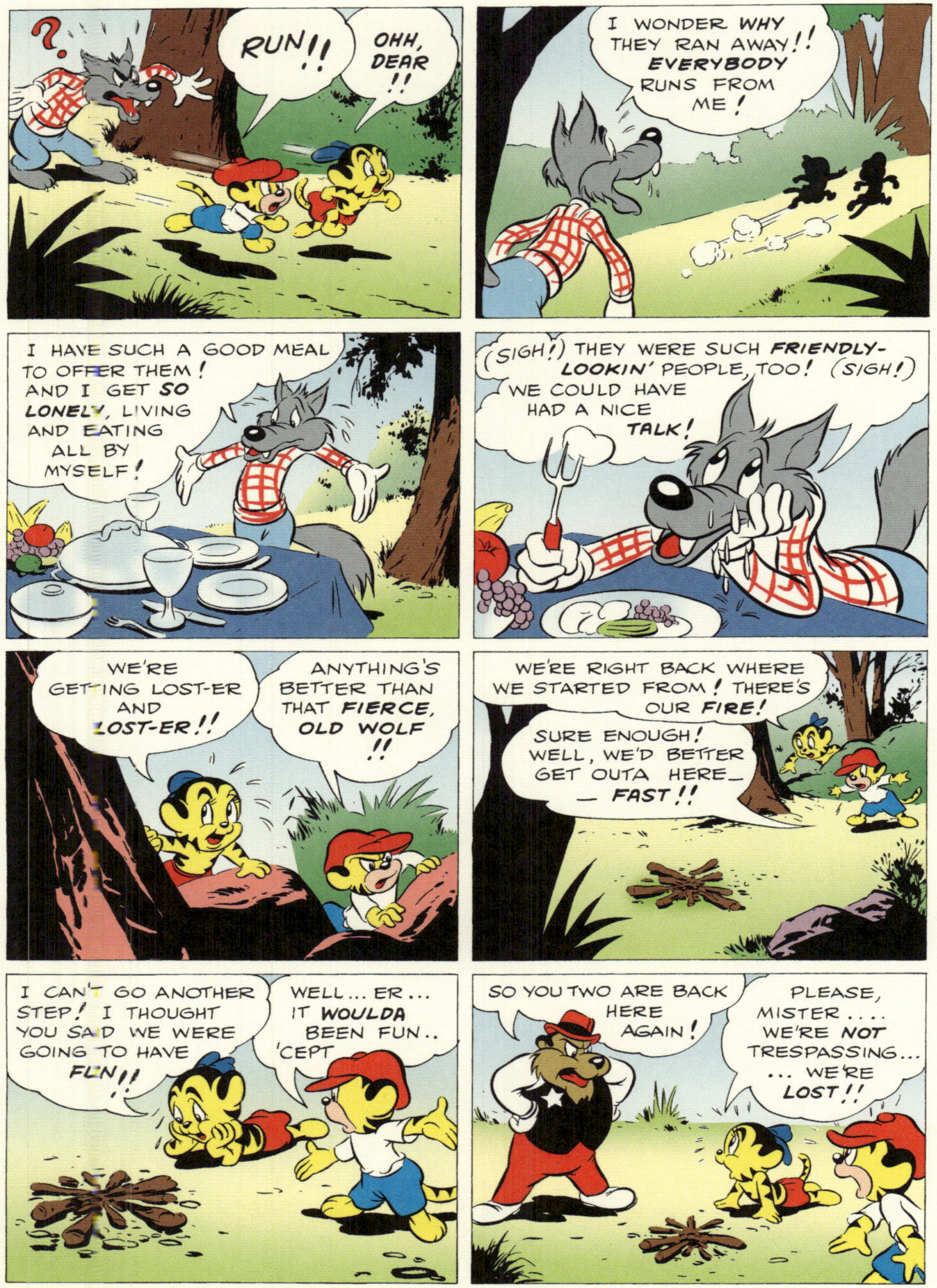
RUN!!
OHH, DEAR!!
I WONDER WHY THEY RAN AWAY!! EVERYBODY RUNS FROM ME!
I HAVE SUCH A GOOD MEAL TO OFFER THEM! AND I GET SO LONELY, LIVING AND EATING ALL BY MYSELF!
(SIGH!) THEY WERE SUCH FRIENDLY-LOOKIN' PEOPLE, TOO! (SIGH!)
WE COULD HAVE HAD A NICE TALK!
WE'RE GETTING LOST-ER AND LOST-ER!!
ANYTHING'S BETTER THAN THAT FIERCE, OLD WOLF!!
WE'RE RIGHT BACK WHERE WE STARTED FROM! THERE'S OUR FIRE!
SURE ENOUGH! WELL, WE'D BETTER GET OUTA HERE — FAST!!
I CAN'T GO ANOTHER STEP! I THOUGHT YOU SAID WE WERE GOING TO HAVE FUN!!
WELL... ER... IT WOULDA BEEN FUN.. 'CEPT
SO YOU TWO ARE BACK HERE AGAIN!
PLEASE, MISTER.... WE'RE NOT TRESPASSING... ...WE'RE LOST!!

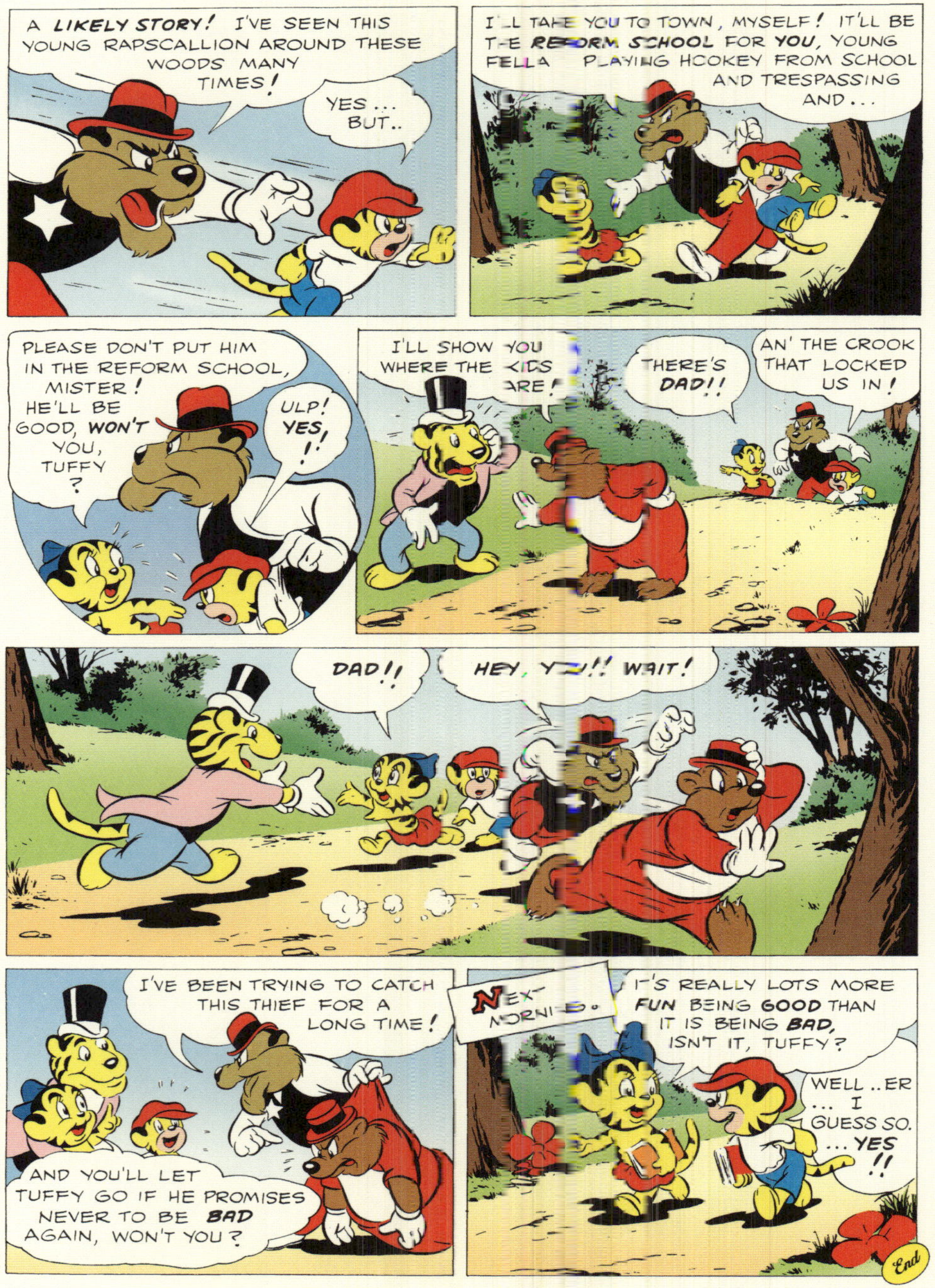
A LIKELY STORY! I'VE SEEN THIS YOUNG RAPSCALLION AROUND THESE WOODS MANY TIMES!
YES... BUT..
I'LL TAKE YOU TO TOWN, MYSELF! IT'LL BE THE REFORM SCHOOL FOR YOU, YOUNG FELLA PLAYING HOOKEY FROM SCHOOL AND TRESPASSING AND...
PLEASE DON'T PUT HIM IN THE REFORM SCHOOL, MISTER! HE'LL BE GOOD, WON'T YOU, TUFFY?
ULP! YES!
I'LL SHOW YOU WHERE THE KIDS ARE!
THERE'S DAD!!
AN' THE CROOK THAT LOCKED US IN!
DAD!!
HEY, YOU!! WAIT!
I'VE BEEN TRYING TO CATCH THIS THIEF FOR A LONG TIME!
AND YOU'LL LET TUFFY GO IF HE PROMISES NEVER TO BE BAD AGAIN, WON'T YOU?
NEXT MORNING.
IT'S REALLY LOTS MORE FUN BEING GOOD THAN IT IS BEING BAD, ISN'T IT, TUFFY?
WELL.. ER... I GUESS SO. ...YES!!
End